Social Intelligence

Dong Wang • Lanyu Shang • Yang Zhang

Social Intelligence

The New Frontier of Integrating Human Intelligence and Artificial Intelligence in Social Space

Springer

Dong Wang
School of Information Sciences and Siebel School of Computing and Data Science (affiliated)
University of Illinois Urbana-Champaign
Champaign, IL, USA

Lanyu Shang
Computer Science
Loyola Marymount University
Los Angeles, CA, USA

Yang Zhang
Computer Science and Software Engineering
Miami University
Oxford, OH, USA

ISBN 978-3-031-90079-2 ISBN 978-3-031-90080-8 (eBook)
https://doi.org/10.1007/978-3-031-90080-8

This Springer imprint is published by the registered company Springer Nature Switzerland AG
The registered company address is: Gewerbestrasse 11, 6330 Cham, Switzerland

To Na and David
D.W.
To my family, who believed
L.S.
To J.C.
Y.Z.

Preface

The rise of Artificial Intelligence (AI) and its tight interactions with humans and our society leads to the emergence of a new field called Social Intelligence (SI). The SI is motivated by the complementary strengths of AI and humans. For example, AI is observed to excel at tasks that require high speed, run at a large scale, and generate accurate quantitative results. In contrast, humans often outperform machines at tasks that require critical thinking, creative works, and excellent social skills. Different from many existing works that take AI and humans as competitors in a zero-sum game, this book presents an exciting vision of SI that allows humans and AI to collaborate with each other and build a novel paradigm of collective and hybrid intelligence by fully exploring their complementary strengths and interactions in the social space. The SI will empower human-centered AI solutions in many critical application domains by fully unleashing the power of integrating human intelligence with AI. Examples of such application domains include truth discovery and explanation, healthcare analytics, disaster response, online education, face recognition, intelligent transportation, urban sensing, and smart cities.

The SI paradigm introduces a set of critical challenges for research. Examples include human-centered data heterogeneity and sparsity, model generality and adaptability, explainability, fairness and bias, privacy, and hybrid intelligence integration. This book addresses these challenges by presenting a series of principled analytical frameworks and real-world system designs that fully explore the collective strengths of AI and human intelligence, while explicitly addressing the unique concerns and constraints of humans. The book first presents a set of novel human-centered AI solutions (e.g., multimodal approaches, robust and generalizable models, socially empowered explainable AI designs) to address the aforementioned SI challenges. The book then presents several human-AI collaborative learning frameworks that jointly integrate the strengths of collective human intelligence from people and AI to address the limitations of human-only or AI-only solutions. Finally, the book discusses the pressing societal and human-centered issues in SI such as fairness, bias, and privacy. The book also offers extensive evaluation of the discussed SI systems in real-world applications and case studies to demonstrate the effectiveness and performance gains of the presented solutions in comparison to state-of-the-art baselines in different aspects such as model accuracy, generalizability, explainability, algorithmic fairness, and system robustness.

Leveraging the models, techniques, and systems presented in this book, the reader is offered with analytical foundations, optimized frameworks, and system prototypes needed to explore the power of social intelligence. The SI paradigm generalizes the current trends of human-AI interactions, human-assisted AI, and AI for social good into a holistic human-AI ecosystem with social context. The book takes the reader on a journey of discovery through the analytical and systematic underpinning of developing novel theories, models, and systems in the domain of social intelligence. The uniqueness of human-centered nature and integration of human intelligence and AI makes this journey more exciting and challenging. The authors hope that techniques developed in this book will become part of the solution space in dealing with challenges in future social intelligence systems. These techniques can help fully unleash the power of both AI and humans in the next generation of computing, intelligence, and information systems.

Champaign, IL, USA — Dong Wang
Los Angeles, CA, USA — Lanyu Shang
Oxford, OH, USA — Yang Zhang
January, 2025

Acknowledgments

This book would not have been possible without the encouragement, support, and hard work of many individuals who contributed in different ways to the journey of discovery described within. The authors are grateful to all the colleagues, students, and researchers who dedicated their time to developing theory, building systems, running experiments, and generally advancing the state of the art in social intelligence, as well as the agencies funding their work.[1]

In a brainstorm session among Dong Wang, Lanyu Shang, and Yang Zhang, the research leading to this book was started. The core ideas of this book are rooted at the intersection of multiple research communities: Artificial Intelligence (AI), Human-centered Computing (HCC), Estimation Theory, and Statistical Learning. During their discussions and debate, the authors realize there exist a new interdisciplinary research direction that explore the collective strengths of both human intelligence and AI by investigating their interaction and integration in a social context. The authors coined the term Social Intelligence (SI) to refer to this new direction, which is the theme of this book. The authors are grateful to their colleagues in AI, machine learning, social computing, human-computer interaction communities who shared their thoughts and provided feedback for the work in this direction.

The authors would further like to acknowledge, Zhenrui Yue, Ziyi Kou, Daniel (Yue) Zhang, Ruohan Zong, Yeaeun Gong, YeonJung Choi, Frank Stinar, Nigel Bosch, and Siyu Duan for taking part in building systems, developing theory, and

[1] Research reported in this book was sponsored, in part, by the NSF grants CNS-2427070, IIS-2331069, IIS-2202481, IIS-2130263, CNS-2131622, CNS-2140999. The views and conclusions contained in this document are those of the authors and should not be interpreted as representing the official policies, either expressed or implied of the U.S. government. The U.S. government is authorized to reproduce and distribute reprints for Government purposes notwithstanding any copyright notation here on.

running experiments described in this book. Special thanks goes to Yeaeun Gong who also helped proofread the book and offered suggestions for improvement.

Finally, the book would not have been possible without the support of our friends and family, who encouraged us to complete this work, and put up with the late nights, missed promises, and rescheduled obligations it took to do so.

Declarations

Competing Interests The authors have no conflicts of interest to declare that are relevant to the content of book other than the funding acknowledge reported in the Acknowledgment section.

Ethics Approval The studies with online crowdsourcing experiments presented in the chapters of the book were performed in line with the approved Institute Review Board (IRB) protocols granted by Office for the Protected of Research Subjects at University of Illinois Urbana-Champaign: IRB24-1120 (9/27/2-24), IRB24-1125 (8/9/2024), IRB24-1083 (8/6/2024), IRB24-0654 (4/30/2024), IRB21-981(6/17/2021).

Contents

About the Authors

Dong Wang is a professor in School of Information Sciences and Siebel School of Computing and Data Science (affiliated) at the University of Illinois at Urbana Champaign (UIUC). His research interests lie in social sensing and intelligence, human-centered AI, and big data analytics. Dong Wang has published over 200 technical papers in peer reviewed conferences and journals. His work has been applied in a wide range of real-world applications such as data reliability, social network analysis, disaster response, AI for science, and AI for social good. His research on social sensing and intelligence resulted in software tools that found applications in academia, industry, and government research labs. He also authored three books: "Social Intelligence" to be published by Springer in 2025, "Social Edge Computing" published by Springer in 2023, and "Social Sensing" published by Elsevier in 2015. He is the recipient of NSF CAREER Award, Google Faculty Research Award, ARO Young Investigator Program (YIP), the Best Paper Award of 2022 ACM/IEEE International Conference on Advances in Social Networks Analysis and Mining (ASONAM), the Best Paper Award of 16th IEEE Real-Time and Embedded Technology and Applications Symposium (RTAS) and the Best Paper Honorable Mention of 2025 ACM CHI and 8th IEEE SmartComp. He serves as an associate editor of IEEE Transactions on Big Data, Frontiers in Big Data, and Social Network and Analysis Journal (SNAM). He is also an IEEE Senior Member and ACM and AAAI Member.

Lanyu Shang is an assistant professor in Computer Science at Loyola Marymount University. She earned her Ph.D. in information sciences from the University of Illinois Urbana-Champaign. Prior to this, she received an M.S. in Data Science from New York University and a B.S. in Applied Mathematics from the University of California, Los Angeles. Her research interest lies in human-centric AI, human-AI collaboration, social media analysis, AI for social good, and applied AI. Her work has been published in top venues in data mining and machine learning/AI, such as The WebConf, ICWSM, AAAI, IJCAI, and IEEE Big Data. She is also the recipient of the Best Paper Award at ACM/IEEE ASONAM 2022, the Best Paper Honorable Mention at IEEE SmartComp 2022, the Outstanding Graduate Student Teaching Award from the University of Notre Dame, and the N2Women Young Researcher Fellowship.

Yang Zhang is an assistant professor in Computer Science and Software Engineering at Miami University. Previously, he was a Postdoctoral Research Associate at UIUC and a W. J. Cody Research Associate at Argonne National Laboratory. Yang earned his Ph.D. in Computer Science & Engineering from the University of Notre Dame, an M.S. in Data Science from Indiana University Bloomington, and a B.S. in Software Engineering from Wuhan University. His research focuses on human-centered AI, human-AI collaboration, deep learning, and generative AI. He has authored over 80 peer-reviewed conference and journal papers published in top venues such as ACM CSCW, ACM Web Conference, AAAI, IJCAI, and IEEE BigData. His work has been recognized with prestigious honors, including the Outstanding Graduate Research Award from the University of Notre Dame and the W. J. Cody Research Associateship at Argonne National Laboratory.

Acronyms

ADA	AI-based Damage Assessment
AFDB	Accuracy-Fairness-aware Dataset Balancer
AI	Artificial Intelligence
AMT	Amazon Mechanical Turk
API	Application Programming Interface
ASUS	AI-based Smart Urban Sensing
BERT	Bidirectional Encoder Representations from Transformers
biGRU	bidirectional Gated Recurrent Unit
bPFG	bi-relational Partial Face Graph
CBBE	Crowdsourcing Batch Bias Estimator
CBC	Crowd-guided Bias Calibration
CCF	Community-Contributed Fact
CDEG	Comment-Driven Explanation Generator
CDKG	Community-driven Distributed Knowledge Graph
CGMD	Claim-Graph-based Multi-relational Detector
CHKG	Crowdsourced Hierarchical Knowledge Graph
CHST	Crowd-manageable Hyperparameter Space Transformation
CKGC	Crowdsourced Knowledge Graph Constructor
CKU	Crowdsourcing-based Knowledge Updater
CLIP	Contrastive Language-Image Pre-training
CNN	Convolutional Neural Network
COAS	Crowd-guided Optimal Architecture Search
COHI	Crowd-driven Optimal Hyperparameter Identification
CollabGeneral	Collaborative Generality
ContrastFaux	Contrastive Fauxtography detector
CoviDKG	Covid-19 Distributed Knowledge Graph
CPGC	Crowdsource Partial Graph Constructor
CrowdAdapt	Crowdsourcing-based domain Adaptation
CrowdNAS	Crowd-guided Neural Network Architecture Search
CrowdOptim	Crowd-driven neural network hyperparameter Optimization
CS	Convolutional operation sub-search Space

CSKP	Claim-guided Specific Knowledge Propagator
CSSD	Crowd-manageable Search Space Design
CV	Computer Vision
DAKI	Domain-Aware Knowledge Integrator
DANN	Domain-Adversarial Neural Networks
DDA	Disaster Damage Assessment
DebiasEdu	Debias AI for online Education
DExFC	Dual Explainable Fauxtography detection under Constrained supervision
DGCN	Dual Graph Convolutional Network
DGFE	Dual Graph convolutional Feature Encoder
DKGC	Distributed Knowledge Graph Constructor
DMD	Dual Modality-level false content Discriminator
DRL	Domain-invariant Representation Learning
DS	Dense layer sub-search Space
DualGen	Dual-modal Generation
EM	Expectation Maximization
FaceCrowd	Face partition based on Crowdsourcing
FairCrowd	Fair Crowdsourcing-based data sampling
FAP	Face Attractiveness Prediction
FFD	Final Fauxtography Discriminator
FMR	False Match Rate
FS	Feature extraction sub-search Space
GAN	Generative Adversarial Network
GBI	Gradient-based Bias Identification
GCN	Graph Convolutional Network
GDO	Generality-aware Deep Optimization
GKE	Graph-based Knowledge Encoder
GMM	Gaussian Mixture Model
GNN	Graph Neural Network
GPT	Generative Pre-trained Transformer
GPU	Graphics Processing Unit
GRU	Gated Recurrent Unit
HC-COVID	Hierarchical Crowdsourced Knowledge Graph for COVID-19 truth discovery
HCC	Human-Centered Computing
HCI	Human-Computer Interaction
HI	Human Intelligence
HIT	Human Intelligence Task
HMM	Hidden Markov Model
HPO	HyperParameter Optimization
ICC	Intraclass Correlation Coefficient
IFE	Image Feature Encode
LiDAR	Light Detection And Ranging
ITFD	Image-guided Textual Feature Decoder

LFM	Large Foundation Model
LLaMA	Large Language Model Meta AI
LLM	Large Language Model
LS	Least Squares
LSTM	Long Short-Term Memory
MAML	Model-Agnostic Meta-Learning
MBP	Multi-armed Bandits Problem
MCA	Multimodal Co-Attention
MCC	Matthews Correlation Coefficient
MCFN	Multi-view Contrastive Fauxtography-aware Network
MGR	Modality-level Graph Refinement
MKIN	Medical Knowledge Information Network
MLD	Modality-Level Discriminator
MLE	Maximum Likelihood Estimation
MLP	Multi-Layer Perceptions
MMD	Maximum Mean Discrepancy
MoM	Method of Moments
MPID	Metric-based Partial Identity Discriminator
MRGN	Multi-Relational Graph neural Network
MRI	Minimum Reading Index
NAS	Neural Architecture Search
NLP	Natural Language Processing
NN	Neural Network
NT-Xent	Normalized Temperature-scaled Cross-entropy loss
OMFE	Object-aware Multimodal Feature Encoder
OG-LSTM	Object-Guided Long Short-Term Memory
PAKG	Privacy-Aware Knowledge Generator
PFS	Potential Face Similarity
PGDG	Partial Graph Denoising Generator
ReLU	Rectified Linear Unit
ResNet	Residual Network
RGCN	Relational Graph Convolutional Network
RNN	Recurrent Neural Network
SASO	Sparse Annotation and Similarity-driven Optimization
SBDS	Service-specific Batch Data Sampler
SCF	Subjective logic-driven Crowd-AI Fusion
SCIM	Smart City Infrastructure Monitoring
SDLP	Similarity-based Demographic Label Predictor
SGD	Stochastic Gradient Descent
SI	Social Intelligence
TFE	Text Feature Encoder
TGKI	Topic-based Generalized Knowledge Integrator
TMR	True Match Rate
TVFG	Text-guided Visual Feature Generator
UECA	Urban Environment Cleanliness Assessment

ViT	Vision Transformer
VKAE	Variational Knowledge AutoEncoder
WFE	Word Feature Encoder
XAI	eXplainable AI
XGBoost	eXtreme Gradient Boosting

Chapter 1
Introduction

Abstract In this chapter, we introduce the new paradigm of Social Intelligence (SI) where the goal is to explore the collective intelligence of both humans and machines by understanding their complementary strengths and interactions in the social space. We highlight the uniqueness of the social intelligence paradigm in the context of related literature. We further discuss the motivation of SI from both the challenge and application perspectives. Examples of some key challenges in SI include data heterogeneity, model generality, explainability, fairness and bias, privacy, and hybrid intelligence integration. Finally, we conclude the chapter by summarizing the contributions of this book and presenting the structure for the rest of the book.

Keywords Social intelligence · Human-centered AI · Human-AI collaboration · AI for social good

1.1 Overview

Given the rise of artificial intelligence (AI) and the advent of online social collaboration opportunities (e.g., social media, crowdsourcing), emerging research has started investigating the integration of AI and human intelligence, especially in a collaborative social context. This opens up unprecedented challenges and opportunities in the field of Social Intelligence (SI), where the goal is to explore the collective intelligence of both humans and machines by understanding their complementary strengths and interactions in the social space. Social intelligence can be applied to a wide range of human-centered applications in the real world, such as truth discovery, disaster response, explainable AI, online education, and smart cities, to enhance human well-being and promote social good. For example, in an online truth discovery application, SI-based solutions address the limitations of existing AI approaches by not only detecting the false information accurately but also presenting convincing explanation of the detected false information with expert-validated evidence and justification [18]. With real-world case studies, this

D. Wang et al., *Social Intelligence*, https://doi.org/10.1007/978-3-031-90080-8_1

book systematically presents the concepts, fundamental research challenges, state-of-the-art techniques, and open-ended research questions in this emerging domain. The book highlights several critical challenges in social intelligence applications, such as data heterogeneity, data sparsity, model generalizability, explainability, human-AI collaboration, fairness, and privacy. The book addresses these challenges by presenting a series of principled models and real-world systems that jointly explore the collective intelligence of humans and AI, while explicitly addressing their respective limitations and constraints.

This book offers a comprehensive guide to understand the nature of human intelligence and AI. Novel human-centered AI techniques are presented to address the challenges of social intelligence applications, including multimodal approaches, robust and generalizable frameworks, and socially empowered explainable AI designs. The book then presents several human-AI collaborative learning frameworks that jointly integrate the strengths of crowd wisdom and AI to address the limitations inherent in standalone solutions. The book also emphasizes pressing societal issues in social intelligence, such as fairness, bias, and privacy. Real-world case studies from different application domains in social intelligence are presented to demonstrate the effectiveness of the proposed solutions in achieving substantial performance gains in various aspects, such as prediction accuracy, model generalizability and explainability, algorithmic fairness, and system robustness.

Compared to existing literature in related fields (e.g., social computing, human-centered AI, crowdsourcing, AI for social good), the vision of this book is unique: we focus on social intelligence, an emerging direction at the intersection of human intelligence and AI in the context of social space, aiming to jointly integrate the complementary strengths of human intelligence and AI with novel human-AI collaborative designs and systems. It highlights the unique role of humans in enabling socially intelligent applications that prioritize human needs and values in the core design of such human-AI collaborative systems. To our knowledge, the collaborative integration of human intelligence and AI for social good has not been systematically reviewed and studied in an existing book. The social intelligence vision generalizes current works in human-centered AI (e.g., Human-Computer Interaction (HCI) and AI for social good literature) and collective human intelligence (e.g., social media and crowdsourcing literature) into a comprehensive human-AI collaboration paradigm in the social space. Such a paradigm integrates emerging human-centered applications (e.g., healthcare, disaster response, smart cities, online education), state-of-the-art AI challenges (e.g., heterogeneity, sparsity, generalizability, explainability), and related societal concerns (e.g., fairness, privacy, robustness) into a holistic human-AI ecosystem, as shown in Fig. 1.1.

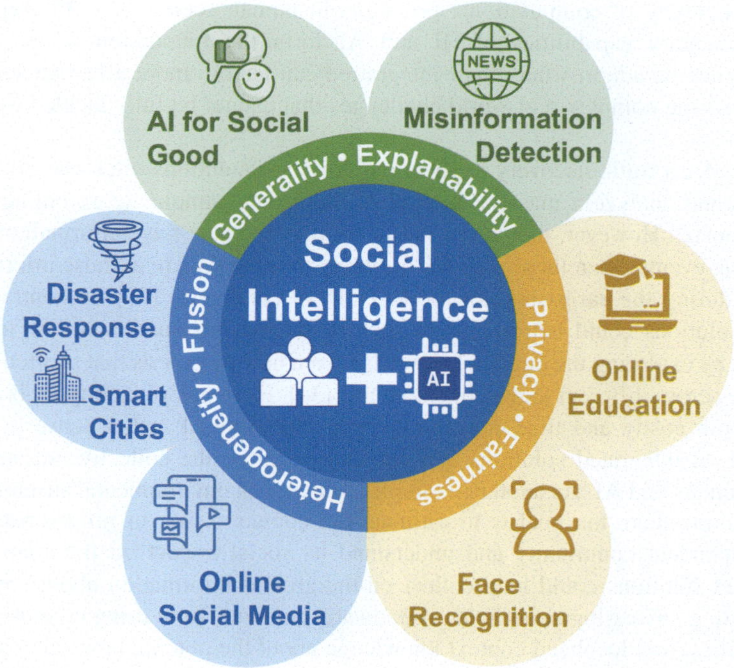

Fig. 1.1 An overview of the social intelligence paradigm

1.2 Motivation and Challenges

1.2.1 Motivation

This book introduces a new paradigm called Social Intelligence (SI). This paradigm is motivated by the observation that human intelligence (HI) and artificial intelligence (AI) have complementary strengths in addressing complex real-world issues in the social space. In particular, HI refers to the cognitive abilities of humans, such as reasoning, planning, problem-solving, abstract thinking, complex idea comprehension, and learning from experience [15]. In contrast, AI refers to the simulation of human intelligence processes by machines that may include computation-based learning, reasoning, problem-solving, perception, and language understanding [16]. It is observed that HI and AI excel at tasks that are complementary to each other. For example, HI is often good at providing specific context, domain expertise, creative and abstract thinking, and human-centered insights, which are essential for understanding the complex social and physical factors in social intelligence applications [1, 12, 27]. In contrast, AI excels at tasks such as processing large amounts of data, complex calculations, and simulations, identifying latent patterns, and quantitative analysis with high accuracy, which can help address the scalability and complexity of computational problems in human society [25, 35, 39]. Such complementary capabilities of HI and AI form the foundation of the Social Intelligence paradigm where their integration can lead to more effective solutions to address the complex real-world challenges that cannot be fully tackled by HI or AI alone.

Consider a truth discovery application, AI-based solutions often can efficiently process and analyze a massive amount of input data samples (e.g., online social media posts). However, they often fail to identify the new false information about emerging events when there is a lack of timely training data (e.g., false information spread during the early stage of the COVID-19 pandemic) [47]. In contrast, HI-based solutions could better capture such new false information in an "unseen" domain by exploring the domain knowledge from human experts that is often generalizable across different knowledge domains [34]. However, obtaining HI is known to be both costly and time-consuming [52]. Therefore, it makes sense to create new HI-AI integrated solutions that can fully explore the collective strengths of both humans and AI. As another example, consider an environmental sustainability application where the goal is to estimate the contamination of groundwater in a well-dependent community and understand its social impact on the community. HI-based solutions could help collect on-the-ground information about the water quality (e.g., assessing household groundwater contamination using crowdsourcing approaches) and localized context knowledge about the potential pollution sources (e.g., identifying the nearby farms and patterns of fertilizer applications that may affect the groundwater contamination) [36]. However, individual inputs from unvetted human users often suffer from uncertainty and noise due to the inherent subjectivity and variability in human observations. In contrast, AI-based solutions could help mitigate these limitations of HI by effectively quantifying the uncertainty of individual observations from the collective yet noisy human inputs and capturing the hidden patterns between these observations [32]. Therefore, an integrated HI-AI paradigm could better address the above problem by providing a more reliable and trustworthy social intelligence solution. While the SI paradigm is promising, there exist a few fundamental challenges in integrating HI and AI, which we elaborate on below.

1.2.2 The Heterogeneity Challenge

Data heterogeneity is one of the fundamental challenges in social intelligence, where many of its applications are characterized by the heterogeneous nature of human and AI-generated contents that encompass diverse data modalities such as text, images, videos, and user interactions [4]. Many existing multimodal solutions have been developed to address the data heterogeneity in different application contexts (e.g., online social media, healthcare, disaster response) [13, 45, 52]. However, these solutions often struggle to effectively capture the intricate interplay among different data modalities and sources due to the implicit nature of such interplays and interactions. The fauxtography generation tools have taken advantage of such limitations and leveraged the multimodal data and the interaction between different data modalities to present a incorrect narrative [54]. For example, a multimodal social media post shows a photo of a wild forest fire that is accompanied by a brief text statement that reports the forest fire in the image as a severe one in Tennessee [51]. While both the image and texts are real (i.e., the image is not edited and there is indeed a forest fire in Tennessee), the narrative from the multimodal post is incorrect in the sense that the image was borrowed from an earlier event (i.e., wildfires in the Bitterroot National Forest in west-central Montana and eastern Idaho of United States) and used to exaggerate the severity of the forest fire in Tennessee. While AI-based solutions can be leveraged to verify the truthfulness of the claim from individual modality (e.g., text or image), it is still challenging for AI solutions to detect such fauxtography posts that hide incorrect information in the connection and interaction between different modalities. In contrast, HI can be helpful in addressing such a problem if it is integrated with AI in an appropriate way. For example, people living in Tennessee may be able to note that these tree species in the wildfire image are not those commonly found in their state. If the crowd intelligence (HI from a group of people) is utilized, some individuals may also be able to identify these trees in the image are species commonly found in the northwestern United States. More recently, multimodal large foundation models (e.g., GPT-4, PaLM-E, Flamingo, CLIP) have also been developed and shown promise in processing and analyzing data of different modalities. However, they still face significant challenges in fully capturing, integrating, and interpreting the complex and context-dependent association and interplay between different modalities, especially when dealing with the dynamic and potentially contradictory nature of human-generated contents in the social intelligence context [24]. Therefore, it remains a critical challenge to fully understand, model, and evaluate data heterogeneity in social intelligence applications.

1.2.3 The Generality Challenge

In social intelligence applications, the developed systems are often applied across different domains (e.g., topics, events, locations) and the generality of the human-AI integration model is critical for the social intelligence system to achieve reliable and robust performance across domains [3]. The current AI solutions are often trained and fine-tuned on labeled data samples from a given domain to achieve optimized performance [10]. However, the annotation process to obtain the labeled data in a specific domain is often known to be both time-consuming and expensive [53]. This usually results in the limited generality of the AI models and their suboptimal performance when they are applied to new or different target domains other than the original source domain they were trained in [23]. For example, consider an AI model that has been trained to assess the severity of damage based on social media posts in the aftermath of an earthquake in California. The model may excel at assessing the severity of damage caused by the earthquake through the training process by leveraging the annotated data samples in the source domain (earthquake). However, the model is likely to achieve suboptimal performance when it is applied to assess the damage severity in different types of natural disasters such as hurricanes in North Carolina and Florida and flash floods in the Midwest [53]. One major reason for such performance degradation is the domain discrepancy between the source domain where the model is trained and the target domain where the model is applied. For example, the model may not be able to correctly understand hurricane-related terms like "storm surge" or "eye of the storm" and misclassify them as irrelevant or non-critical in the damage severity assessment process as the model has never seen such terms in the earthquake contexts. It is not a trivial task to develop generalizable social intelligence models that can overcome the domain discrepancy given the potential different data distributions and label shifts across domains as well as the unique characteristics, languages, and patterns of the data samples in each domain.

1.2.4 The Explainability Challenge

Explainability is another interesting challenge in social intelligence applications where AI and humans closely interact with each other. Ideally, people often prefer a clear, understandable, justifiable, and evidence-based explanation in addition to the AI-generated outcomes from the social intelligence systems [11]. For example, consider an AI-based metacognitive calibration system in education where the goal is to predict students' performance (e.g., final grade) at an early stage of a class and help students better calibrate their self-assessments of the class performance and improve their time management and final education outcome. In such an application, it will not be sufficient to only provide students with an AI-based prediction of their final grades without any explanations. Instead, students will find the prediction results more informative and become motivated to calibrate their self-assessments of class performance if the AI predictions come with a well-designed explanation. For example, such an explanation could include details on (1) what data does the AI system use to generate the prediction result? (2) What is the confidence of the AI-generated prediction? (3) What chapters/sections of the course play a more critical role in the prediction? However, it is not a trivial task to generate such an explanation due to several challenges in integrating AI and HI in social intelligence. First, the "black-box" nature of the AI models contributes to the lack of explainability of the generated results [50]. For example, when an AI model gives an inaccurate prediction on the student performance, what is the reason—is it due to the lack of training data or the AI model itself? Such questions make it difficult for human intelligence to effectively improve the black-box AI model. Second, many current explainable AI (XAI) solutions mainly focus on extracting the relevant content (e.g., specific words or image regions) from the input data as explanations, which often lack appropriate contexts to clearly articulate the reasons behind the prediction results in natural human language [19]. In the above meta-cognitive calibration example, students often prefer an understandable human language-based explanation to their performance prediction over some scattered terms extracted from the course materials or their assignments. More recently, the progress on generative large language models (e.g., GPT-4, Llama) also shows promising performance on general natural language tasks, such as summarizing, translating, and generating natural language text [29]. However, such large language models often require a significant amount of training data and computational resources which limit their application to emerging or new tasks in social intelligence applications such as truth discovery and explanations in emerging domains [21, 37].

1.2.5 The Fairness and Bias Challenge

In social intelligence applications, it is important to ensure fairness and mitigate potential bias when AI and HI are integrated [20]. One challenge in addressing the bias of AI models lies in the fundamental trade-off between the fairness and accuracy of the AI models. It is well observed that mitigating the bias (i.e., improving fairness) of AI models often leads to model accuracy degradation [2, 41]. The fairness and accuracy trade-offs become much more complicated when the fairness across multiple demographic groups is considered simultaneously. Consider the metacognitive calibration application we discussed above where there exists more training data from males than females in the collected dataset. To achieve fairness for the "female" demographic group, the model should be trained on more balanced data by reducing the number of male data samples in the training process. However, if it happens that the male data samples are mostly from a minority group (e.g., African American students), the data samples for them will decrease as well, leading to lower prediction accuracy and potential unfairness for the minority students (e.g., African American male students) [49]. It remains an open challenge to achieve a good balance between fairness and accuracy among different demographic groups in social intelligence applications. Another challenge lies in the fact humans also have their own biases when HI is leveraged to improve the AI model fairness in social intelligence. For example, humans have the confirmation bias of selecting the option that aligns with their preexisting beliefs or hypotheses about the outcome that is expected [17]. Similarly, humans also have the effect of heuristic bias, where humans are prone to selecting options based on their immediate positive or negative reactions [6]. These human-based biases could also negatively affect the overall fairness of the social intelligence system if they are not addressed carefully. An open question in this direction is: how to leverage the collective strengths of AI and HI in social intelligence to improve system fairness by jointly mitigating their individual bias and investigating their potential interactions?

1.2.6 The Privacy Challenge

Privacy is a non-negligible challenge in human-centered paradigms like social intelligence where data are collected from humans or devices on their behalf [14]. The collected human data often contain sensitive information about the individuals and the contexts they are involved and such information is at substantial risk to individual privacy if it is not protected appropriately [5, 33]. For example, consider a social intelligence application where the goal is to study public health trends using human-centered data from social media and location services (e.g., online check-ins). While the outcomes of this application can contribute to the prediction of epidemic and disease spread, it also raises serious privacy concerns [31]. For instance, attackers could identify sensitive health information (e.g., medical conditions, lifestyles, health history) of users by mining their online posts and estimating their home locations by leveraging their check-in traces online. In another example of AI for education, students' study behavior data, quiz, and exam scores, and demographic information are often collected to train AI models for accurate prediction of the student's performance in a certain class [55]. However, students may not feel comfortable sharing such sensitive information with AI models or anyone they do not trust. It remains a critical challenge in education to build reliable AI models without posing additional risks to student's private data. Several solutions have been proposed to address the privacy challenge. Examples include data anonymization [44] and federated learning [42]. However, these techniques have their own limitations. For example, the data anonymization scheme is vulnerable to re-identification attacks when the attacker can get access to additional publicly available information (e.g., rich contextual information from social media) [9]. Additionally, federated learning requires the training data to be stored locally and only accessible to the clients (individual users) to protect their privacy [7]. However, the data at each client could be sparse and the data distributions across different clients could be different [49]. Such data sparsity and data heterogeneity often significantly affect the performance of AI models in federated learning settings [48]. With recent advancements in conversational AI and large language models, users are increasingly sharing their data during interactions with these systems. The privacy issue becomes a potential concern due to the conversational nature of such AI systems and the lack of awareness of how the data exchanged during the conversation is stored or used [46]. Similar challenges also exist in human-AI collaborative decision-making systems that can effectively learn from human feedback, which can include sensitive information being unintentionally shared during the collaboration process [22]. Therefore, it remains an open challenge in social intelligence to ensure the privacy of users and protect their data while maintaining desirable system performance.

1.2.7 *The Hybrid Intelligence Integration Challenge*

The integration of AI and HI showcases both the opportunities and the challenges of leveraging the strengths of HI and AI to address complex technical and social challenges. HI has the ability to contextualize data, bring domain-specific knowledge to bear, and make moral judgments, all of which are crucial for better understanding the dynamics of complex real-world applications in the social context [28]. However, human judgments can be influenced by biases, and HI scales only up to human cognitive, time, and cost constraints [40]. AI, on the other hand, has powerful data-processing and analysis capacities, and is usually consistent, objective, and scalable [26]. However, AI often suffers from a lack of contextual awareness, is often task/domain-specific, and its decisions can be opaque, leading to moral and ethical concerns. Motivated by the above observations, collaborative decision-making frameworks can be developed where AI focuses on data processing and preliminary analysis while humans provide contextual interpretation and ethical oversight [38]. However, several challenges exist in integrating AI and HI in social intelligence applications. The challenges are rooted in the complex interdependence between AI and HI. A "chicken-and-egg" dilemma arises when one form of intelligence relies on the reliable outputs of the other [30]. Specifically, AI models often require accurate human inputs to identify and correct biases and errors of the models. For example, when detecting false claims about vaccine efficacy, expert-annotated unbiased data—grounded in verified scientific evidence, covering diverse viewpoints, and adhering to consistent annotation criteria—helps AI models identify fine-grained false information patterns, facilitating bias correction during training. On the other hand, human workers can also rely on AI-generated feedback to highlight patterns they may have missed, such as recurring incorrect phrases or fabricated statistics, thereby reducing annotation errors [43]. However, the lack of systematic study and modeling of this mutual dependency between HI and AI makes it challenging to ensure accurate and reliable outputs from human-AI collaborative systems. The integrated intelligence can better tackle complex challenges in ways that are more reliable and aligned better with societal needs. The synergy between HI and AI can also facilitate the adaptive learning paradigm where AI systems are improved continually with human feedback, and humans also improve their decisions with AI-driven insights, leading to a more robust and effective co-learning framework [8].

1.3 Contributions

This book introduces a new paradigm in the era of human-centered AI: Social Intelligence (SI). The SI paradigm unleashes the collective power of human intelligence (HI) and AI by exploring their complementary strengths and interactions in the social space. The main contributions of the book can be summarized as follows.

First, this book presents a set of novel SI frameworks to address several fundamental technical challenges in integrating HI with AI. Examples of these challenges include data heterogeneity, data sparsity, model generality, and model explainability. The presented solutions are interdisciplinary in nature and include techniques from AI, machine learning, social computing, human-computer interaction, estimation theory, and statistical learning. Second, this book also offers a comprehensive exploration of critical human-centered issues in social intelligence. Examples of such issues include fairness, bias, and privacy. The book presents several human-AI integrated systems that are designed specifically to address these pressing issues of social concerns and provide a holistic approach to designing robust and ethical SI systems that can be deployed responsibly in our society. Third, this book provides real-world case studies from different application domains to thoroughly evaluate the presented frameworks and solutions and demonstrate their effectiveness in real-world settings. Examples of the application domains include (but are not limited to) truth discovery and explanation, disaster damage assessment, smart cities, human face recognition, and AI for online education. These case studies provide valuable insights for the readers to understand the practical applicability and limitations of social intelligence solutions in a real-world context. Overall, to the best of our knowledge, this book presents the first comprehensive SI paradigm for harnessing the collective intelligence from both HI and AI towards addressing emerging problems in our society for the common good.

The remaining chapters of the book are structured as follows. In Chap. 2, we discuss the background, interdisciplinary nature, and emerging applications of the SI paradigm. In Chap. 3, we review a series of mathematical foundations that are essential to understand the principles of the presented SI techniques. Examples of such foundations include estimation theory, deep learning, and AI optimizations. In Chap. 4, we present two examples of SI frameworks (i.e., DualGen and ContrastFaux) to address the data heterogeneity challenge in social intelligence. In Chap. 5, we introduce CrowdAdapt and CollabGeneral, two representative SI solutions to address the data sparsity and model generality challenges in social intelligence. In Chap. 6, we investigate the critical aspect of explainable AI (XAI) in social intelligence and present two XAI frameworks (i.e., HC-COVID and DExFC) to demonstrate the concept of collaborative explanations that integrate the strengths of both HI and AI. Chapter 7 studies the problem of integrating AI and HI from crowdsourcing systems and presents two human-AI collaboration frameworks (i.e., CrowdNAS and CrowdOptim) to address several fundamental problems in AI design and optimization (e.g., neural network architecture search and hyperparameter optimization). In Chap. 8, we discuss the critical challenge of fairness and bias mitigation in social intelligence systems and present two fairness-aware SI systems (i.e., FairCrowd and DebiasEdu) that specifically address the fairness issue of SI systems by exploring the collective power of HI and AI. Chapter 9 studies the topic of privacy in social intelligence and presents two privacy-preserving solutions (i.e., CoviDKG and FaceCrowd) that particularly target at addressing the privacy issue in SI by leveraging the integrated intelligence from both humans and AI. In Chap. 10, we provide further readings on several important directions that are closely related to SI (e.g., human-AI systems, AI for social good, fairness and privacy in SI, ethics of AI, generative AI in SI). The book concludes with Chap. 11 which summarizes the key findings of the book and discusses the remaining challenges for future research in this exciting field of social intelligence.

References

1. A. E. Aiello, A. Renson, and P. Zivich. Social media-and internet-based disease surveillance for public health. *Annual review of public health*, 41:101, 2020.
2. M. T. Al Amin, T. Abdelzaher, D. Wang, and B. Szymanski. Crowd-sensing with polarized sources. In *Distributed Computing in Sensor Systems (DCOSS), 2014 IEEE International Conference on*, pages 67–74. IEEE, 2014.
3. T. R. Besold and U. Schmid. Why generality is key to human-level artificial intelligence. *Advances in Cognitive Systems*, 4:13–24, 2016.
4. G. Chandrasekaran, T. N. Nguyen, and J. Hemanth D. Multimodal sentimental analysis for social media applications: A comprehensive review. *Wiley Interdisciplinary Reviews: Data Mining and Knowledge Discovery*, 11(5):e1415, 2021.
5. U. A. Ciftci, G. Yuksek, and I. Demir. My face my choice: Privacy enhancing deepfakes for social media anonymization. In *Proceedings of the IEEE/CVF Winter Conference on Applications of Computer Vision*, pages 1369–1379, 2023.
6. T. Draws, A. Rieger, O. Inel, U. Gadiraju, and N. Tintarev. A checklist to combat cognitive biases in crowdsourcing. In *Proceedings of the AAAI Conference on Human Computation and Crowdsourcing*, volume 9, pages 48–59, 2021.
7. M. Duan. Astraea: Self-balancing federated learning for improving classification accuracy of mobile deep learning applications. *arXiv preprint arXiv:1907.01132*, 2019.
8. L. Edwards and M. Veale. Slave to the algorithm? why a 'right to an explanation' is probably not the remedy you are looking for. *Duke Law & Technology Review*, 16:18–84, 2017.
9. K. El Emam, E. Jonker, L. Arbuckle, and B. Malin. A systematic review of re-identification attacks on health data. *PloS one*, 6(12):e28071, 2011.
10. A. Farahani, S. Voghoei, K. Rasheed, and H. R. Arabnia. A brief review of domain adaptation. *Advances in data science and information engineering: proceedings from ICDATA 2020 and IKE 2020*, pages 877–894, 2021.
11. Y. Gong, L. Shang, and D. Wang. Integrating social explanations into explainable artificial intelligence (xai) for combating misinformation: Vision and challenges. *IEEE Transactions on Computational Social Systems*, 2024.
12. G. Grill. Future protest made risky: Examining social media based civil unrest prediction research and products. *Computer Supported Cooperative Work (CSCW)*, 30(5-6):811–839, 2021.
13. S. Hangloo and B. Arora. Combating multimodal fake news on social media: methods, datasets, and future perspective. *Multimedia systems*, 28(6):2391–2422, 2022.
14. A. Hanlon and K. Jones. Ethical concerns about social media privacy policies: do users have the ability to comprehend their consent actions? *Journal of Strategic Marketing*, pages 1–18, 2023.
15. E. Hunt. *Human intelligence*. Cambridge University Press, 2010.
16. E. B. Hunt. *Artificial intelligence*. Academic Press, 2014.
17. J. Klayman. Varieties of confirmation bias. *Psychology of learning and motivation*, 32:385–418, 1995.
18. Z. Kou, L. Shang, Y. Zhang, and D. Wang. Hc-covid: A hierarchical crowdsource knowledge graph approach to explainable covid-19 misinformation detection. *Proceedings of the ACM on Human-Computer Interaction*, 6(GROUP):1–25, 2022. https://doi.org/10.1145/3492855.

19. Z. Kou, D. Y. Zhang, L. Shang, and D. Wang. Exfaux: A weakly supervised approach to explainable fauxtography detection. In *2020 IEEE International Conference on Big Data (Big Data)*, pages 631–636. IEEE, 2020.
20. M. K. Lee, N. Grgić-Hlača, M. C. Tschantz, R. Binns, A. Weller, M. Carney, and K. Inkpen. Human-centered approaches to fair and responsible ai. In *Extended Abstracts of the 2020 CHI Conference on Human Factors in Computing Systems*, pages 1–8, 2020.
21. P. Lee, S. Bubeck, and J. Petro. Benefits, limits, and risks of gpt-4 as an ai chatbot for medicine. *New England Journal of Medicine*, 388(13):1233–1239, 2023.
22. T. Li, S. Das, H.-P. Lee, D. Wang, B. Yao, and Z. Zhang. Human-centered privacy research in the age of large language models. In *Extended Abstracts of the CHI Conference on Human Factors in Computing Systems*, pages 1–4, 2024.
23. X. Li, D. Caragea, C. Caragea, M. Imran, and F. Ofli. Identifying disaster damage images using a domain adaptation approach. In *Proceedings of the 16th International conference on information systems for crisis response and management*, 2019.
24. P. P. Liang, A. Zadeh, and L.-P. Morency. Foundations & trends in multimodal machine learning: Principles, challenges, and open questions. *ACM Computing Surveys*, 56(10):1–42, 2024.
25. M. T. Linaza, J. Posada, J. Bund, P. Eisert, M. Quartulli, J. Döllner, A. Pagani, I. G. Olaizola, A. Barriguinha, T. Moysiadis, et al. Data-driven artificial intelligence applications for sustainable precision agriculture. *Agronomy*, 11(6):1227, 2021.
26. M. L. Littman and J. W. Crandall. Coordinating human and ai decisions. *Nature Machine Intelligence*, 3(1):1–3, 2021.
27. S. Mahajan, P. Kumar, J. A. Pinto, A. Riccetti, K. Schaaf, G. Camprodon, V. Smári, A. Passani, and G. Forino. A citizen science approach for enhancing public understanding of air pollution. *Sustainable Cities and Society*, 52:101800, 2020.
28. T. W. Malone and M. S. Bernstein. *Handbook of Collective Intelligence*. MIT Press, 2015.
29. OpenAI. Gpt-4 technical report, 2023.
30. M. Ponti and A. Seredko. Human-machine-learning integration and task allocation in citizen science. *Humanities and Social Sciences Communications*, 9(1):1–15, 2022.
31. M. T. Rashid and D. Wang. Covidsens: a vision on reliable social sensing for covid-19. *Artificial Intelligence Review*, pages 1–25, 2020.
32. L. Shang, Y. Zhang, Q. Ye, N. Wei, and D. Wang. Smartwatersens: A crowdsensing-based approach to groundwater contamination estimation. In *2022 IEEE International Conference on Smart Computing (SMARTCOMP)*, pages 48–55. IEEE, 2022.
33. L. Shang, Y. Zhang, C. Youn, and D. Wang. Sat-geo: A social sensing based content-only approach to geolocating abnormal traffic events using syntax-based probabilistic learning. *Information Processing & Management*, 59(2):102807, 2022.
34. L. Shang, Y. Zhang, Z. Yue, Y. Choi, H. Zeng, and D. Wang. A domain adaptive graph learning framework to early detection of emergent healthcare misinformation on social media. In *Proceedings of the International AAAI Conference on Web and Social Media*, volume 18, pages 1408–1421, 2024, https://doi.org/10.1609/icwsm.v18i1.31398.
35. F. Shi, J. Wang, J. Shi, Z. Wu, Q. Wang, Z. Tang, K. He, Y. Shi, and D. Shen. Review of artificial intelligence techniques in imaging data acquisition, segmentation, and diagnosis for covid-19. *IEEE reviews in biomedical engineering*, 14:4–15, 2020.
36. S. L. Speir, L. Shang, D. Bolster, J. L. Tank, C. J. Stoffel, D. M. Wood, B. W. Peters, N. Wei, and D. Wang. Solutions to current challenges in widespread monitoring of groundwater quality via crowdsensing. *Groundwater*, 60(1):15–24, 2022.
37. G. Spitale, N. Biller-Andorno, and F. Germani. Ai model gpt-3 (dis) informs us better than humans. *arXiv preprint arXiv:2301.11924*, 2023.
38. M. Taddeo and L. Floridi. How ai can be a force for good. *Science*, 361(6404):751–752, 2018.
39. N. Tomašev, J. Cornebise, F. Hutter, S. Mohamed, A. Picciariello, B. Connelly, D. C. Belgrave, D. Ezer, F. C. v. d. Haert, F. Mugisha, et al. Ai for social good: unlocking the opportunity for positive impact. *Nature Communications*, 11(1):2468, 2020.

40. G. von Krogh and E. von Hippel. The promise of research on open source software. *Management Science*, 52(7):975–983, 2006.
41. D. Wang, B. K. Szymanski, T. Abdelzaher, H. Ji, and L. Kaplan. The age of social sensing. *Computer*, 52(1):36–45, 2019.
42. J. Wen, Z. Zhang, Y. Lan, Z. Cui, J. Cai, and W. Zhang. A survey on federated learning: challenges and applications. *International Journal of Machine Learning and Cybernetics*, 14(2):513–535, 2023.
43. Y. Yan, G. M. Fung, R. Rosales, and J. G. Dy. Active learning from crowds. In *Proceedings of the 28th international conference on machine learning (ICML-11)*, pages 1161–1168, 2011.
44. L. Yang, M. Tian, D. Xin, Q. Cheng, and J. Zheng. Ai-driven anonymization: Protecting personal data privacy while leveraging machine learning. *arXiv preprint arXiv:2402.17191*, 2024.
45. Y. Yang, C. Zhang, C. Fan, W. Yao, R. Huang, and A. Mostafavi. Exploring the emergence of influential users on social media during natural disasters. *International Journal of Disaster Risk Reduction*, 38:101204, 2019.
46. Y. Yao, J. Duan, K. Xu, Y. Cai, Z. Sun, and Y. Zhang. A survey on large language model (llm) security and privacy: The good, the bad, and the ugly. *High-Confidence Computing*, page 100211, 2024.
47. Z. Yue, H. Zeng, Z. Kou, L. Shang, and D. Wang. Contrastive domain adaptation for early misinformation detection: A case study on covid-19. *arXiv preprint arXiv:2208.09578*, pages 2423–2433, 2022.
48. H. Zeng, Z. Yue, Z. Kou, Y. Zhang, L. Shang, and D. Wang. Fairness-aware training of face attribute classifiers via adversarial robustness. *Knowledge-Based Systems*, 264:110356, 2023.
49. D. Y. Zhang, Z. Kou, and D. Wang. Fairfl: A fair federated learning approach to reducing demographic bias in privacy-sensitive classification models. In *2020 IEEE International Conference on Big Data (Big Data)*, pages 1051–1060. IEEE, 2020.
50. D. Y. Zhang, Q. Li, H. Tong, J. Badilla, Y. Zhang, and D. Wang. Crowdsourcing-based copyright infringement detection in live video streams. In *2018 IEEE/ACM International Conference on Advances in Social Networks Analysis and Mining (ASONAM)*, pages 367–374. IEEE, 2018.
51. D. Y. Zhang, L. Shang, B. Geng, S. Lai, K. Li, H. Zhu, M. T. Amin, and D. Wang. Fauxbuster: A content-free fauxtography detector using social media comments. In *2018 IEEE international conference on big data (big data)*, pages 891–900. IEEE, 2018.
52. Y. Zhang, L. Shang, R. Zong, H. Zeng, Z. Yue, and D. Wang. Collabequality: A crowd-ai collaborative learning framework to address class-wise inequality in web-based disaster response. In *Proceedings of the ACM Web Conference 2023*, pages 4050–4059, 2023.
53. Y. Zhang, R. Zong, L. Shang, H. Zeng, Z. Yue, N. Wei, and D. Wang. On optimizing model generality in ai-based disaster damage assessment: A subjective logic-driven crowd-ai hybrid learning approach. In *IJCAI*, pages 6317–6325, 2023, https://doi.org/10.24963/ijcai.2023/701. Copyright owner: IJCAI Organization, all rights reserved.
54. R. Zong, Y. Zhang, L. Shang, and D. Wang. Contrastfaux: Sparse semi-supervised fauxtography detection on the web using multi-view contrastive learning. In *Proceedings of the ACM Web Conference 2023*, pages 3994–4003, New York, NY, USA, 2023. ACM. https://doi.org/10.1145/3543507.3583869.
55. R. Zong, Y. Zhang, F. Stinar, L. Shang, H. Zeng, N. Bosch, and D. Wang. A crowd–ai collaborative approach to address demographic bias for student performance prediction in online education. In *Proceedings of the AAAI Conference on Human Computation and Crowdsourcing*, volume 11, pages 198–210, 2023. https://doi.org/10.1609/hcomp.v11i1.27560.

Chapter 2
Social Intelligence Backgrounds and Applications

Abstract In this chapter, we discuss the root of social intelligence from the perspective of human intelligence (HI), artificial intelligence (AI), and their integration. The interdisciplinary nature of social intelligence is also highlighted with a detailed discussion on closely related domains, such as natural language processing and text mining, computer vision and image processing, social computing and human-computer interaction, estimation theory, and statistical learning. Additionally, we present a few emerging social intelligence applications in real-world scenarios to further demonstrate the necessity of this new intelligence paradigm. Examples of these applications include social media misbehavior identification and mitigation, multimodal truth discovery, explainable AI and machine learning, disaster response and damage assessment, AI and crowdsourcing for education, and social sensing in smart city applications.

Keywords Social intelligence · Human intelligence · Artificial intelligence · Interdisciplinary · Applications

2.1 Social Intelligence: Integrating Human Intelligence and AI

2.1.1 Human Intelligence

Human intelligence (HI) often refers to the intellectual or cognitive capabilities of human beings. Examples of such capabilities include problem solving, abstract thinking, reasoning, creativity, adapting to new situations, emotions, and social understanding [18]. More recently, with the ubiquity of network connections and the proliferation of collective intelligence platforms (e.g., online crowdsourcing), HI could be obtained at an unprecedented speed and scale [23]. Collective HI from a large cohort of individuals has been leveraged to address critical real-world problems. One example of using HI in the healthcare domain is a platform called PatientsLikeMe where people with chronic conditions, rare diseases, and other health issues can share their experiences, track their symptoms, and exchange

D. Wang et al., *Social Intelligence*, https://doi.org/10.1007/978-3-031-90080-8_2

health-related insights with others [71]. The goal of this platform is to improve the health outcomes of its users by harnessing the collective intelligence of patients and providing an opportunity for peer-to-peer support and research. The patients' self-reported outcomes and personalized experiences help build a broader understanding of their medical conditions and how they manifest in real life. This HI-centered approach provides a much richer set of human-derived knowledge that greatly supplements the traditional clinical datasets that are often sparse and incomplete. Another example of using HI in the information space is called "Community Notes" from X (previously known as "Birdwatch" from Twitter) where users on X are empowered to review tweets and identify incorrect claims on the platform [46]. X users can also provide additional contexts and explanations to justify why they believe a certain claim is false. The platform then takes into account the inputs from a large crowd of participating users by considering their report consistency and individual reputations to decide the veracity of the relevant claims. The "Community Notes" represents a new paradigm of decentralized fact-checking that gets rid of the reliance on centralized authorities or external organizations by leveraging the power of collective intelligence from humans. HI has also been leveraged to address complex and widespread challenges in other application domains (e.g., astronomy, biology, environmental sustainability, history) by fully harnessing the collective wisdom of diverse individuals [72], which will essentially complement the power of AI in the social intelligence paradigm.

2.1.2 Artificial Intelligence

AI is one of the major technology revolutions that is believed to significantly improve productivity in this new century. Compared to HI, AI has its unique strength in domains that process large volumes of data, perform precise computational tasks, and identify trends and patterns from complex data patterns [14]. One example is in the domain of AI for health where AI systems have shown increased accuracy in disease diagnoses (e.g., breast cancer, eye diseases) by analyzing a massive amount of medical imaging data. In a recent study, a collaboration team of Google Health researchers and physician scientists have developed a deep learning based AI prediction model that can outperform radiologists in detecting breast cancer from mammograms by achieving reduced rates of both false positives and false negatives [24]. Moreover, AI also shows a clear advantage in areas like financial trading where AI models process a tremendous amount of transaction data samples in real-time to make critical decisions at speeds and scales beyond human's capabilities. For example, Robo-advisors are AI-powered automated financial advisors that offer financial planning and advice to clients [6]. Such systems have the advantage of avoiding conflict of interest and providing significantly lower and more transparent cost structures than human financial advisors. They can also provide 24/7 continuous monitoring of market conditions and automatically adjust clients' portfolios based on their investment preferences and risk tolerance. Additionally,

AI has also been successfully applied to autonomous driving. For example, AI systems in autonomous cars make real-time decisions by leveraging data inputs from cameras, radar, and LiDAR (Light Detection And Ranging) and improve the safety of driving compared to human drivers, who are often limited by slower reflexes and attention spans [59]. Thus, AI can effectively augment human capabilities to build a more accurate, scalable, and efficient social intelligence system.

2.1.3 Social Intelligence

In the above discussion, we note that HI and AI have unique advantages in their specific application domains. However, we also observe that these two types of intelligence suffer from their intrinsic limitations. For example, human intelligence, while adaptable and creative, is often constrained by human cognitive capacity and biases [18]. Similarly, artificial intelligence, while computationally scalable and efficient, often lacks an in-depth understanding of correct contexts and the ability to generalize knowledge across diverse domains. Motivated by the complementary strengths of HI and AI, social intelligence emerges as a new paradigm that integrates human expertise and AI capabilities to address complex societal challenges more effectively. For example, social intelligence has been applied to detect false health information during health crises by jointly incorporating the crowdsourced domain knowledge from expert workers and the inference capabilities of deep learning algorithms to accurately identify incorrect information on social and news media [25]. Additionally, social intelligence has been applied to improve disaster damage assessment accuracy across different types of disasters by collectively exploring the generalizable knowledge from common individuals and the precision and specificity of AI models in correctly assessing the severity of disaster damage situations [86]. Such hybrid social intelligence solutions effectively harness the joint power of HI and AI while addressing their individual limitations, ultimately enhancing the decision-making processes and problem-solving capabilities of humans in complex real-world SI applications.

2.2 Interdisciplinary Nature of Social Intelligence

The interdisciplinary nature of social intelligence requires an integration of knowledge and methodology from a diverse set of research disciplines to fully address the technical challenges within social intelligence applications. For example, the data heterogeneity in SI requires techniques from natural language processing and computer vision to extract information from multimodal SI data. To provide better model explainability and systems accessibility, methods from human-computer interaction and social computing can be leveraged to facilitate the human-AI interactions in SI. Additionally, principles from estimation theory and statistical learning lay out a solid foundation for SI to integrate the hybrid intelligence from both HI and AI. In this section, we highlight several key research fields and disciplines that are closely related to the development and understanding of social intelligence systems, including: (1) *Natural Language Processing and Text Mining* that enables the understanding and generation of natural language for social intelligence applications in human society; (2) *Computer Vision and Image Processing* that support the analysis and interpretation of visual content and non-verbal communications in the social contexts; (3) *Social Computing and Human-Computer Interaction* that facilitates the modeling of social dynamics and the designing of effective human-AI interfaces; and (4) *Estimation Theory and Statistical Learning* that ensures the rigorous development of analytical social intelligence models that can effectively integrate HI with AI. We elaborate on each of these related fields below.

2.2.1 Natural Language Processing and Text Mining

Social intelligence data encompasses a variety of textual information, ranging from social media posts and online discussions to digital messages and news articles. Recent advancements in natural language processing (NLP) and text mining play a crucial role in encoding, analyzing, and understanding rich and informative textual data in social intelligence applications [12]. For example, sentiment analysis techniques can be used to explore public opinion on pressing issues on social media (e.g., health crises, natural disasters, social unrest) [51], topic modeling can identify emerging trends in online discussions [52], and named entity recognition can track the mention and influence of specific entities (e.g., individuals, organizations) across various data sources [74]. These techniques greatly enhance the capability of machines to extract meaningful insights from large volumes of unstructured textual data. More recently, with the advent of deep learning-based language models and transformer architectures, large language models (e.g., GPTs, LLaMA) have demonstrated unparalleled performance in natural language understanding and generation [3]. Despite these models offering significant improvements in language processing capabilities, their application in social intelligence presents unique challenges and opportunities. For example, human-centric data in social intelligence applications often includes multimodal content beyond text, such as images, videos, and audio. Such multimodal data requires the development of integrated social intelligence systems that are capable of analyzing information across different data modalities. For instance, to accurately detect multimodal incorrect information that is intentionally crafted by sophisticated malicious content creators, it is often required to not only analyze content in individual data modalities (e.g., text, image) but also explicitly examine their cross-modal associations to identify the incorrect content that is implicitly conveyed by the multimodal content [55]. Therefore, while NLP and text mining techniques build a solid foundation for analyzing textual content in social intelligence applications, these techniques still need to be integrated with advancements in other disciplines (e.g., computer vision, multimedia) to fully capture and understand the complex multimodal human-centric content in social intelligence.

2.2.2 Computer Vision and Image Processing

Social intelligence also closely relates to computer vision (CV) and image processing given the observation that images and videos are increasingly prevalent in social media, news outlets, and online communications [62]. CV and image processing techniques are essential in extracting and learning from the diverse visual content in social intelligence applications. For example, convolutional neural networks (CNNs) and other deep learning architectures in CV have shown remarkable performance in image-driven tasks. Examples of such tasks include image classification, object detection, and facial recognition [5]. These advanced techniques empower social intelligence systems to automatically categorize visual content, capture salient objects, identify individuals in images, and infer emotions from facial expressions. Additionally, image processing methods, such as style transfer and super-resolution, also expand the visual analysis capability of social intelligence. For example, a social intelligence application for public policy adherence may leverage super-resolution techniques to enhance low-quality images or videos captured in public spaces, revealing critical details such as face masks and social distancing compliance [85]. However, the integration of these advanced CV and image processing techniques in social intelligence systems also presents new challenges. In particular, bias and fairness issues in CV models pose significant concerns for social intelligence applications [27]. These models may exhibit biased performance across different demographic groups due to imbalanced training data or inherent algorithmic biases [76]. For instance, facial recognition systems have been shown to have higher error rates for certain racial and gender groups, which can lead to unfair results for individuals or groups from vulnerable populations in social intelligence applications [75]. These challenges lie not only in developing more equitable CV models but also in ensuring transparency and accountability in their deployment in social intelligence applications, which is especially true when the outcome of these models may negatively affect certain individuals and communities.

2.2.3 Social Computing and Human-Computer Interaction

Social computing and human-computer interaction (HCI) are two other fields that are in a close connection to social intelligence. Social Computing examines how people interact with each other through computing technologies, while HCI studies the design and use of computer interfaces for human users [32, 36]. In the context of social intelligence, these disciplines contribute to the development of human-AI integrated systems that can effectively interpret, respond to, and influence human behaviors in the social space. For example, social computing techniques, such as AI-driven social network analysis [13] and social dynamic modeling [60], could be leveraged to identify influential users or detect community structures in online platforms. HCI principles could guide the design of interactive user interfaces with AI systems to engage users for effective information sharing and collaborative problem-solving. However, the integration of social computing and HCI with social intelligence also faces several critical challenges. One significant issue is the ethical consideration of user privacy and data protection when integrating human intelligence with AI. As social intelligence increasingly collects and adopts user information (e.g., social media activities, profile information) to analyze and model social behaviors, there is a growing concern about the potential incorrect use of this information and the erosion of individual privacy [20]. For example, while community-contributed medical knowledge is helpful for assessing the integrity of health information, the incorrect personal health information could be abused by potential employers to discriminate against job candidates [53]. Thus, it remains an important challenge how to balance the needs of social data and the responsibility of protecting user data privacy in computational social intelligence applications. Moreover, another challenge lies in the development of HCI interfaces in social intelligence applications that could effectively transform abstract prediction results generated by AI algorithms into contextualized and actionable insights that could be easily understood by end users with varying levels of expertise. For example, explainable AI (XAI) could identify key features or model decision paths that lead to a particular prediction. However, such technical explanations often lack natural language context that could be adopted by non-expert end users for critical decision-making (e.g., health decisions, financial investments). Thus, it is also crucial for HCI designs in social intelligence applications to effectively bridge the gap between complex AI-generated insights and practical, actionable information for humans with diverse backgrounds and expertise levels.

2.2.4 Estimation Theory and Statistical Learning

Estimation theoretical approaches form a basis for many machine learning and statistical models and offer ways to infer parameters of a model given a set of data samples [29]. These approaches also provide the foundation for developing rigorous analytical models that support integration of HI and AI with uncertainty quantification in social intelligence applications. Maximum Likelihood Estimation (MLE) is a statistical method for estimating the parameters of a model by maximizing the likelihood of the observed data being least surprising to the model [43]. MLE can be used in truth discovery where it identifies probabilistic parameters for detecting false narratives from the true ones by analyzing patterns in target datasets to optimize model accuracy and adaptability. The Expectation-Maximization (EM) algorithm is an iterative method for finding the maximum likelihood estimates of parameters in models with latent variables. The EM algorithm alternates between two steps: the

Expectation (E) step and the Maximization (M) step [15]. For example, in a hateful meme detection application, it leverages latent sentiment clusters to iteratively improve the accuracy of classifier predictions by incorporating unobserved data dimensions. Hidden Markov Models (HMMs) are another set of statistical models that are often used to represent dynamic systems whose states follow a Markov process. Such models are commonly used in temporal pattern recognition tasks (e.g., speech, handwriting, and gesture recognition) [48]. For example, in smart city applications, the HMM-based models can predict and optimize traffic flow by modeling sequential vehicle movement patterns and detecting anomalies in urban transit systems. Subjective Logic is a probabilistic logic framework that leverages logic and probability theory to handle subjective opinions, explicitly accounting for uncertainty and belief ownership [22]. For instance, in health truth discovery, it evaluates the credibility of sources by combining probabilistic opinions and user-generated trust scores to assess information integrity under uncertainty. Therefore, estimation theory and statistical learning provide the key to creating analytically sound social intelligence systems with rigorous mathematical foundations.

2.3 Emerging Social Intelligence Applications

While being an interdisciplinary field, the social intelligence paradigm is also motivated by several emerging issues and applications in real world that are elaborated below. These issues span the information, social, health, education, and environmental dimensions, and highlight the need for innovative, adaptive, and integrated solutions that prioritize the collective intelligence from both humans and AI.

2.3.1 Social Media Misbehavior Identification and Mitigation

Social media misbehavior has become a severe issue on online platforms [67–69]. Examples of social media misbehaviors include cyberbullying [17, 63], trolling [42], hate speech [37, 50], rumors [10], and offensive memes [61]. For example, Yao et al. proposed an online approach with sequential hypothesis testing to detect cyberbullying events in a timely manner [73]. Cheng et al. developed a machine learning based scheme to detect troll posts by exploring users' mood and context information on online news discussion communities [9]. Relia et al. developed a multi-level classifier to automatically identify targeted and self-narration of discrimination on social media [49]. Kumar et al. designed a multi-task learning scheme that exploits the reply stance of social media posts to identify rumors [31]. Mathew et al. developed a user behavior based solution to classify hateful users on social media by characterizing social connections of hateful users and the diffusion patterns of content posted by these users [38]. Zhu designed a visual-linguistic transformer framework to integrate the pre-trained visual and linguistic features for detecting the abuse of memes [87]. While the above solutions identify or mitigate certain social media misbehaviors to some extent, the potential of human intelligence remains largely under-explored (e.g., human inputs are mainly used for data annotations, which suffer from the cost and scalability challenges). The social intelligence paradigm provides a new perspective to address the social media misbehavior identification and mitigation problem by fully exploring the strength of human intelligence (e.g., rich prior knowledge, social context awareness, ethical judgment) and integrating human intelligence with AI solutions to provide a more comprehensive and reliable solution. For example, Shang et al. designed a human-AI collaborative hatred-vulnerable video detector by jointly modeling the topological patterns and semantic features in user comment networks on online video-sharing platforms [56]. In particular, the crowd wisdom embedded in the user comment network has been effectively extracted and integrated with a deep learning model to accurately identify hatred-vulnerable videos that are difficult to be detected with AI-only solutions. We believe that SI can be explored to address other emerging social media misbehavior problems in future by fully harnessing the power of HI and AI.

2.3.2 Multimodal Truth Discovery

Faulty and ungrounded information have raised many concerns in recent years, especially for the multimodal news and user-generated content on social platforms and the Web [2]. Researchers have made significant efforts to detect online false information [25, 54, 79]. Specifically, Popat et al. proposed the CredEye system that assesses the credibility of social media claims by exploiting the language style and stance characteristics of the textual content [44]. Chen et al. developed a cross-model ambiguity learning approach to learn multimodal feature representation from image and text for truth discovery [8]. Choi et al. proposed a context-aware multi-modal data fusion approach that utilizes user comments to assess the information integrity of YouTube videos [11]. Min et al. designed a graph-based health truth discovery solution that explores the social context information from social media users to detect false health information [39]. Weinzierl et al. utilized a domain-specific language model to detect COVID-19 vaccine false information on social media [70]. Gonzalez et al. proposed a machine learning based detection system that incorporates health experts' perceptions to detect false information on health-related websites [19]. While the above AI or machine learning driven approaches can identify false information in textual or visual content, they often fall short of capturing the misalignment between the multimodal news content or are unreliable in detecting the deliberately manipulated content targeting audiences who often lack professional knowledge to make reliable decisions [64]. Social intelligence provides an alternative paradigm to address the multimodal truth discovery problem by exploring the collective strengths of both human intelligence (e.g., both specialized and generalized domain knowledge) and AI (e.g., the capability to process and analyze a tremendous amount of data). For example, Kou et al. developed a human-centered AI framework exploring the collective intelligence from both humans and AI to detect multimodal fauxtography (a type of multimodal false information) with structured explanations [26, 28]. Their approach effectively captures the implicit relations and attributes of different subjects in a multimodal post by creating a multimodal knowledge graph that integrates human intelligence and AI. We expect social intelligence to play an increasingly important role in addressing such multimodal truth discovery and explanation problems in future research.

2.3.3 Disaster Response and Damage Assessment

Previous efforts have been made to address the disaster response and damage assessment in AI and deep learning [30, 34, 40, 41]. As an example, Nguyen et al. developed a convolutional neural network approach to quantify the damage severity of affected areas from social media imagery data for disaster response [41]. Li et al. proposed a deep transfer learning approach for disaster damage assessment of an unfolding disaster event using a domain adaptation approach [34]. Mouzannar et al. developed a deep neural network framework that utilizes both text and image data from social media posts for damage identification via multimodal convolutional neural networks [40]. Kumar et al. developed an end-to-end deep learning based image processing system to detect disaster-affected cultural heritage sites using online social media images [30]. Current disaster response and damage assessment solutions rely on neural network architectures designed by AI experts, which often introduce non-negligible costs and errors into the design process [16]. There also exist several crowd-AI integrated approaches (e.g., CrowdLearn [77], Hybrid Para [21]) that leverage human intelligence to troubleshoot and retrain a single neural network architecture in disaster damage assessment applications [21, 78]. Those approaches, however, rely heavily on the pre-defined neural network architecture and are subject to the suboptimal performance caused by the manual neural network selection process [66]. In contrast, social intelligence creates the possibility of leveraging the human intelligence of common individuals to improve the design and configuration of AI systems. For example, Zhang et al. developed a novel social intelligence system by exploring the integrated intelligence from both humans (i.e., crowd workers from Amazon Mechanical Turk) and AI to automatically identify the optimal neural network architecture in the design space without the inputs from the AI experts [81]. We expect SI to be further applied to optimize other components (e.g., data collection, information processing, and decision-making) in future disaster response and damage assessment systems.

2.3.4 AI and Crowdsourcing for Education

Researchers have made significant progress to improve learning experiences and outcomes in education with the recent advances in AI and crowdsourcing. For example, Abdi et al. designed a crowdsourcing-based learning system to assess students' knowledge state by tracing their performance on crowdsourcing knowledge assessment tasks [1]. Prihar et al. utilized crowdsourced tutoring to increase students' next-problem accuracy in online learning and developed a method to rank the tutoring effectiveness of different crowd workers [45]. Wambsganss et al. developed a deep-learning-based student argumentation self-evaluation system that leverages nudging theory techniques to help students write convincing texts [65]. Qadir et al. analyzed how to use large language models to benefit students (e.g., customized explanations) while minimizing negative impacts (e.g., false information) [47]. A comprehensive survey of using AI and crowdsourcing in education can be found in [4]. This survey discusses several challenges of current solutions that are solely based on AI or crowdsourcing and highlighted a hybrid solution that combines both AI and crowdsourcing is promising to address these challenges. Among the challenges discussed, a prominent one is the fairness issue in education where bias from both AI (e.g., demographic bias, model bias) and humans (e.g., confirmation bias, affect heuristic bias) can negatively affect the AI model performance in the education context and potentially has a negative impact on the learning outcomes of students who use such AI-assisted learning tools. In social intelligence, the collective intelligence from both humans and AI can provide a new paradigm to address the complex bias in education context effectively. For example, Zong et al. has recently developed a crowd-AI collaborative debias framework that integrates AI and crowd intelligence to achieve accurate and fair student performance prediction in online education [88]. In their framework, they designed a novel bias-aware crowdsourcing interface and a crowd-AI fusion mechanism to address the demographic bias of AI and the cognitive bias of the crowd, respectively. Future research opportunities include further investigate the potential interactions between different types of bias from both AI and HI and create a comprehensive SI solution for AI in Education applications.

2.3.5 Social Sensing in Smart City Applications

Social (human-centric) sensing presents a new sensing paradigm, where timely observations of the physical world are collected from human sensors (e.g., people or devices on their behalf) [67, 69]. With the pervasive network connections, the prevalence of digital devices, and the mass data dissemination opportunities, social sensing has been increasingly applied in smart city applications [57, 82, 84]. For example, Liang et al. leveraged social sensing data from crowdsourced PurpleAir sensor networks to assess the wildfire smoke impact on indoor air quality in

California [35]. Silva et al. designed a crowd-driven vehicle pollution monitoring system that couples social sensing with an onboard diagnostic carbon dioxide reader to estimate vehicle emission in smart cities [58]. Zhang et al. proposed a multi-view learning framework to identify risky traffic locations in smart transportation systems [80]. Breuer et al. developed HydroCrowd, a social sensing based water sampling strategy that recruited crowd participants to collect surface water samples for a hydrological study that assesses the spatial distribution of stream solutes and demonstrated the effectiveness of social sensing as a sampling method in hydrology [7]. Lee et al. proposed a social sensing noise mapping framework to monitor urban environmental noise in smart cities by utilizing crowdsourced noise data from calibrated smartphones [33]. The above social sensing solutions, however, mainly focus on humans' roles as sensors for data generation or collection purposes. Social intelligence provides a more comprehensive paradigm that also unleashes the full power of human intelligence that complements AI well in many smart city applications. For example, Zhang et al. developed a social intelligence system that leverages human contributions in two separate roles (i.e., sensing and intelligence) in a smart urban sensing application [83]. In their framework, they first collected and analyzed the image data contributed by human users on social media (i.e., human sensing ability) and built a human-AI collaboration system to optimize the hyperparameter configuration of the AI model via a novel fusion scheme that integrates AI and HI to generate desirable predictions for the smart urban sensing application. In future research, it will be an exciting direction to develop a human-AI integrated SI system for smart city applications where human roles (e.g., data contributor, AI optimizer, decision makers) are fully explored and optimized.

References

1. S. Abdi, H. Khosravi, and S. Sadiq. Modelling learners in crowdsourcing educational systems. In *International Conference on Artificial Intelligence in Education*, pages 3–9. Springer, 2020.
2. F. Alam, S. Cresci, T. Chakraborty, F. Silvestri, D. Dimitrov, G. D. S. Martino, S. Shaar, H. Firooz, and P. Nakov. A survey on multimodal disinformation detection. *arXiv preprint arXiv:2103.12541*, 2021.
3. M. Alawida, S. Mejri, A. Mehmood, B. Chikhaoui, and O. Isaac Abiodun. A comprehensive study of chatgpt: advancements, limitations, and ethical considerations in natural language processing and cybersecurity. *Information*, 14(8):462, 2023.
4. H. S. Alenezi and M. H. Faisal. Utilizing crowdsourcing and machine learning in education: Literature review. *Education and Information Technologies*, 25(4):2971–2986, 2020.
5. Y. Bi, B. Xue, P. Mesejo, S. Cagnoni, and M. Zhang. A survey on evolutionary computation for computer vision and image analysis: Past, present, and future trends. *IEEE Transactions on Evolutionary Computation*, 27(1):5–25, 2022.
6. L. Brenner and T. Meyll. Robo-advisors: A substitute for human financial advice? *Journal of Behavioral and Experimental Finance*, 25:100275, 2020.
7. L. Breuer, N. Hiery, P. Kraft, M. Bach, A. H. Aubert, and H.-G. Frede. Hydrocrowd: a citizen science snapshot to assess the spatial control of nitrogen solutes in surface waters. *Scientific reports*, 5(1):1–10, 2015.

8. Y. Chen, D. Li, P. Zhang, J. Sui, Q. Lv, L. Tun, and L. Shang. Cross-modal ambiguity learning for multimodal fake news detection. In *Proceedings of the ACM Web Conference 2022*, pages 2897–2905, New York, NY, USA, 2022. ACM.
9. J. Cheng, M. Bernstein, C. Danescu-Niculescu-Mizil, and J. Leskovec. Anyone can become a troll: Causes of trolling behavior in online discussions. In *Proceedings of the 2017 ACM conference on computer supported cooperative work and social computing*, pages 1217–1230, 2017.
10. D. Choi, S. Chun, H. Oh, J. Han, et al. Rumor propagation is amplified by echo chambers in social media. *Scientific Reports*, 10(1):1–10, 2020.
11. H. Choi and Y. Ko. Effective fake news video detection using domain knowledge and multimodal data fusion on youtube. *Pattern Recognition Letters*, 154:44–52, 2022.
12. K. Chowdhary and K. Chowdhary. Natural language processing. *Fundamentals of artificial intelligence*, pages 603–649, 2020.
13. N. N. Daud, S. H. Ab Hamid, M. Saadoon, F. Sahran, and N. B. Anuar. Applications of link prediction in social networks: A review. *Journal of Network and Computer Applications*, 166:102716, 2020.
14. T. H. Davenport. *The AI advantage: How to put the artificial intelligence revolution to work.* mit Press, 2018.
15. A. P. Dempster, N. M. Laird, and D. B. Rubin. Maximum likelihood from incomplete data via the em algorithm. *Journal of the Royal Statistical Society: Series B (Methodological)*, 39(1):1–22, 1977.
16. T. Elsken, J. H. Metzen, F. Hutter, et al. Neural architecture search: A survey. *J. Mach. Learn. Res.*, 20(55):1–21, 2019.
17. E. Englander, E. Donnerstein, R. Kowalski, C. A. Lin, and K. Parti. Defining cyberbullying. *Pediatrics*, 140(Supplement 2):S148–S151, 2017.
18. R. Fjelland. Why general artificial intelligence will not be realized. *Humanities and Social Sciences Communications*, 7(1):1–9, 2020.
19. C. González-Fernández, A. Fernández-Isabel, I. M. de Diego, R. R. Fernández, and J. V. Pinheiro. Experts perception-based system to detect misinformation in health websites. *Pattern Recognition Letters*, 152:333–339, 2021.
20. W. Hollingshead, A. Quan-Haase, and W. Chen. Ethics and privacy in computational social science: A call for pedagogy. In *Handbook of Computational Social Science, Volume 1*, pages 171–185. Routledge, 2021.
21. J. Jarrett, I. Saleh, M. B. Blake, R. Malcolm, S. Thorpe, and T. Grandison. Combining human and machine computing elements for analysis via crowdsourcing. In *10th IEEE International Conference on Collaborative Computing: Networking, Applications and Worksharing*, pages 312–321. IEEE, 2014.
22. A. Jøsang. *Subjective Logic: A Formalism for Reasoning Under Uncertainty.* Springer, 2016.
23. R. Karachiwalla and F. Pinkow. Understanding crowdsourcing projects: A review on the key design elements of a crowdsourcing initiative. *Creativity and innovation management*, 30(3):563–584, 2021.
24. D. Killock. Ai outperforms radiologists in mammographic screening. *Nature Reviews Clinical Oncology*, 17(3):134–134, 2020.
25. Z. Kou, L. Shang, Y. Zhang, and D. Wang. Hc-covid: A hierarchical crowdsource knowledge graph approach to explainable covid-19 misinformation detection. *Proceedings of the ACM on Human-Computer Interaction*, 6(GROUP):1–25, 2022. https://doi.org/10.1145/3492855.
26. Z. Kou, D. Zhang, L. Shang, and D. Wang. What and why? towards duo explainable fauxtography detection under constrained supervision. *IEEE Transactions on Big Data*, 9(1):133–146, 2023, https://doi.org/10.1109/TBDATA.2021.3130165.
27. Z. Kou, Y. Zhang, L. Shang, and D. Wang. Faircrowd: Fair human face dataset sampling via batch-level crowdsourcing bias inference. In *2021 IEEE/ACM 29th International Symposium on Quality of Service (IWQOS)*, pages 1–10. IEEE, 2021, https://doi.org/10.0.4.85/IWQOS52092.2021.9521312, Reprinted with permission from IEEE.

28. Z. Kou, Y. Zhang, D. Zhang, and D. Wang. Crowdgraph: A crowdsourcing multi-modal knowledge graph approach to explainable fauxtography detection. *Proceedings of the ACM on Human-Computer Interaction*, 6(CSCW2):1–28, 2022.
29. L. Kubácek. *Foundations of estimation theory*. Elsevier, 2012.
30. P. Kumar, F. Ofli, M. Imran, and C. Castillo. Detection of disaster-affected cultural heritage sites from social media images using deep learning techniques. *Journal on Computing and Cultural Heritage (JOCCH)*, 13(3):1–31, 2020.
31. S. Kumar and K. M. Carley. Tree lstms with convolution units to predict stance and rumor veracity in social media conversations. In *Proceedings of the 57th Annual Meeting of the Association for Computational Linguistics*, pages 5047–5058, 2019.
32. D. M. Lazer, A. Pentland, D. J. Watts, S. Aral, S. Athey, N. Contractor, D. Freelon, S. Gonzalez-Bailon, G. King, H. Margetts, et al. Computational social science: Obstacles and opportunities. *Science*, 369(6507):1060–1062, 2020.
33. H. P. Lee, S. Garg, and K. M. Lim. Crowdsourcing of environmental noise map using calibrated smartphones. *Applied Acoustics*, 160:107130, 2020.
34. X. Li, D. Caragea, C. Caragea, M. Imran, and F. Ofli. Identifying disaster damage images using a domain adaptation approach. In *Proceedings of the 16th International conference on information systems for crisis response and management*, 2019.
35. Y. Liang, D. Sengupta, M. J. Campmier, D. M. Lunderberg, J. S. Apte, and A. H. Goldstein. Wildfire smoke impacts on indoor air quality assessed using crowdsourced data in california. *Proceedings of the National Academy of Sciences*, 118(36):e2106478118, 2021.
36. I. S. MacKenzie. *Human-computer interaction: An empirical research perspective*. Elsevier, 2024.
37. R. Magu, K. Joshi, and J. Luo. Detecting the hate code on social media. In *Proceedings of the international AAAI conference on web and social media*, volume 11, pages 608–611, 2017.
38. B. Mathew, R. Dutt, P. Goyal, and A. Mukherjee. Spread of hate speech in online social media. In *Proceedings of the 10th ACM conference on web science*, pages 173–182, 2019.
39. E. Min, Y. Rong, Y. Bian, T. Xu, P. Zhao, J. Huang, and S. Ananiadou. Divide-and-conquer: Post-user interaction network for fake news detection on social media. In *Proceedings of the ACM Web Conference 2022*, pages 1148–1158, 2022.
40. H. Mouzannar, Y. Rizk, and M. Awad. Damage identification in social media posts using multimodal deep learning. In *ISCRAM*, 2018.
41. D. T. Nguyen, F. Ofli, M. Imran, and P. Mitra. Damage assessment from social media imagery data during disasters. In *Proceedings of the 2017 IEEE/ACM International Conference on Advances in Social Networks Analysis and Mining 2017*, pages 569–576, 2017.
42. J. Paavola, T. Helo, H. Jalonen, M. Sartonen, and A. Huhtinen. Understanding the trolling phenomenon: The automated detection of bots and cyborgs in the social media. *Journal of Information Warfare*, 15(4):100–111, 2016.
43. Y. Pawitan. *All Likelihood: Statistical Modelling and Inference Using Likelihood*. Oxford University Press, 2013.
44. K. Popat, S. Mukherjee, J. Strötgen, and G. Weikum. Credeye: A credibility lens for analyzing and explaining misinformation. In *Companion Proceedings of the The Web Conference 2018*, pages 155–158, 2018.
45. E. Prihar, T. Patikorn, A. Botelho, A. Sales, and N. Heffernan. Toward personalizing students' education with crowdsourced tutoring. In *Proceedings of the Eighth ACM Conference on Learning@ Scale*, pages 37–45, 2021.
46. N. Pröllochs. Community-based fact-checking on twitter's birdwatch platform. In *Proceedings of the International AAAI Conference on Web and Social Media*, volume 16, pages 794–805, 2022.
47. J. Qadir. Engineering education in the era of chatgpt: Promise and pitfalls of generative ai for education. In *2023 IEEE Global Engineering Education Conference (EDUCON)*, pages 1–9. IEEE, 2023.
48. L. R. Rabiner. A tutorial on hidden markov models and selected applications in speech recognition. *Proceedings of the IEEE*, 77(2):257–286, 1989.

49. K. Relia, Z. Li, S. H. Cook, and R. Chunara. Race, ethnicity and national origin-based discrimination in social media and hate crimes across 100 us cities. In *Proceedings of the International AAAI Conference on Web and Social Media*, volume 13, pages 417–427, 2019.
50. M. H. Ribeiro, P. H. Calais, Y. A. Santos, V. A. Almeida, and W. Meira Jr. “like sheep among wolves”: Characterizing hateful users on twitter. *arXiv preprint arXiv:1801.00317*, 2017.
51. A. Saroj and S. Pal. Use of social media in crisis management: A survey. *International Journal of Disaster Risk Reduction*, 48:101584, 2020.
52. L. Shang, B. Chen, A. Vora, Y. Zhang, X. Cai, and D. Wang. Socialdrought: A social and news media driven dataset and analytical platform towards understanding societal impact of drought. In *Proceedings of the International AAAI Conference on Web and Social Media*, volume 18, pages 2051–2062, 2024.
53. L. Shang, Z. Kou, Y. Zhang, J. Chen, and D. Wang. A privacy-aware distributed knowledge graph approach to qois-driven covid-19 misinformation detection. In *2022 IEEE/ACM 30th International Symposium on Quality of Service (IWQoS)*, pages 1–10. IEEE, 2022. https://doi.org/10.1109/IWQoS54832.2022.9812879, Reprinted with permission from IEEE.
54. L. Shang, Z. Kou, Y. Zhang, and D. Wang. A multimodal misinformation detector for covid-19 short videos on tiktok. In *2021 IEEE International Conference on Big Data (Big Data)*, pages 899–908. IEEE, 2021.
55. L. Shang, Z. Kou, Y. Zhang, and D. Wang. A duo-generative approach to explainable multimodal covid-19 misinformation detection. In *Proceedings of the ACM Web Conference 2022*, pages 3623–3631, New York, NY, USA, 2022. ACM. https://doi.org/10.1145/3485447.3512257.
56. L. Shang, D. Y. Zhang, M. Wang, and D. Wang. Vulnercheck: a content-agnostic detector for online hatred-vulnerable videos. In *2019 IEEE International Conference on Big Data (Big Data)*, pages 573–582. IEEE, 2019.
57. L. Shang, Y. Zhang, C. Youn, and D. Wang. Sat-geo: A social sensing based content-only approach to geolocating abnormal traffic events using syntax-based probabilistic learning. *Information Processing & Management*, 59(2):102807, 2022.
58. M. Silva, G. Signoretti, J. Oliveira, I. Silva, and D. G. Costa. A crowdsensing platform for monitoring of vehicular emissions: A smart city perspective. *Future Internet*, 11(1):13, 2019.
59. J. Singh. The future of autonomous driving: Vision-based systems vs. lidar and the benefits of combining both for fully autonomous vehicles. *Journal of Artificial Intelligence Research and Applications*, 1(2):333–376, 2021.
60. J. Skarding, B. Gabrys, and K. Musial. Foundations and modeling of dynamic networks using dynamic graph neural networks: A survey. *iEEE Access*, 9:79143–79168, 2021.
61. S. Suryawanshi, B. R. Chakravarthi, M. Arcan, and P. Buitelaar. Multimodal meme dataset (multioff) for identifying offensive content in image and text. In *Proceedings of the Second Workshop on Trolling, Aggression and Cyberbullying*, pages 32–41, 2020.
62. R. Szeliski. *Computer vision: algorithms and applications*. Springer Nature, 2022.
63. C. Van Hee, G. Jacobs, C. Emmery, B. Desmet, E. Lefever, B. Verhoeven, G. De Pauw, W. Daelemans, and V. Hoste. Automatic detection of cyberbullying in social media text. *PloS one*, 13(10):e0203794, 2018.
64. E. K. Vraga and L. Bode. Using expert sources to correct health misinformation in social media. *Science Communication*, 39(5):621–645, 2017.
65. T. Wambsganss, A. Janson, T. Käser, and J. M. Leimeister. Improving students argumentation learning with adaptive self-evaluation nudging. *Proceedings of the ACM on Human-Computer Interaction*, 6(CSCW2):1–31, 2022.
66. A. Wan, X. Dai, P. Zhang, Z. He, Y. Tian, S. Xie, B. Wu, M. Yu, T. Xu, K. Chen, et al. Fbnetv2: Differentiable neural architecture search for spatial and channel dimensions. In *Proceedings of the IEEE/CVF Conference on Computer Vision and Pattern Recognition*, pages 12965–12974, 2020.
67. D. Wang, T. Abdelzaher, and L. Kaplan. *Social sensing: building reliable systems on unreliable data*. Morgan Kaufmann, 2015.

68. D. Wang, L. Kaplan, H. Le, and T. Abdelzaher. On truth discovery in social sensing: A maximum likelihood estimation approach. In *Information Processing in Sensor Networks (IPSN), 2012 ACM/IEEE 11th International Conference on*, pages 233–244. IEEE, 2012.
69. D. Wang, B. K. Szymanski, T. Abdelzaher, H. Ji, and L. Kaplan. The age of social sensing. *Computer*, 52(1):36–45, 2019.
70. M. A. Weinzierl and S. M. Harabagiu. Automatic detection of covid-19 vaccine misinformation with graph link prediction. *Journal of biomedical informatics*, 124:103955, 2021.
71. P. Wicks, M. Massagli, J. Frost, C. Brownstein, S. Okun, T. Vaughan, R. Bradley, J. Heywood, et al. Sharing health data for better outcomes on patientslikeme. *Journal of medical Internet research*, 12(2):e1549, 2010.
72. D. H. Wolpert and K. Tumer. An introduction to collective intelligence. *arXiv preprint cs/9908014*, 1999.
73. M. Yao, C. Chelmis, and D. S. Zois. Cyberbullying ends here: Towards robust detection of cyberbullying in social media. In *The World Wide Web Conference*, pages 3427–3433, 2019.
74. J. Yu, Z. Li, J. Wang, and R. Xia. Grounded multimodal named entity recognition on social media. In *Proceedings of the 61st Annual Meeting of the Association for Computational Linguistics (Volume 1: Long Papers)*, pages 9141–9154, 2023.
75. H. Zeng, Z. Yue, Z. Kou, Y. Zhang, L. Shang, and D. Wang. Fairness-aware training of face attribute classifiers via adversarial robustness. *Knowledge-Based Systems*, 264:110356, 2023.
76. H. Zeng, Z. Yue, L. Shang, Y. Zhang, and D. Wang. On adversarial robustness of demographic fairness in face attribute recognition. In *Proceedings of the Thirty-Second International Joint Conference on Artificial Intelligence*, pages 527–535, 2023.
77. D. Zhang, Y. Zhang, Q. Li, T. Plummer, and D. Wang. Crowdlearn: A crowd-ai hybrid system for deep learning-based damage assessment applications. In *2019 IEEE 39th International Conference on Distributed Computing Systems (ICDCS)*, pages 1221–1232, 2019.
78. D. Zhang, Y. Zhang, Q. Li, T. Plummer, and D. Wang. Crowdlearn: A crowd-ai hybrid system for deep learning-based damage assessment applications. In *2019 IEEE 39th International Conference on Distributed Computing Systems (ICDCS)*, pages 1221–1232. IEEE, 2019.
79. D. Y. Zhang, L. Shang, B. Geng, S. Lai, K. Li, H. Zhu, M. T. Amin, and D. Wang. Fauxbuster: A content-free fauxtography detector using social media comments. In *2018 IEEE international conference on big data (big data)*, pages 891–900. IEEE, 2018.
80. Y. Zhang, Y. Lu, D. Zhang, L. Shang, and D. Wang. Risksens: A multi-view learning approach to identifying risky traffic locations in intelligent transportation systems using social and remote sensing. In *2018 IEEE International Conference on Big Data (Big Data)*, pages 1544–1553. IEEE, 2018.
81. Y. Zhang, R. Zong, Z. Kou, L. Shang, and D. Wang. Crowdnas: A crowd-guided neural architecture searching approach to disaster damage assessment. *Proceedings of the ACM on Human-Computer Interaction*, 6(CSCW2):1–29, 2022. https://doi.org/10.1145/3555179.
82. Y. Zhang, R. Zong, L. Shang, Z. Kou, and D. Wang. A deep contrastive learning approach to extremely-sparse disaster damage assessment in social sensing. In *Proceedings of the 2021 IEEE/ACM International Conference on Advances in Social Networks Analysis and Mining*, pages 151–158, New York, NY, USA, 2021. ACM.
83. Y. Zhang, R. Zong, L. Shang, Z. Kou, H. Zeng, and D. Wang. Crowdoptim: A crowd-driven neural network hyperparameter optimization approach to ai-based smart urban sensing. *Proceedings of the ACM on Human-Computer Interaction*, 6(CSCW2):1–27, 2022. https://doi.org/10.1145/3555536.
84. Y. Zhang, R. Zong, L. Shang, M. T. Rashid, and D. Wang. Superclass: A deep duo-task learning approach to improving qos in image-driven smart urban sensing applications. In *2021 IEEE/ACM 29th International Symposium on Quality of Service (IWQOS)*, pages 1–6. IEEE, 2021.
85. Y. Zhang, R. Zong, L. Shang, H. Zeng, Z. Yue, and D. Wang. Symlearn: A symbiotic crowd-ai collective learning framework to web-based healthcare policy adherence assessment. In *Proceedings of the ACM on Web Conference 2024*, pages 2497–2508, 2024.

86. Y. Zhang, R. Zong, L. Shang, H. Zeng, Z. Yue, N. Wei, and D. Wang. On optimizing model generality in ai-based disaster damage assessment: A subjective logic-driven crowd-ai hybrid learning approach. In *IJCAI*, pages 6317–6325, 2023, https://doi.org/10.24963/ijcai.2023/701. Copyright owner: IJCAI Organization, all rights reserved.
87. R. Zhu. Enhance multimodal transformer with external label and in-domain pretrain: Hateful meme challenge winning solution. *arXiv preprint arXiv:2012.08290*, 2020.
88. R. Zong, Y. Zhang, F. Stinar, L. Shang, H. Zeng, N. Bosch, and D. Wang. A crowd–ai collaborative approach to address demographic bias for student performance prediction in online education. In *Proceedings of the AAAI Conference on Human Computation and Crowdsourcing*, volume 11, pages 198–210, 2023. https://doi.org/10.1609/hcomp.v11i1.27560.

Chapter 3
Mathematical Foundations of Social Intelligence

Abstract The chapter outlines the mathematical aspects of social intelligence and covers major estimation theory techniques such as Maximum Likelihood Estimation (MLE), Expectation-Maximization (EM), Hidden Markov Models (HMM), Bayesian Estimation, and Subjective Logic. With our understanding of their mathematics and application, we seek to shed light on their utility in parameter inference and uncertainty-based decision-making in social intelligence settings. Furthermore, the chapter transitions into an analysis of deep learning models such as Multilayer Perceptrons (MLP), Convolutional Neural Networks (CNN), Graph Neural Networks (GNN), and Transformers, emphasizing their architectural innovations and application-specific optimizations. This comprehensive synthesis provides a unified framework for understanding and leveraging advanced computational methods in Social Intelligence, setting the stage for future research and applications in this interdisciplinary domain.

Keywords Mathematical foundation · Estimation theory · Deep learning · AI optimization

3.1 Basics of Estimation Theoretical Approaches

Estimation theoretical approaches form a basis for many machine learning and statistical models, and offer ways to infer parameters of models given a set of data samples. In this chapter, we will review some foundational estimation techniques that are related to social intelligence (SI): Maximum Likelihood Estimation (MLE), the Expectation-Maximisation (EM) algorithm, Hidden Markov Models (HMM), Bayesian Estimation, and Subjective Logic. We will present both mathematical formulations and technical details of these reviewed methods.

D. Wang et al., *Social Intelligence*, https://doi.org/10.1007/978-3-031-90080-8_3

3.1.1 Maximum Likelihood Estimation (MLE)

Maximum Likelihood Estimation (MLE) is a method for estimating the parameters of a statistical model by maximizing the likelihood function that measures how well the model explains the observed data [86].

Given a dataset $\mathcal{D} = \{x_1, x_2, \ldots, x_n\}$ and a parameterized model with parameter vector θ, the likelihood function $\mathcal{L}(\theta)$ is defined as:

$$\mathcal{L}(\theta) = P(\mathcal{D} \mid \theta) = \prod_{i=1}^{n} P(x_i \mid \theta)$$

The log-likelihood function, which is often more convenient to work with, is:

$$\ell(\theta) = \log \mathcal{L}(\theta) = \sum_{i=1}^{n} \log P(x_i \mid \theta)$$

The MLE for the parameter θ is obtained by maximizing the log-likelihood function:

$$\hat{\theta}_{\text{MLE}} = \arg\max_{\theta} \ell(\theta)$$

This involves taking the derivative of the log-likelihood with respect to θ, setting it to zero, and solving for θ:

$$\frac{\partial \ell(\theta)}{\partial \theta} = 0$$

Consider the example of a Gaussian distribution with observations $\mathcal{D} = \{x_1, x_2, \ldots, x_n\}$, mean μ, and variance σ^2. The likelihood function is:

$$\mathcal{L}(\mu, \sigma^2) = \prod_{i=1}^{n} \frac{1}{\sqrt{2\pi\sigma^2}} \exp\left(-\frac{(x_i - \mu)^2}{2\sigma^2}\right)$$

The log-likelihood function is:

$$\ell(\mu, \sigma^2) = -\frac{n}{2} \log(2\pi\sigma^2) - \frac{1}{2\sigma^2} \sum_{i=1}^{n} (x_i - \mu)^2$$

To find the MLEs, we take the partial derivatives of $\ell(\mu, \sigma^2)$ with respect to μ and σ^2 and set them to zero:

$$\frac{\partial \ell}{\partial \mu} = \frac{1}{\sigma^2} \sum_{i=1}^{n} (x_i - \mu) = 0 \implies \hat{\mu} = \frac{1}{n} \sum_{i=1}^{n} x_i$$

$$\frac{\partial \ell}{\partial \sigma^2} = -\frac{n}{2\sigma^2} + \frac{1}{2(\sigma^2)^2} \sum_{i=1}^{n} (x_i - \mu)^2 = 0 \implies \hat{\sigma}^2 = \frac{1}{n} \sum_{i=1}^{n} (x_i - \hat{\mu})^2$$

MLE enjoys a set of advantages compared to other estimation methods, such as the method of moments (MoM), least squares (LS), and regularized estimation methods like ridge regression and LASSO. One is its simplicity and generality [61]: MLE provides a unified approach to parameter estimation that works across a broad class of statistical models. Under certain regularity conditions, MLEs are also asymptotically efficient [115]—meaning that they are the estimator with the lowest possible variance among all unbiased estimators—and they are often reparameterisation invariant: a good estimator that will maintain its desirable properties even when a model is reparameterised [17].

Yet MLE has its own issues as well. One important problem is that the likelihood function is often hard to maximize [77], especially for complex models with large model parameter search space, such as slow convergence and local optima, necessitating the use of advanced optimization methods [14]. Another downside is that MLE can be very sensitive to outliers; the likelihood function gives unusually large weights to extreme values [52]. This can be a problem when the sample size is small, where MLEs might be biased and perform poorly, and often require correction or alternative methods to validate results and ensure robustness [71].

MLE is well-suited to being applied in contexts where the model for the data is well-specified, and adequate data are available so that the estimates produced are likely to be reliable. Examples include inference about parameters of distributions, fitting models in regression problems, and machine learning algorithms such as logistic regression and hidden Markov models [11]. In practice, MLE is usually applied as a step in conjunction with other methods to check robustness of results [44].

MLE can be applied to several social intelligence applications as it facilitates strong probabilistic decision modeling. For example, in truth discovery, MLE generates parameter estimates of models to evaluate the accuracy of information by making the best use of the data the model see (e.g., trends in the spread of incorrect information or interactions among users) [87]. MLE also plays a significant role in training NLP models to detect hateful speech, by optimizing patterns and feature weights of words to identify toxic messages accurately [98]. Furthermore, in smart city applications, MLE helps parameterize models of urban data analysis, including traffic forecasting, environmental monitoring, and social behavior prediction, so that probabilistic predictions are close to real observations [105]. By offering a principle-based approach to parameter estimation, MLE is highly reliable and versatile in multiple social intelligence contexts.

3.1.2 Expectation-Maximization (EM) Algorithm

The Expectation-Maximization (EM) algorithm is an iterative method for finding the maximum likelihood estimates of parameters in models with latent variables. The EM algorithm alternates between two steps: the expectation (E) step and the maximization (M) step [21].

Given observed data $\mathcal{D}$ and latent variables Z, the goal is to maximize the marginal likelihood $P(\mathcal{D} \mid \theta)$. The EM algorithm proceeds as follows:

In the E-step, we compute the expected value of the log-likelihood function with respect to the current estimate of the distribution of the latent variables:

$$Q(\theta \mid \theta^{(t)}) = \mathbb{E}_{Z|\mathcal{D},\theta^{(t)}} \left[\log P(\mathcal{D}, Z \mid \theta) \right]$$

In the M-step, we maximize $Q(\theta \mid \theta^{(t)})$ to update the parameter estimates:

$$\theta^{(t+1)} = \arg\max_{\theta} Q(\theta \mid \theta^{(t)})$$

The process is repeated until convergence, where the parameter estimates do not change significantly between iterations [77].

Consider the example of a Gaussian Mixture Model (GMM) with K components. The likelihood function for this model is:

$$L(\theta; \mathbf{x}) = \prod_{i=1}^{n} \sum_{k=1}^{K} \pi_k \mathcal{N}(x_i \mid \mu_k, \sigma_k^2)$$

In the context of the EM algorithm for GMMs, the steps are as follows:

During the E-step, we calculate the responsibility $\gamma(z_{ik})$:

$$\gamma(z_{ik}) = \frac{\pi_k \mathcal{N}(x_i \mid \mu_k, \sigma_k^2)}{\sum_{j=1}^{K} \pi_j \mathcal{N}(x_i \mid \mu_j, \sigma_j^2)}$$

During the M-step, we update the parameters π_k, μ_k, and σ_k^2 based on the calculated responsibilities:

$$\pi_k = \frac{1}{n} \sum_{i=1}^{n} \gamma(z_{ik})$$

$$\mu_k = \frac{\sum_{i=1}^{n} \gamma(z_{ik}) x_i}{\sum_{i=1}^{n} \gamma(z_{ik})}$$

$$\sigma_k^2 = \frac{\sum_{i=1}^{n} \gamma(z_{ik})(x_i - \mu_k)^2}{\sum_{i=1}^{n} \gamma(z_{ik})}$$

EM algorithm has several advantages compared to other optimization techniques such as variational inference, stochastic expectation-maximization, and reinforcement learning [81]. For example, the EM provides a solution for incomplete or missing data, and is useful in a wide range of latent variable models, (e.g., Gaussian Mixture Models (GMMs), Hidden Markov Models (HMMs), and Factor Analysis). The EM solution is particularly useful when it is difficult to directly maximize the likelihood function. While the EM algorithm aims to achieve a local maximum of the likelihood function, its performance depends on the initial parameter estimates, and it may converge to suboptimal solutions or local optima in certain cases [121]. The EM algorithm works well with latent variables, in which the likelihood can not be calculated directly. EM algorithm gives a reliable and iterative parameter estimation for these models by exploring the latent variables structure, which helps refine the model's fit to the observed data [78].

However, the EM algorithm comes with its own limitations. For example, it could settle in to a local rather than a global maximum, when the first estimates of parameters are not close to the true values [95]. This may lead to unsatisfactory parameter estimations. Additionally, the convergence of the EM algorithm can be slow, especially when the data is multidimensional or the parameter space of the model is complex [10].

EM algorithm offers an efficient solution to handle incomplete or noisy data in social intelligence applications. For example, in social media sentiment analysis, EM can be employed to find unlabeled sentiment distributions in incomplete or poorly labeled datasets and optimize model performance to capture emotional patterns [101]. EM gleans preferences from partial-interactions—such as clicks, views, or time spent on an item—that do not fully capture a user's final decision to generate precise, adaptive recommendations for recommendation engines such as e-commerce or personalized content engines [82]. Similarly, in community detection applications in social intelligence, EM can locate individuals or groups based on partially-available interaction data (such as incomplete records of public transport usage or electricity consumption), which arise due to privacy constraints or data collection limitations, to optimize infrastructure development and resource allocation. As the EM algorithm iteratively updates the probabilistic models, it helps ensure that predictions remain effective and reliable, even when social intelligence applications face uncertainty due to incomplete, noisy, or conflicting data.

3.1.3 *Hidden Markov Models (HMMs)*

Hidden Markov Models (HMMs) are statistical models used to represent systems that follow a Markov process with hidden states [27]. HMMs are widely used in temporal pattern recognition tasks such as speech, handwriting, and gesture recognition[88]. An HMM consists of a set of hidden states $S = \{S_1, S_2, \ldots, S_N\}$, an initial state distribution $\pi = \{\pi_i\}$, state transition probabilities $A = \{a_{ij}\}$, and observation probabilities $B = \{b_i(o_t)\}$. These components define the probabilistic structure of the model [11].

The Forward-Backward algorithm is used to compute the posterior probabilities of the hidden states. This algorithm consists of two main procedures: the forward procedure and the backward procedure [5].

In the forward procedure, we compute the probability of the partial observation sequence up to time t and state S_i:

$$\alpha_t(i) = P(O_1, O_2, \ldots, O_t, S_t = S_i \mid \lambda)$$

The forward probabilities are recursively calculated as:

$$\alpha_{t+1}(j) = \left[\sum_{i=1}^{N} \alpha_t(i) a_{ij} \right] b_j(O_{t+1})$$

In the backward procedure, we compute the probability of the partial observation sequence from time $t + 1$ to the end, given state S_i at time t:

$$\beta_t(i) = P(O_{t+1}, O_{t+2}, \ldots, O_T \mid S_t = S_i, \lambda)$$

The backward probabilities are recursively calculated as:

$$\beta_t(i) = \sum_{j=1}^{N} a_{ij} b_j(O_{t+1}) \beta_{t+1}(j)$$

This is done using the Baum-Welch algorithm (one variation of the EM algorithm) to compute an HMM's unknown parameters. It iteratively changes the model parameters to maximize the likelihood that the observed data is generated by the model[119].

One key advantage of HMM is that they can be used to describe temporal dependence in continuous data, which makes them ideal for problems where the sequence of observations is of interest [60]. HMMs can also handle missing/incomplete values by using the hidden state model to extrapolate missing values [89]. Furthermore, HMMs present a probabilistic way of modelling data sequences where prior information and uncertainty are implicitly considered [34].

However, the HMMs have their own drawbacks. One key limitation lies in the computational complexity of algorithms for training and inference, especially when it involves big data or more complex models , where the exponential growth of computational complexity can hinder scalability and real-time applicability [9]. Another drawback is that HMMs assume a first-order Markov property where the future state depends solely on the current state, which is not necessarily realistic in many real-world scenarios [89]. Furthermore, HMMs is also sensitive to the initial parameters selection, which can influence the final model convergence [66].

HMMs are particularly appropriate for sequence data where the aim is to simulate the process that produces the observations. Common use cases are speech recognition (using HMMs to emulate phonemes and words), handwriting recognition (using HMMs to simulate stroke progression), and gesture recognition (using HMMs to emulate motions of the hand) [88]. HMMs are also employed in bio-informatics to model biological DNA, RNA, and protein sequences to detect genes, regulatory features, and structural patterns [34].

In social intelligence, HMMs are commonly used to describe sequential and time-dependent processes by modeling the interplay between observations and hidden states [35]. For example, in truth discovery, HMMs can observe the history of narratives and determine trends in the propagation of false information through social networks by modeling user behavior and content consumption [80]. In damage assessment, HMMs can simulate the temporal progression of damage patterns—including the transitions between different severity levels—which leads to more accurate assessments [79]. Furthermore, in human-face applications, HMMs allow predictive modeling of facial expressions and identity recognition by learning the hidden patterns behind facial movements or changes [13]. Additionally, by synchronizing observed and latent variables in the inference process, HMMs is capable of revealing knowledge and predicting trends in complicated social intelligence situations.

3.1.4 Subjective Logic

Subjective Logic is a probabilistic logic framework that extends traditional logic and probability theory to handle subjective opinions, explicitly accounting for uncertainty and belief ownership [55]. In Subjective Logic, an opinion is defined by a belief mass b, disbelief mass d, and uncertainty mass u, constrained by the relationship:

$$b + d + u = 1$$

Each opinion also includes a base rate a, which represents the prior probability of the proposition [59].

Subjective opinions can be modeled using Dirichlet distributions. A Dirichlet distribution is parameterized by a concentration parameter vector $\boldsymbol{\alpha}$ =

$(\alpha_1, \alpha_2, \ldots, \alpha_K)$. The probability density function for the Dirichlet distribution is given by:

$$f(\mathbf{p} \mid \boldsymbol{\alpha}) = \frac{\Gamma\left(\sum_{i=1}^{K} \alpha_i\right)}{\prod_{i=1}^{K} \Gamma(\alpha_i)} \prod_{i=1}^{K} p_i^{\alpha_i - 1}$$

where $\mathbf{p}$ is a probability vector and $\Gamma(\cdot)$ is the Gamma function [7].

Subjective Logic provides various operators for combining opinions, such as the consensus operator for combining independent opinions and the discounting operator for combining dependent opinions [59].

The consensus operator combines two independent opinions $\omega_A = (b_A, d_A, u_A, a)$ and $\omega_B = (b_B, d_B, u_B, a)$ as follows:

$$\omega_{A \wedge B} = \left(\frac{b_A u_B + u_A b_B}{u_A + u_B - u_A u_B}, \frac{d_A u_B + u_A d_B}{u_A + u_B - u_A u_B}, \frac{u_A u_B}{u_A + u_B - u_A u_B} \right)$$

The discounting operator combines an opinion $\omega_B = (b_B, d_B, u_B, a)$ with a trust discount $\omega_A = (b_A, d_A, u_A, a)$:

$$\omega_{A \circ B} = (b_A b_B, d_A + b_A d_B, u_A + b_A u_B, a)$$

An important feature of subjective logic is that it can implicitly express and control ownership of uncertainty and belief, and therefore can be used for applications where such factors are relevant [58]. Subjective logic combines autonomous and dependent viewpoints in a mathematically rigorous manner, which enables robust decision-making under uncertainty [76]. Additionally, subjective logic goes a step further than standard probability theory by capturing beliefs in a more complex way by incorporating the qualitative measurement of uncertainty through the use of opinions that express degrees of belief, disbelief, and uncertainty [103].

However, subjective logic comes with its own limitations. First, combination operators in subjective logic requires extensive computing resources and are notoriously hard for modeling large-scale dataset [84]. Second, another limitation of subjective logic is its requirement of specialized knowledge to set base rates and translate the opinions (e.g., determining initial trust levels often relies on subjective or domain-specific criteria). In addition, the assumption that underlies the Dirichlet distribution is not always accurate, as it assumes fixed positive correlations and proportional relationships, which may not hold in real-world scenarios with independent, negatively correlated, or heterogeneous data, limiting its generalizability[56].

Subjective logic is ideal for scenarios in which uncertainty and ownership of beliefs must be ruled out , as it accounts for uncertainty and attributes beliefs to specific sources[57]. One common application of subjective logic is the truth discovery problem in social intelligence, for which subjective logic is used to model and merge multiple opinions of trust by leveraging opinion tuples (belief, disbelief, and uncertainty) to effectively aggregate conflicting information and identify the reliable consensus. When used in decision making for online education, subjective logic offers an approach to assessing the reliability of different learning resources and student feedback, helping educators manage uncertainty and conflicting perspectives to design more effective and personalized learning experiences [69]. Additionally, for disaster response, subjective logic can evaluate the trustworthiness of incoming reports from various sources, such as eyewitness accounts, sensor data, and social media, allowing response teams to make rational decisions under uncertainty, prioritize actions, and allocate resources more effectively [128].

3.2 Basics of Deep Learning Models

3.2.1 Multilayer Perceptron (MLP)

Multilayer Perceptron (MLP) is a basic type of deep learning model, where it has multiple layers of neurons, with each neuron mapping to all neurons in the next layer. The elementary component of an MLP is the artificial neuron that performs a weighted sum of its inputs and a non-linear activation function [11]. In particular, the output y of a single neuron can be described mathematically as:

$$y = \sigma \left(\sum_{i=1}^{n} w_i x_i + b \right) \tag{3.1}$$

where w_i are the weights, x_i are the inputs, b is the bias, and σ is the activation function, commonly a ReLU (Rectified Linear Unit), sigmoid, or tanh function [38].

For a network with L layers, the output of layer l is given by:

$$\mathbf{a}^{(l)} = \sigma \left(\mathbf{W}^{(l)} \mathbf{a}^{(l-1)} + \mathbf{b}^{(l)} \right) \tag{3.2}$$

where $\mathbf{a}^{(l-1)}$ is the activation from the previous layer, $\mathbf{W}^{(l)}$ is the weight matrix, and $\mathbf{b}^{(l)}$ is the bias vector for layer l [46].

The primary advantage of MLP is that they are easy to implement and are considered as the basis of deep learning and can be adopted as a reference architecture [45]. MLPs also have the universal approximation potential—theoretically, they can approximate any continuous function if sufficient neurons are included in the hidden layer[50]. Furthermore, MLPs are usable for different tasks such as classification and regression, where the input-output correlation is not always linear or sequential [96]. However, MLPs have their own limitations. Their biggest weakness is that they are not effective in the context of large-dimensional data that contain spatially complex representations, like images, as every neuron in one layer is connected to every neuron in the next layer [70]. As a result, the network will encounter a large number of parameters, leading to increased computational complexity and a higher risk of overfitting [49]. Additionally, MLPs are often incapable of exploiting local correlation in unstructured data, such as the sequential dependencies in natural language (where words are contextually related to each other) [125]. Finally, MLPs typically need hyperparameter fine-tuning and can be opportunistic about activation functions and initialization schemes, as the choices of hyperparameters directly influence their ability to mitigate vanishing/exploding gradients and achieve optimal convergence during training[37].

MLPs are particularly appropriate for applications where input data are not ordered spatially or temporally, and input-output relations can be encoded via dense connections [1]. MLP can be used for tabular data analysis, where each feature does not depend on one another spatially or temporally. MLPs are also used when the dataset is relatively small and features interactions are simple enough to capture without having to use any more complex architectures. Multilayer Perceptrons (MLPs) continue to be fundamental models in machine learning, serving as the backbone for various applications such as image and speech recognition, natural language processing, and financial forecasting [109].

3.2.2 Convolutional Neural Networks (CNNs)

Convolutional Neural Networks (CNNs) are deep learning models which are designed to process the grid-based data, such as images, time-series data, and video frames. They have significantly advanced computer vision by leveraging their unique structure to identify spatial hierarchies. CNNs use convolutional layers that perform a convolutional filter of the data to extract fundamental visual features, such as edges, textures, and simple shapes [38]. The core idea of a convolutional layer is to use filters (or kernels) that slide over the input data and perform element-wise multiplications, followed by a summation, to produce a feature map. This operation allows CNNs to be translation invariant, meaning that the learned features can be recognized regardless of their position in the image. The mathematical representation of the output of a convolutional layer is given by [65]:

$$\mathbf{y}_{i,j,k} = \sigma\left(\sum_{m=0}^{M-1}\sum_{n=0}^{N-1}\sum_{c=0}^{C-1} \mathbf{W}_{m,n,c,k}\mathbf{x}_{i+m,j+n,c} + b_k\right) \tag{3.3}$$

where $\mathbf{W}_{m,n,c,k}$ represents the filter weights. Here, m and n are indices spanning the height and width of the filter, c is the index over the input channels, and k denotes the k-th output filter. $\mathbf{x}_{i+m,j+n,c}$ is the input data, and b_k is the bias term for the k-th filter.

In addition to convolutional layers, CNNs typically incorporate pooling layers to reduce the spatial dimensions of the feature maps, which helps in reducing the computational load and controlling overfitting. The most common type of pooling is max pooling, which selects the maximum value within a defined window, as shown in the equation below[126]:

$$\mathbf{y}_{i,j,k} = \max_{m,n} \mathbf{x}_{i+m,j+n,k} \tag{3.4}$$

One of the major advantages of CNNs is their learning of spatial hierarchy, i.e., being able to perceive complicated patterns by joining simpler patterns learned at lower levels. This kind of sequential learning method is especially suitable for data analysis using pictures and videos [8]. Furthermore, CNNs simplify the number of parameters over full-connectivity networks using convolutional filters where weights are allocated among various segments of the input [48]. This parameter sharing scheme not only makes CNNs more effective but also helps reduce the overfitting issue. The other important feature of CNNs is translation invariance—CNNs will recognize features independent of their original locations in the input data, making them remarkably strong for visual tasks [38]. However, CNNs have their own limitations. First, CNNs can be very expensive to train, requiring fast hardware accelerators such as GPUs to train and infer. The requirement of computations may also be an obstacle to those without such hardware. Second, CNNs generally require a good amount of labeled data for training purpose. If training data are in short supply or too costly to obtain, this constraint might inhibit their applications[97]. Moreover, CNN architecture design and tuning is not trivial and typically require extensive deep learning experience, which can be problematic for less experienced users [107].

CNNs are especially good for image/video data driven applications since they can explicitly model spatial correlations in image data [94]. CNNs are commonly used in AI and machine learning tasks such as image classification (identifying the class of an object in an image), object detection (locating and recognizing objects in a picture), and image segmentation (splitting an image into portions or regions according to features)[18, 53, 74]. Additionally, CNNs are also widely used in medical imaging applications such as detecting tumors and segmenting organs [67], and autonomous driving applications by processing camera data to detect objects like vehicles and pedestrians and enable actions such as lane changing and obstacle avoidance[12].

3.2.3 Graph Neural Networks (GNNs)

Graph Neural Networks (GNNs) are popular neural network architectures that operate on graph-structured data, utilizing nodes and edges to model and capture the dependencies and relationships between entities [123]. GNNs have been widely applied for modeling relational data in applications such as social network analysis, recommendation, and molecular biology [63]. In GNNs, the node representation $\mathbf{h}_v^{(k)}$ at layer k is updated based on the representations of its neighbors:

$$\mathbf{h}_v^{(k)} = \sigma\left(\mathbf{W}^{(k)} \sum_{u \in \mathcal{N}(v)} \mathbf{h}_u^{(k-1)} + \mathbf{b}^{(k)}\right) \tag{3.5}$$

where $\mathcal{N}(v)$ denotes the set of neighbors of node v, $\mathbf{W}^{(k)}$ is the weight matrix, and $\mathbf{b}^{(k)}$ is the bias at layer k [42].

A common variation of GNN is the Graph Convolutional Network (GCN), where the update rule is normalized:

$$\mathbf{h}_v^{(k)} = \sigma\left(\mathbf{W}^{(k)} \sum_{u \in \mathcal{N}(v) \cup \{v\}} \frac{1}{\sqrt{\deg(v)\deg(u)}} \mathbf{h}_u^{(k-1)}\right) \tag{3.6}$$

where $\deg(v)$ is the degree of node v [63].

GNNs have their pros and cons. Their most obvious asset is their capability to directly approximate deep relationships and dependencies in graph-based data. This feature makes GNNs appropriate for applications where the data itself is a network (such as social networks, biological networks, and knowledge graphs) [122]. Furthermore, GNNs are adaptable to different types of graphs, such as directed, undirected, weighted, and dynamic graphs [4]. However, GNNs have their own drawbacks. For example, one of the notable problems is that the computational demands of GNNs increase significantly as the number of nodes and edges in the graph increases [124]. Such computation demand can make training and inference of GNNs on big graphs expensive. Another drawback of GNNs is over-smoothing, which happens if the GNNs are stacked with too many graph convolutional layers. The consequence of over-smoothing is a loss of structural information of the input graph data [72]. Moreover, designing effective GNN architectures often requires careful consideration of the specific properties of the graph and task at hand, which can also be complex and time-consuming [123].

GNNs are well-suited for data processing on graphs—where entity relationships matter as much as entities themselves [122]. GNNs are commonly used for social network analysis, in which GNNs are used to predict connections, detect communities, and recommend friends [42]. GNNs can also provide accurate recommendations in recommendation systems by explicitly modeling the user-item relationships [124]. GNNs have been used in molecular biology to predict the activity of proteins, simulate chemical reactions, and design novel molecules [36]. In natural language processing (NLP), GNNs have also been used in semantic role labeling and machine translation, where the data can be represented as a dependency or constituency parse tree [4].

3.2.4 Transformers

Transformers are models of deep learning which have rewritten the game for natural language processing and a few other fields as they successfully process the sequential data without the need for recurrence or convolutions [43]. The transformers exploit an architecture known as self-attention to store dependencies among successive positions in a sequence and therefore perform training and inference in parallel. Transformers are the core to state-of-the-art models, such as BERT, GPT, T5 LNet, and RoBERTa [113].

The key innovation in transformers is the self-attention mechanism, which computes the importance of each element in a sequence relative to others. This is achieved using three main components: queries (Q), keys (K), and values (V). The self-attention operation is defined as:

$$\text{Attention}(Q, K, V) = \text{softmax}\left(\frac{QK^T}{\sqrt{d_k}}\right)V \tag{3.7}$$

where d_k is the dimension of the key vectors. The scaled dot-product attention [26] allows the model to weigh the relevance of different words in a sentence, providing a more comprehensive understanding of the context [113].

Transformers are typically composed of an encoder and a decoder. The encoder consists of multiple layers of self-attention and feed-forward neural networks, while the decoder has a similar structure but includes additional mechanisms to handle sequential generation of outputs. The architecture can be represented as:

$$\mathbf{Z}_l = \text{LayerNorm}(\mathbf{H}_l + \text{SelfAttention}(\mathbf{H}_l)) \tag{3.8}$$

$$\mathbf{H}_{l+1} = \text{LayerNorm}(\mathbf{Z}_l + \text{FeedForward}(\mathbf{Z}_l)) \tag{3.9}$$

where $\mathbf{H}_l$ represents the input to layer l, and $\mathbf{Z}_l$ is the intermediate representation after the self-attention layer [113]. *LayerNorm* refers to the layer normalization, which is a technique that normalizes the inputs across all features in a layer, stabilizing the training process and improving convergence by reducing internal covariate shift.

Transformers have several advantages. The primary one is that they support long-range dependencies which is not a strength of RNNs and LSTMs [22]. Its self-attention allows transformers to extract context from the entire sequence at once, and thus excels at machine translation, text summarization, and question-answering [91]. In addition, since transformers are parallelizable, we can train and infer them much faster than with recurrent models [15]. However, there exist some limitations of transformers as well. For example, the transformers often require significant computational resources, especially to train large models on a massive amount of data. This self-attention mechanism becomes four times as complicated as the input data, as its complexity scales quadratically with the sequence length, leading to low efficiency for very long sequences [6]. Furthermore, transformers require a massive amount of labeled data to train, which can be a challenge in low-resource scenarios (e.g., medical image analysis, low-resource language translation, and rare disease diagnosis) where labeled datasets are often scarce [73].

Transformers do particularly well with tasks that require natural language processing since they can interpret temporal correspondences. They have been widely used for large language models (LLMs) to produce well-formed, context-dependent texts [92]. In machine translation, BERT's bidirectional transformer architecture pre-trains deep contextual embeddings, enabling accurate language translation by effectively capturing cross-lingual syntactic and semantic relationships [22]. Transformers are utilized in speech recognition to analyze audio files for transcribing spoken words [23]. In computer vision, models like Vision Transformers (ViTs) apply self-attention to image patches to capture global dependencies in visual information [24].

3.3 Basics of Optimization Techniques

Deep learning has transformed many tasks from image and speech recognition to natural language analysis and autonomous driving, which greatly improves the efficiency and effectiveness in processing the massive multimodal data in social intelligence applications. However, deep learning models are difficult to train effectively. In this section, we review some of the advanced optimization strategies that have been adopted for optimizing the training process and model performance of deep learning models.

3.3.1 Contrastive Learning

Contrastive learning is a self-supervised learning technique designed to learn effective representations of input data by distinguishing between similar and dissimilar pairs of data points. The primary objective is to bring similar pairs closer together in the feature space while pushing dissimilar pairs apart. This method has proven to be highly effective in learning rich and meaningful representations without the need for labeled data [19].

The core idea of contrastive learning is captured by the contrastive loss function. In its simplest form, the contrastive loss is defined as follows:

$$\mathcal{L}_{contrastive} = \sum_{i=1}^{N} \Big(y_i \cdot d(f(x_i), f(x_i^+)) + (1 - y_i) \cdot \max(0, m - d(f(x_i), f(x_i^-)))\Big) \tag{3.10}$$

where y_i is 1 if x_i and x_i^+ are similar and 0 otherwise. The value of y_i is determined based on predefined criteria for similarity, such as shared class labels in supervised settings or similarity through data augmentation in unsupervised settings [54]. The term $f(x)$ represents the feature representation of input x, while $d(\cdot, \cdot)$ is a distance metric, such as the Euclidean distance. The parameter m is a margin that defines how far apart dissimilar pairs should be [41].

In frameworks like SimCLR [19], the contrastive loss is defined as the normalized temperature-scaled cross-entropy loss (NT-Xent):

$$\mathcal{L}_{NT-Xent} = -\log \frac{\exp(\text{sim}(\mathbf{z}_i, \mathbf{z}_j)/\tau)}{\sum_{k=1}^{2N} \mathbf{1}_{[k \neq i]} \exp(\text{sim}(\mathbf{z}_i, \mathbf{z}_k)/\tau)} \tag{3.11}$$

where $\text{sim}(\mathbf{z}_i, \mathbf{z}_j) = \frac{\mathbf{z}_i \cdot \mathbf{z}_j}{\|\mathbf{z}_i\|\|\mathbf{z}_j\|}$ is the cosine similarity between vectors $\mathbf{z}_i$ and $\mathbf{z}_j$. The parameter τ is a temperature parameter, and $\mathbf{1}_{[k \neq i]}$ is an indicator function which equals 1 if $k \neq i$, and 0 otherwise [19].

Contrastive learning offers several advantages. One of its key advantages is that it can learn useful representations of input features from the unlabeled data (especially when labeled data is different or costly to obtain) [112]. Taking advantage of the natural hierarchy of the data, contrastive learning can create representations that are suitable for many downstream tasks such as image classification, object detection, natural language understanding, and bioinformatics, where robust and semantically meaningful embeddings are crucial for performance and generalization [51]. Moreover, the portability of contrastive learning to other fields and data sets makes it a versatile method for AI model generalization [47]. However, contrastive learning has its own limitations. One of the key limitations is that contrastive learning requires many negative samples (e.g., e.g., a pair of data samples that do not share the same class label in a classification problem) to learn how to discriminate between dissimilar pairs [20]. Moreover, the performance of contrastive learning models can be sensitive to the choice of augmentations and hyperparameters, requiring careful tuning and experimentation [62].

Contrastive learning is well suited for representation learning tasks in both computer vision and natural language processing [127]. In image representation learning, models like SimCLR and MoCo leverage contrastive learning to learn sufficient image representations without labeled data for desirable application performance[19, 47]. Contrastive learning is also employed in mutlimodal learning field in approaches such as CLIP (Contrastive Language-Image Pre-training), which aligns visual and textual representations that enables models to effectively comprehend images and generate corresponding textual descriptions [90].

3.3.2 Domain Adaptation

Domain adaptation seeks to transfer knowledge from a source domain (from which labeled data are abundant) to a target domain (which carries little or no labeled data). This is essential for applying machine learning and AI models to real-world scenarios where labeled data is scarce in new and unseen domains [83]. Domain adaptation has different variants depending on the amount of labeled data in the target domain. For example, in the unsupervised domain adaptation, no labeled data is available in the target domain. In semi-supervised domain adaptation, a few labeled data samples exist in the target domain. In supervised domain adaptation, by contrast, labeled samples exist in both source and target domains, although with different distributions [85]. One of the key steps in domain adaptation is to measure the discrepancy between two domains. Maximum Mean Discrepancy (MMD) is a widely used approach to measure the difference between two domains. It is defined as:

$$\mathrm{MMD}^2(\mathcal{D}_s, \mathcal{D}_t) = \left\| \frac{1}{n_s} \sum_{i=1}^{n_s} \phi(x_i^s) - \frac{1}{n_t} \sum_{j=1}^{n_t} \phi(x_j^t) \right\|_{\mathcal{H}}^2 \tag{3.12}$$

where $\mathcal{D}_s$ and $\mathcal{D}_t$ are the source and target domain distributions, n_s and n_t are the number of samples in the source and target domains, and $\phi(x)$ is a feature mapping function to map the input features into the kernel Hilbert space $\mathcal{H}$ [40].

The squared MMD can be further expanded as:

$$\mathrm{MMD}^2(\mathcal{D}_s, \mathcal{D}_t) = \frac{1}{n_s^2} \sum_{i,j=1}^{n_s} k(x_i^s, x_j^s) + \frac{1}{n_t^2} \sum_{i,j=1}^{n_t} k(x_i^t, x_j^t) - \frac{2}{n_s n_t} \sum_{i=1}^{n_s} \sum_{j=1}^{n_t} k(x_i^s, x_j^t) \tag{3.13}$$

where $k(x, y) = \langle \phi(x), \phi(y) \rangle$ is the kernel function [40].

Domain-Adversarial Neural Networks (DANN) use an adversarial loss to make the features indistinguishable between the source and target domains:

$$\mathcal{L}_{DANN} = \mathcal{L}_{task} - \lambda \mathcal{L}_{domain} \tag{3.14}$$

where $\mathcal{L}_{task}$ is the loss for the main task (e.g., classification), $\mathcal{L}_{domain}$ is the domain classification loss, and λ is a trade-off parameter [33].

The domain classification loss $\mathcal{L}_{domain}$ can be expressed as:

$$\mathcal{L}_{domain} = -\frac{1}{n_s + n_t} \sum_{i=1}^{n_s+n_t} (d_i \log D(f(x_i)) + (1 - d_i) \log(1 - D(f(x_i)))) \tag{3.15}$$

where d_i is 1 if x_i is from the source domain and 0 if from the target domain, and $D(\cdot)$ is the domain discriminator [33].

Domain adaptation offers several advantages. One of the key advantages is its ability to leverage existing labeled data from a source domain to enhance performance of the model in a target domain with limited or weakly labeled data [29]. The domain adaptation reduces the need of expensive and time-intensive data labeling in the target domain. Moreover, domain adaptation has been shown to be effective in strengthening and generalizing models for real-world applications, where the test data distributions are often different from training data [117]. However, domain adaptation has its own limitations. For example, one major challenge in domain adaptation is that it could be difficult to align the source and target domains if domain distributions are highly divergent [102]. This might lead to poor performance of the adapted models if the features learned in the source domain do not transfer well to the target domain. Additionally, domain adaptation techniques can be computationally intensive and may require heavy hyperparameter tuning for results optimization [111].

Domain adaptation is particularly useful for applications where labeled data is either difficult or costly to obtain in the target domain. A typical use case is cross-domain sentiment analysis where a model trained on labeled reviews in one domain (e.g., electronics) is adapted to a model in another domain (e.g., books). As another example, in medical image analysis, domain adaptation allows models trained on annotated images of one type of medical scans to generalize to another type, e.g., from CT scans to MRI scan [25]. Additionally, domain adaptation has also been applied in speech recognition where models trained on one accent or dialect are adapted to work well on another [106].

3.3.3 Few-Shot Learning

Few-shot learning is a learning approach that can create models for generalizing from very few examples. This is especially effective when data collection is prohibitively expensive, time-consuming, or otherwise unattainable [30]. Few-shot learning uses various methods to accomplish the above goals. One popular approach is meta-learning (or "learning to learn"), where the model is trained across many tasks to quickly adopt to a new task with a finite amount of data samples [32]. Another well-known technique is Siamese networks, which rely on twin networks with shared weights to compare input pairs, such as images or text sequences, and discover their similarity in terms of features or semantics [64].

In Model-Agnostic Meta-Learning (MAML), the objective is to find a good initialization of the model parameters that can quickly adapt to new tasks with just a few gradient steps [32]. This process is formalized as:

$$\theta = \arg\min_{\theta} \sum_{T_i \sim p(T)} \mathcal{L}_{T_i}\left(\theta - \alpha \nabla_{\theta} \mathcal{L}_{T_i}(\theta)\right) \tag{3.16}$$

where θ represents the model parameters, T_i is a task sampled from the task distribution $p(T)$, and α is the learning rate for the inner loop. The goal is to minimize the loss across tasks, ensuring that the model parameters are well-initialized for rapid adaptation to new and unseen tasks.

The adaptation process in MAML involves two steps: inner-loop adaptation and outer-loop optimization. The inner-loop adaptation updates the model parameters for each task T_i:

$$\theta_i' = \theta - \alpha \nabla_\theta \mathcal{L}_{T_i}(\theta) \tag{3.17}$$

where θ_i' are the task-specific parameters after the inner-loop adaptation. The outer-loop optimization then updates the initial parameters θ based on the performance of the adapted parameters θ_i':

$$\theta \leftarrow \theta - \beta \nabla_\theta \sum_{T_i \sim p(T)} \mathcal{L}_{T_i}(\theta_i') \tag{3.18}$$

where β is the learning rate for the outer loop [32].

Siamese networks are another effective approach for few-shot learning. These networks use a pair of identical sub-networks with shared weights to process input pairs of data samples. The network learns to determine the similarity between the inputs by minimizing a few-shot loss:

$$\mathcal{L}_{few-shot} = \frac{1}{2N} \sum_{i=1}^{N} \left[y_i \cdot d(\mathbf{h}_i^1, \mathbf{h}_i^2)^2 + (1 - y_i) \cdot \max(0, m - d(\mathbf{h}_i^1, \mathbf{h}_i^2))^2 \right] \tag{3.19}$$

where $\mathbf{h}_i^1$ and $\mathbf{h}_i^2$ are the embeddings of the input pair, y_i is 1 if the inputs are similar and 0 otherwise, $d(\cdot, \cdot)$ is a distance metric (e.g., Euclidean distance), and m is a margin that defines how far apart dissimilar pairs should be [64].

Few-shot learning offers several advantages. One major advantage is that it works extremely well with minimal training data and therefore can be a viable choice for applications with small or costly data to access. This feature can save considerable time and resources for data collection and annotation. Aside from that, few-shot learning methods are also generalizable to multiple tasks such as multi-class classification, sequence labeling, and anomaly detection, demonstrating its adaptability [104]. Yet few-shot learning does not work without constraints. One issue is that it is challenging to select or design appropriate meta-tasks to train the model because the performance of the model often depends heavily on the variety and usefulness of tasks [118]. Also, few-shot learning models are hyperparameter dependent and might require extensive fine-tuning to achieve a desirable performance [93].

Few-shot learning works particularly well when it comes to situations where it is necessary to classify new, unseen classes using only *a few* labeled examples.

For example, few-shot learning can be applied in the image classification where the goal is to discover an unknown class by looking at a small number of labeled images [114]. Few-shot learning can also be used in natural language processing to train models for tasks such as text classification and sentiment analysis, thereby facilitating adaptation to new domains with minimal labeled data from unknown classes [15]. Additionally, few-shot learning has also been applied in areas such as medical diagnosis where labels for rare disorders are not always available [118].

3.3.4 Adversarial Training

Adversarial training is developed to enhance the model robustness by training it on adversarial examples, which are input examples specifically designed to deceive the model into making incorrect predictions [3]. This method aims to improve the model's ability to handle such deceptive inputs, thereby increasing the overall robustness and reliability of the model [108]. In particular, adversarial examples are generated by adding small perturbations to the original input data that cause the model to produce incorrect predictions. The perturbation can be computed as follows:

$$\mathbf{x}^{adv} = \mathbf{x} + \epsilon \cdot \text{sign}(\nabla_{\mathbf{x}} \mathcal{L}(\mathbf{x}, y)) \tag{3.20}$$

In this equation, $\mathbf{x}$ represents the original input, ϵ denotes the perturbation magnitude, $\mathcal{L}$ is the loss function, and y is the true label. The perturbation is calculated by taking the sign of the gradient of the loss function with respect to the input, scaled by ϵ [39].

The adversarial training process involves generating adversarial examples during training and including these adversarial examples in the training set. This process ensures that the model is exposed to adversarial inputs and learns to correctly classify them, thereby improving the model robustness. By addressing these challenging cases during training, the model becomes better equipped to handle unexpected or malicious inputs in real-world scenarios [2]. The objective function for adversarial training is given by:

$$\mathcal{L}_{adv} = \mathbb{E}_{(x,y)\sim\mathcal{D}} \left[\max_{\|\delta\| \le \epsilon} \mathcal{L}(f(x+\delta), y) \right] \tag{3.21}$$

where δ represents the perturbation constrained by $\|\delta\| \le \epsilon$, ensuring that the perturbation remains within a specified magnitude [75]. This constraint is essential because it ensures the adversarial examples are both realistic and imperceptible, thereby simulating practical adversarial attacks that could occur in real-world settings [100].

Adversarial training offers several advantages. A major advantage is that the model is better protected from adversarial attacks, making it more robust and trustworthy in real-world situations where malicious inputs can occur [3]. The training of the model with adversarial examples teaches it to recognize and correctly categorize such adversarial inputs and avoid being misled by subtle perturbations [68]. Additionally, adversarial training can boost generalization of the model because it learns to handle a wider variety of inputs, including those that are deliberately designed to be challenging [110]. However, challenges exist in adversarial training. A major drawback is that it is computationally expensive to build adversarial examples and train against them [99]. In addition, adversarial training demands careful configurations of hyperparameters (e.g., perturbation magnitude, learning rate, and norm constraints) to ensure robustness as well as model performance [120].

Adversarial training is best suited for situations where model robustness is of primary concern like security-based applications and systems vulnerable to adversarial attacks [116]. For example, in cyber security, adversarial training can be used to boost the resilience of intrusion detection systems against adversarial retaliation [16]. Similarly, adversarial training has been proven to be effective in healthcare applications, such as medical image analysis, where it helps enhance the robustness of diagnostic models against adversarial perturbations that could mislead disease detection systems [31]. When applied to autonomous driving, it can increase the stability of models employed for object recognition and navigation so that the car has the correct information to interpret the physical world even when adversarial inputs are present [28].

References

1. L. B. Almeida. Multilayer perceptrons. In *Handbook of Neural Computation*, pages C1–2. CRC Press, 2020.
2. M. Andriushchenko and N. Flammarion. Understanding and improving fast adversarial training. *Advances in Neural Information Processing Systems*, 33:16048–16059, 2020.
3. T. Bai, J. Luo, J. Zhao, B. Wen, and Q. Wang. Recent advances in adversarial training for adversarial robustness. *arXiv preprint arXiv:2102.01356*, 2021.
4. P. W. Battaglia, J. B. Hamrick, V. Bapst, A. Sanchez-Gonzalez, V. Zambaldi, M. Malinowski, A. Tacchetti, D. Raposo, A. Santoro, R. Faulkner, et al. Relational inductive biases, deep learning, and graph networks. *arXiv preprint arXiv:1806.01261*, 2018.
5. L. E. Baum and T. Petrie. A maximization technique occurring in the statistical analysis of probabilistic functions of markov chains. *The Annals of Mathematical Statistics*, 41(1):164–171, 1970.
6. I. Beltagy, M. E. Peters, and A. Cohan. Longformer: The long-document transformer. *arXiv preprint arXiv:2004.05150*, 2020.
7. J. O. Berger. *Statistical Decision Theory and Bayesian Analysis*. Springer Science & Business Media, 1985.
8. D. Bhatt, C. Patel, H. Talsania, J. Patel, R. Vaghela, S. Pandya, K. Modi, and H. Ghayvat. Cnn variants for computer vision: History, architecture, application, challenges and future scope. *Electronics*, 10(20):2470, 2021.
9. J. Bilmes. Graphical models and automatic speech recognition. In *Mathematical Foundations of Speech and Language Processing*, pages 191–245. Springer, 2006.

10. J. A. Bilmes. A gentle tutorial of the em algorithm and its application to parameter estimation for gaussian mixture and hidden markov models. *International Computer Science Institute*, 4:126, 1998.
11. C. M. Bishop. *Pattern Recognition and Machine Learning*. Springer, 2006.
12. M. Bojarski, D. Del Testa, D. Dworakowski, B. Firner, B. Flepp, P. Goyal, L. D. Jackel, M. Monfort, U. Muller, J. Zhang, et al. End to end learning for self-driving cars. *arXiv preprint arXiv:1604.07316*, 2016.
13. D. Bouchaffra. Conformation-based hidden markov models: Application to human face identification. *IEEE transactions on neural networks*, 21(4):595–608, 2010.
14. S. Boyd and L. Vandenberghe. *Convex Optimization*. Cambridge University Press, 2004.
15. T. B. Brown, B. Mann, N. Ryder, M. Subbiah, J. D. Kaplan, P. Dhariwal, A. Neelakantan, P. Shyam, G. Sastry, A. Askell, et al. Language models are few-shot learners. *arXiv preprint arXiv:2005.14165*, 2020.
16. N. Carlini and D. Wagner. Adversarial examples are not easily detected: Bypassing ten detection methods. *Proceedings of the 10th ACM Workshop on Artificial Intelligence and Security*, pages 3–14, 2017.
17. G. Casella and R. L. Berger. *Statistical Inference*. Duxbury, 2002.
18. R. Chandana and A. Ramachandra. Real time object detection system with yolo and cnn models: A review. *arXiv Prepr. arXiv2208*, 773, 2022.
19. T. Chen, S. Kornblith, M. Norouzi, and G. Hinton. A simple framework for contrastive learning of visual representations. In *International Conference on Machine Learning (ICML)*, pages 1597–1607, 2020.
20. X. Chen and K. He. Improved baselines with momentum contrastive learning. In *arXiv preprint arXiv:2003.04297*, 2020.
21. A. P. Dempster, N. M. Laird, and D. B. Rubin. Maximum likelihood from incomplete data via the em algorithm. *Journal of the Royal Statistical Society: Series B (Methodological)*, 39(1):1–22, 1977.
22. J. Devlin, M.-W. Chang, K. Lee, and K. Toutanova. Bert: Pre-training of deep bidirectional transformers for language understanding. *arXiv preprint arXiv:1810.04805*, 2018.
23. L. Dong, B. Xu, and B. Xu. Speech-transformer: A no-recurrence sequence-to-sequence model for speech recognition. *2018 IEEE International Conference on Acoustics, Speech and Signal Processing (ICASSP)*, pages 5884–5888, 2018.
24. A. Dosovitskiy, L. Beyer, A. Kolesnikov, D. Weissenborn, X. Zhai, T. Unterthiner, M. Dehghani, M. Minderer, G. Heigold, S. Gelly, et al. An image is worth 16x16 words: Transformers for image recognition at scale. *arXiv preprint arXiv:2010.11929*, 2020.
25. Q. Dou, C. Ouyang, C. Chen, and P.-A. Heng. Unsupervised cross-modality domain adaptation of convnets for biomedical image segmentations with adversarial loss. In *International Conference on Medical Image Computing and Computer-Assisted Intervention*, pages 338–346. Springer, 2018.
26. Y. Du, B. Pei, X. Zhao, and J. Ji. Deep scaled dot-product attention based domain adaptation model for biomedical question answering. *Methods*, 173:69–74, 2020.
27. S. R. Eddy. What is a hidden markov model? *Nature biotechnology*, 22(10):1315–1316, 2004.
28. K. Eykholt, I. Evtimov, E. Fernandes, B. Li, A. Rahmati, C. Xiao, A. Prakash, T. Kohno, and D. Song. Robust physical-world attacks on deep learning models. In *Proceedings of the IEEE Conference on Computer Vision and Pattern Recognition (CVPR)*, pages 1625–1634, 2018.
29. A. Farahani, S. Voghoei, K. Rasheed, and H. R. Arabnia. A brief review of domain adaptation. *Advances in data science and information engineering: proceedings from ICDATA 2020 and IKE 2020*, pages 877–894, 2021.
30. L. Fei-Fei, R. Fergus, and P. Perona. One-shot learning of object categories. In *IEEE Transactions on Pattern Analysis and Machine Intelligence*, pages 594–611, 2006.
31. S. G. Finlayson, J. D. Bowers, J. Ito, J. L. Zittrain, A. L. Beam, and I. S. Kohane. Adversarial attacks on medical machine learning. *Science*, 363(6433):1287–1289, 2019.
32. C. Finn, P. Abbeel, and S. Levine. Model-agnostic meta-learning for fast adaptation of deep networks. In *International conference on machine learning*, pages 1126–1135. PMLR, 2017.

33. Y. Ganin and V. Lempitsky. Unsupervised domain adaptation by backpropagation. In *International Conference on Machine Learning (ICML)*, pages 1180–1189, 2015.
34. Z. Ghahramani. An introduction to hidden markov models and bayesian networks. In *International School on Neural Networks, Initiated by IIASS and EMFCSC*, pages 9–42. Springer, 2001.
35. S. Ghassempour, F. Girosi, and A. Maeder. Clustering multivariate time series using hidden markov models. *International journal of environmental research and public health*, 11(3):2741–2763, 2014.
36. J. Gilmer, S. S. Schoenholz, P. F. Riley, O. Vinyals, and G. E. Dahl. Neural message passing for quantum chemistry. *International Conference on Machine Learning (ICML)*, pages 1263–1272, 2017.
37. X. Glorot and Y. Bengio. Understanding the difficulty of training deep feedforward neural networks. In *Proceedings of the Thirteenth International Conference on Artificial Intelligence and Statistics*, pages 249–256. JMLR Workshop and Conference Proceedings, 2010.
38. I. Goodfellow, Y. Bengio, and A. Courville. *Deep Learning*. MIT Press, 2016.
39. I. J. Goodfellow, J. Shlens, and C. Szegedy. Explaining and harnessing adversarial examples. In *International Conference on Learning Representations (ICLR)*, 2014.
40. A. Gretton, K. M. Borgwardt, M. J. Rasch, B. Schölkopf, and A. Smola. A kernel two-sample test. *Journal of Machine Learning Research*, 13(3):723–773, 2012.
41. R. Hadsell, S. Chopra, and Y. LeCun. Dimensionality reduction by learning an invariant mapping. In *IEEE Conference on Computer Vision and Pattern Recognition (CVPR)*, pages 1735–1742, 2006.
42. W. Hamilton, Z. Ying, and J. Leskovec. Inductive representation learning on large graphs. In *Advances in Neural Information Processing Systems (NIPS)*, pages 1024–1034, 2017.
43. K. Han, Y. Wang, H. Chen, X. Chen, J. Guo, Z. Liu, Y. Tang, A. Xiao, C. Xu, Y. Xu, et al. A survey on vision transformer. *IEEE transactions on pattern analysis and machine intelligence*, 45(1):87–110, 2022.
44. T. Hastie, R. Tibshirani, and J. Friedman. *The Elements of Statistical Learning: Data Mining, Inference, and Prediction*. Springer, 2009.
45. T. Hastie, R. Tibshirani, and J. Friedman. *The Elements of Statistical Learning: Data Mining, Inference, and Prediction*. Springer, 2009.
46. S. Haykin. *A Comprehensive Foundation*. Neural Networks, 2004.
47. K. He, H. Fan, Y. Wu, S. Xie, and R. Girshick. Momentum contrast for unsupervised visual representation learning. In *IEEE/CVF Conference on Computer Vision and Pattern Recognition (CVPR)*, pages 9729–9738, 2020.
48. K. He, X. Zhang, S. Ren, and J. Sun. Deep residual learning for image recognition. In *Proceedings of the IEEE conference on computer vision and pattern recognition*, pages 770–778, 2016.
49. G. E. Hinton. Neural networks for machine learning. *Coursera Video Lectures*, 2012.
50. K. Hornik, M. Stinchcombe, and H. White. Multilayer feedforward networks are universal approximators. *Neural Networks*, 2(5):359–366, 1989.
51. H. Hu, X. Wang, Y. Zhang, Q. Chen, and Q. Guan. A comprehensive survey on contrastive learning. *Neurocomputing*, page 128645, 2024.
52. P. J. Huber. *Robust Statistics*. John Wiley & Sons, 1981.
53. M. Hussain, J. J. Bird, and D. R. Faria. A study on cnn transfer learning for image classification. In *Advances in Computational Intelligence Systems: Contributions Presented at the 18th UK Workshop on Computational Intelligence, September 5–7, 2018, Nottingham, UK*, pages 191–202. Springer, 2019.
54. A. Jaiswal, A. R. Babu, M. Z. Zadeh, D. Banerjee, and F. Makedon. A survey on contrastive self-supervised learning. *Technologies*, 9(1):2, 2020.
55. A. Jøsang. *Subjective Logic: A Formalism for Reasoning Under Uncertainty*. Springer, 2016.
56. A. Jøsang, M. Araujo, and G. Alzobaidi. Modelling uncertainty in subjective logic. In *Proceedings of the 6th International Conference on Trust, Privacy and Security in Digital Business*, pages 39–48. Springer, 2009.

57. A. Jøsang and R. Ismail. Beta reputation systems. *Proceedings of the 15th Bled Electronic Commerce Conference*, 5(1):2502–2511, 2002.
58. A. Jøsang, R. Ismail, and C. Boyd. Reasoning about trust in information sources. *International Journal of Approximate Reasoning*, 53(3):453–469, 2007.
59. A. Jøsang and S. Pope. Subjective logic: Principles and applications. In *Proceedings of the 4th European Conference on Information Warfare and Security*, pages 113–122, 2018.
60. D. Jurafsky and J. H. Martin. *Speech and Language Processing: An Introduction to Natural Language Processing, Computational Linguistics, and Speech Recognition.* Prentice Hall, 2000.
61. M. G. Kendall and A. Stuart. *Advanced Theory of Statistics*, volume 2. Charles Griffin & Company Limited, 1979.
62. P. Khosla, P. Teterwak, C. Wang, A. Sarna, Y. Tian, P. Isola, A. Maschinot, C. Liu, and S. Belongie. Supervised contrastive learning. In *Advances in Neural Information Processing Systems (NIPS)*, 2020.
63. T. N. Kipf and M. Welling. Semi-supervised classification with graph convolutional networks. *arXiv preprint arXiv:1609.02907*, 2016.
64. G. Koch, R. Zemel, and R. Salakhutdinov. Siamese neural networks for one-shot image recognition. In *ICML Deep Learning Workshop*, 2015.
65. A. Krizhevsky, I. Sutskever, and G. E. Hinton. Imagenet classification with deep convolutional neural networks. In *Advances in neural information processing systems*, pages 1097–1105, 2012.
66. A. Krogh, B. Larsson, G. von Heijne, and E. L. Sonnhammer. Predicting transmembrane protein topology with a hidden markov model: Application to complete genomes. *Journal of Molecular Biology*, 305(3):567–580, 2001.
67. S. Kumar, R. Dhir, and N. Chaurasia. Brain tumor detection analysis using cnn: a review. In *2021 international conference on artificial intelligence and smart systems (ICAIS)*, pages 1061–1067. IEEE, 2021.
68. A. Kurakin, I. Goodfellow, and S. Bengio. Adversarial machine learning at scale. *arXiv preprint arXiv:1611.01236*, 2016.
69. T. Largillier. Using subjective logic to divide learners into groups. In *International Symposium on Web AlGorithms*, 2015.
70. Y. LeCun, Y. Bengio, and G. Hinton. Deep learning. *Nature*, 521(7553):436–444, 2015.
71. E. L. Lehmann and G. Casella. *Theory of Point Estimation.* Springer Science & Business Media, 2006.
72. Q. Li, Z. Han, and X.-M. Wu. Deeper insights into graph convolutional networks for semi-supervised learning. In *AAAI Conference on Artificial Intelligence*, 2018.
73. Y. Liu, M. Ott, N. Goyal, J. Du, M. Joshi, D. Chen, O. Levy, M. Lewis, L. Zettlemoyer, and V. Stoyanov. Roberta: A robustly optimized bert pretraining approach. *arXiv preprint arXiv:1907.11692*, 2019.
74. J. Long, E. Shelhamer, and T. Darrell. Fully convolutional networks for semantic segmentation. In *Proceedings of the IEEE conference on computer vision and pattern recognition*, pages 3431–3440, 2015.
75. A. Madry, A. Makelov, L. Schmidt, D. Tsipras, and A. Vladu. Towards deep learning models resistant to adversarial attacks. In *International Conference on Learning Representations (ICLR)*, 2017.
76. D. L. McGuinness and F. Van Harmelen. Owl web ontology language: Overview. In *W3C Recommendation*, volume 10, page 2004. W3C, 2005.
77. G. J. McLachlan and T. Krishnan. The em algorithm. *The EM Algorithm and Extensions*, 382, 2007.
78. G. J. McLachlan and D. Peel. *F*inite Mixture Models. John Wiley & Sons, 2004.
79. H. Mei, S. Yuan, L. Qiu, and J. Zhang. Damage evaluation by a guided wave-hidden markov model based method. *S*mart Materials and Structures, 25(2):025021, 2016.
80. C. Naumzik and S. Feuerriegel. Detecting false rumors from retweet dynamics on social media. In *P*roceedings of the ACM web conference 2022, pages 2798–2809, 2022.

81. R. M. Neal and G. E. Hinton. View of the em algorithm that justifies incremental, sparse, and other variants. *Learning in Graphical Models*, pages 355–368, 1998.
82. M. Nilashi, O. bin Ibrahim, N. Ithnin, and N. H. Sarmin. A multi-criteria collaborative filtering recommender system for the tourism domain using expectation maximization (em) and pca–anfis. *Electronic Commerce Research and Applications*, 14(6):542–562, 2015.
83. S. J. Pan and Q. Yang. A survey on transfer learning. *IEEE Transactions on Knowledge and Data Engineering*, 22(10):1345–1359, 2009.
84. S. Parsons. Current approaches to handling imperfect information in data and knowledge bases. *IEEE Transactions on Knowledge and Data Engineering*, 10(6):977–993, 1998.
85. V. M. Patel, R. Gopalan, R. Li, and R. Chellappa. Visual domain adaptation: A survey of recent advances. *IEEE Signal Processing Magazine*, 32(3):53–69, 2015.
86. Y. Pawitan. *All Likelihood: Statistical Modelling and Inference Using Likelihood*. Oxford University Press, 2013.
87. V. Qazvinian, E. Rosengren, D. Radev, and Q. Mei. Rumor has it: Identifying misinformation in microblogs. In *Proceedings of the 2011 conference on empirical methods in natural language processing*, pages 1589–1599, 2011.
88. L. R. Rabiner. A tutorial on hidden markov models and selected applications in speech recognition. *Proceedings of the IEEE*, 77(2):257–286, 1989.
89. L. R. Rabiner and B. Juang. An introduction to hidden markov models. *IEEE ASSP Magazine*, 3(1):4–16, 1986.
90. A. Radford, J. W. Kim, C. Hallacy, A. Ramesh, G. Goh, S. Agarwal, G. Sastry, A. Askell, P. Mishkin, J. Clark, et al. Learning transferable visual models from natural language supervision. In *International Conference on Machine Learning*, pages 8748–8763. PMLR, 2021.
91. A. Radford, K. Narasimhan, T. Salimans, and I. Sutskever. Improving language understanding by generative pre-training. In *arXiv preprint arXiv:1801.06146*, 2018.
92. A. Radford, J. Wu, R. Child, D. Luan, D. Amodei, and I. Sutskever. Language models are unsupervised multitask learners. In *OpenAI Blog*, 2019.
93. S. Ravi and H. Larochelle. Optimization as a model for few-shot learning. In *International Conference on Learning Representations (ICLR)*, 2017.
94. W. Rawat and Z. Wang. Deep convolutional neural networks for image classification: A comprehensive review. *Neural computation*, 29(9):2352–2449, 2017.
95. R. A. Redner and H. F. Walker. Mixture densities, maximum likelihood and the em algorithm. *SIAM Review*, 26(2):195–239, 1984.
96. D. E. Rumelhart, G. E. Hinton, and R. J. Williams. *Learning Representations by Back-Propagating Errors*. Nature Publishing Group, 1986.
97. O. Russakovsky, J. Deng, H. Su, J. Krause, S. Satheesh, S. Ma, Z. Huang, A. Karpathy, A. Khosla, M. Bernstein, et al. Imagenet large scale visual recognition challenge. *International Journal of Computer Vision*, 115(3):211–252, 2015.
98. E. Scharwächter and E. Müller. Does terrorism trigger online hate speech? on the association of events and time series. *arXiv e-prints*, 2020.
99. A. Shafahi, M. Najibi, A. Ghiasi, Z. Xu, J. Dickerson, L. Davis, G. Taylor, and T. Goldstein. Adversarial training for free! In *Advances in Neural Information Processing Systems (NeurIPS)*, 2019.
100. A. Shafahi, M. Najibi, Z. Xu, J. Dickerson, L. S. Davis, and T. Goldstein. Universal adversarial training. In *Proceedings of the AAAI Conference on Artificial Intelligence*, volume 34, pages 5636–5643, 2020.
101. N. M. Shelke, S. Deshpande, and V. Thakre. Exploiting expectation maximization algorithm for sentiment analysis of product reviews. In *2017 International Conference on Inventive Communication and Computational Technologies (ICICCT)*, pages 390–396. IEEE, 2017.
102. P. Singhal, R. Walambe, S. Ramanna, and K. Kotecha. Domain adaptation: challenges, methods, datasets, and applications. *IEEE access*, 11:6973–7020, 2023.
103. P. Smets. The nature of the unnormalized belief structure. *International Journal of Approximate Reasoning*, 10(2):81–124, 1994.

104. J. Snell, K. Swersky, and R. Zemel. Prototypical networks for few-shot learning. In *Advances in Neural Information Processing Systems (NIPS)*, pages 4077–4087, 2017.
105. H. B. Sta. Quality and the efficiency of data in "smart-cities". *Future Generation Computer Systems*, 74:409–416, 2017.
106. B. Sun and K. Saenko. Unsupervised domain adaptation through self-supervision. In *Advances in Neural Information Processing Systems (NIPS)*, 2017.
107. C. Szegedy, W. Liu, Y. Jia, P. Sermanet, S. Reed, D. Anguelov, D. Erhan, V. Vanhoucke, and A. Rabinovich. Going deeper with convolutions. In *Proceedings of the IEEE Conference on Computer Vision and Pattern Recognition*, pages 1–9, 2015.
108. C. Szegedy, W. Zaremba, I. Sutskever, J. Bruna, D. Erhan, I. Goodfellow, and R. Fergus. Intriguing properties of neural networks. *arXiv preprint arXiv:1312.6199*, 2013.
109. W. L. Tong and C. Pehlevan. Mlps learn in-context. *arXiv preprint arXiv:2405.15618*, 2024.
110. F. Tramèr, A. Kurakin, N. Papernot, I. Goodfellow, D. Boneh, and P. McDaniel. Ensemble adversarial training: Attacks and defenses. In *International Conference on Learning Representations (ICLR)*, 2018.
111. E. Tzeng, J. Hoffman, K. Saenko, and T. Darrell. Adversarial discriminative domain adaptation. In *IEEE Conference on Computer Vision and Pattern Recognition (CVPR)*, pages 7167–7176, 2017.
112. A. van den Oord, Y. Li, and O. Vinyals. Representation learning with contrastive predictive coding. In *arXiv preprint arXiv:1807.03748*, 2018.
113. A. Vaswani, N. Shazeer, N. Parmar, J. Uszkoreit, L. Jones, A. N. Gomez, Ł. Kaiser, and I. Polosukhin. Attention is all you need. *Advances in neural information processing systems*, 30, 2017.
114. O. Vinyals, C. Blundell, T. Lillicrap, K. Kavukcuoglu, and D. Wierstra. Matching networks for one-shot learning. In *Advances in Neural Information Processing Systems (NIPS)*, pages 3630–3638, 2016.
115. A. Wald. Note on the consistency of the maximum likelihood estimate. *Annals of Mathematical Statistics*, 20(4):595–601, 1949.
116. J. Wang and H. Zhang. Bilateral adversarial training: Towards fast training of more robust models against adversarial attacks. In *Proceedings of the IEEE/CVF international conference on computer vision*, pages 6629–6638, 2019.
117. M. Wang, J. Shao, C. Sun, Y. Wang, and P. S. Yu. Deep visual domain adaptation: A survey. *Neurocomputing*, 312:135–153, 2018.
118. Y. Wang, Q. Yao, J. T. Kwok, and L. M. Ni. Generalizing from a few examples: A survey on few-shot learning. *ACM computing surveys (csur)*, 53(3):1–34, 2020.
119. L. R. Welch. Hidden markov models and the baum-welch algorithm. *IEEE Information Theory Society Newsletter*, 53(4):10–13, 2003.
120. E. Wong, L. Rice, and J. Z. Kolter. Fast is better than free: Revisiting adversarial training. In *International Conference on Learning Representations (ICLR)*, 2020.
121. C.-F. Wu. On the convergence properties of the em algorithm. *The Annals of Statistics*, 11(1):95–103, 1983.
122. Z. Wu, S. Pan, F. Chen, G. Long, C. Zhang, and S. Y. Philip. A comprehensive survey on graph neural networks. *IEEE transactions on neural networks and learning systems*, 32(1):4–24, 2020.
123. K. Xu, W. Hu, J. Leskovec, and S. Jegelka. How powerful are graph neural networks? In *International Conference on Learning Representations (ICLR)*, 2019.
124. R. Ying, R. He, K. Chen, P. Eksombatchai, W. Hamilton, and J. Leskovec. Graph convolutional neural networks for web-scale recommender systems. In *Proceedings of the 24th ACM SIGKDD International Conference on Knowledge Discovery & Data Mining*, pages 974–983, 2018.
125. R. Yu, W. Yu, and X. Wang. Kan or mlp: A fairer comparison. *arXiv preprint arXiv:2407.16674*, 2024.
126. M. D. Zeiler and R. Fergus. Visualizing and understanding convolutional networks. In *European Conference on Computer Vision*, pages 818–833. Springer, 2014.

127. R. Zhang, Y. Ji, Y. Zhang, and R. J. Passonneau. Contrastive data and learning for natural language processing. In *P*roceedings of the 2022 Conference of the North American Chapter of the Association for Computational Linguistics: Human Language Technologies: Tutorial Abstracts, pages 39–47, 2022.
128. Y. Zhang, R. Zong, L. Shang, H. Zeng, Z. Yue, N. Wei, and D. Wang. On optimizing model generality in ai-based disaster damage assessment: A subjective logic-driven crowd-ai hybrid learning approach. In *I*JCAI, pages 6317–6325, 2023, https://doi.org/10.24963/ijcai.2023/701. Copyright owner: IJCAI Organization, all rights reserved.

Chapter 4
Data Heterogeneity

Abstract Data heterogeneity is a fundamental issue in social intelligence, where the data is often obtained from diverse sources, modalities, and contexts, due to the varying nature of human interactions and behaviors. Addressing the data heterogeneity problem in social intelligence encounters several unique challenges, such as cross-modal information inconsistency, sparse multimodal data annotation, and heterogeneous feature fusion. To overcome these challenges, this chapter reviews state-of-the-art multimodal solutions that address the data heterogeneity challenge in social intelligence applications. In particular, we present two case studies: one on generative learning based multimodal truth discovery and another on contrastive learning based fauxtography detection. These case studies demonstrate the superiority and potential of advanced deep learning techniques in addressing data heterogeneity issues in social intelligence tasks, paving the way for more accurate and reliable analysis of diverse data modalities.

Keywords Multimodal · Data modality · Heterogeneous data · Multi-view learning · Contrastive learning · Truth Discovery

4.1 The Data Heterogeneity Problem in Social Intelligence

In social intelligence, the data heterogeneity problem arises when the data is obtained from diverse sources (e.g., social media, human behavioral data, sensor data), consists of various data modalities (e.g., text, image, video), and originates from different contexts (e.g., locations, events, time). While the heterogeneous data in social intelligence offers a comprehensive view of human intelligence, it also poses unique challenges in integrating and mining data from diverse sources, modalities, and contexts. Existing solutions to address the data heterogeneity challenge can be mainly classified into three categories: content-based, content-independent, and hybrid solutions [1]. First, content-based approaches have primarily focused on fusing multimodal content (e.g., combining the latent features of textual and visual features) to capture the complementary information across

D. Wang et al., *Social Intelligence*, https://doi.org/10.1007/978-3-031-90080-8_4

different modalities [13]. However, these approaches often struggle to effectively handle the semantic gap and association between different modalities. Moreover, content-independent solutions often rely on a set of auxiliary features (e.g., user attitude/comments [43], user profiles [37], propagation patterns [20]) to characterize the aggregated information of heterogeneous data without considering the actual content. However, these methods may not fully capture the semantics and dynamics of the heterogeneous data, leading to suboptimal performance in downstream tasks. Additionally, hybrid methods aim to address the limitations of content-based and content-independent solutions by leveraging both content and auxiliary features to learn more comprehensive representations of heterogeneous data. However, the effectiveness of hybrid methods depends on the careful design of fusion strategies and the availability of high-quality auxiliary information, which may not always be readily available in real-world scenarios. More recently, the advancement of large foundation models (LFM) has also shown promising performance in understanding multimedia content [47]. However, these pre-trained large models primarily focus on fusing the multimodal content but often fall short in capturing and reasoning about the complex relationships and inter-dependencies between different modalities in heterogeneous social intelligence data. Specifically, three unique challenges exist in the data heterogeneity of social intelligence, including *cross-modal information inconsistency*, *sparse multimodal data annotation*, and *heterogeneous feature fusion* [28, 51]. We elaborate on them below.

Cross-Modal Information Inconsistency

The first challenge lies in the inconsistency across the varied data modalities of social intelligence data. Let us consider a multimodal truth discovery problem where incorrect information may be embedded not only in the textual or visual component of the multimodal news articles but also in their associations. For example, Fig. 4.1 shows four examples of incorrect multimodal COVID-19 news where the cross-modal information is inconsistent. A straightforward solution to assess the cross-modal information consistency is to directly compare the latent features extracted from each modality using deep learning models (e.g., convolutional neural network models for visual features [7] and natural language processing models for textual features [5]). However, such a solution ignores the intrinsic difference between the visual and textual content (e.g., a composition of pixels vs. a sequence of words). Thus, it is impractical to directly compare the extracted visual and textual features that belong to different latent feature spaces. In addition, we observe that the visual content (i.e., image) in multimodal news articles often contains multiple salient objects. It is challenging to accurately extract representative information from the visual content without knowing the explicit intention of the news creator [44]. For example, the syringe and vial in Fig. 4.1c show an important visual hint (e.g., vaccine) for the COVID-19 vaccination described in the news. However, such important visual information will likely be under-represented in the extracted visual features due to the large and colorful caption on the left of the image.

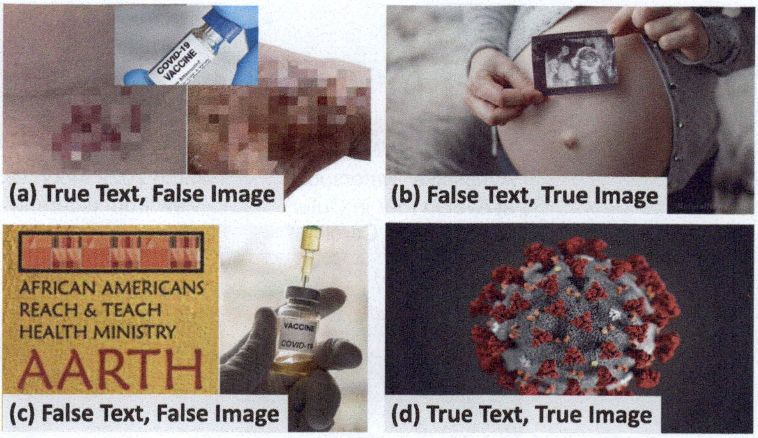

Fig. 4.1 Multimodal truth discovery examples. (**a**) was titled "Side effects of COVID-19 vaccine." It abuses an image of shingles (a painful rash caused by the chickenpox virus) to exaggerate the side effects (e.g., itchy rash) of COVID-19 vaccines. (**b**) was titled "Sterilization of most US girls and women is the next phase for mRNA vaccine technology." It shows a true image of a pregnant woman but a false text that indicates mRNA vaccines will cause sterilization. (**c**) was titled "White people are denied shots under COVID-19 vaccine regime." It utilizes a manipulated image (i.e., the name of AARTH with a hand holding a vial) to support incorrect news text. (**d**) was titled "Ivermectin has been FDA approved for human use since 1996." It aims to mislead the audience to believe that Ivermectin, a treatment for tropical skin disease, is authorized to treat COVID-19

Sparse Multimodal Data Annotation

The second challenge lies in the lack of multimodal data annotations in social intelligence applications due to the high cost of obtaining reliable annotations which often require domain expertise and significant human effort [29]. Several semi-supervised learning approaches have been studied to address the annotation sparsity challenge in social intelligence applications, such as truth discovery [2, 9], hate speech recognition [40], and social disparity identification [22]. A representative category of solutions is leveraging the weak labels (e.g., pseudo labels from pre-trained image or text classification models, crowdsourcing annotations) [17, 21] to complement the lack of high-quality annotations in the training of social intelligence models (e.g., truth discovery, disaster damage assessments). However, such approaches often highly depend on the quality of the pseudo labels and are insufficient to address the multimodal social intelligence problem. This is because the truthfulness of the multimodal social media post is not only dependent on the truthfulness of individual modalities (i.e., image and text) but also determined by the association between them (e.g., Fig. 4.2d). More importantly, existing semi-supervised truth discovery solutions often require a non-trivial amount of well-annotated ground-truth annotations of the social media posts and cannot be directly adapted to the multimodal detection problem where the multimodal data annotations are quite sparse (i.e., only 10% of the data is annotated [43]). Additionally, few-shot and zero-shot learning approaches leverage pre-trained models' transferability to new tasks

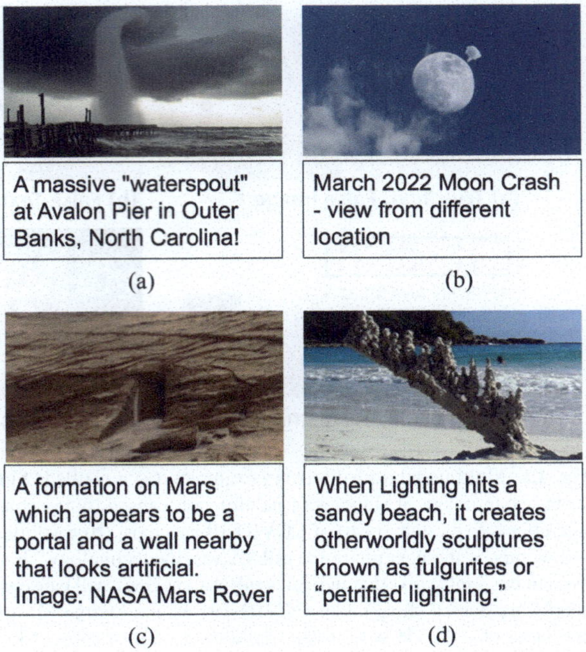

Fig. 4.2 Examples of multimodal false information on social media. (**a**) Fake image and text. (**b**) Fake image. (**c**) Fake text. (**d**) Unmatched image and text

with a few or no task-specific annotations [35]. However, these approaches often struggle with complex multimodal social intelligence tasks due to the significant domain discrepancy between pre-training and target tasks, as well as their limited reasoning ability to capture cross-modal relationships.

Heterogeneous Feature Fusion

The third challenge lies in the heterogeneous feature fusion where different modalities such as text and images must be effectively combined and integrated to capture the heterogeneous patterns relevant to the specific task in social intelligence. Existing methods [6, 32, 33] apply state-of-the-art image and text feature extraction neural networks (e.g., EfficientNet [36], BERT [5], and RoBERTa [19]) to learn feature representations for social intelligence tasks (e.g., multimodal misinformation detection, hate speech recognition). However, such image and text feature extraction models are often trained on conventional tasks (e.g., object detection and text classification) and are insufficient to capture task-specific multimodal semantic features. For example, in multimodal emotion recognition, while pre-trained vision models can detect basic facial expressions and language models can process textual sentiment, they often fail to capture the implicit relations between different modalities. A social media post with a smiling selfie and a sarcastic or distressed caption requires understanding both cross-modal patterns and social context to accurately interpret the user's true emotional state. Such heterogeneous and complicated multimodal features in the multimodal posts make this problem more challenging.

4.2 Two Multimodal Approaches: DualGen and ContrastFaux

In this section, we present two novel multimodal learning approaches, namely DualGen (Dual-Modal Generation) [28] and ContrastFaux (Contrastive Fauxtography Detector) [51], to address the above data heterogeneity challenges in social intelligence. We will start with two more AI-focused solutions with human inputs (e.g., user comments) in this chapter and present more human-AI integrated SI solutions in the following chapters. In particular, DualGen designs a dual-generative learning strategy to examine the cross-modal relation in multimodal social intelligence data. ContrastFaux develops a multi-view contrastive learning method that aims to effectively capture the multimodal features with sparse multimodal data annotations.

4.2.1 DualGen: A Dual-Generative Approach

An overview of DualGen is shown in Fig. 4.3. DualGen consists of four modules: (1) an *object-aware multimodal feature encoder (OMFE)* that extracts key information from the news content and news comments, (2) a *text-guided visual feature generator (TVFG)* that aims to effectively generate comprehensive visual features from the news text, (3) an *image-guided textual feature decoder (ITFD)* that is designed to generate the corresponding textual features from the news image, and (4) a *comment-driven explanation generator (CDEG)* that is developed to exploit the original and generated multimodal features and user comments to detect incorrect multimodal COVID-19 news articles and obtain the content and comment explanation. We elaborate on each module below.

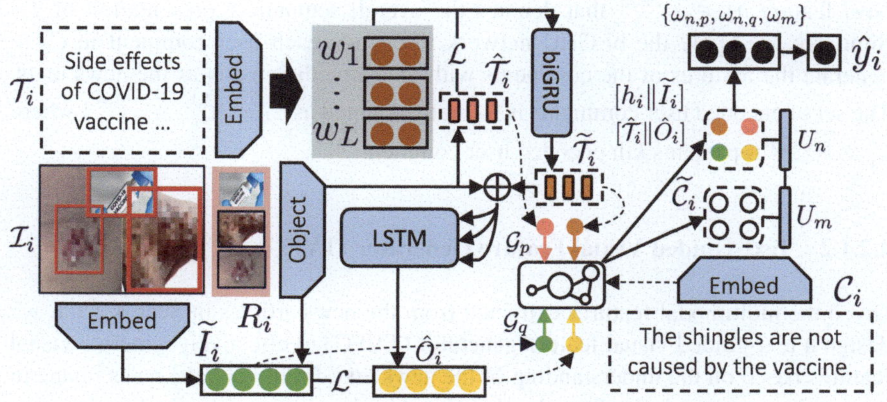

Fig. 4.3 An overview of the DualGen framework

4.2.1.1 Object-Aware Multimodal Feature Encoder (OMFE)

The object-aware multimodal feature encoder (OMFE) encodes the content (e.g., images, texts) and user comments of input news articles to extract useful information as effective evidence for explainable multimodal COVID-19 truth discovery. First, we design an object-aware visual feature encoder that effectively learns abstract visual information from news images. The encoder contains a deep learning based image embedding component that embeds the entire news image to high-dimensional visual features. The intuition is that the encoded features are extracted from image pixels and can be leveraged to effectively validate the pixel-level inconsistency of news images (e.g., human forgery of adding incorrect visual patterns) [12]. Moreover, we observe that objects in news images often contain informative clues about the news event/topic in the articles. Therefore, we also extract the fine-grained object-level visual features from the news images. Formally, given a COVID-19 news article $\mathcal{P}_i$, we first extract a set of potential object regions $\mathcal{R}_i = \{r_1, \ldots, r_K\}$ from the image $\mathcal{I}_i$ by applying the deep learning based object detection neural networks [27]. We then develop a deep image embedding component $\mathcal{F}$ to encode both $\mathcal{R}_i$ and $\mathcal{I}_i$. The process is denoted as $\widetilde{I}_i = \text{Avg}_{feat}(\mathcal{F}(\mathcal{I}_i), \sum_{k=1}^{K} \mathcal{F}(R_{i,k}))$ where $\widetilde{I}_i \in \mathbb{R}^{2d}$ is the encoded visual feature, $\mathcal{F}$ is the image embedding component and Avg_{feat} is the average operation in the feature dimension.

Second, we design a bi-directional gated recurrent unit (bi-GRU) network to encode textual features and learn the semantic representation from the news texts. Given the news text $\mathcal{T}_i = \{w_{i,1}, \cdots, w_{i,L}\}$ of $\mathcal{P}_i$ with L words, we expect the bi-GRU network to retrieve both forward and backward semantic information from the word sequence, which strengthens the semantic connection between different words. In particular, the forward bi-GRU reads from the first word embedding to the last one while the backward bi-GRU reads them reversely. We aggregate the updated forward and backward word embeddings as $\widetilde{\mathcal{T}}_i = \{\widetilde{w}_{i,1}, \ldots, \widetilde{w}_{i,L}\}$ where $\widetilde{w}_{i,l} = [\overrightarrow{w}_{i,l}, \overleftarrow{w}_{i,l}] \in \mathbb{R}^{2d}$. We apply the max-pooling operation to obtain the *claim-level* feature $h_i \in \mathbb{R}^{1\times 2d}$ that denotes the overall semantic representation of $\mathcal{T}_i$. Similarly, we apply the bi-GRU network to encode each user comment in C_i to generate the features of the comments with the same dimension as the news texts. The set of encoded user comments is formally denoted as $\widetilde{C}_i = \{\widetilde{C}_i^1, \ldots, \widetilde{C}_i^K\}$ where $\widetilde{C}_i^k \in \mathbb{R}^{1\times 2d}$ represents kth encoded user comment.

4.2.1.2 Text-Guided Visual Feature Generator (TVFG)

Given the multimodal features extracted from the news articles in Sect. 4.2.1.1, we design a text-guided visual feature generator (TVFG) to effectively generate visual features based on the understanding of the news text. Intuitively, the news image in a credible news article is often closely related to the content described in the news text. For example, a news article about the COVID-19 outbreak is often published with a real picture taken from a health facility. One possible solution is to aggregate the embedded text words of the input news article and directly transform the word embeddings back to the raw news image using text-to-image synthesis tools [23]. However, the news text usually only contains a limited number of words that are not efficient in accurately generating a news image that contains various COVID-19-related objects. Moreover, the news images may contain a non-trivial amount of pixel-level noise that prevents the generation algorithm from generating high-quality raw images. To address the problem, TVFG leverages the image objects as input features and learns to generate the latent visual features of the raw images. The intuition is that the latent visual features contain less pixel-level noise while the image objects provide effective visual information to complement the semantic information in the news texts.

In particular, we design an object-guided long short-term memory (OG-LSTM) network in TVFG that encodes each word and each image object in the news to recurrently generate visual features of the entire news image. Given the embedded words $\widetilde{\mathcal{T}}_i$ and the encoded image objects $\widetilde{\mathcal{R}}_i$ of a COVID-19 news article $\mathcal{P}_i$, we first equalize the number of features with different modalities by duplicating the features of either text words or image objects. We then concatenate each pair of embedded word and image object to jointly encode the multimodal information, which is denoted as $(\widetilde{\mathcal{TR}})_i = \{\widetilde{wr}_{i,1}, \ldots, \widetilde{wr}_{i,L}\}$. OG-LSTM recurrently encodes each element in $(\widetilde{\mathcal{TR}})_i$ and decodes visual features of the entire image. The process is denoted as $\widetilde{o}_{i,l} = \text{OB-LSTM}(\widetilde{wr}_{i,1}, \phi)$ and $\widetilde{O}_i = \{\widetilde{o}_{i,l}, \ldots, \widetilde{o}_{i,L}\}$, where ϕ is the hidden state vector of OG-LSTM. We aggregate the features in $\widetilde{O}_i$ to generate a single feature denoted as the generated visual feature of the entire news image $\hat{O}_i$. The loss function between the generated visual feature and the feature of the original image I_i is denoted as $\mathcal{L}(\hat{O}_i, \mathcal{F}(I_i)) = \sum_{j=1}^{2d} |\hat{O}_{i,j} - \mathcal{F}(I_i)_j|$. If the news text and image are less consistent with each other, we expect a lower similarity between the encoded image and the generated visual feature.

4.2.1.3 Image-Guided Textual Feature Decoder (ITFD)

Given the fact that the textual content of the news articles can convey the visual information in Sect. 4.2.1.2, we reverse the relation between the textual and visual content and develop an image-guided textual feature decoder (ITFD) to learn the corresponding textual information from the news images. We observe that, in a incorrect news article, the visual information expressed in the news images often deviates from the news texts. In particular, given a COVID-19 news article $\mathcal{P}_i$, ITFD first designs an object-based self-attention encoder to encode pairwise relationships of all extracted visual objects in Sect. 4.2.1.1, which are denoted as $A(\mathcal{R}_i) = U\sigma(\text{Attention}(W_q\mathcal{R}_i, W_k\mathcal{R}_i, W_v\mathcal{R}_i))$. Attention(Q,K,V) $= \text{Softmax}(\frac{QK^T}{\sqrt{d}})V$ is the scaled dot-product attention function and U is a linear transformation matrix. We create a stack of N encoders to recurrently consume the previously encoded outputs and produce a multi-level output $\mathbb{R}_i = \{\mathcal{R}_i^1, \ldots, \mathcal{R}_i^N\}$.

After encoding the visual objects and their internal relations, the ITFD then develops a cross-modal self-attention decoder to decode the image-associated textual features based on the news text $\mathcal{T}_i$. Formally, the process is denoted below.

$$\hat{\mathcal{T}}_i = U\sigma(\sum_{n=1}^{N} \text{Attention}(W_q \text{Mask}(\mathcal{T}_i), W_k \mathcal{R}_i^n, W_v \mathcal{R}_i^n)) \tag{4.1}$$

where Mask$(\cdot)$ denotes the mask operation on $\mathcal{T}_i$ to hide the one-step ground-truth sequential words from the input text. The loss function between the decoded words and the corresponding ground-truth words is denoted as $\mathcal{L}(\mathcal{T}_i, \hat{\mathcal{T}}_i) = \sum_{l=1}^{L} \text{CrossEntropy}(w_{i,l}, \hat{\mathcal{T}}_{i,l})$. If the news texts and news images are less consistent with each other, we expect a lower similarity between the encoded news texts and the generated textual features.

4.2.1.4 Comment-Driven Explanation Generator (CDEG)

After generating the cross-modal features $\hat{O}_i$ and $\hat{\mathcal{T}}_i$ based on the original text and image of the news article $\mathcal{P}_i$, the comment-driven explanation generator (CDEG) aims to leverage both the original and generated features of $\mathcal{P}_i$ to provide content and comment explanations on the truth discovery results of $\mathcal{P}_i$. In particular, CDEG jointly exploits the information embedded in multimodal content and user comments of $\mathcal{P}_i$ to provide accurate explanations. One possible solution is to apply the co-attention mechanism [30] to aggregate the encoded features of the content and comment from $\mathcal{P}_i$. However, such a solution can not solve the problem because it ignores the generated features from TVFG and ITFD that are useful to explain the complex association between multimodal content of $\mathcal{P}_i$. Moreover, the co-attention mechanism considers each user comment in C_i as independent and ignores the close relations between them to accurately retrieve the comment explanation. For example, comment A "Agree!" replying to another comment B "These shingles are not caused by the vaccine" will be incorrectly used as an endorsing comment to the news article instead of comment B if the hierarchical relationship between the comments is ignored. To address the above limitations, we design the dual content-comment graphs to explicitly model the relationship between the multimodal content and the user comments to detect and explain the multimodal COVID-19 false information. We first define the content-comment graph below.

Definition 4.1 (Content-Comment Graph ($\mathcal{G}$)) We define the content-comment graph $\mathcal{G}$ as $\mathcal{G} = (\mathcal{V}, \mathcal{E})$ where $\mathcal{V} = \{\mathcal{V}_n, \mathcal{V}_m\}$ is a set of graph entities that include the content-level entity subset $\mathcal{V}_n$ and the comment-level entity subset $\mathcal{V}_m$. $\mathcal{E} = \{\mathcal{E}_n, \mathcal{E}_m\}$ is a set of graph edges that connect content and comment features. In particular, the edges in $\mathcal{E}_n$ connect the content features (i.e., source features) to the comment features (i.e., target features). Edges in $\mathcal{E}_m$ connect different comment features based on their "reply relations".

Based on Definition 4.1, we develop two content-comment graphs that focus on the original and generated multimodal contents of the news article, respectively. We formally define the two graphs as $\mathcal{G}_p = \{\mathcal{V}_p, \mathcal{E}_p\}$ and $\mathcal{G}_q = \{\mathcal{V}_q, \mathcal{E}_q\}$ where $\mathcal{V}_p = \{h_i, \widetilde{I}_i, \widetilde{C}_i\}$ contains the encoded text feature h_i, the encoded visual feature $\widetilde{I}_i$ and the encoded user comments $\widetilde{C}_i$. Similarly, $\mathcal{V}_q = \{\hat{\mathcal{T}}_i, \hat{O}_i, \widetilde{C}_i\}$ contains the generated text feature $\hat{\mathcal{T}}_i$, the generated visual feature $\hat{O}_i$ and the encoded user comments $\widetilde{C}_i$. We then design a graph-based information aggregation strategy that fully aggregates the multimodal information in each graph based on the graph edges. The process is formally defined below.

$$v_i^{(l)} = \sigma(W_1 v_i^{(l-1)} + \sum_{j \in \mathcal{V}_k} \alpha_{k,j} W_2 \Delta_{k,j}^{(l-1)}) \tag{4.2}$$

where v_i represents ith graph entity from the content-comment graph. $l-1$ and l denote the $(l-1)$th and lth graph aggregation layers. $\mathcal{V}_k$ denotes the set of graph entities that are connected with v_i based on the graph edges. $\Delta_{i,j}^{(l-1)} = v_i^{(l-1)} - v_j^{(l-1)}$ is the embedding difference between the ith and jth graph node embeddings. $\alpha_{i,j}$ is the normalized attention score between ith and jth graph node embeddings. After the aggregation, we develop learnable parameters $U_n \in \mathbb{R}^{2d \times 1}$ to learn the possibility of each content feature (i.e., text or image feature) to be incorrect. Similarly, we develop $U_m \in \mathbb{R}^{2d \times 1}$ to learn the possibility of each comment feature that can explain the reasons for the content features being incorrect. The process is formally denoted as:

$$\begin{gathered} \omega_{n,p} = \text{Softmax}([h_i \| \widetilde{I}_i] U_n); \quad \omega_{n,q} = \text{Softmax}([\hat{\mathcal{T}}_i \| \hat{O}_i] U_n) \\ \omega_m = \text{Softmax}(\widetilde{C}_i U_m) \end{gathered} \tag{4.3}$$

where $\omega_{n,p} \in \mathbb{R}^2$, $\omega_{n,q} \in \mathbb{R}^2$ and $\omega_m \in \mathbb{R}^K$ are generated possibility scores for the original content, generated content and user comments, respectively. To accurately estimate the truthfulness of each modality in the news content, we average $\omega_{n,p}$ and $\omega_{n,q}$ in the feature dimension to compute the possibility of textual and visual modalities being incorrect (denoted as φ_t and φ_v), respectively. We average the similarity score from TVFG and ITFD to compute the possibility φ_a of the multimodal association being false.

Given the aggregated multimodal features and the corresponding possibility scores, we summarize all the features based on their scores to generate a single *article-level* feature $z_n \in \mathbb{R}^{2d}$. Let $\hat{y}_i \in \{0, 1\}$ be the estimated label of a multimodal news article being incorrect ($\hat{y}_i = 0$) or not ($\hat{y}_i = 1$). We obtain $\hat{y}_i$ by applying the linear transformation matrix $W_f \in \mathbb{R}^{2d \times 2}$ to z_n as $\hat{y}_i = \text{Softmax}(W_f z_n + b_n)$.

We optimize the DualGen framework based on the cross-entropy loss [46] as follows.

$$\mathcal{L} = \sum_{i=1}^{N} \big(-y_i \log(\hat{y}_i)_1 - (1 - y_i) \log(1 - (\hat{y}_i)_0)\big) \tag{4.4}$$

where y_i and $\hat{y}_i$ are the ground-truth and estimated labels of each multimodal COVID-19 news article $\mathcal{P}_i$. The final output of DualGen includes: (1) the estimated label $\hat{y}_i \in \{0, 1\}$ that $\mathcal{P}_i$ is incorrect or not, (2) the possibility scores $\varphi_t, \varphi_v, \varphi_a$ that identify if the textual content, visual content, and their association are incorrect, respectively and (3) the set of comments that achieve the highest possibility scores ω_m in explaining why the specific content is incorrect.

4.2.2 *ContrastFaux: A Multi-View Contrastive Learning Method*

An overview of the ContrastFaux framework is shown in Fig. 4.4. In particular, the framework consists of two core modules:

- *Multi-view Contrastive Fauxtography-aware Network (MCFN)*: it introduces a novel multi-view contrastive deep network architecture to capture the deeply embedded fauxtography features from multi-view social media posts. The identified fauxtography features are then used to detect the fauxtography using sparse annotations of the social media posts.

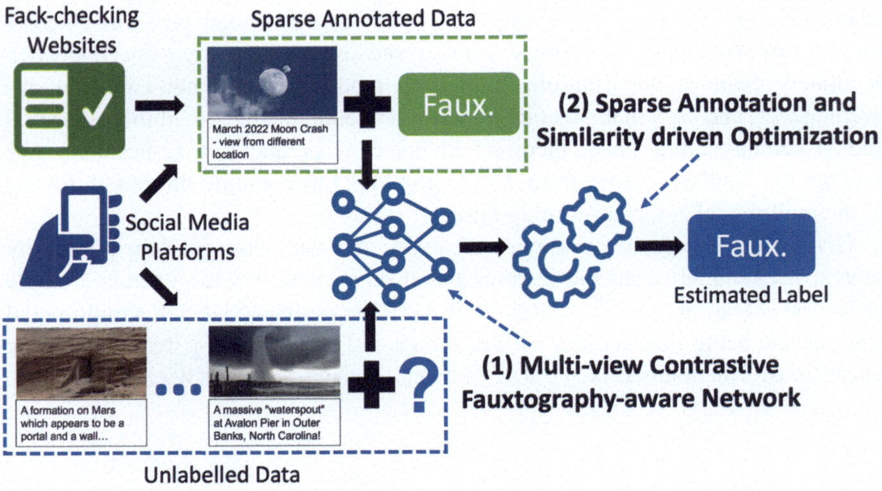

Fig. 4.4 Overview of the ContrastFaux framework

- *Sparse Annotation and Similarity-driven Optimization (SASO)*: it explicitly leverages the sparse annotations and the cross-modal fauxtography feature similarity between the image and text of a social media post to derive the optimal instance of the multi-view contrastive deep neural network from MCFN for accurate fauxtography detection.

4.2.2.1 Multi-View Contrastive Fauxtography-aware Network (MCFN)

We first present the MCFN module that designs a principled multi-view contrastive deep network to address the *sparse fauxtography annotation* challenge. The design of MCFN module is motivated by the limitations of current truth discovery approaches that can not effectively identify the fauxtography features from the multi-view text and image post when the training data is sparse. We first introduce a few key definitions that will be used in the MCFN module as follows:

Definition 4.2 (Fauxtography Features (F)) We define $\boldsymbol{F^I} = \{F_1^I, F_2^I, \ldots, F_N^I\}$ and $\boldsymbol{F^T} = \{F_1^T, F_2^T, \ldots, F_N^T\}$ to be the visual features in the image and the semantic features in the text, respectively. The fauxtography features can capture the key fauxtography-related characteristics for identifying incorrect content or incorrect cross-modal association in multi-view social media posts. F_k^I and F_k^T represent the visual and textual fauxtography features of social media post X_k for $k \in \{1, 2, \ldots, N\}$. An effective fauxtography feature extraction network architecture will provide the module with key fauxtography features to accurately identify different types of fauxtography.

Definition 4.3 (Paired Image and Text Entity $\{\boldsymbol{Z^I}, \boldsymbol{Z^T}\}^+$) we define $\{\boldsymbol{Z^I}, \boldsymbol{Z^T}\}^+$ to be the paired social media image and text entities for all studied social media posts, where $\{Z_k^I, Z_k^T\}$ includes the pair of image Z_k^I and text Z_k^T posted in the *same* social media post X_k. Formally, we have $\boldsymbol{X} = \{\boldsymbol{Z^I}, \boldsymbol{Z^T}\}^+$. An example of paired image and text entities is shown in Fig. 4.5a. Given the fact that the paired image and text entities essentially come with the same fauxtography annotation, the

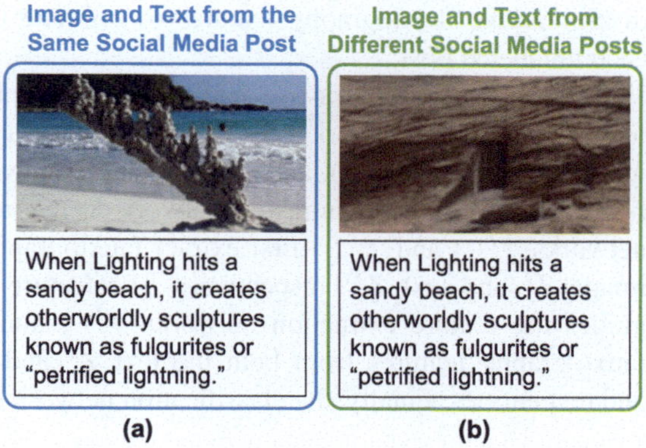

Fig. 4.5 Examples of paired and unpaired image and text entities. (**a**) Paired image and text entity. (**b**) Unpaired image and text entity

paired image and text entities supervise the multi-view contrastive deep network to learn the multi-view fauxtography features from the image and text of the post for accurate fauxtography detection.

Definition 4.4 (Unpaired Image and Text Entity $\{\boldsymbol{Z^I}, \boldsymbol{Z^T}\}^-$) We define $\{\boldsymbol{Z^I}, \boldsymbol{Z^T}\}^-$ to be the image and text entities selected from *different* social media posts, where $Z^I_{k_1}$ is the image in a social media post X_{k_1} and $Z^T_{k_2}$ is the text in another social media post X_{k_2}. Given the notations, we have $\{Z^I_{k_1}, Z^T_{k_2} \big| k_1 \neq k_2\}$ for $k_1, k_2 \in \{1, 2, \ldots, N\}$ to represent all unpaired image and text entities selected from different social media posts. An example of the unpaired image and text entities is shown in Fig. 4.5b. The unpaired text and image entities are used to train the multi-view contrastive deep network by preventing it from learning the fauxtography-irrelevant visual and textual features from the image and text of the unpaired entities.

Given the above definitions, we further define the pair indicator $\boldsymbol{P}$ as a binary variable to indicate the paired and unpaired entities as follows:

$$P_{k_1,k_2} = \begin{cases} 1 & \text{for } \{Z^I_{k_1}, Z^T_{k_2} \big| k_1 = k_2\} \\ 0 & \text{for } \{Z^I_{k_1}, Z^T_{k_2} \big| k_1 \neq k_2\} \end{cases} \tag{4.5}$$

To effectively perform fauxtography detection with sparse annotations, the MCFN module leverages the paired and unpaired image and text entities to supervise the contrastive multi-view network to learn the discriminative fauxtography features from the multi-view social media posts. We observe that the image and text from the paired entities often share the discriminative fauxtography features that are essential for the fauxtography detection task. On the other hand, the shared semantic features between the text and image from the unpaired entities often appear to be irrelevant to fauxtography detection, which should be clearly distinguished by the deep network from the discriminative fauxtography features learned from the paired entities. The MCFN module leverages such a unique characteristic to supervise the deep network to identify the discriminative fauxtography features from both the image and text of a social media post. The MCFN module then utilizes the identified discriminative fauxtography features to estimate the fauxtography annotation of each unlabeled post.

The multi-view contrastive network consists of the following core networks: feature extraction networks $f^I(\cdot)$ for the image and $f^T(\cdot)$ for the text, a feature matching network $m(\cdot, \cdot)$, and a classification network $c(\cdot, \cdot)$. We show an illustration of the multi-view contrastive network design in Fig. 4.6. The feature extraction networks $f^I(\cdot)$ and $f^T(\cdot)$ first extract fauxtography features $\boldsymbol{F^I}$ and $\boldsymbol{F^T}$ for the image $\boldsymbol{Z^I}$ and text $\boldsymbol{Z^T}$, respectively. The feature matching network $m(\cdot, \cdot)$ then guides the feature extraction networks $f^I(\cdot)$ and $f^T(\cdot)$ to learn discriminative fauxtography features from both the text $\boldsymbol{Z^I}$ and image $\boldsymbol{Z^T}$ of a pair of image and text entities. Finally, the classification network $c(\cdot, \cdot)$ classifies unlabeled social

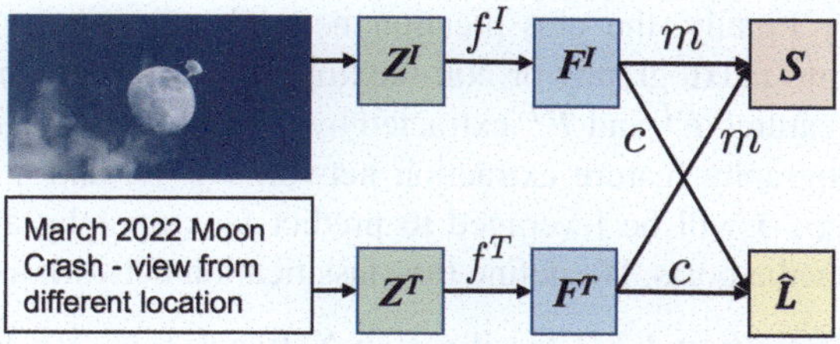

Fig. 4.6 Overview of the multi-view contrastive fauxtography-aware network (MCFN) module

media post into fauxtography or non-fauxtography using the fauxtography features $\boldsymbol{F^I}$ and $\boldsymbol{F^T}$ extracted by the feature extraction networks $f^I(\cdot)$ and $f^T(\cdot)$ and the sparse fauxtography labels. We elaborate each core network in the MCFN module as follows. In particular, we first define feature extraction networks as follows.

Definition 4.5 (Feature Extraction Networks ($f^I(\cdot)$ and $f^T(\cdot)$)) We define $f^I(\cdot)$ and $f^T(\cdot)$ as feature extraction networks that focus on extracting fauxtography features from image $\boldsymbol{Z^I}$ and text $\boldsymbol{Z^T}$ of a social media post as:

$$\begin{aligned} \boldsymbol{F^I} &= f^I(\boldsymbol{Z^I}) \\ \boldsymbol{F^T} &= f^T(\boldsymbol{Z^T}) \end{aligned} \tag{4.6}$$

In particular, we utilize representative ResNet [11] as the image feature extraction networks $f^I(\cdot)$ and leverage the widely used BERT [5] as the text feature extraction network $f^T(\cdot)$. The objective of this design is to provide the feature extraction networks with deep network architecture to effectively learn the complicated multi-view fauxtography features.

Given the extracted features $\boldsymbol{F^I}$ and $\boldsymbol{F^T}$, the feature matching network $m(\cdot,\cdot)$ then supervises the feature extraction networks $f^I(\cdot)$ and $f^T(\cdot)$ to learn the similar fauxtography features between $\boldsymbol{Z^I}$ and $\boldsymbol{Z^T}$. In particular, the feature matching network is defined as follows.

Definition 4.6 (Feature Matching Network ($m(\cdot,\cdot)$)) We define $m(\cdot,\cdot)$ as a feature matching network that aims to identify the discriminative fauxtography features from paired image and text entities by computing the feature similarity $\boldsymbol{S}$ as follows:

$$\boldsymbol{S} = m(\boldsymbol{F^I}, \boldsymbol{F^T}) \tag{4.7}$$

The feature matching network $m(\cdot,\cdot)$ includes a set of fully connected layers, which compute the feature similarity between the image and text features. In particular, the feature matching network $m(\cdot,\cdot)$ guides the feature extraction networks $f^I(\cdot)$ and $f^T(\cdot)$ to extract fauxtography features effectively by capturing the discriminative fauxtography features from the social media posts of the same fauxtography annotation. We will introduce a feature matching loss to learn the feature similarity in the next subsection.

Finally, the classification network $c(\cdot, \cdot)$ categorizes each social media post into fauxtography or non-fauxtography by leveraging the multi-view fauxtography features $\boldsymbol{F^I}$ and $\boldsymbol{F^T}$ extracted by the feature extraction networks. The learned fauxtography feature extraction networks $f^I(\cdot)$ and $f^T(\cdot)$ and classification network $c(\cdot, \cdot)$ will be leveraged to predict fauxtography annotations for unlabeled social media posts. We define the classification network as follows.

Definition 4.7 (Classification Network ($c(\cdot, \cdot)$)) We define $c(\cdot, \cdot)$ to be a classification network that utilizes the extracted features $\boldsymbol{F^I}$ and $\boldsymbol{F^T}$ for the text and image $\boldsymbol{Z^I}$ and $\boldsymbol{Z^T}$ to identify the fauxtography annotation $\widehat{\boldsymbol{L}}$ as follows:

$$\widehat{\boldsymbol{L}} = c(\boldsymbol{F^I}, \boldsymbol{F^T}) \tag{4.8}$$

In particular, the $c(\cdot, \cdot)$ consists of a concatenation layer followed by several fully connected layers to predict the fauxtography annotation by examining the fauxtography features extracted by $f^I(\cdot)$ and $f^T(\cdot)$.

To conclude, the core feature extraction networks $f^I(\cdot)$ and $f^T(\cdot)$, feature matching network $m(\cdot, \cdot)$, and classification network $c(\cdot, \cdot)$ in the MCFN module collaboratively learn an effective fauxtography detection model given the sparse fauxtography annotations by designing a multi-view contrastive neural network architecture.

4.2.2.2 Sparse Annotation and Similarity-Driven Optimization (SASO)

Given the multi-view contrastive network designed in the MCFN module, the SASO module aims to utilize the sparse fauxtography annotations to learn the optimal instance of the multi-view contrastive deep network from the MCFN module. To that end, we design two sets of novel loss functions (i.e., fauxtography-aware feature matching loss function and sparse data-driven classification loss) to guide the multi-view contrastive deep network to effectively identify the fauxtography features from both text and image for fauxtography detection using the sparse training data. We elaborate on the two loss functions below.

We first define the fauxtography-aware feature matching loss for $f^I(\cdot)$, $f^T(\cdot)$, and $m(\cdot, \cdot)$ as:

$$\begin{aligned} \mathcal{L}_m = \mathcal{L}_{\text{contrastive}}\left(P_{k_1,k_2}, m\left(f^I(Z^I_{k_1}), f^T(Z^T_{k_2})\right)\right), \\ \forall k_1, k_2 \in \{1, 2, \ldots, N\} \end{aligned} \tag{4.9}$$

where $\mathcal{L}_m$ represents the fauxtography-aware feature matching loss. $\mathcal{L}_{\text{contrastive}}$ is a contrastive learning loss function that calculates the cross-entropy between feature similarity predicted by the feature matching network $m(\cdot)$ and the pair indicator P_{k_1,k_2}. The objective of the feature matching loss function is to supervise the MCFN module to learn accurate fauxtography features for fauxtography detection.

The second loss function focuses on supervising the MCFN module to effectively predict the fauxtography labels $\boldsymbol{L}$ from the fauxtography features extracted by $f^I(\cdot)$ and $f^T(\cdot)$. To that end, we define the sparse data-driven classification loss function for $f^I(\cdot)$, $f^T(\cdot)$, and $c(\cdot,\cdot)$ as:

$$\mathcal{L}_c = \mathcal{L}_{\text{cross-entropy}}\left(L_i^A, c\left(f^I(Z_i^I), f^T(Z_i^T)\right)\right), \quad \forall\{Z_i^I, Z_i^T\} \in \boldsymbol{X^A} \tag{4.10}$$

where $\mathcal{L}_c$ is the sparse data-driven classification loss function. $\mathcal{L}_{\text{cross-entropy}}$ is the cross entropy loss [18] that computes the difference between ground truth and predicted fauxtography annotations generated by the classification network $c(\cdot,\cdot)$. The objective of the sparse data-driven classification loss $\mathcal{L}_c$ is to supervise the classification network $c(\cdot,\cdot)$ to effectively quantify the identified fauxtography features and generate accurate fauxtography annotations accordingly.

Given the two loss functions defined above, we then combine them to generate the overall loss function $\mathcal{L}_{overall}$ for all the networks $f^I(\cdot)$, $f^T(\cdot)$, $m(\cdot,\cdot)$, and $c(\cdot,\cdot)$ in the MCFN module to collaboratively optimize the sparse semi-supervised fauxtography detection performance as follows:

$$\mathcal{L}_{overall} = \mathcal{L}_m + \mathcal{L}_c \tag{4.11}$$

Using the overall loss function in the SASO module, we can optimize all the networks to generate the optimal network instances (i.e., f_*^I, f_*^T, m_*, and c_*) using the Adam optimizer [14]. We then apply f_*^I, f_*^T, and c_* to obtain the predicted fauxtography label $\widehat{\boldsymbol{L^U}}$ for unlabeled social media posts $\boldsymbol{X^U}$ as follows:

$$\widehat{L_j^U} = c_*\left(f_*^I(Z_j^I), f_*^T(Z_j^T)\right), \ \forall\{Z_j^I, Z_j^T\} \in \boldsymbol{X^U} \tag{4.12}$$

The final output of the ContrastFaux includes predicted fauxtography annotations $\widehat{\boldsymbol{L^U}}$ for unlabeled social media posts $\boldsymbol{X^U}$.

4.3 Real-World Case Studies

We evaluate the effectiveness of the DualGen and ContrastFaux using two real-world case studies with multiple datasets. Specifically, we evaluate DualGen under the application scenario of multimodal truth discovery where the goal is to assess the truthfulness of news articles that combine text and images. To evaluate ContrastFaux, we adopt the application scenario of fauxtography detection that aims to detect multimodal social media posts where the image and associated text jointly convey a questionable or false sense.

4.3.1 Multimodal Truth Discovery

We evaluate the performance of DualGen using two real-world datasets of online news articles that are related to COVID-19 and its vaccines. Evaluation results show that DualGen achieves significant performance gains compared to state-of-the-art baselines for multimodal truth discovery.

4.3.1.1 Data

First, we describe the datasets to be used in the case study. We collect the multimodal COVID-19 news datasets from two publicly available COVID-19 news repositories—ReCOVery [48] and MMCoVaR [4]. ReCOVery contains the multimodal COVID-19 news articles collected from Jan. 2020 to May. 2020. MMCoVaR contains the multimodal COVID-19 vaccine-related news articles collected from Feb. 2020 to May. 2021. We adopt the ground-truth labels provided in the original data repositories.After removing invalid news articles (i.e., the ones where the original news articles are no longer available), we obtain 1868 and 2534 multimodal COVID-19 news articles in the ReCOVery and MMCoVaR datasets, respectively. A summary of the datasets is reported in Table 4.1.

4.3.1.2 Baseline Methods and Experimental Setting

We compare DualGen with several state-of-the-art multimodal truth discovery solutions, described below.

- **MVAE [13]:** MVAE is a bimodal variational autoencoder approach that utilizes the encoded representation of multimodal news data to assess its integrity.
- **SpotFake [34]:** SpotFake is a multimodal truth discovery scheme that utilizes a pre-trained natural language model (i.e., BERT) and visual feature extraction model (i.e., VGG-19) to encode multimodal news articles for truth discovery.

Table 4.1 Dataset summary

	ReCOVery		MMCoVaR	
Data trace	Correct	Incorrect	Correct	Incorrect
# of articles	1311	557	1626	908
# of unique publishers	21	31	52	39
Avg. # of comments per article	29	12	13	12
News topic	COVID-19 Pandemic		COVID-19 Vaccine	
Collection period	Jan. 2020–May. 2020		Feb. 2020–May. 2021	

- **EANN [39]:** EANN is an event adversarial neural network approach that leverages the text and image features in social media news posts to train an event-based discriminator for multimodal truth discovery.
- **SAFE [49]:** SAFE is a similarity-aware method that jointly learns the news representation from textual and visual information to detect false posts on social media.
- **BTIC [45]:** BTIC is a BERT-based learning framework that extracts the latent visual and textual features for unreliable multimodal news article detection.
- **dEFEND [30]:** dEFEND is an explainable truth discovery method that leverages the association between the news text and user comments to classify credible news and identify user comments to explain the classification results.
- **ExFaux [15]:** ExFaux is a graph-based explainable fauxtography detection solution that provides content explanations for fauxtography detection results.
- **HSA [10]:** HSA is a hierarchical social attention network solution that incorporates social media user comments to detect rumors.

In the experiments, we use 80 and 20% of the dataset as the training and testing set, respectively. To ensure a fair comparison, we use the same input (i.e., text, image, and user comments) to all the content-based baselines (i.e., MVAE, SpotFake, EANN, SAFE, BTIC, dEFEND, and ExFaux). In particular, for the baselines that only use text content (e.g., dEFEND), we add the visual features as new features in addition to the textual features of the models. In addition, we use comment-only baseline HSA to evaluate the comment explainability and keep the input the same as that in their paper (i.e., user comments). We strictly follow the model configuration of all schemes as documented in their paper and carefully tune the hyperparameters for the best results.

4.3.1.3 Truth Discovery Performance

In the first set of experiments, we evaluate the classification performance on detecting false information in multimodal COVID-19 news. We use the following metrics to evaluate the performance of all compared methods: *Accuracy*, *Precision*, *Recall*, and *F1 Score*. The evaluation results are summarized in Table 4.2. We observe that DualGen consistently outperforms all compared baseline methods on all evaluation metrics. In particular, we observe that DualGen achieves a performance gain of 4.9 and 4.3% compared to the best-performing baselines (i.e., EANN and dEFEND) in terms of F1 score on the ReCOVery and MMCoVaR datasets, respectively. The performance gains are attributed to the accurate cross-modal feature generation and the effective consistency measurement and validation between the generated and original multimodal features in DualGen. Moreover, the design of the content-comment graph in DualGen also greatly enhances the aggregation of generated and original multimodal features and the user comments for identifying incorrect information. We also observe that the performance of feature fusion based methods (i.e., MVAE, SpotFake, EANN, dEFEND, and ExFaux) is less desirable in detecting

Table 4.2 Truth discovery performance

	ReCOVery				MMCoVaR			
Method	Accuracy	Precision	Recall	F1 score	Accuracy	Precision	Recall	F1 score
DualGen	**0.897**	**0.890**	**0.861**	**0.873**	**0.895**	**0.896**	**0.871**	**0.881**
MVAE	0.825	0.813	0.755	0.774	0.815	0.805	0.834	0.808
SpotFake	0.681	0.637	0.650	0.641	0.699	0.670	0.620	0.623
EANN	0.847	0.816	0.834	0.824	0.833	0.819	0.810	0.814
SAFE	0.831	0.803	0.789	0.795	0.788	0.773	0.749	0.757
BTIC	0.763	0.719	0.695	0.704	0.829	0.823	0.791	0.803
dEFEND	0.856	0.826	0.813	0.823	0.856	0.847	0.831	0.838
ExFaux	0.763	0.719	0.695	0.704	0.769	0.784	0.694	0.707
HSA	0.779	0.737	0.736	0.736	0.803	0.782	0.785	0.784

The bold values indicate the best performing results in each evaluation metric

Table 4.3 Ablation study results

	ReCOVery				MMCoVaR			
Method	Accuracy	Precision	Recall	F1	Accuracy	Precision	Recall	F1
DualGen	**0.897**	**0.890**	**0.861**	**0.873**	**0.895**	**0.896**	**0.871**	**0.881**
DualGen w/o text	0.850	0.820	0.841	0.829	0.856	0.839	0.851	0.844
DualGen w/o image	0.852	0.835	0.803	0.816	0.869	0.857	0.852	0.855
DualGen w/o graph	0.886	0.870	0.857	0.863	0.871	0.866	0.846	0.854

The bold values indicate the best performing results in each evaluation metric

false information in multimodal COVID-19 news articles. The reason is that these methods directly infer the truthfulness of the news article from the fused multimodal news content but ignore the interdependence between the visual and textual content in the news articles.

4.3.1.4 Ablation Study

We also conduct an ablation study to investigate the contribution of generated visual and textual features, and the dual content-comment graphs in the DualGen framework. In particular, we consider three types of ablations of DualGen in the experiments: (1) *DualGen w/o Text* that does not generate textual features, (2) *DualGen w/o Image* that does not generate visual features, (3) *DualGen w/o Graph* that directly concatenates user comments with the multimodal content features rather than propagating the user comments information via the dual content-comment graphs. The results are shown in Table 4.3. We observe that DualGen achieves the best performance when it incorporates all components. The results demonstrate the necessity of the generated visual and textual features as well as the graph-based comment information propagation in detecting false information in multimodal COVID-19 news articles.

4.3.2 *Fauxtography Detection*

In this section, we study the performance of the ContrastFaux framework with two real-world social media fauxtography datasets. Evaluation results show that ContrastFaux consistently outperforms state-of-the-art deep learning and semi-supervised learning baselines by accurately detecting fauxtography posts on social media with sparse annotations.

4.3.2.1 Data

We collected two real-world datasets from widely used social media platforms Twitter and Reddit. Given the fact that a huge amount of posts are generated on Twitter and Reddit in real-time, it is challenging to collect and annotate fauxtography data directly from these social media platforms. Therefore, we utilize three online fact-checking platforms (i.e., snopes.com, factcheck.org, and truthorfiction.com) to obtain fauxtography annotations. In particular, we collect images of social media posts and their fauxtography annotations from these fact-checking platforms following the standard procedure [16]. The collected fauxtography and non-fauxtography images were posted between 2010 and 2019. To ensure the quality of the fauxtography annotations, the ground-truth annotations are generated using the majority voting results of the three fact-checking platforms. Using the collected images and fauxtography annotations, we then utilize the Google Vision API [8] to reversely search for social media post URLs. Using the obtained URLs, we crawl the texts of the posts from the Twitter API [38] and Reddit API [26]. We summarize the statistics of the two real-world datasets in Table 4.4. In the experiments, we set the sparsely annotated social media post ratio α to be 10% for all compared schemes. We also vary the value of α to evaluate the robustness of the framework in Sect. 4.3.2.4.

4.3.2.2 Baseline Methods and Experimental Setting

Baseline Methods

In the evaluation, we compare the proposed ContrastFaux with a rich set of representative deep learning and semi-supervised learning fauxtography detection baselines.

Table 4.4 Statistics of fauxtography detection datasets

Datasets	Twitter	Reddit
Total number of posts	883	958
Percent of fauxtography	20.8%	42.4%
Percent of non-fauxtography	79.2%	57.5%

- **FCMF [50]**: FCMF is a multi-view classification approach that integrates various image features (e.g., Google tags, URL categories) and text features (e.g., text contents, text embedding similarities) to achieve sizable improvements in fauxtography detection.
- **dEFEND [30]**: dEFEND is a co-attention deep neural network that jointly captures check-worthy social media sentences and user comments for explainable fauxtography detection.
- **MMFND [6]**: MMFND is a multimodal deep neural network model that utilizes an image branch and a text branch to combine textual and visual modalities using representative feature representation networks BERT [5] and VGG-16 [31] to detect online fauxtography.
- **SpotFake [33]**: SpotFake is a multimodal deep learning approach that leverages textual and visual features to detect fauxtography using pre-trained transformer-based language networks and deep convolutional image networks, respectively.
- **PredictCredibility [32]**: PredictCredibility is a efficient multimodal deep neural network that leverages a sentence transformer for the text and a convolutional neural network for the image and then fuses the two modalities for fauxtography detection.
- **Gen. to Adapt [41]**: Gen. to Adapt is a semi-supervised learning approach that induces a symbolic relationship and a generative adversarial network to achieve generalization among different data domains in fauxtography detection.
- **VAT [24]**: VAT is a semi-supervised learning method that proposes a virtual adversarial loss to measure the robustness of the conditional label distribution for the generalizable fauxtography detection.
- **Billion-scale [42]**: Billion-scale is a semi-supervised learning convolutional neural network that leverages a large collection of unlabeled data using a training and fine-tuning pipeline to improve the fauxtography detection performance.
- **CL [3]**: CL is a resilient semi-supervised learning method that utilizes pseudo-labeling and curriculum learning to improve the generalizability of fauxtography detection model.

Experimental Setting

For a fair comparison, we keep the input data to all compared approaches to be the same: (1) all studied social media posts, and (2) fauxtography labels for the sparsely annotated social media post subset. Social media posts in the sparsely annotated subset are randomly sampled from all posts in the dataset. ContrastFaux is implemented using PyTorch 1.1.0 libraries [25] on NVIDIA Quadro RTX 6000 GPUs. The network is optimized by the Adam optimizer [14] with the learning rate of 1×10^{-5}. The batch size is set to 60 and the number of epochs is set to 100. To evaluate the performance of all compared schemes, we utilize four different metrics that are widely used in binary classification tasks: Accuracy, F1-Score, Precision, and Recall. Higher values of these metrics indicate better detection performance.

Table 4.5 Fauxtography detection performance

	Twitter dataset				Reddit dataset			
Method	Accuracy	F1-score	Precision	Recall	Accuracy	F1-score	Precision	Recall
ContrastFaux	**0.936**	**0.850**	**0.828**	**0.873**	**0.822**	**0.798**	**0.777**	**0.821**
FCMF	0.886	0.688	0.805	0.600	0.728	0.629	0.759	0.537
dEFEND	0.913	0.793	0.786	0.800	0.788	0.763	0.731	0.797
MMFND	0.890	0.701	0.810	0.618	0.794	0.770	0.739	0.805
SpotFake	0.890	0.713	0.783	0.655	0.732	0.639	0.756	0.553
PredictCredibility	0.867	0.607	0.794	0.491	0.767	0.712	0.755	0.675
Gen. to adapt	0.852	0.519	0.808	0.382	0.655	0.508	0.654	0.415
VAT	0.788	0.442	0.773	0.309	0.665	0.719	0.731	0.707
Billion-scale	0.856	0.568	0.758	0.455	0.673	0.565	0.656	0.496
CL	0.887	0.694	0.791	0.618	0.784	0.763	0.719	0.813

The bold values indicate the best performing results in each evaluation metric

4.3.2.3 Fauxtography Detection Performance

We first compare the detection accuracy of ContrastFaux with all baselines on the two real-world fauxtography detection datasets collected from Twitter and Reddit. The sparsely annotated social media post ratio α is set to 10%. The comparison results are shown in Table 4.5. We observe that ContrastFaux clearly outperforms all baselines on all metrics. For example, on the Twitter dataset, the ContrastFaux outperforms the best-performing baseline (i.e., dEFEND) by 2.49, 7.16, 5.33, and 9.09% in terms of Accuracy, F1-Score, Precision, and Recall, respectively. Similar results are observed on the Reddit dataset. The consistent performance gains across the two datasets demonstrate that ContrastFaux successfully improves the sparse semi-supervised fauxtography detection performance. Such performance gains are attributed to the explicit design and optimization of the multi-view contrastive network architecture using the sparse fauxtography annotations and the cross-modal fauxtography feature similarity between the image and text.

4.3.2.4 Robustness Study

We conduct a robustness study to evaluate the performance of ContrastFaux on both Twitter and Reddit datasets under different annotated social media post ratios (i.e., α). In particular, we vary α from 1 to 15% for ContrastFaux and the top two best-performing baselines. The comparison results are presented in Fig. 4.7. ContrastFaux consistently and stably outperforms best-performing baselines on both datasets under different annotated social media post ratios. The evaluation results demonstrate the robustness of ContrastFaux in learning heterogeneous and complicated fauxtography features to detect fauxtography given different amounts of annotations.

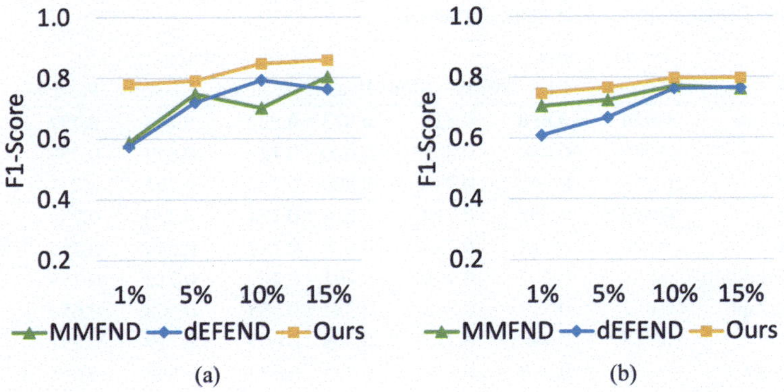

Fig. 4.7 Robustness study of the ContrastFaux framework and the top two best-performing baselines. (**a**) Twitter dataset. (**b**) Reddit dataset

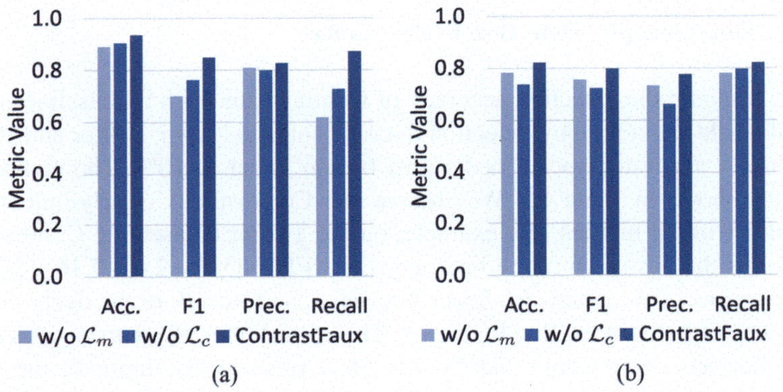

Fig. 4.8 Ablation study of the ContrastFaux framework. (**a**) Twitter dataset. (**b**) Reddit dataset

4.3.2.5 Ablation Study

We further conduct an ablation study to learn the contribution of the two loss functions to the overall ContrastFaux framework on both the Twitter and Reddit datasets. In particular, we present the fauxtography detection performance by removing each of the key loss function terms (i.e., the feature matching loss $\mathcal{L}_m$ and the classification loss $\mathcal{L}_c$). To remove the feature matching loss $\mathcal{L}_m$, we train the model by only using the classification loss $\mathcal{L}_c$ given the sparse fauxtography annotations. For the model without the classification loss $\mathcal{L}_c$, we utilize the K-means clustering algorithm to detect fauxtography based on multi-view features learned by the feature matching loss $\mathcal{L}_m$. The ablation study results are presented in Fig. 4.8. The comparison results demonstrate that both of the loss functions make non-trivial contributions to the performance gain of the overall ContrastFaux framework.

4.4 Discussion

In this chapter, we discussed the data heterogeneity problem and introduced two novel frameworks, DualGen and ContrastFaux, for handling heterogeneous data in social intelligence applications. In particular, DualGen explicitly explores the cross-modal association between the news content in different modalities to examine the cross-model information consistency. Unlike DualGen which relies on ground-truth annotations to supervise the learning process, ContrastFaux alleviates such a requirement and adopts a multi-view contrastive learning approach to effectively capture discriminative features from paired and unpaired image-text entities under sparse annotation settings.

While these solutions have demonstrated the effectiveness of integrating heterogeneous features and examining their relations, they also exhibit certain limitations. First, these solutions rely on a non-trivial amount of training data, with supervised and unsupervised learning objectives, to capture the multimodal features from the heterogeneous multimodal social intelligence data. Such approaches may not be optimal or generalizable across different domains or datasets, limiting their applicability in scenarios where the data distribution shifts over time. In Chap. 5, we will discuss the domain discrepancy issue and review state-of-the-art solutions that further improve the model generality in social intelligence. Furthermore, another limitation of these multimodal approaches lies in the lack of explainability in the sense that the latent multimodal feature representations and decision-making processes of these complex models are often opaque and difficult to interpret, making it challenging to understand the rationale behind the model predictions and support critical decision-making processes or interventions in high-stake applications (e.g., healthcare, criminal justice). In Chap. 6, we introduce explainable social intelligence solutions that are dedicated to tackling the interpretability challenge and enhancing the model's transparency and trustworthiness.

Additionally, a few open research questions and ethical considerations remain in handling data heterogeneity for social intelligence. For example, multimodal social intelligence solutions that process and analyze heterogeneous data might be prone to bias in the source datasets and amplify societal inequities, especially in sensitive domains such as healthcare and criminal justice. We will discuss ethical challenges and review responsible social intelligence designs in Chap. 8. Furthermore, the integration of multiple data modalities raises privacy concerns as the joint analysis of text, images, or other multimedia data could reveal sensitive personal information (e.g., face images, location traces, social relationships) from online users. In Chap. 9, we will review the issue of privacy concerns in social intelligence and present privacy-preserving techniques and mitigation strategies.

References

1. F. Alam, S. Cresci, T. Chakraborty, F. Silvestri, D. Dimitrov, G. D. S. Martino, S. Shaar, H. Firooz, and P. Nakov. A survey on multimodal disinformation detection. *arXiv preprint arXiv:2103.12541*, 2021.
2. A. Benamira, B. Devillers, E. Lesot, A. K. Ray, M. Saadi, and F. D. Malliaros. Semi-supervised learning and graph neural networks for fake news detection. In *2019 IEEE/ACM International Conference on Advances in Social Networks Analysis and Mining (ASONAM)*, pages 568–569, New York, NY, USA, 2019. IEEE, ACM.
3. P. Cascante-Bonilla, F. Tan, Y. Qi, and V. Ordonez. Curriculum labeling: Revisiting pseudo-labeling for semi-supervised learning. In *Proceedings of the AAAI conference on artificial intelligence*, volume 35, pages 6912–6920, 2021.
4. M. Chen, X. Chu, and K. Subbalakshmi. Mmcovar: Multimodal covid-19 vaccine focused data repository for fake news detection and a baseline architecture for classification. In *Proceedings of the 2021 IEEE/ACM International Conference on Advances in Social Networks Analysis and Mining*, pages 31–38, 2021.
5. J. Devlin, M.-W. Chang, K. Lee, and K. Toutanova. Bert: Pre-training of deep bidirectional transformers for language understanding. *arXiv preprint arXiv:1810.04805*, 2018.
6. A. Giachanou, G. Zhang, and P. Rosso. Multimodal multi-image fake news detection. In *2020 IEEE 7th International Conference on Data Science and Advanced Analytics (DSAA)*, pages 647–654. IEEE, 2020.
7. R. Girshick. Fast r-cnn. In *Proceedings of the IEEE international conference on computer vision*, pages 1440–1448, 2015.
8. Google. https://cloud.google.com/vision.
9. G. B. Guacho, S. Abdali, N. Shah, and E. E. Papalexakis. Semi-supervised content-based detection of misinformation via tensor embeddings. In *2018 IEEE/ACM international conference on advances in social networks analysis and mining (ASONAM)*, pages 322–325, New York, NY, USA, 2018. IEEE, ACM.
10. H. Guo, J. Cao, Y. Zhang, J. Guo, and J. Li. Rumor detection with hierarchical social attention network. In *Proceedings of the 27th ACM International Conference on Information and Knowledge Management*, pages 943–951, 2018.
11. K. He, X. Zhang, S. Ren, and J. Sun. Deep residual learning for image recognition. In *Proceedings of the IEEE conference on computer vision and pattern recognition*, pages 770–778, 2016.
12. S. Heller, L. Rossetto, and H. Schuldt. The ps-battles dataset-an image collection for image manipulation detection. *arXiv preprint arXiv:1804.04866*, 2018.
13. D. Khattar, J. S. Goud, M. Gupta, and V. Varma. Mvae: Multimodal variational autoencoder for fake news detection. In *The world wide web conference*, pages 2915–2921, New York, NY, USA, 2019. ACM.
14. D. P. Kingma and J. Ba. Adam: A method for stochastic optimization. *arXiv preprint arXiv:1412.6980*, 2014.
15. Z. Kou, D. Y. Zhang, L. Shang, and D. Wang. Exfaux: A weakly supervised approach to explainable fauxtography detection. In *2020 IEEE International Conference on Big Data (Big Data)*, pages 631–636. IEEE, 2020.
16. D. M. Lazer, M. A. Baum, Y. Benkler, A. J. Berinsky, K. M. Greenhill, F. Menczer, M. J. Metzger, B. Nyhan, G. Pennycook, D. Rothschild, et al. The science of fake news. *Science*, 359(6380):1094–1096, 2018.
17. X. Li, P. Lu, L. Hu, X. Wang, and L. Lu. A novel self-learning semi-supervised deep learning network to detect fake news on social media. *Multimedia Tools and Applications*, 81(14):19341–19349, 2022.
18. W. Liu, Y. Wen, Z. Yu, and M. Yang. Large-margin softmax loss for convolutional neural networks. In *ICML*, volume 2, page 7, 2016.

19. Y. Liu, M. Ott, N. Goyal, J. Du, M. Joshi, D. Chen, O. Levy, M. Lewis, L. Zettlemoyer, and V. Stoyanov. Roberta: A robustly optimized bert pretraining approach. *arXiv preprint arXiv:1907.11692*, 2019.
20. Y. Liu and Y.-F. Wu. Early detection of fake news on social media through propagation path classification with recurrent and convolutional networks. In *Proceedings of the AAAI Conference on Artificial Intelligence*, volume 32, 2018.
21. R. Mansouri, M. Naderan-Tahan, and M. J. Rashti. A semi-supervised learning method for fake news detection in social media. In *2020 28th Iranian Conference on Electrical Engineering (ICEE)*, pages 1–5. IEEE, 2020.
22. M. G. Marmot. Social inequalities in mortality: the social environment. In *Class and health*, pages 21–33. Routledge, 2022.
23. A. Mathews, L. Xie, and X. He. Semstyle: Learning to generate stylised image captions using unaligned text. In *Proceedings of the IEEE Conference on Computer Vision and Pattern Recognition*, pages 8591–8600, 2018.
24. T. Miyato, S.-i. Maeda, M. Koyama, and S. Ishii. Virtual adversarial training: a regularization method for supervised and semi-supervised learning. *IEEE transactions on pattern analysis and machine intelligence*, 41(8):1979–1993, 2018.
25. PyTorch. https://pytorch.org/.
26. Reddit. https://www.reddit.com/dev/api/.
27. S. Ren, K. He, R. Girshick, and J. Sun. Faster r-cnn: Towards real-time object detection with region proposal networks. In *Advances in neural information processing systems*, pages 91–99, 2015.
28. L. Shang, Z. Kou, Y. Zhang, and D. Wang. A duo-generative approach to explainable multimodal covid-19 misinformation detection. In *Proceedings of the ACM Web Conference 2022*, pages 3623–3631, New York, NY, USA, 2022. ACM. https://doi.org/10.1145/3485447.3512257.
29. L. Shang, Y. Zhang, Z. Yue, Y. Choi, H. Zeng, and D. Wang. A knowledge-driven domain adaptive approach to early misinformation detection in an emergent health domain on social media. In *2022 IEEE/ACM International Conference on Advances in Social Networks Analysis and Mining (ASONAM)*, pages 34–41. IEEE, 2022.
30. K. Shu, L. Cui, S. Wang, D. Lee, and H. Liu. defend: Explainable fake news detection. In *Proceedings of the 25th ACM SIGKDD international conference on knowledge discovery & data mining*, pages 395–405, 2019.
31. K. Simonyan and A. Zisserman. Very deep convolutional networks for large-scale image recognition. *arXiv preprint arXiv:1409.1556*, 2014.
32. B. Singh and D. K. Sharma. Predicting image credibility in fake news over social media using multi-modal approach. *Neural Computing and Applications*, pages 1–15, 2021.
33. S. Singhal, R. R. Shah, T. Chakraborty, P. Kumaraguru, and S. Satoh. Spotfake: A multi-modal framework for fake news detection. In *2019 IEEE Fifth International Conference on Multimedia Big Data (BigMM)*, pages 39–47, 2019.
34. S. Singhal, R. R. Shah, T. Chakraborty, P. Kumaraguru, and S. Satoh. Spotfake: A multi-modal framework for fake news detection. In *2019 IEEE fifth international conference on multimedia big data (BigMM)*, pages 39–47. IEEE, 2019.
35. Y. Song, T. Wang, P. Cai, S. K. Mondal, and J. P. Sahoo. A comprehensive survey of few-shot learning: Evolution, applications, challenges, and opportunities. *ACM Computing Surveys*, 55(13s):1–40, 2023.
36. M. Tan and Q. Le. Efficientnet: Rethinking model scaling for convolutional neural networks. In *International conference on machine learning*, pages 6105–6114. PMLR, 2019.
37. A. Tommasel. Friend or foe: Studying user trustworthiness for friend recommendation in the era of misinformation. In *2019 IEEE second international conference on artificial intelligence and knowledge engineering (AIKE)*, pages 273–276. IEEE, 2019.
38. Twitter. https://developer.twitter.com/en/docs/twitter-api.

39. Y. Wang, F. Ma, Z. Jin, Y. Yuan, G. Xun, K. Jha, L. Su, and J. Gao. Eann: Event adversarial neural networks for multi-modal fake news detection. In *Proceedings of the 24th acm sigkdd international conference on knowledge discovery & data mining*, pages 849–857, 2018.
40. P. William, R. Gade, R. esh Chaudhari, A. Pawar, and M. Jawale. Machine learning based automatic hate speech recognition system. In *2022 International conference on sustainable computing and data communication systems (ICSCDS)*, pages 315–318. IEEE, 2022.
41. G. Wilson and D. J. Cook. A survey of unsupervised deep domain adaptation. *ACM Transactions on Intelligent Systems and Technology (TIST)*, 11(5):1–46, 2020.
42. I. Z. Yalniz, H. Jégou, K. Chen, M. Paluri, and D. Mahajan. Billion-scale semi-supervised learning for image classification. *arXiv preprint arXiv:1905.00546*, 2019.
43. D. Y. Zhang, L. Shang, B. Geng, S. Lai, K. Li, H. Zhu, M. T. Amin, and D. Wang. Fauxbuster: A content-free fauxtography detector using social media comments. In *2018 IEEE international conference on big data (big data)*, pages 891–900. IEEE, 2018.
44. L. Zhang, J. Zhang, Z. Lin, H. Lu, and Y. He. Capsal: Leveraging captioning to boost semantics for salient object detection. In *Proceedings of the IEEE/CVF Conference on Computer Vision and Pattern Recognition*, pages 6024–6033, 2019.
45. W. Zhang, L. Gui, and Y. He. Supervised contrastive learning for multimodal unreliable news detection in covid-19 pandemic. *arXiv preprint arXiv:2109.01850*, 2021.
46. Z. Zhang and M. R. Sabuncu. Generalized cross entropy loss for training deep neural networks with noisy labels. In *32nd Conference on Neural Information Processing Systems (NeurIPS)*, 2018.
47. C. Zhou, Q. Li, C. Li, J. Yu, Y. Liu, G. Wang, K. Zhang, C. Ji, Q. Yan, L. He, et al. A comprehensive survey on pretrained foundation models: A history from bert to chatgpt. *International Journal of Machine Learning and Cybernetics*, pages 1–65, 2024.
48. X. Zhou, A. Mulay, E. Ferrara, and R. Zafarani. Recovery: A multimodal repository for covid-19 news credibility research. In *Proceedings of the 29th ACM International Conference on Information & Knowledge Management*, pages 3205–3212, 2020.
49. X. Zhou, J. Wu, and R. Zafarani. Safe: Similarity-aware multi-modal fake news detection. In *Pacific-Asia Conference on Knowledge Discovery and Data Mining*, pages 354–367. Springer, 2020.
50. D. Zlatkova, P. Nakov, and I. Koychev. Fact-checking meets fauxtography: Verifying claims about images. In *Proceedings of the 2019 Conference on Empirical Methods in Natural Language Processing and the 9th International Joint Conference on Natural Language Processing (EMNLP-IJCNLP)*, pages 2099–2108, Hong Kong, China, Nov. 2019. Association for Computational Linguistics.
51. R. Zong, Y. Zhang, L. Shang, and D. Wang. Contrastfaux: Sparse semi-supervised fauxtography detection on the web using multi-view contrastive learning. In *Proceedings of the ACM Web Conference 2023*, pages 3994–4003, New York, NY, USA, 2023. ACM. https://doi.org/10.1145/3543507.3583869.

Chapter 5
Data Sparsity and Model Generality

Abstract Social intelligence systems often face two fundamental limitations, data sparsity and model generality, when the systems need to adapt to new domains or scenarios where training data is limited or unavailable. This is particularly important in critical social intelligence applications such as health truth discovery and disaster damage assessment. This chapter introduces two human-AI hybrid approaches, CrowdAdapt and CollabGeneral, that explore human intelligence and domain expertise to effectively bridge the knowledge gap between data-rich source domains and emergent target domains. Two fundamental challenges exist in developing such hybrid approaches, including: (1) the domain discrepancy where knowledge transfer is degraded by irrelevant or inapplicable information from source domains, and (2) the optimal trade-off between model generality and domain specificity that ensures a social intelligence model can perform well across different domains while maintaining high accuracy for domain-specific characteristics and patterns. Two real-world case studies demonstrate the superiority and great potential of CrowdAdapt and CollabGeneral in addressing these challenges and advancing the development of adaptive social intelligence systems.

Keywords Data sparsity · Model generality · Robustness · Crowdsourcing · Knowledge graph · Human-AI collaboration · Hybrid learning

5.1 Data Sparsity and Model Generality Problems in Social Intelligence

The advancement of artificial intelligence and machine learning has brought unprecedented opportunities to social intelligence, where data from the social space (e.g., social media, online forums) is leveraged to address critical societal challenges, such as public health surveillance [14] and disaster management [25]. However, such data-driven social intelligence systems are often data-intensive and face two fundamental problems: data sparsity and model generality. These problems arise when the systems need to adapt to new domains or scenarios where training data is limited or unavailable. For instance, when a new disease outbreak occurs (e.g., the 2022–2023 Mpox outbreak [31]), social intelligence systems

D. Wang et al., *Social Intelligence*, https://doi.org/10.1007/978-3-031-90080-8_5

trained on previous health crises (e.g., COVID-19) must quickly adapt to detect false information about the new disease, despite having limited domain-specific training data. Similarly, disaster management systems trained to assess damage from hurricane images must generalize their capabilities to different types of disasters, even when the visual characteristics and impact patterns differ significantly.

Current AI and machine learning solutions to address these problems often rely on transfer learning [2] and knowledge adaptation techniques [38]. In particular, transfer learning approaches aim to transfer models from data-rich source domains to data-sparse target domains. For example, pre-trained text representation on general text data (e.g., BERT embeddings [8]) has been utilized to classify false information on social media by fine-tuning the language model with a small set of domain-specific examples [16]. However, such a solution is often prone to overfitting to the limited domain-specific examples and fails to capture the rapidly evolving patterns and domain-specific characteristics of social media data, especially in the emergent target domain. More recently, researchers have explored self-supervised and few-shot learning methods that can learn from limited labeled data by exploiting the inherent structure and patterns in large amounts of unlabeled social media posts. For example, contrastive learning approaches have been used to learn discriminative features from social media posts by treating posts from the same domain as similar examples, while treating topically distant posts as dissimilar examples [43]. While these methods show promise in learning from limited labeled data, they still face significant challenges in capturing domain-specific knowledge, such as the scientifically grounded medical facts for health truth discovery or damage assessment criteria for disaster response, and adapting to rapidly evolving events/topics in social intelligence. In particular, there exist several key challenges in developing generalizable social intelligence systems where the training data is sparse [30, 41]. We elaborate on these challenges below.

Domain Discrepancy in Social Intelligence

Domain discrepancy refers to the fundamental differences in data distribution, contextual features, and domain-specific characteristics between a source domain (e.g., data-rich domains with abundant labeled examples and knowledge resources) and a target domain (e.g., emerging scenarios with limited data and resources). Such domain discrepancy often poses significant challenges for transferring and adapting knowledge in social intelligence systems. Let us consider an example of health truth discovery across different disease outbreaks. A source domain (e.g., COVID-19) often contains a large number of literature resources (e.g., research publications, fact-checking articles) from which the knowledge facts can be extracted for truth discovery [7]. A straightforward solution is to directly use the knowledge facts from the source domain to detect false information in the target domain. However, such a solution often ignores the complex nature of knowledge facts in the source domain, which often contains many knowledge facts that are irrelevant to the target domain. For example, the knowledge facts extracted from fact-checking articles often contain many non-medical entities, such as "5G network" and "RFID chip" in Fig. 5.1a,

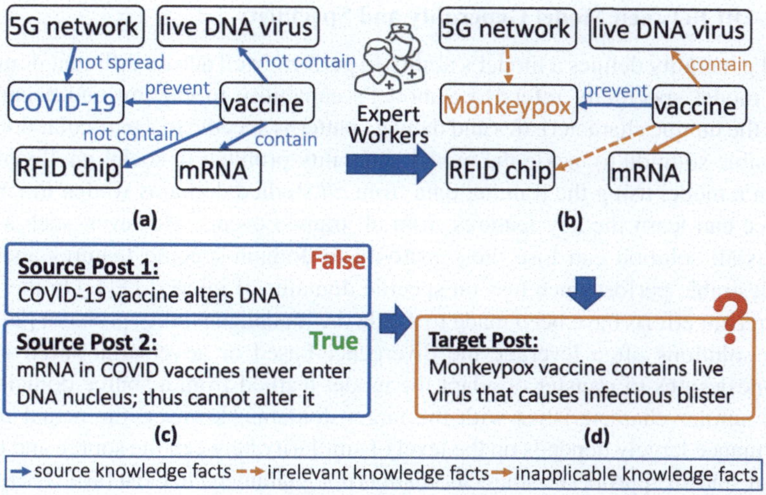

Fig. 5.1 Domain discrepancy in emergent healthcare truth discovery. It shows a crowdsourcing-based strategy in social intelligence to explore the medical knowledge of expert workers (i.e., crowd workers with medical expertise) to adapt the abundant resources from a *source domain* (i.e., the healthcare domain with sufficient annotated data and medical knowledge) to detect incorrect posts in an emergent *target domain* (i.e., the healthcare domain that is short of annotated data and medical knowledge). (**a**) Knowledge facts in source domain. (**b**) Adapted knowledge facts in target domain. (**c**) Annotated posts in source domain. (**d**) Post in target domain

which are often irrelevant to medical science and are rarely seen in false information from the domains other than COVID-19. Such irrelevant knowledge facts can be of little help in detecting false information in the target domain. Thus, it remains a challenge to effectively leverage complex and noisy knowledge facts from the source domain to facilitate the social intelligence task in the target domain.

Moreover, while some knowledge facts from the source domain can be generalized to identify false information in the target domain, there often exists a non-trivial amount of knowledge facts in the source domain that are relevant but inapplicable to the target domain. For example, "vaccine" $\xrightarrow{\text{not contain}}$ "live DNA virus" (Fig. 5.1a) is a widely accepted knowledge fact in the source domain of COVID-19. However, the knowledge fact is inapplicable to the target domain of Mpox, where the vaccine does contain live vaccinia virus (a DNA virus) that can cause serious vaccine adverse events among people with immunocompromising conditions. Such inapplicable knowledge facts have to be identified and corrected to detect false information in the target domain. However, it often requires expertise from medical experts to fully examine the inconsistency of knowledge facts between different domains, which is both labor-intensive and time-consuming [18]. Therefore, it is challenging to efficiently utilize the limited amount of domain experts to adapt and validate the necessary knowledge facts from the source to the target domain.

Trade-Off Between Model Generality and Specificity

Model generality defines a model's ability to perform well across different domains, while model specificity refers to a model's capability to capture and accurately assess the unique characteristics and damage patterns specific to a particular domain. A possible solution to tackle the model generality problem in social intelligence is to train a model using the training data from *all* studied domains so that the model instance can learn the key features from all trained events. However, such a one-size-fits-all solution can lose the sensitivity to domain-specific features and lead to undesirable performance loss on specific domains of interest [11]. On the other hand, recent efforts have been made to tackle the model generality problem [27, 42]. Those solutions often leverage the divergence-based or adversarial-based neural network designs to transfer or adapt the model learned from a source domain that shares similar characteristics with the target domain. However, the actual model performance largely depends on the level of similarity between the source and target domain, and an appropriate source domain is not guaranteed to exist [40]. Therefore, finding the optimal trade-off between model generality and specificity remains a fundamental challenge in social intelligence systems.

5.2 Robust and General Social Intelligence: CrowdAdapt and CollabGeneral

This section presents two novel social intelligence frameworks, CrowdAdapt (Crowdsourcing-based Domain Adaptation) [30] and CollabGeneral (Collaborative Generality) [41], to address the data sparsity and model generality challenge in social intelligence. In particular, CrowdAdapt develops a crowd-AI integrated framework that effectively identifies and adapts relevant knowledge facts from the source knowledge domain to accurately detect false information in the emergent target domain. CollabGeneral designs a subjective logic-driven human-AI collaborative learning framework that exploits AI and HI to address the AI model generality problem in social intelligence.

5.2.1 CrowdAdapt: A Crowdsourcing-Based Domain Adaptation Solution

An overview of the CrowdAdapt framework is shown in Fig. 5.2. In particular, CrowdAdapt consists of three main modules: (1) a *Graph-based Knowledge Encoder (GKE)* module that constructs a graph-based medical knowledge information network to explicitly model the medical knowledge facts and extract the useful knowledge facts related to the posts from different domains; (2) a *Domain-invariant Representation Learning (DRL)* module that aims to jointly learn the domain-

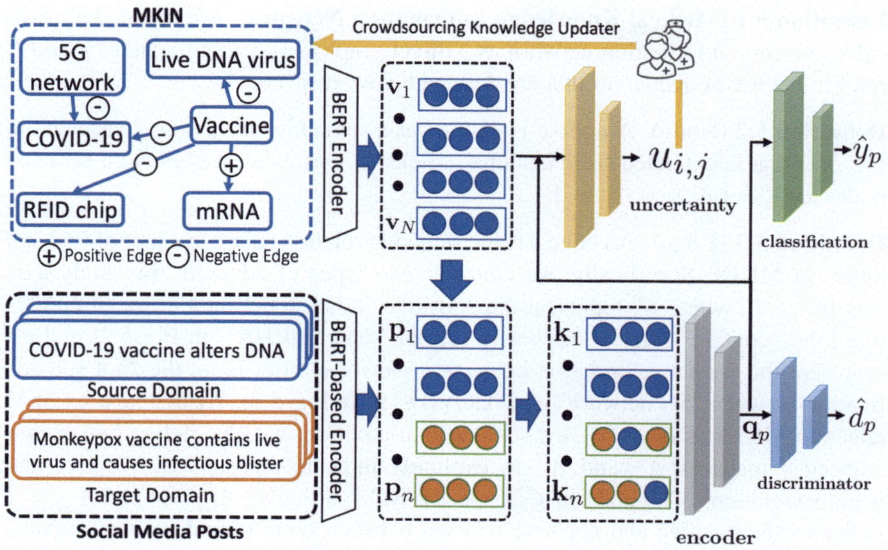

Fig. 5.2 Overview of the CrowdAdapt framework

invariant representation of the posts and their relevant knowledge facts extracted by the GKE module; and (3) a *Crowdsourcing-based Knowledge Updater (CKU)* module that incorporates the medical expertise from expert workers to verify and correct the uncertain medical knowledge facts extracted from GKE and accurately detect incorrect posts in the target domain.

5.2.1.1 Graph-Based Knowledge Encoder

The graph-based knowledge encoder module designs a graph-based knowledge information network to explicitly explore the relationship between different healthcare-related entities and extract useful healthcare knowledge facts that are relevant to the posts from a given domain. We observe that existing domain adaptive truth discovery solutions mainly focus on leveraging the data annotations (i.e., labeled posts) in the source domain to reduce the model's reliance on the data annotations in the target domain [21, 39]. However, such solutions largely ignore the healthcare knowledge facts associated with the posts, which is particularly important for identifying incorrect posts in emergent healthcare domains. Therefore, to mitigate such a limitation, a graph-based medical knowledge information network is developed to explicitly extract the medical knowledge information from the widely available articles in the source domain (i.e., source articles) to facilitate the detection of false information in the target domain. We first define the medical knowledge information network (MKIN) as follows.

Definition 5.1 (Medical Knowledge Information Network) We define the medical knowledge information network as a direct graph $\mathcal{G} = \{\mathcal{V}, \mathcal{E}\}$, where $\mathcal{V}$ and $\mathcal{E}$ refer to the *nodes* and *edges* that are defined below, respectively.

Definition 5.2 (Node) A node v is defined as a semantic entity (e.g., "vaccine" in Fig. 5.2) that is extracted from a source article. In particular, we denote a set of N nodes as $\mathcal{V} = \{v_1, v_2, \cdots, v_N\}$.

Definition 5.3 (Edge) An edge e is the semantic relation between a pair of relevant nodes in MKIN. Specifically, we consider two types of edges in this study, i.e., $e \in \{e^+, e^-\}$, where e^+ represent the "positive" relation between a pair of entities (e.g., the "contain" relation between "vaccine" and "mRNA" in Fig. 5.2) and e^- represent the "negative" relation between a pair of entities (e.g., the "not spread" relation between "5G network" and "COVID-19" in Fig. 5.2). We denote a set of M edges in MKIN as $\mathcal{E} = \{e_1, e_2, \cdots, e_M\}$. In addition, we also define two *binary* adjacency matrices A^+ and A^- to explicitly indicate the pairwise positive and negative relations of all nodes in $\mathcal{G}$, respectively. In particular, $A^+_{i,j} = 1$ and $A^-_{i,j} = 1$ indicates the positive and negative relation between node v_i and v_j, respectively. Otherwise, $A^+_{i,j}$ and $A^-_{i,j}$ are 0, indicating no relation between node v_i and v_j.

Definition 5.4 (Knowledge Triple) We also define a knowledge triple $t = (v, e, v')$ as a pair of relevant nodes v and v' that are connected via an edge e in $\mathcal{G}$.

With the medical knowledge information network $\mathcal{G}$ constructed as above, the next objective is to learn the context-aware semantic representation of each node in MKIN by exploring its semantic dependency on other relevant nodes in MKIN. In particular, we first develop a BERT-based semantic encoder to extract the semantic representation of each node in MKIN. Formally, let $v_i = [w_1, w_2, \cdots, w_{n_i}]$ be the semantic entity of node $v_i \in \mathcal{V}$, where w_k for $1 \leq k \leq n_i$ is the kth word in node v_i. We first adopt a pre-trained BERT model [8] to retrieve the word embedding $\mathbf{u}_k$ of each word w_k, where $\mathbf{u}_k \in \mathbb{R}^d$ and d is the dimension of the word embedding. We then apply the mean-pooling and max-pooling to the word embeddings of each node and concatenate the pooled embeddings to obtain the final node embedding $\mathbf{v}_i \in \mathbb{R}^{2d}$ that aggregates the semantic representation of each node $v_i \in \mathcal{V}$. We also define a node embedding matrix $V \in \mathbb{R}^{N \times 2d}$ as the matrix that contains the node embeddings of all nodes in MKIN.

While the node embeddings can capture the semantic meaning of each node in MKIN, it remains a challenge to effectively extract the key knowledge triples from MKIN to identify the false information in the target domain. This is because MKIN is constructed from a number of articles in the source domain and often contains many knowledge triples that are irrelevant to the topics discussed in the posts from a target domain. For example, the knowledge triple ("vaccine", ⊖, "RFID chip") in Fig. 5.2 is of little help for identifying the incorrect post "Mpox vaccine contains live virus and causes infectious blister" in the target domain of Mpox. To address such a challenge, we design a post-based knowledge triple refinement strategy to explicitly capture the critical knowledge triples that are relevant to the given post.

For example, the knowledge triples related to the "live DNA virus" can be captured in MKIN to facilitate the detection of the incorrect post that the live DNA virus in the Mpox vaccine causes an infectious blister. Thus, we explicitly measure the semantic relevance between a post and each node in $\mathcal{V}$ to obtain the knowledge triples that are more relevant to a given post. In particular, we adopt the same BERT-based encoding strategy to encode each post $p \in \{P_s, P_t\}$ and denote the encoded vector representation of p as $\mathbf{p} \in \mathbb{R}^{1\times 2d}$. Finally, the post-based knowledge triple refinement strategy to obtain the refined adjacency matrices $\hat{A}^+$ and $\hat{A}^-$ are as follows.

$$\hat{A}_p^+ = f\left((V\mathbf{p}^\top W_a^+) \odot A^+\right); \hat{A}_p^- = f\left((V\mathbf{p}^\top W_a^-) \odot A^-\right) \tag{5.1}$$

where $V \in \mathbb{R}^{N\times 2d}$ is node embedding matrix. $f(\cdot)$ is the softmax function, and W_a^+ and W_a^- are learnable weights.

5.2.1.2 Domain-Invariant Representation Learning

Given the fact that there are often no ground-truth labels for the post in an emergent target domain to supervise the learning, the next objective is to learn the domain-invariant representations of the posts and their relevant medical knowledge triples in the refined MKIN from the GKE module by only using the available ground-truth labels of the posts from the source domain. Existing domain adaptive learning frameworks mainly focus on the domain discrepancy of the post content between the source and target domains and target to map the post content from different domains to a domain-invariant feature space. However, such solutions ignore the domain discrepancy of medical knowledge information in MKIN, which is critical to identify incorrect posts in different healthcare domains. To overcome such a limitation, we present a joint representation learning framework to jointly learn the domain-invariant representations of the posts from different domains as well as their relevant knowledge triples. In particular, we first aggregate the medical knowledge information from the refined MKIN by propagating the node information based on their relations captured in the refined adjacency matrices $\hat{A}^+$ and $\hat{A}^-$ (Eq. (5.1)). Formally, the knowledge aggregation process is defined as

$$\hat{\mathbf{v}}_i = \sigma\left(\sum_{\mathbf{v}_j \in \mathcal{N}_i^+} \frac{1}{\omega_i^+} W^+ \mathbf{v}_j + \sum_{\mathbf{v}_j \in \mathcal{N}_i^+} \frac{1}{\omega_i^-} W^- \mathbf{v}_j + \mathbf{v}_i\right) \tag{5.2}$$

where $\hat{\mathbf{v}}_i$ is the learned node representation of $v_i \in \mathcal{V}$ with the knowledge information propagated from neighborhood nodes of v_i. $\sigma(\cdot)$ is the non-linear ReLU activation function. $\mathbf{v}_i$ and $\mathbf{v}_j$ are the node embeddings of v_i and v_j in $\mathcal{V}$, respectively. $\mathcal{N}_i^+$ and $\mathcal{N}_i^-$ refer to the set of neighborhood nodes of $v_i \in \mathcal{V}$ under the edge e^+ and e^-, respectively. W^+, W^-, and W are the learnable weight parameters. ω_i^+ and ω_i^- are the normalization factors of W^+ and W^-, respectively. We further aggregate the node representation for $v_i \in \mathcal{V}$ to obtain the representation of knowledge triples that are relevant to a post $p \in \{P_s, P_t\}$ based on the score measured in $\hat{A}_p^+$ and $\hat{A}_p^-$ (Eq. (5.1)), followed by an average operation. The aggregated knowledge triple representation is defined as $\mathbf{t}_p = [\mathbf{t}_p^+ || \mathbf{t}_p^-]$, where $||$ denotes the concatenation operation. $\mathbf{t}_p^+$ and $\mathbf{t}_p^-$ are the knowledge triple representations computed based on the learned node representation $\hat{\mathbf{v}}_i$ of all $v_i \in \mathcal{V}$ and the refined adjacency matrices $\hat{A}_p^+$ and $\hat{A}_p^-$, respectively.

Using the aggregated representations of the knowledge triples, we design a discriminative encoder network with an adversarial loss to jointly learn the knowledge-enriched representation of the posts from the source and target domains while minimizing the domain divergence of the learned features. In particular, the discriminative encoder network consists of two main components: (1) a two-layer *encoder network* that aims to learn the key information from the input posts and relevant knowledge triples in MKIN; (2) a two-layer *discriminator network* that targets at accurately distinguishing the domain of the encoded posts and their relevant knowledge triples. Formally, the encoder network and discriminator network are defined as follows.

$$\mathbf{q}_p = \mathbf{encoder}([\mathbf{p}||\mathbf{t}_p]) \quad \text{and} \quad \hat{d}_p = \mathbf{discriminator}(\mathbf{q}_p) \tag{5.3}$$

where $\mathbf{p}$ and $\mathbf{t}_p$ are the encoded vector representation and the aggregated knowledge triple representation of posts p, respectively. $\mathbf{q}_p$ is the knowledge-enriched representation of a post p and $\hat{d}_p$ is the estimated domain of $\mathbf{q}_p$.

With the discriminative encoder network defined above, we adopt the adversarial loss to effectively regulate the encoder network (Eq. (5.3)) to learn the domain-invariant representation from the posts and their relevant knowledge triples that cannot be distinguished by the discriminator network (Eq. (5.3)). Formally, the adversarial loss is defined as follows:

$$\mathcal{L}_{adv} = \sum_{p \in \{P_s, P_t\}} -d_p \log(\hat{d}_p)_1 - (1 - d_p) \log(1 - (\hat{d}_p)_0) \tag{5.4}$$

where d_p and $\hat{d}_p$ are the true and estimated domain of post $p \in \{P_s, P_t\}$, respectively.

The latent representation learned from the discriminative encoder network effectively captures the domain-invariant knowledge-enriched features of the posts from the source and target domains. Such domain-invariant features with minimized domain discrepancy can be leveraged to detect incorrect posts regardless of the domain of the posts. In particular, we employ a two-layer classification network to accurately predict the truthfulness of each post. Formally, the classification network is defined as $\hat{y}_p = MLP(\mathbf{q}_p)$. We optimize the classification network with cross-entropy loss:

$$\mathcal{L}_{cla} = -\sum_{p \in P_s} (1 - y_p) \log(1 - (\hat{y}_p)) + y_i \log(\hat{y}_p) \tag{5.5}$$

where y_p is the ground-truth label of the source post $p \in P_s$.

The overall learning objective $\mathcal{L}$ is to jointly optimize the discriminative encoder network and the classification network by maximizing the adversarial loss $\mathcal{L}_{adv}$ and minimizing the classification loss $\mathcal{L}_{cla}$ as $\mathcal{L} = \mathcal{L}_{cla} - \lambda \mathcal{L}_{adv}$, where λ is a hyperparameter to be tuned for optimizing the trade-off between $\mathcal{L}_{adv}$ and $\mathcal{L}_{cla}$.

5.2.1.3 Crowdsourcing-Based Knowledge Updater

The crowdsourcing-based knowledge updater (CKU) module is designed to leverage the medical expertise of the domain experts to verify and correct any uncertain knowledge triples in MKIN from the GKE module that may only be applicable in the source domain but cannot be directly adapted to detect false information in the target domain. We observe that the MKIN constructed from the articles in the source domain also contains knowledge triples that are not applicable to examining the truthfulness of posts in the target domain. For example, the knowledge triple (“vaccine”, $\ominus$, “live DNA virus”) in MKIN from the source domain of COVID-19 (Fig. 5.2) could lead to the incorrect prediction result on the true claim that “Mpox vaccine contains live virus that causes infectious blister,” due to the conflicting fact that the Mpox vaccine is made with attenuated live DNA virus while the COVID-19 vaccine is not. Therefore, it is critical to identify and correct such inapplicable knowledge triples in MKIN to ensure that the medical knowledge obtained from the source domain can be applied to accurately detect false information in the target domain.

To address the above problem, we design a crowdsourcing-based knowledge updating strategy that incorporates the efforts of expert workers (i.e., domain experts from the crowdsourcing platform) to effectively identify and correct the knowledge triples in MKIN to accurately detect false information in the target domain. However, verifying the correctness of knowledge triples in a specific domain often requires background knowledge from domain experts who are often expensive and may not always be available [18]. Therefore, it is impractical to ask expert workers to annotate all knowledge triples in MKIN. To this end, we design a post-driven knowledge triple retrieval process to identify a set of uncertain knowledge triples in MKIN that can be sent to the expert workers to verify their applicability in the target domain. Intuitively, the knowledge-enriched domain-invariant representation of a post learned in the DRL module contains the semantic features of relevant knowledge triples in MKIN for examining the truthfulness of the post, which can also be leveraged to estimate the relationship between a pair of nodes in MKIN. For example, the knowledge-enriched representation of the post “COVID-19 vaccine alters DNA" can capture the critical knowledge features extracted from the knowledge triple ("vaccine", ⊖, "live DNA virus") for examining the truthfulness of the post. Such knowledge-enriched representation is expected to confidently infer the relationship (i.e., edge label) between the corresponding nodes in the knowledge triple. Therefore, we train an MLP-based edge classifier to classify the edge label $e_{i,j}^{p}$ between a pair of nodes (v_i, v_j) in MKIN based on the context of a post p. In particular, we consider three categories of $e_{i,j}^{p}$, including "positive", "negative", and "no relation" as the edges identified in MKIN, and define the edge classifier as $\Pr(\hat{e}_{i,j}^{p}) = MLP([\mathbf{q}_p||\mathbf{v}_i||\mathbf{v}_j])$ where $\hat{e}_{i,j}^{p}$ is the estimated edge label of $e_{i,j}^{p}$. $\mathbf{q}_p$ is the domain-invariant representation of a post $p \in P_s$ and $\mathbf{v}_i$ and $\mathbf{v}_j$ are the BERT-encoded representation of nodes $v_i, v_j \in \mathcal{V}$, respectively. We optimize the edge classifier with cross-entropy loss between $e_{i,j}^{p}$ and $\hat{e}_{i,j}^{p}$.

We then measure the overall uncertainty of each knowledge triple in MKIN in the target domain based on the entropy of the estimated edge labels obtained from the edge classifier. Formally, let $t_{i,j} = (v_i, e_{i,j}, v_j)$ be the knowledge triple containing nodes v_i and v_j, and the uncertainty of each knowledge triple $t_{i,j}$ is computed as

$$u_{i,j} = -\sum_{p \in P_t} \Pr(\hat{e}_{i,j}^{p}) \times \log \Pr(\hat{e}_{i,j}^{p}) \tag{5.6}$$

We further retrieve the top K knowledge triples with the highest uncertainty scores and K is a tunable hyperparameter to be determined based on the model performance and budget. The retrieved knowledge triples are then sent to the expert workers for applicability verification. We show the details of the crowdsourcing task in the Evaluation section. Finally, we update MKIN with the expert-verified knowledge triples (i.e., the knowledge triples verified by the crowd experts) and further optimize the discriminative encoder network and classification network in DRL to accurately detect false information in the target domain.

5.2.2 CollabGeneral: A Crowd-AI Hybrid Learning Framework

CollabGeneral is a crowd-AI hybrid learning framework that integrates AI and crowd intelligence to optimize model generality in AI-based Damage Assessment (ADA) applications.

1. *Generality-aware Deep Optimization (GDO)*: It designs a novel deep model optimization scheme that effectively learns a set of ADA model instances to achieve a good trade-off between AI model generality and specificity through a novel generality-aware network optimization design. The learned ADA model instances are then used to identify the subset of image samples for crowd intelligence query.

2. *Subjective Logic-driven Crowd-AI Fusion (SCF)*: It develops a principled subjective logic-driven crowd-AI fusion framework to effectively integrate the class labels generated by the ADA model instances from GDO module and the crowd labels returned by crowd intelligence query to derive accurate ADA results for each studied disaster event.

5.2.2.1 Generality-Aware Deep Optimization

We first present the generality-aware deep network optimization design to learn a set of ADA model instances that have a high likelihood of achieving an optimized trade-off between the model generality and specificity in ADA applications. We first introduce a key definition for the module.

Definition 5.5 (Deep Estimation Network (Φ)**)** We define Φ to be the deep estimation network (i.e., AI model) in the GDO module that estimates the class labels from the input image samples. Rather than reinventing the wheel, we set Φ to be a representative convolutional neural network (e.g., ResNet, VGG, DenseNet) that is designed to perform the image-based multi-class classification tasks.

Given the deep estimation network Φ, the next step is to learn the optimal network instance of Φ for accurate event-wise ADA performance. To that end, the GDO module introduces two sets of loss functions to explicitly supervise the network optimization process and derive the optimal network instance that can achieve a good trade-off between ADA model generality and specificity. We first define the accuracy-aware loss function for Φ as:

$$\mathcal{L}_1 = \sum_{\forall D_t \in \boldsymbol{D}} \sum_{k=1}^{K} || \Pr(\widehat{Y_{D_t}^{\Phi}} \neq k | Y_{D_t} = k) ||_2 \tag{5.7}$$

where $\mathcal{L}_1$ denotes the accuracy-aware loss function for Φ. D_t is a disaster event from the set of studied events $\boldsymbol{D}$. K denotes the number of unique classes in the ADA application of interest. $\widehat{Y_{D_t}^{\Phi}}$ and Y_{D_t} indicate the *estimated* class labels from Φ and *ground-truth* class labels for all imagery data from disaster event D_t, respectively. $|| \cdot ||_2$ is the L2-norm of a matrix. The objective of the accuracy-aware loss is to supervise Φ to accurately estimate the class labels from all input imagery data. However, a limitation of $\mathcal{L}_1$ loss function is that $\mathcal{L}_1$ only focuses on the overall ADA performance but may not supervise Φ to achieve optimized ADA performance on each individual disaster event. Therefore, we further define the generality-aware loss function for Φ to address such a limitation as:

$$\begin{aligned} \mathcal{L}_2 = \sum_{\forall D_{t_1}, D_{t_2} \in \boldsymbol{D}, D_{t_1} \neq D_{t_2}} \sum_{k=1}^{K} || &\Pr(\widehat{Y_{D_{t_1}}^{\Phi}} = k | D_{t_1}, Y_{D_{t_1}} = k) \\ &- \Pr(\widehat{Y_{D_{t_2}}^{\Phi}} = k | D_{t_2}, Y_{D_{t_2}} = k) ||_2 \end{aligned} \tag{5.8}$$

where $\mathcal{L}_2$ is the generality-aware loss function for Φ. D_{t_1}, D_{t_2} represent any two different disaster events from the set of studied disaster events $\boldsymbol{D}$. $\widehat{Y^{\Phi}_{D_{t_1}}}$ and $\widehat{Y^{\Phi}_{D_{t_2}}}$ indicate the *estimated* class labels for all imagery data from event D_{t_1} and D_{t_2}, respectively. $Y_{D_{t_1}}$ and $Y_{D_{t_2}}$ indicate the *ground-truth* class labels for all imagery data from event D_{t_1} and D_{t_2}, respectively. We then combine the two loss functions to derive the overall loss function for Φ to learn the optimal network instance of Φ as:

$$\mathcal{L}_{Overall} = \mathcal{L}_1 + \mathcal{L}_2 \tag{5.9}$$

Using the overall loss function above, the optimal network instances of Φ can be learned by investigating the trade-off between the exploitation and exploration during the network optimization process through a budget-constrained multi-armed bandit learning process [10]. On the one hand, we keep tuning the same network instance that achieves the low value for $\mathcal{L}_{Overall}$. On the other hand, we take action to attempt new network instances to prevent the model from being trapped in a local optimum. Such an optimization strategy could jointly explore the large network instance space while finding the optimal network instance for Φ.

After performing the budget-constrained multi-armed bandit learning process, one possible solution to obtain the optimal network instance is to use the network instance with the lowest value of $\mathcal{L}_{Overall}$ as the optimal network instance. However, the optimized network instance could be overfitted to the training/validation data and lead to non-negligible performance degradation when it is applied to the testing data due to the potential feature discrepancy between the training/validation and testing sets [28]. To address such an issue, the GDO module not only exploits the network instances with the lowest value of $\mathcal{L}_{Overall}$ but also explores other candidate network instances with low values of $\mathcal{L}_{Overall}$. We formally define the network instances generated by the GDO module as follows.

Definition 5.6 (Optimized Network Instance Set ($\boldsymbol{M}$)) We define the set of network instances learned by the GDO module as $\boldsymbol{M} = \{M_1, M_2, \cdots, M_J\}$, which includes network instances with top J lowest values in $\mathcal{L}_{Overall}$. In addition, M_j indicates the jth learned network instance.

Note that all network instances in $\boldsymbol{M}$ are the instances of the deep estimation network Φ. To generate different network instances in $\boldsymbol{M}$, the GDO module keeps tracking the $\mathcal{L}_{Overall}$ of different network instances generated during *one* budget-constrained multi-armed bandit learning process. The GDO module then adds the network instances with top J lowest values in $\mathcal{L}_{Overall}$ to $\boldsymbol{M}$. The above design avoids the low computational efficiency of performing the budget-constrained multi-armed bandit learning process J times to generate different network instances in $\boldsymbol{M}$.

CollabGeneral then jointly leverages the identified network instances and crowd intelligence to derive accurate ADA results for all studied disaster events, which will be discussed in the next subsection.

5.2.2.2 Subjective Logic-Driven Crowd-AI Fusion

In this module, we design a novel subjective logic-driven crowd-AI fusion framework to fuse the AI and crowd intelligence to derive the accurate ADA results for all studied disaster events to address the ADA model generality problem.

We first discuss how to perform crowd intelligence query Q to collect crowd intelligence for the SCF module. We observe that it is impractical to query the crowd intelligence for all studied image samples due to the budget and resource constraints, which is especially challenging in ADA applications with massive social media data inputs [19]. Therefore, the SCF module samples a subset of image samples for Q in which different network instances in $\boldsymbol{M}$ (Definition 5.6) cannot reach a consensus on. We first measure the *divergence* of the class labels estimated by all network instances in $\boldsymbol{M}$ for each image sample X_i using Shannon entropy [22]. The divergence indicates the degree of disagreement between different network instances in $\boldsymbol{M}$ on the estimated class label for X_i. We then select the image samples with top $\delta \times I$ highest divergence for Q. Here, δ indicates the percentage of studied disaster-related imagery data that are sampled for Q. δ is determined by the trade-off between the ADA model performance and the crowdsourcing cost in the ADA application of interest. I is the total number of studied images.

The next step is to effectively fuse the crowd labels returned by Q with the estimated labels generated by different network instances in $\boldsymbol{M}$. In particular, we define:

Definition 5.7 (Crowd-AI Fusion Committee (S)) We define $\boldsymbol{S} = \{S_1, S_2, \ldots, S_C\}$ as a crowd-AI fusion committee, which contains all J different optimized network instances $\boldsymbol{M}$ learned by the GDO module and all B different crowd workers $\boldsymbol{W}$ in an ADA application. In particular, we have $\boldsymbol{S} = \boldsymbol{M} \cup \boldsymbol{W}$, where $C = J + B$. C is the size of committee $\boldsymbol{S}$, and S_c is a committee member in $\boldsymbol{S}$ (i.e., either an AI network instance or a crowd worker.

The goal of the SCF module is to effectively fuse the inputs from all members in $\boldsymbol{S}$ to derive the accurate ADA labels for the studied disaster events. To that end, we first define the "opinion" of each committee member towards the class label of each image sample through subjective logic, a probabilistic logic that models the epistemic uncertainty and source trust when combining the opinions from different sources [15]. The subjective logic was leveraged to explicitly model each committee member's uncertainty and reliability in estimating the ADA labels for all disaster events.

Definition 5.8 (Committee Member Opinion Entity (E)) For a member S_c, we define $E^k_{S_c} = \{T^k_{S_c}, F^k_{S_c}, U^k_{S_c}\}$ as the member's opinion on whether an image sample belongs to a particular class k or not. In particular, we have:

$$T^k_{S_c}, F^k_{S_c}, U^k_{S_c} \in [0, 1], T^k_{S_c} + F^k_{S_c} + U^k_{S_c} = 1 \tag{5.10}$$

where $T_{S_c}^k$ and $F_{S_c}^k$ indicates S_c's belief and disbelief in the class label of an image sample to be k, respectively. $U_{S_c}^k$ indicates S_c's uncertainty in determining if the class label of an image sample is k or not.

Given the opinion entity of each committee member, we can utilize the consensus operation from subjective logic to combine the opinions of different committee members. Consensus operation is a key operation in subjective logic that is used to determine the shared belief and uncertainty of two sources by considering the individual belief and uncertainty of each source. In particular, we can use the consensus operation $\oplus$ to combine the opinions from any two committee member S_p and S_q as follows:

$$E_{S_p,S_q}^K = \{T_{S_p,S_q}^k, F_{S_p,S_q}^k, U_{S_p,S_q}^k\} = E_{S_p}^k \oplus E_{S_q}^k \tag{5.11}$$

where E_{S_p,S_q}^K indicates the opinion entity after combining the opinions from both S_p and S_q, which indicates their collective opinions on whether an image sample belongs to a particular class k or not.

Then, we can recursively adopt the consensus operation $\oplus$ to combine the opinions from all committee members in the crowd-AI fusion committee as follows:

$$E_{\boldsymbol{S}}^k = \{T_{\boldsymbol{S}}^k, F_{\boldsymbol{S}}^k, U_{\boldsymbol{S}}^k\} = E_{S_1}^k \oplus E_{S_2}^k \oplus, \ldots, \oplus E_{S_C}^k \tag{5.12}$$

Given the combined opinion $E_{\boldsymbol{S}}^k$ from all committee members in the crowd-AI fusion committee $\boldsymbol{S}$, we can leverage it to derive the accurate class label for each image sample. In particular, we set the class label estimated by the CollabGeneral framework to be the one that has the highest belief value $T_{\boldsymbol{S}^{i,k}}^k$ among all possible class labels k for each studied image sample X_i as follows:

$$\arg\max_{k^*} T_{\boldsymbol{S}^{i,k}}^k, \text{ where } k \in \{1, 2, \ldots, K\}, \text{ set } k^* \text{ as } \widehat{Y}_i \tag{5.13}$$

where $\boldsymbol{S}^{i,k}$ indicates the set of committee members who estimate the class label for X_i as k.

However, $E_{S_c}^k$ for each committee member S_c in $\boldsymbol{S}$ is unknown *a priori* and we need to infer the value for each $E_{S_c}^k$ before estimating the accurate class label for each image sample. To that end, we further design an iterative learning framework in the SCF module to obtain the accurate value for each $E_{S_c}^k$. In particular, we first introduce two important concepts in the iterative learning framework.

Definition 5.9 (Committee Member Reliability ($\boldsymbol{R}$)) We define R_c^k to be the probability of a committee member S_c in correctly estimating the class label of an image from class k.

Definition 5.10 (Image Sample Discriminative Score (Z)) We define Z_i^k as the discriminative score of an image sample X_i in terms of identifying the reliable committee member that can correctly estimate the label for image samples of class k.

Given the above two definitions, we note that the values of both committee member reliability $\boldsymbol{R}$ and the image sample discriminative score $\boldsymbol{Z}$ are unknown and depend on each other. Therefore, we optimize $\boldsymbol{R}$ and $\boldsymbol{Z}$ alternately as follows.

First, we optimize the image sample discriminative score $\boldsymbol{Z}$ given the committee member reliability $\boldsymbol{R}$ as follows:

$$Z_i^k = \frac{\sum_{S_p, S_q \in \boldsymbol{S}^{i,k}} R_p^k \times R_q^k \times \frac{N_{S_p,S_q}^k}{N_{S_q}^k}}{\sum_{S_p, S_q \in \boldsymbol{S}^{i,k}} R_p^k \times R_q^k} \tag{5.14}$$

where $\boldsymbol{S}^{i,k}$ is the set of crowd-AI committee members who estimate the class label of X_i to be k. S_p and S_q are any two committee members in $\boldsymbol{S}^{i,k}$. R_p^k and R_q^k are the reliability of S_p and S_q, respectively. N_{S_p,S_q}^k is the number of image samples where both S_p and S_q estimate the class label to be k. $N_{S_q}^k$ is the number of image samples where S_q estimates the class label to be k. In addition, Z_i^k is set to be 0 if there is only 1 or no committee member label X_i to be k. Intuitively, a high value of Z_i^k indicates a high likelihood that the estimated class label for X_i is to be k, and vice versa.

Then, we compute the committee member reliability $\boldsymbol{R}$ using the updated image sample discriminative score $\boldsymbol{Z}$ as:

$$R_c^k = \frac{\sum_{\forall i \in \boldsymbol{\Delta}_k^{S_c}} \left(Z_i^k \times \sum_{S_p \in \boldsymbol{S}^{i,k}} \frac{N_{S_p,S_c}^k}{N_{S_c}^k}\right)}{\sum_{\forall i \in \boldsymbol{\Delta}_k^{S_c}} Z_i^k} \tag{5.15}$$

where $\boldsymbol{\Delta}_k^{S_c}$ indicates the set of all image samples where S_c estimates the class label to be k. Intuitively, a high value of R_c^k indicates that the class labels estimated by S_c are more likely to be correct.

Given the above two definitions, we can obtain the optimal value for all Z_i^{k*} and R_c^{k*} by iteratively updating all Z_i^k and R_c^k until their values convergence (e.g., the values of Z_i^k and R_c^k remains unchanged between two consecutive iterations). We then leverage Z_i^{k*} and R_c^{k*} to derive the optimal opinion entity $E_{S_c}^{k\ *}$ for each committee member as follows:

$$U_{S_c}^{k\ *} = 1 - \Omega(\mathcal{Z}),\ T_{S_c}^{k\ *} = \Omega(\mathcal{Z}) \times R_c^{k*},\ F_{S_c}^{k\ *} = 1 - T_{S_c}^{k\ *} - U_{S_c}^{k\ *} \tag{5.16}$$

where $\Omega(\cdot)$ is a normalization function to normalize the input between 0 and 1. $\mathcal{Z} = \sum_{\forall i \in \Delta_k^{S_c}} Z_i^{k*}$ indicates the likelihood that S_c is certain about estimated labels for images of class k.

The learned opinion entity $E_{S_c}^{k\ *}$ is then plugged in Eq. (5.12) to derive the accurate class labels for all imagery data in each studied disaster event.

5.3 Real-World Case Studies

5.3.1 Emergent Healthcare Truth Discovery

In this section, we evaluate the healthcare truth discovery performance of CrowdAdapt in various domain adaptation scenarios. In particular, we adopt *COVID-19* as the source domain, and choose *Mpox* and *Polio* as the target domains to evaluate the domain adaptation effectiveness of CrowdAdapt. COVID-19 has been a popular healthcare domain of false information since the beginning of the global pandemic, and many efforts have been made to combat the spread of COVID-19 false information. The recent outbreaks of Mpox (in May 2022) and Polio (in July 2022) are trending healthcare domains that have attracted a non-trivial amount of false information but lack sufficient timely resources for truth discovery. Therefore, we consider Mpox and Polio as the target healthcare domains in the study. Evaluation results from extensive experiments show that CrowdAdapt achieves significant performance gains compared to state-of-the-art baselines in terms of early healthcare truth discovery accuracy.

5.3.1.1 Data

Source Articles

We focus on two types of source articles, including the *medical news articles* and *fact-checking articles*. The medical news articles are online articles from reliable medical news publishers (e.g., CDC, Mayo Clinic) discussing the up-to-date medical information (e.g., official guidance, treatments, precautions) related to the source domain. The fact-checking articles are the reports published by professional journalists and scholars on mainstream fact-checking websites (e.g., FactCheck.org, Politifact) concerning the false information related to the source domain. We finally collected 259 source articles in the study.

Posts

We collect social media posts from both the source and target domains to study the domain adaptation performance of CrowdAdapt.

Source Posts

The goal of CrowdAdapt is to leverage existing annotated datasets in the source domain (i.e., source posts) to detect false information in an emergent healthcare domain that has limited or no annotated data (i.e., target posts). Therefore, we use five widely adopted public COVID-19 false information datasets with ground-truth labels as the source post datasets, including Constraint [26], COVIDRumor [5], MMCoVar [4], ANTiVax [12], and CMU-MisCov19 [23]. We use the ground-truth labels provided in each dataset and remove invalid posts that are duplicates or cannot be retrieved. We note that existing COVID-19 false information datasets (i.e., Constraint, COVIDRumor, MMCoVar, ANTiVax) primarily annotate the source posts into binary classes (i.e., correct or incorrect). Following such a conventional practice, we adopt the original binary labels in each dataset for the experiments. For the dataset with non-binary ground-truth labels, such as CMU-MisCov19 which also categorizes COVID-19 posts into topic-based classes (e.g., "True Prevision", "False Fact or Prevention"), we further group these non-binary labels into binary classes in terms of their veracity meaning. A summary of the source post datasets is presented in Table 5.1. While we focus on binary classification in the experiments, we also acknowledge that healthcare truth discovery is a complex problem where certain posts may not be sufficiently classified into binary classes. We believe the designed framework of CrowdAdapt can be further extended to address the multi-class healthcare truth discovery problem. The details about the generalization of CrowdAdapt will be discussed in the Discussion section.

Target Posts

We collect the target posts from Twitter based on the relevant keywords in the Mpox and Polio domains. For each dataset, we randomly select 500 posts as the test set to evaluate the early truth discovery performance and use the remaining data for the unsupervised training in CrowdAdapt. We invite three independent healthcare

Table 5.1 Summary of source post datasets

Dataset	# Posts	# Incorrect	# Correct
Constraint	10,700	5600	5100
COVIDRumor	5505	3661	1844
MMCoVaR	2791	1315	1476
ANTiVax	12,326	4156	8170
CMU-MisCov19	3114	1269	1845

Table 5.2 Summary of target post datasets

	Mpox	Polio
# Posts	9156	12,893
# Annotated posts	500	500
# Incorrect	168	141
# Correct	332	359
Date range	5/1–5/31, 2022	7/1–7/31, 2022

experts to annotate the target posts in the test sets and obtain the ground-truth labels based on their majority votes to ensure the label quality. We summarize the target post datasets in Table 5.2.

5.3.1.2 Baseline Methods and Experimental Setting

Baselines and Implementation Details

We compare CrowdAdapt with state-of-the-art baselines in domain adaptive and knowledge graph based truth discovery.

- **BDANN** [39]: BDANN is a BERT-based domain adaptation solution for multi-modal truth discovery. We exclude the visual features in BDANN and leverage the BERT-based feature extraction model trained on the source posts to classify target posts.
- **MDA-WS** [21]: MDA-WS is a weakly supervised domain adaptive truth discovery framework that leverages labeled source domain news articles and the word frequency based weak labels of target domain news articles to distinguish truthful news from the false ones in the target domain.
- **EANN** [35]: EANN is an event adversarial network framework that learns transferable features from source news events for truth discovery on emerging news events.
- **DETERRENT** [7]: DETERRENT is a graph attention network solution that utilizes relational medical knowledge to detect incorrect healthcare news.
- **CompGCN** [34]: CompGCN is an advanced multi-relational knowledge graph solution that exploits the entity and their relations to extract key information from graph data.

To ensure a fair comparison, we keep the source and target posts to all compared methods the same in the evaluation. In addition, for the knowledge graph based methods (i.e., DETERRENT, CompGCN, CrowdAdapt), we use the same MKIN constructed in CrowdAdapt as the medical knowledge graph for classifying misleading posts. We strictly follow the model configurations of all baselines as documented in the original papers and carefully tune the hyperparameters to obtain the best results. In the experiments, we utilize all the source posts and unlabeled target posts for the unsupervised training of the encoder network and the domain discriminator network. Additionally, we use the labeled source posts for the supervised training of the classification network. We adopt the commonly used metrics for classification evaluation, including *Accuracy (Acc.)*, *Precision (Prec.)*, *Recall*, and *F1 Score (F1)*.

In the model implementation, we set the dimensions of the node embeddings and post embeddings as 768. The total number of epochs is set to 80 with a batch size of 32. We adopt an initial learning rate of 0.0001 with a decay of 0.95. We set the total number of retrieved uncertain knowledge triples K as 100. We run the experiments on Ubuntu 20.04 with four NVIDIA A40 GPUs.

Crowdsourcing Platform

We choose Amazon Mechanical Turk (AMT) as the crowdsourcing platform to acquire expert knowledge in the target domain from healthcare professionals. AMT is one of the largest crowdsourcing platforms that provides 24/7 crowdsourcing services from a large number of crowd workers with diversified expertise. In particular, we recruit the expert workers who have been verified by AMT as "healthcare experts" to participate in the study [33]. In addition, we also developed a domain screening test for each studied target domain to ensure the qualification of the expert workers. The qualified expert workers will be assigned to the knowledge triple verification tasks (Fig. 5.3). To ensure the quality of the response, we only select qualified expert workers with 95% or higher Human Intelligence Task (HIT) rate. To reduce the potential bias in the crowdsourcing responses, we recruited 5 expert workers for each knowledge triple verification task and applied the majority voting to resolve any conflicts between the responses. The inter-rater agreement of the responses for the Mpox and Polio datasets are 0.74 and 0.71 in terms of the kappa score, and 0.87 and 0.85 in terms of intraclass correlation coefficient (ICC), respectively. A kappa score above 0.60 and an ICC above 0.75 indicate substantial agreement among the annotators [3]. We pay $0.47 per knowledge triple in the experiment, including the payment to both the expert worker and AMT.

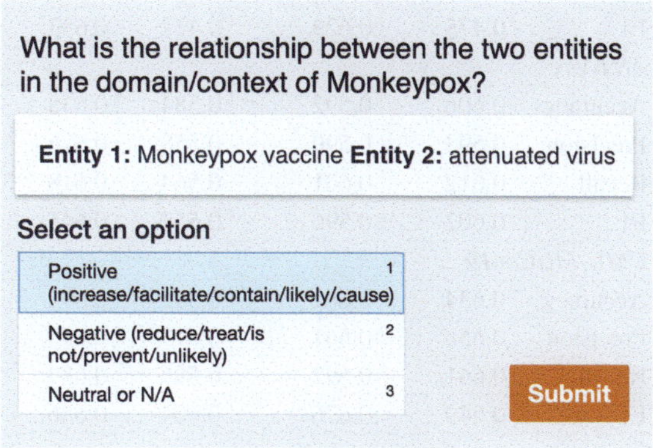

Fig. 5.3 Example of knowledge triple verification task

5.3.1.3 Truth Discovery Performance

We first compare the truth discovery performance of CrowdAdapt with all baseline schemes for detecting incorrect posts in the Mpox and Polio target domains. The evaluation results on the Mpox and Polio datasets are shown in Tables 5.3 and 5.4, respectively. We observe that CrowdAdapt consistently outperforms all compared baselines on all source datasets for detecting false information in both Mpox and Polio datasets. For example, on the Mpox dataset, CrowdAdapt achieves a 1.2, 7.1, 9.1, 6.5, and 5.2% performance improvements against the best-performing baseline (i.e., DETERRENT) in terms of the F1 score on the Constraint, COVIDRumor, MMCoVar, ANTiVax, and CMU-MisCov19, respectively. We also observe similar performance gains on the Polio dataset. The performance gains can be attributed to the crowdsourcing-based domain adaptive knowledge verification strategy in CrowdAdapt that leverages the medical knowledge of expert workers to examine and

Table 5.3 Detection performance in target domain—Mpox

	BDANN	MDA-WA	EANN	DETERRENT	CompGCN	CrowdAdapt
Constraint						
Accuracy	0.554	0.624	0.576	0.636	0.622	**0.640**
Precision	0.443	0.667	0.596	0.682	0.651	**0.688**
Recall	0.587	0.614	0.606	0.643	0.609	**0.652**
F1	0.505	0.639	0.601	0.662	0.630	**0.670**
COVIDRumor						
Accuracy	0.658	0.628	0.534	0.672	0.648	**0.682**
Precision	0.638	0.626	0.558	0.668	0.659	**0.702**
Recall	0.733	0.748	0.563	0.727	0.677	**0.793**
F1	0.683	0.682	0.560	0.696	0.668	**0.745**
MMCoVaR						
Accuracy	0.532	0.604	0.548	0.628	0.588	**0.642**
Precision	0.483	0.627	0.471	0.617	0.625	**0.699**
Recall	0.467	0.619	0.474	0.649	0.603	**0.682**
F1	0.475	0.623	0.472	0.633	0.614	**0.691**
ANTiVax						
Accuracy	0.606	0.592	0.584	0.638	0.618	**0.648**
Precision	0.593	0.590	0.558	0.676	0.637	**0.693**
Recall	0.612	0.601	0.564	0.618	0.607	**0.681**
F1	0.602	0.596	0.557	0.645	0.621	**0.687**
CMU-MisCov19						
Accuracy	0.634	0.681	0.592	0.697	0.676	**0.727**
Precision	0.658	0.661	0.613	0.683	0.669	**0.708**
Recall	0.641	0.692	0.596	0.689	0.702	**0.736**
F1	0.649	0.676	0.604	0.686	0.685	**0.722**

The bold values indicate the best performing results in each evaluation metric

Table 5.4 Detection performance in target domain—Polio

	BDANN	MDA-WA	EANN	DETERRENT	CompGCN	CrowdAdapt
Constraint						
Accuracy	0.642	0.636	0.644	0.674	0.652	**0.692**
Precision	0.681	0.673	0.618	0.687	0.635	**0.706**
Recall	0.613	0.625	0.652	0.667	0.661	**0.687**
F1	0.645	0.649	0.634	0.677	0.648	**0.697**
COVIDRumor						
Accuracy	0.702	0.658	0.664	0.688	0.660	**0.722**
Precision	0.688	0.678	0.681	0.671	0.657	**0.709**
Recall	0.701	0.646	0.629	0.693	0.673	**0.744**
F1	0.694	0.661	0.654	0.682	0.665	**0.726**
MMCoVaR						
Accuracy	0.616	0.602	0.626	0.664	0.642	**0.712**
Precision	0.602	0.635	0.617	0.641	0.639	**0.703**
Recall	0.617	0.591	0.631	0.677	0.655	**0.726**
F1	0.609	0.612	0.624	0.659	0.647	**0.714**
ANTiVax						
Accuracy	0.634	0.652	0.676	0.672	0.668	**0.706**
Precision	0.619	0.643	0.651	0.674	0.683	**0.693**
Recall	0.657	0.659	0.685	0.698	0.659	**0.716**
F1	0.638	0.651	0.667	0.686	0.671	**0.704**
CMU-MisCov19						
Accuracy	0.669	0.681	0.676	0.708	0.692	**0.731**
Precision	0.675	0.696	0.663	0.689	0.661	**0.728**
Recall	0.684	0.672	0.680	0.703	0.686	**0.719**
F1	0.679	0.684	0.671	0.696	0.673	**0.723**

The bold values indicate the best performing results in each evaluation metric

correct the knowledge triples in MKIN for the accurate detection of incorrect posts in the target domain. In addition, the significant performance improvements over knowledge-agnostic domain adaption solutions also highlight the importance of medical knowledge in detecting false information in emergent healthcare domains.

5.3.1.4 Ablation Study

We study the importance of the key components in the CrowdAdapt framework. In particular, we consider three variants of CrowdAdapt, including: (1) **CrowdAdapt\G** that excludes the MKIN and only extracts the domain-invariant representation from the post content to detect false information, (2) **CrowdAdapt\P** that removes the post-based knowledge refinement and only applies the mean-pooling layer to obtain the knowledge representation from MKIN, (3) **CrowdAdapt\U** that

Table 5.5 Results of ablation study

Target domain	Method	Constraint		COVIDRumor		MMCoVaR		ANTiVax	
		Acc.	F1	Accuracy	F1	Accuracy	F1	Accuracy	F1
MPox	CrowdAdapt	**0.640**	**0.670**	**0.682**	**0.745**	**0.642**	**0.691**	**0.648**	**0.687**
	CrowdAdapt\G	0.602	0.647	0.644	0.713	0.612	0.653	0.616	0.659
	CrowdAdapt\P	0.616	0.655	0.658	0.726	0.620	0.664	0.628	0.663
	CrowdAdapt\U	0.624	0.661	0.662	0.721	0.632	0.676	0.634	0.671
Polio	CrowdAdapt	**0.692**	**0.706**	**0.722**	**0.726**	**0.712**	**0.714**	**0.706**	**0.704**
	CrowdAdapt\G	0.668	0.677	0.684	0.691	0.688	0.697	0.678	0.687
	CrowdAdapt\P	0.672	0.683	0.688	0.679	0.696	0.701	0.684	0.688
	CrowdAdapt\U	0.676	0.681	0.692	0.681	0.702	0.709	0.692	0.698

The bold values indicate the best performing results in each evaluation metric

excludes knowledge triples verified and corrected by expert workers, and only uses the original knowledge triples in MKIN to guide the truth discovery.

The results of the ablation study on the Mpox and Polio datasets are summarized in Table 5.5. We observe that CrowdAdapt achieves its best truth discovery performance when it incorporates all key components in the framework. In particular, we observe that the incorporation of the expert-verified knowledge triples in MKIN greatly enhances the domain adaptive truth discovery on the target domain which further validates the effectiveness of crowdsourced expert knowledge in CrowdAdapt.

5.3.1.5 Effect of Expert-Verified Knowledge Triples

We further investigate the effect of expert-verified knowledge triples on the detection performance of CrowdAdapt in the target domain. In particular, we vary the number of expert-verified knowledge facts to be annotated by the expert workers from 0 to 100% of the K retrieved knowledge triples in the CKU module. The results are reported in Fig. 5.4. We use the COVIDRumor dataset as the dataset in the source

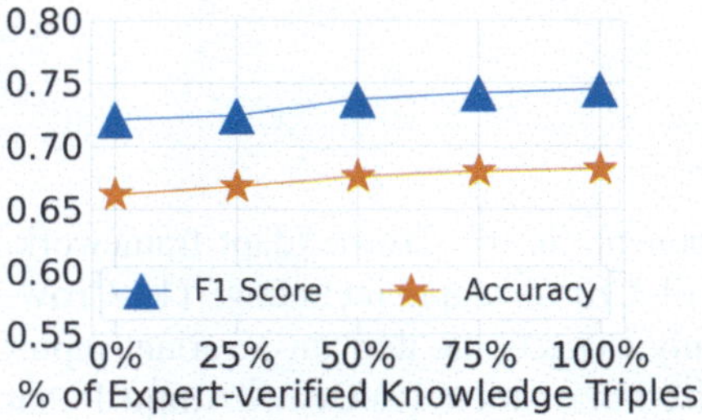

(a)

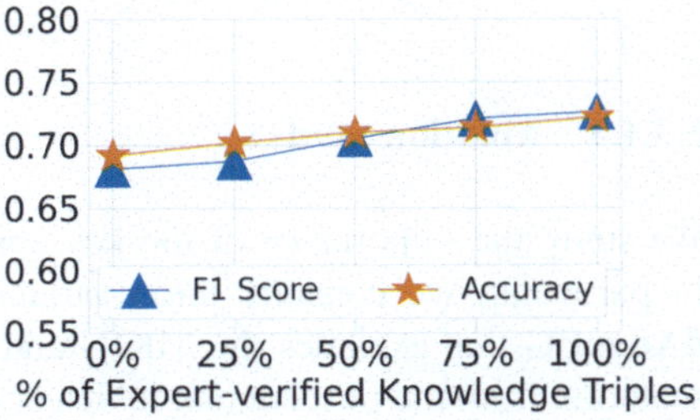

(b)

Fig. 5.4 Effect of expert-verified knowledge triples. (**a**) Mpox. (**b**) Polio

domain of COVID-19 and evaluate the domain adaptive truth discovery performance in the target domains of both Mpox and Polio. We observed similar performance gains on other COVID-19 datasets and omitted the evaluation results due to the page limit. In particular, we observe the overall performance of CrowdAdapt improves as the number of expert-verified knowledge triples increases and gradually plateaus after the number of expert-verified knowledge triples reaches 75% of the retrieved knowledge triples. A possible reason is that, as we retrieve additional knowledge triples from MKIN to be verified by the domain experts, the newly retrieved knowledge triples have lower uncertainty scores (i.e., the entropy of the prediction results of edge classifier), which are less likely to be corrected by domain experts and contribute less to CrowdAdapt for identifying incorrect posts in the target domain.

5.3.2 Disaster Damage Assessment

5.3.2.1 Data

In the experiments, we use four publicly available real-world ADA datasets.[1] The datasets consist of social media images collected from four different disaster events: Hurricane Irma (2017), Ecuador Earthquake (2016), Nepal Earthquake (2015), and Sri Lanka Flooding (2017). Images in each dataset reflect disaster-specific visual characteristics of a disaster (e.g., structure damage vs. flooding damage, urban layout vs. rural layout, plateau landscape vs. coastal landscape). Following the standard practice in ADA applications [24], we classify the disaster damages into three classes including *severe damage*, *medium damage*, and *no/minor damage*. Each image is annotated by three independent annotators, with the majority voting as the aggregated label. We invited domain experts to cross-validate the aggregated label to obtain the final ground-truth annotation. A summary of all datasets is presented in Table 5.6. Additionally, we split the training and test sets with a ratio of 7:3 and used the training sets to train all compared schemes for ADA tasks and evaluate their performance on the testing sets.

Table 5.6 Statistics of four ADA datasets

Event	Images	No/Minor damage	Medium damage	Severe damage
Hurricane Irma	893	34.6%	39.6%	25.8%
Ecuador earthquake	670	41.0%	5.7%	53.3%
Nepal earthquake	666	41.9%	13.5%	44.6%
Sri Lanka flooding	144	40.4%	40.3%	19.3%

[1] https://crisisnlp.qcri.org/.

5.3.2.2 Baseline Methods and Experimental Setting

In the evaluation, we compare CollabGeneral with a set of state-of-the-art baselines, including: (1) Deep Neural Network (DNN): **ResNet** [32], **DenseNet** [13], and **VGG** [20]; (2) AI Model Generalization: **GTA** [27], **VS** [17], **SL** [36]; (3) Crowd-AI Collaboration: **Deep Active** [29], **CrowdLearn** [37], **SL** [36].

In the experiments, to ensure the fairness of comparison, we use the same inputs for all compared methods. In particular, the inputs to each scheme include: (1) the social media images for all studied disaster events in both training and testing datasets; (2) the ground-truth labels for social media images in the training dataset, where the number of training images from each disaster event is proportional to the total number of images from that event as shown in Table 5.6; and (3) the labeled social media images returned by the crowd workers. In particular, we use the crowd labels to retrain the DNN and AI model generalization baselines to ensure all baselines have the same inputs and the performance of compared baselines is optimized. For the DNN baselines, we consider two different training settings: (1) training a single DNN model for *all* studied disaster events, which is referred as *DNN-A* (e.g., ResNet-A for ResNet); (2) training four DNN models, one for each *specific* disaster event, which is referred as *DNN-S* (e.g., ResNet-S for ResNet).

We use three evaluation metrics that are commonly used to quantify the performance of multi-class text classification: (1) *F1-score*, and (2) *Matthews Correlation Coefficient (MCC)*, (3) *kappa score (Kappa)*. We use MCC and Kappa in the evaluation because the datasets are imbalanced, and these two metrics are known to be reliable on imbalanced data [6]. The higher values of the above metrics demonstrate better ADA performance.

We leverage the widely used AMT to acquire crowd intelligence in the experiments. AMT is one of the largest crowdsourcing platforms offering 24/7 crowdsourcing services from a massive amount of crowd workers around the world. For each task on AMT, we recruit crowd workers who have finished at least 1000 approved tasks with an overall task approval rate of 95% or above to ensure the crowdsourcing label quality. We pay $0.05 per image to the crowd workers and follow the IRB protocol approved for this project.

5.3.2.3 Model Generality on Different Types of Disaster Events

First we study the ADA model generality with a challenging evaluation setting, where the studied disaster events are of *completely different types*: Ecuador Earthquake and Sri Lanka Flooding. We summarize the evaluation results in Table 5.7. We observe that CollabGeneral consistently outperforms all compared baselines in terms of the ADA performance on each individual event and the overall performance across two different types of events. For example, the performance gains of CollabGeneral compared to the best-performing baseline (i.e., VS) on the Sri Lanka Flooding event on F1-Score, MCC, and Kappa are 5.22, 6.52, and 8.41%, respectively.

Table 5.7 Evaluation results (different types of events)

Algorithm	Ecuador earthquake F1	Ecuador earthquake MCC	Ecuador earthquake Kappa	Sri Lanka flooding F1	Sri Lanka flooding MCC	Sri Lanka flooding Kappa	Overall F1	Overall MCC	Overall Kappa
ResNet-A	0.8032	0.6658	0.6513	0.5214	0.4582	0.3732	0.7326	0.6138	0.5851
DenseNet-A	0.7999	0.6529	0.6444	0.5519	0.4607	0.3942	0.7384	0.6098	0.5904
VGG-A	0.8023	0.6469	0.6319	0.7105	0.5647	0.5323	0.7785	0.6505	0.6330
ResNet-S	0.8315	0.6849	0.6833	0.6434	0.5507	0.4850	0.7779	0.6518	0.6426
DenseNet-S	0.7975	0.6527	0.6399	0.6913	0.5796	0.5372	0.7758	0.6539	0.6363
VGG-S	0.8132	0.6569	0.6493	0.4837	0.4232	0.3264	0.7270	0.5875	0.5639
GTA	0.7117	0.4523	0.4516	0.5545	0.4106	0.3733	0.6666	0.4498	0.4488
VS	0.7724	0.5457	0.5334	0.7502	0.6212	0.5950	0.7561	0.5940	0.5820
SL	0.8309	0.7058	0.7034	0.6406	0.4897	0.4622	0.7870	0.6668	0.6607
Deep Active	0.7986	0.6524	0.6452	0.4347	0.4184	0.3329	0.7112	0.5912	0.5695
CrowdLearn	0.8145	0.6574	0.6552	0.5263	0.4796	0.3955	0.7425	0.6074	0.5938
LL4AL	0.7886	0.6133	0.6123	0.4177	0.3830	0.3110	0.7018	0.5565	0.5459
CollabGeneral	**0.8574**	**0.7267**	**0.7266**	**0.8024**	**0.6864**	**0.6791**	**0.8436**	**0.7388**	**0.7384**

The bold values indicate the best performing results in each evaluation metric

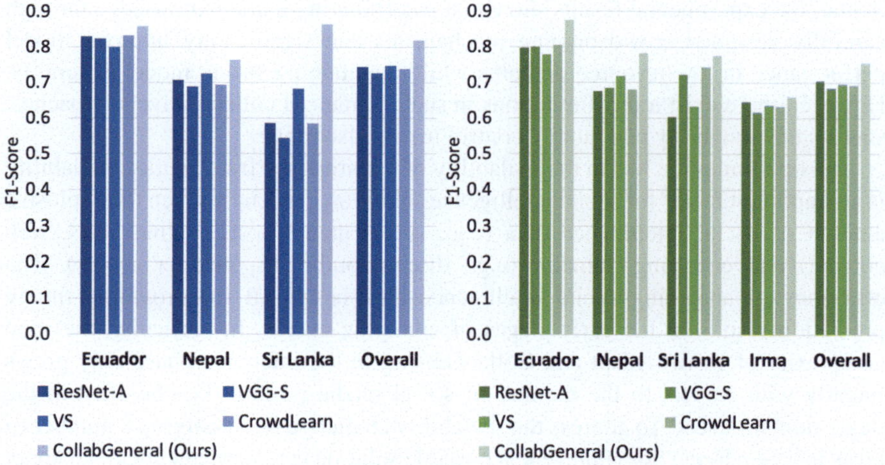

Fig. 5.5 Performance comparisons on different number of events

5.3.2.4 Model Generality on Different Number of Events

Second we evaluate the ADA performance of CollabGeneral when there exist more than two disaster events. In particular, we evaluate CollabGeneral up to four different disaster events by leveraging all possible disaster events available in the datasets. In the experiments, we evaluate the ADA performance by comparing CollabGeneral with the best-performing baselines in each category. The results are presented in Fig. 5.5. Note that we only show the evaluation results on the F1-Score due to the page limit. The evaluation results on other metrics are similar.

We observe that CollabGeneral continuously outperforms all compared baselines on both individual events and overall performance when the number of studied disaster events increases. This is because the subjective logic-based crowd-AI framework design effectively improves the ADA model generality without sacrificing the model's specificity on each studied disaster event.

5.4 Discussion

This chapter has examined the critical challenges of data sparsity and model generality in social intelligence applications. We reviewed two representative frameworks, CrowdAdapt and CollabGeneral, to demonstrate the great potential of leveraging collective human intelligence to address the data sparsity and model generality problems in social intelligence. Two real-world case studies on emergent health truth discovery and disaster damage assessment demonstrated the effectiveness of integrating the domain expertise of expert workers with advanced AI techniques through knowledge adaptation strategies and principled crowdsourcing mechanisms. In particular, the experimental results show that incorporating human knowledge through carefully designed crowdsourcing mechanisms can significantly improve model performance in low-resource domains while maintaining strong model generality. However, there exist a few limitations in such human-AI collaborative approaches, such as the scalability and quality control in crowdsourcing.

The first limitation lies in the scalability of the proposed frameworks. Scalability is an important factor for social intelligence solutions, especially given the explosive amount of social intelligence data (e.g., social media posts, online news, web content) and emerging domains (e.g., disease outbreaks, disaster events). The efficiency of analyzing social intelligence data is critical for providing timely prediction results in the early stages of emerging events. In particular, the time complexity of CrowdAdapt and CollabGeneral in the inference phase only grows linearly with respect to the number of social media posts to be classified in the target domain/event. To address the scalability challenge of classifying a number of posts in an emergent domain/event, a possible solution is to implement CrowdAdapt and CollabGeneral on distributed GPU clusters or cloud computing platforms to improve computing efficiency. For example, the knowledge graph construction and neural network inference can be parallelized across multiple GPUs, while the crowdsourcing tasks can be distributed through cloud-based task scheduling [1] to enable real-time processing of large-scale social media data streams.

The second limitation lies in the unknown expertise of the crowd workers. The case studies recruit expert workers with premium qualifications or high task approval rates to finish the human intelligence tasks. While majority voting and interrater agreement are considered to reduce the uncertainty in the crowdsourcing responses, it is still possible that some expert workers have less relevant experience or knowledge to provide accurate responses to the crowdsensing tasks (e.g., knowledge triple verification, damage assessment annotation). To lift the assumption that the crowdsourcing responses are equally valid and accurate, a potential solution is to explicitly quantify the confidence and certainty of each crowdsourcing response, such as asking expert workers to provide their confidence level in each response. Such confidence-aware responses can be further integrated into the knowledge adaptation framework via the uncertainty-aware information aggregation strategy [9] to reduce the overall uncertainty of crowdsourcing responses.

We envision that future research in human-AI collaborative systems will continue to grow and advance in social intelligence. First, more sophisticated knowledge adaptation mechanisms can be developed to automatically transfer and update domain knowledge with minimal and efficient human interventions. For example, meta-learning approaches could be developed to learn generalizable patterns across different domains and reduce the number of human-labeled data in the target domain/event. Second, large language models (LLMs) can be integrated into these social intelligence frameworks to assist with knowledge extraction, domain adaptation, and human-AI interaction. For example, LLMs may help with validating crowd responses, generating preliminary knowledge graphs for emerging domains/events, or facilitating more natural interactions between crowd workers and AI systems. These advances will help realize the full potential of human-AI collaboration in addressing emerging societal challenges across diverse domains in social intelligence.

References

1. A. Amini Motlagh, A. Movaghar, and A. M. Rahmani. Task scheduling mechanisms in cloud computing: A systematic review. *International Journal of Communication Systems*, 33(6):e4302, 2020.
2. S. Bozinovski. Reminder of the first paper on transfer learning in neural networks, 1976. *Informatica*, 44(3), 2020.
3. S. Chaturvedi and R. Shweta. Evaluation of inter-rater agreement and inter-rater reliability for observational data: an overview of concepts and methods. *Journal of the Indian Academy of Applied Psychology*, 41(3):20–27, 2015.
4. M. Chen, X. Chu, and K. Subbalakshmi. Mmcovar: Multimodal covid-19 vaccine focused data repository for fake news detection and a baseline architecture for classification. In *Proceedings of the 2021 IEEE/ACM International Conference on Advances in Social Networks Analysis and Mining*, pages 31–38, 2021.
5. M. Cheng, S. Wang, X. Yan, T. Yang, W. Wang, Z. Huang, X. Xiao, S. Nazarian, and P. Bogdan. A covid-19 rumor dataset. *Frontiers in Psychology*, 12, 2021.
6. D. Chicco and G. Jurman. The advantages of the matthews correlation coefficient (mcc) over f1 score and accuracy in binary classification evaluation. *BMC genomics*, 21(1):6, 2020.
7. L. Cui, H. Seo, M. Tabar, F. Ma, S. Wang, and D. Lee. Deterrent: Knowledge guided graph attention network for detecting healthcare misinformation. In *Proceedings of the 26th ACM SIGKDD International Conference on Knowledge Discovery & Data Mining*, pages 492–502, 2020.
8. J. Devlin, M.-W. Chang, K. Lee, and K. Toutanova. Bert: Pre-training of deep bidirectional transformers for language understanding. *arXiv preprint arXiv:1810.04805*, 2018.

9. B. Feng, Y. Wang, and Y. Ding. Uag: Uncertainty-aware attention graph neural network for defending adversarial attacks. In *Proceedings of the AAAI Conference on Artificial Intelligence*, volume 35, pages 7404–7412, 2021.
10. M. Feurer and F. Hutter. Hyperparameter optimization. In *Automated Machine Learning*, pages 3–33. Springer, 2019.
11. M. Ghifary, D. Balduzzi, W. B. Kleijn, and M. Zhang. Scatter component analysis: A unified framework for domain adaptation and domain generalization. *IEEE transactions on pattern analysis and machine intelligence*, 39(7):1414–1430, 2016.
12. K. Hayawi, S. Shahriar, M. A. Serhani, I. Taleb, and S. S. Mathew. Anti-vax: a novel twitter dataset for covid-19 vaccine misinformation detection. *Public health*, 203:23–30, 2022.
13. G. Huang, Z. Liu, L. Van Der Maaten, and K. Q. Weinberger. Densely connected convolutional networks. In *CVPR*, page 3, 2017.
14. P. Jia, S. Liu, and S. Yang. Innovations in public health surveillance for emerging infections. *Annual Review of Public Health*, 44(1):55–74, 2023.
15. A. Jøsang. *Subjective Logic: A Formalism for Reasoning Under Uncertainty*. Springer, 2016.
16. M. G. Kim, M. Kim, J. H. Kim, and K. Kim. Fine-tuning bert models to classify misinformation on garlic and covid-19 on twitter. *International Journal of Environmental Research and Public Health*, 19(9):5126, 2022.
17. G. R. Kini, O. Paraskevas, S. Oymak, and C. Thrampoulidis. Label-imbalanced and group-sensitive classification under overparameterization. *Advances in Neural Information Processing Systems*, 34:18970–18983, 2021.
18. Z. Kou, L. Shang, Y. Zhang, and D. Wang. Hc-covid: A hierarchical crowdsource knowledge graph approach to explainable covid-19 misinformation detection. *Proceedings of the ACM on Human-Computer Interaction*, 6(GROUP):1–25, 2022. https://doi.org/10.1145/3492855.
19. X. Li, D. Caragea, C. Caragea, M. Imran, and F. Ofli. Identifying disaster damage images using a domain adaptation approach. In *Proceedings of the 16th International conference on information systems for crisis response and management*, 2019.
20. X. Li, D. Caragea, H. Zhang, and M. Imran. Localizing and quantifying damage in social media images. In *2018 IEEE/ACM International Conference on Advances in Social Networks Analysis and Mining (ASONAM)*, pages 194–201. IEEE, 2018.
21. Y. Li, K. Lee, N. Kordzadeh, B. Faber, C. Fiddes, E. Chen, and K. Shu. Multi-source domain adaptation with weak supervision for early fake news detection. In *2021 IEEE International Conference on Big Data (Big Data)*, pages 668–676. IEEE, 2021.
22. J. Lin. Divergence measures based on the shannon entropy. *IEEE Transactions on Information theory*, 37(1):145–151, 1991.
23. S. A. Memon and K. M. Carley. Characterizing covid-19 misinformation communities using a novel twitter dataset. *arXiv preprint arXiv:2008.00791*, 2020.
24. D. T. Nguyen, F. Ofli, M. Imran, and P. Mitra. Damage assessment from social media imagery data during disasters. In *Proceedings of the 2017 IEEE/ACM International Conference on Advances in Social Networks Analysis and Mining 2017*, pages 569–576, 2017.
25. R. S. Oktari, K. Munadi, R. Idroes, and H. Sofyan. Knowledge management practices in disaster management: Systematic review. *International Journal of Disaster Risk Reduction*, 51:101881, 2020.
26. P. Patwa, S. Sharma, S. Pykl, V. Guptha, G. Kumari, M. S. Akhtar, A. Ekbal, A. Das, and T. Chakraborty. Fighting an infodemic: Covid-19 fake news dataset. In *International Workshop on Combating Online Hostile Posts in Regional Languages during Emergency Situation*, pages 21–29. Springer, 2021.
27. S. Sankaranarayanan, Y. Balaji, C. D. Castillo, and R. Chellappa. Generate to adapt: Aligning domains using generative adversarial networks. In *Proceedings of the IEEE conference on computer vision and pattern recognition*, pages 8503–8512, 2018.
28. D. Saunders. Domain adaptation and multi-domain adaptation for neural machine translation: A survey. *Journal of Artificial Intelligence Research*, 75:351–424, 2022.
29. O. Sener and S. Savarese. Active learning for convolutional neural networks: A core-set approach. In *International Conference on Learning Representations*, 2018.

30. L. Shang, Y. Zhang, Z. Yue, Y. Choi, H. Zeng, and D. Wang. A domain adaptive graph learning framework to early detection of emergent healthcare misinformation on social media. In *Proceedings of the International AAAI Conference on Web and Social Media*, volume 18, pages 1408–1421, 2024, https://doi.org/10.1609/icwsm.v18i1.31398.
31. N. Sharif, N. Sharif, K. J. Alzahrani, I. F. Halawani, F. M. Alzahrani, I. D. l. T. Díez, V. Lipari, M. A. L. Flores, A. K. Parvez, and S. K. Dey. Molecular epidemiology, transmission and clinical features of 2022-mpox outbreak: A systematic review. *Health science reports*, 6(10):e1603, 2023.
32. S. Targ, D. Almeida, and K. Lyman. Resnet in resnet: Generalizing residual architectures. *arXiv preprint arXiv:1603.08029*, 2016.
33. A. M. Turk. Introducing premium qualifications, 2016.
34. S. Vashishth, S. Sanyal, V. Nitin, and P. Talukdar. Composition-based multi-relational graph convolutional networks. In *ICLR*, 2020.
35. Y. Wang, F. Ma, Z. Jin, Y. Yuan, G. Xun, K. Jha, L. Su, and J. Gao. Eann: Event adversarial neural networks for multi-modal fake news detection. In *Proceedings of the 24th acm sigkdd international conference on knowledge discovery & data mining*, pages 849–857, 2018.
36. Y. Wang, X. Ma, Z. Chen, Y. Luo, J. Yi, and J. Bailey. Symmetric cross entropy for robust learning with noisy labels. In *Proceedings of the IEEE/CVF International Conference on Computer Vision*, pages 322–330, 2019.
37. D. Zhang, Y. Zhang, Q. Li, T. Plummer, and D. Wang. Crowdlearn: A crowd-ai hybrid system for deep learning-based damage assessment applications. In *2019 IEEE 39th International Conference on Distributed Computing Systems (ICDCS)*, pages 1221–1232. IEEE, 2019.
38. L. Zhang and X. Gao. Transfer adaptation learning: A decade survey. *IEEE Transactions on Neural Networks and Learning Systems*, 2022.
39. T. Zhang, D. Wang, H. Chen, Z. Zeng, W. Guo, C. Miao, and L. Cui. Bdann: Bert-based domain adaptation neural network for multi-modal fake news detection. In *2020 international joint conference on neural networks (IJCNN)*, pages 1–8. IEEE, 2020.
40. Y. Zhang, R. Zong, L. Shang, Z. Kou, and D. Wang. A deep contrastive learning approach to extremely-sparse disaster damage assessment in social sensing. In *Proceedings of the 2021 IEEE/ACM International Conference on Advances in Social Networks Analysis and Mining*, pages 151–158, New York, NY, USA, 2021. ACM.
41. Y. Zhang, R. Zong, L. Shang, H. Zeng, Z. Yue, N. Wei, and D. Wang. On optimizing model generality in ai-based disaster damage assessment: A subjective logic-driven crowd-ai hybrid learning approach. In *IJCAI*, pages 6317–6325, 2023, https://doi.org/10.24963/ijcai.2023/701. Copyright owner: IJCAI Organization, all rights reserved.
42. Y. Zhang, R. Zong, and D. Wang. A hybrid transfer learning approach to migratable disaster assessment in social media sensing. In *2020 IEEE/ACM International Conference on Advances in Social Networks Analysis and Mining (ASONAM)*, pages 131–138. IEEE, 2020.
43. R. Zong, Y. Zhang, L. Shang, and D. Wang. Contrastfaux: Sparse semi-supervised fauxtography detection on the web using multi-view contrastive learning. In *Proceedings of the ACM Web Conference 2023*, pages 3994–4003, New York, NY, USA, 2023. ACM. https://doi.org/10.1145/3543507.3583869.

Chapter 6
Explainable AI (XAI) in Social Intelligence

Abstract Explainability has been a critical aspect in social intelligence applications that analyze human-centered data and can directly impact human decision-making and well-being. This chapter presents two graph-based AI-driven explanation approaches, HC-COVID and DExFC, that address several fundamental challenges in developing explainable social intelligence systems. These challenges include the varying knowledge fact quality contributed by humans with diverse expertise, lack of modality-level annotations, and diverse cross-modal explanations. Through extensive experiments on real-world social intelligence case studies, including COVID-19 news truth discovery and fauxtography detection, both frameworks demonstrate significant performance gains in both prediction accuracy and explanation quality compared to state-of-the-art baselines.

Keywords Explainable AI · XAI · Black box · Interpretability · Hybrid knowledge graph · Multimodal explanation · Fauxtography

6.1 Collaborative Explanation for AI

The explainability of AI is the capability of intelligent systems to provide clear and understandable explanations about the rationale behind their decisions and predictions [4]. Such capability is particularly important in social intelligence applications that analyze human-centered data and can directly impact human decision-making and well-being. For example, a health truth discovery model has to provide accurate and well-justified explanations to common social media users who often do not have sufficient medical knowledge to accurately identify false claims about health issues. Such explanations help users understand why certain health claims are identified as true or false and support their better-informed health decisions. More importantly, with the proliferation of multimodal content (e.g., text, image, video) on online and social media, the explainability of social intelligence solutions becomes more and more critical. For example, when analyzing multimodal social media posts that combine text and images, a social intelligence system needs to explain how the textual claims and/or the visual elements contribute to the prediction results (e.g., false information, hate speech). Such an explanation is

D. Wang et al., *Social Intelligence*, https://doi.org/10.1007/978-3-031-90080-8_6

essential not only for building user trust in AI-driven social intelligence systems but also for identifying potential biases and failure cases in these complex multimodal social intelligence models.

Recent efforts have made significant progress in developing explainable AI solutions for social intelligence applications. Existing solutions have focused on content-based features (e.g., textual content [30], visual information [21]), context-based factors (e.g., user comments [49], social interaction [38]), and auxiliary information (e.g., news cascade patterns [37]). Recently, a few initial efforts have been made to leverage knowledge graphs to enhance the explainability of social intelligence systems by exploring the implicit relationship between diverse entities and/or data modalities [11, 27, 39]. However, current knowledge graph-based solutions often fall short in handling emerging phenomena and novel content patterns in social intelligence. This is because these solutions mainly rely on static knowledge facts extracted from existing documents (e.g., literature, archives), which often fail to capture rapidly evolving events or topics in social intelligence applications (e.g., disaster response, emerging truth discovery). We elaborate on a few fundamental challenges in developing effective explainable social intelligence systems.

Varied Knowledge Fact Quality

The extraction of knowledge facts (i.e., a pair of entities and their relation as shown in Fig. 6.1) in social intelligence systems often requires human efforts due to high-quality standards and the complexity and ambiguity of social intelligence data. Crowdsourcing has been a widely adopted approach for acquiring such human annotations. However, the expertise of human crowd workers often varies due to

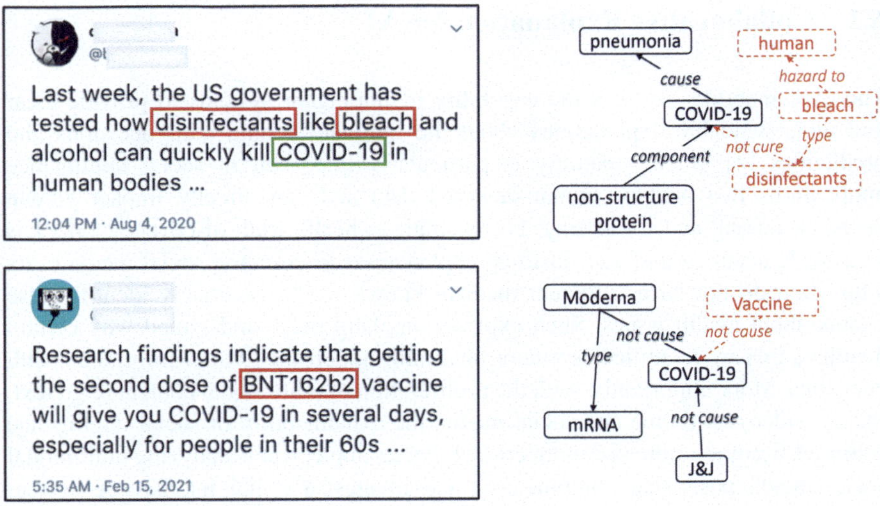

Fig. 6.1 Explainable truth discovery problem

their diverse backgrounds, domain knowledge, and familiarity with specific social intelligence tasks. In particular, expert workers (e.g., workers with professional domain knowledge or extensive task experience) typically provide high-quality but costly annotations, while non-expert workers offer more affordable but potentially noisy inputs due to their unvetted nature [34]. Therefore, it remains a challenging problem how to effectively coordinate and integrate the efforts from both expert and non-expert workers to extract useful knowledge facts to generate accurate explanations for social intelligence solutions.

Lack of Modality-Level Annotations

As discussed in Chap. 4, social intelligence systems often handle input from different data modalities, and so do their explanations. A possible way to solve the explainability problem in social intelligence is to annotate each component of the input, such as true or false for a truth discovery problem, and then train a *fully supervised* learning model to identify the false component. However, it is extremely time-consuming and expensive to obtain such a large fine-grained training set with modality-level labels, even with crowdsourcing [31]. For example, the annotators need to annotate all components of a post by considering the text, image, and the association between the text and image in addition to the binary ground-truth label of the entire post. Moreover, a fully supervised training pipeline with modality-level annotations will add a non-trivial amount of overheads to the training process (e.g., a longer training time and a more complex parameter adjustment procedure). Therefore, it is more desirable to develop an explainable social intelligence scheme under constrained supervision (e.g., by utilizing a very limited amount of modality-level annotations in the training), which is not a trivial task.

Diverse Cross-Modal Explanations

Another possible solution to solve the explainable problem in multimodal social intelligence systems is to apply modality-specific models that generate explanations tailored to each modality's unique characteristics. For instance, when analyzing a social media post containing both text and images, the system can employ separate explanation mechanisms where the text-based model identifies the key phrases and the image-based scheme captures the salient visual components. However, such a modality-specific approach largely ignores the association between text and images. For example, Fig. 6.2d shows an example of fauxtography where the image itself is authentic but is used out of context with a piece of true text to convey incorrect information. Therefore, the problem of generating diverse cross-modal explanations and identifying the exact modality component in multimodal social intelligence remains a challenge to be addressed [24, 25].

Fig. 6.2 Examples of fauxtography. Example (**a**) includes both a fake picture and a incorrect text description. In example (**b**), the description tries to fool people by a real photo with a camera close to a normal rat. In example (**c**), though there is such a kind of creature in the world, the color of the picture is manipulated by computer software. For example (**d**), both the text description and the image are true. However, the woman mentioned in the text is not the one in the image

6.2 Social XAI: HC-COVID and DExFC

This section presents two novel social explainable AI frameworks, HC-COVID (Hierarchical Crowdsourced Knowledge Graph for COVID-19 Truth Discovery) [24] and DExFC (Dual Explainable Fauxtography Detection under Constrained Supervision) [25], to tackle the explainability challenge in social intelligence. In particular, HC-COVID develops a hierarchical crowdsourced knowledge graph-based framework that explicitly models the varied knowledge fact quality to accurately explain the prediction results in social intelligence applications. DExFC designs a weakly supervised modality-aware explanation mechanism that aims to generate cross-modal explanations in multimodal social intelligence with constrained modality-level annotation.

6.2.1 HC-COVID: A Crowdsourced Knowledge Graph Approach

The overview of the HC-COVID scheme is shown in Fig. 6.3. HC-COVID consists of four modules: (1) a Crowdsourced Knowledge Graph Constructor (CKGC), (2) a Claim-guided Specific Knowledge Propagator (CSKP), (3) a Topic-based Generalized Knowledge Integrator (TGKI), and (4) a Joint Claim-Graph-based Multi-relational Detector (CGMD). First, CKGC constructs the crowdsourced hierarchical knowledge graph (CHKG) by leveraging a group of expert and non-expert crowd workers to collaboratively identify specific and generalized knowledge facts from domain-specific news articles (e.g., COVID-19). Second, the CSKP module develops a multi-relational graph neural network to encode input social

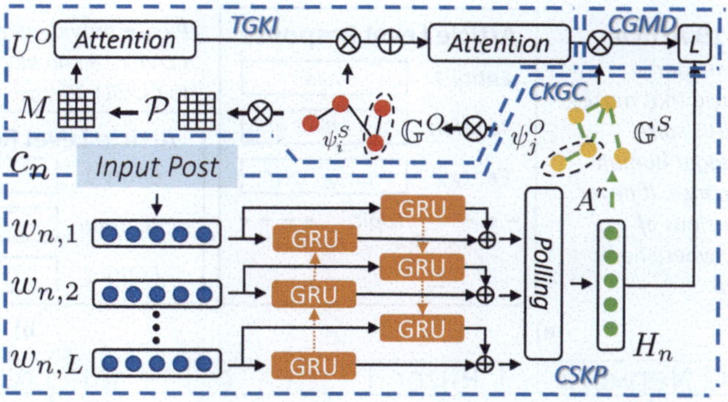

Fig. 6.3 Overview of HC-COVID

media claims and integrate the claim information with the specific knowledge facts in CHKG. Third, the TGKI module explores the generalized knowledge facts in CHKG that are strongly correlated with input claims by designing a dual hierarchical attention-based neural network. The attention outputs are used to retrieve informative graph triples from CHKG as explanations for the social intelligence prediction results (e.g., truth discovery). Finally, the CGMD module classifies an input claim (e.g., true or false for truth discovery) by jointly exploring the encoded claims and CHKG.

6.2.1.1 Crowdsourced Knowledge Graph Constructor (CKGC)

The CKGC module aims to construct a crowdsourced hierarchical knowledge graph (CHKG) that contains both specific and generalized knowledge facts from domain-specific news articles. In particular, two novel crowdsourcing tasks for a group of expert workers and non-expert workers to analyze a set of domain-specific news articles. Unlike traditional crowdsourcing tasks that only assign workers simple annotation tasks (e.g., image annotation [8, 48], text classification [15, 41]), CKGC designs a novel crowdsourcing task that expects crowd workers to understand and summarize the content of domain-specific news articles by leveraging their background knowledge. In particular, HC-COVID designs two crowdsourcing task interfaces (i.e., the *article-level* interface and the *topic-level* interface) for the crowd workers. Examples of the two interfaces are shown in Fig. 6.4. The *article-level* interface helps workers explore specific knowledge facts in relevant news articles. The *topic-level* interface lets crowd workers focus on the summarized topics from the article-level interface and propose generalized knowledge facts that can help identify incorrect claims with similar topics. The responses from crowd workers are defined as *article-level* responses and *topic-level* responses, respectively.

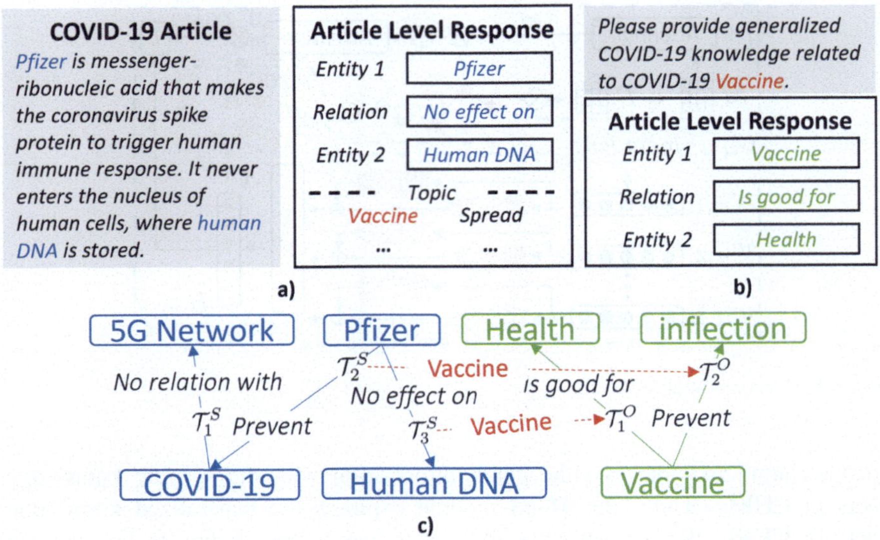

Fig. 6.4 Crowdsourcing interface and example result. (**a**) Article level interface. (**b**) Topic level interface. (**c**) Example CHKG

Article-Level Response

The article-level interface requires the non-expert crowd workers to provide specific knowledge facts based on a single news article. To integrate the crowd responses into CHKG, we specify the following requirements for the crowd worker's responses.

- A worker needs to provide a 3-tuple statement as shown in Fig. 6.4a (e.g., "Entity 1" $\xrightarrow{\text{relation}}$ "Entity 2").
- The input entities should match existing terms in the news article. The reason is that non-expert workers usually do not have enough domain-specific background knowledge to propose novel concepts. However, they can extract key terms from the news article to summarize the specific knowledge facts [32].
- The input relation should be selected from the pre-defined relation pool that includes a set of frequently used relations (e.g., "is", "close relation to", "no effect on") identified by crowd workers in the pilot study.

For example, an article-level response from a non-expert worker could be "Pfizer" $\xrightarrow{\text{no effect on}}$ "human DNA", which is a specific knowledge fact for the Pfizer vaccine. However, such the COVID-19 knowledge fact summarized from a single news article is insufficient to cover the information from other COVID-19 vaccine-related articles (e.g., articles discussing Moderna or J&J vaccine). To address this problem, the non-expert workers are then asked to submit the potential topics of the news article they read.

Topic-Level Response

While the article-level responses only focus on the specific knowledge within a single news article, the topic-level response serves as a complementary measure to assign expert workers to propose generalized knowledge. There are two key advantages of the topic-level interface: (1) it is both cost- and time-efficient for expert workers to focus on abstract topics and propose generalized knowledge that can cover the information of different news articles; (2) it significantly improves the robustness of the constructed hierarchical knowledge graph because the generalized knowledge can cover unseen concepts that are embedded in news articles with similar topics. For example, the generalized knowledge fact for Fig. 6.4b could be "Vaccine" $\xrightarrow{\text{no effect on}}$ "DNA" that covers not only the current major COVID-19 vaccines (e.g., Pfizer, Moderna) but also the unseen and emerging ones (e.g., BNT162b2 in Fig. 6.1b). In particular, the topic-level interface first collects the topics from responses of the article-level interface. Then the topic-level interface shows the topics to the expert workers and expects the workers to propose generalized knowledge facts related to the given topics. To ensure the quality of both article-level and topic-level responses from crowd workers, we leverage a set of crowd quality control mechanisms (e.g., HITs worker filtering, entity matching) [5, 40] to obtain high-quality responses.

After collecting all responses from both interfaces, the next step is to construct CHKG. The responses from both article-level and topic-level interfaces serve as triples in the knowledge graph. In particular, the entities in the 3-tuple responses are used to construct graph entities, and the relations are used to construct the graph edges. We show an example constructed crowdsourcing knowledge graph in Fig. 6.4c. Formally, CHKG and its two sub-graphs are defined as below.

Definition 6.1 (Crowdsourced Article-Level Knowledge Graph ($\mathbb{G}^S$)**)** the crowdsourced article-level knowledge graph $\mathbb{G}^S = \{\mathcal{V}^S, \mathcal{E}^S, \mathcal{T}^S\}$ (e.g., the blue subgraph in Fig. 6.4c) contains specific knowledge constructed only by the triples from the article-level responses where $\mathcal{V}^S$, $\mathcal{E}^S$ and $\mathcal{T}^S$ represent the graph entities, graph edges and graph triples, respectively. We further split $\mathcal{E}^S$ as $\mathcal{E}^S = \{\mathcal{E}^{S,r_1}, \cdots, \mathcal{E}^{S,r_Q}\}$ where $\mathcal{R} = \{r_1, \cdots, r_Q\}$ represents all relations in the relation pool and $\mathcal{E}^{S,r_q}$ denotes the graph edges belonging to the relation of r_q.

Definition 6.2 (Crowdsourced Topic-Level Knowledge Graph ($\mathbb{G}^O$)**)** the crowdsourced topic-level knowledge graph $\mathbb{G}^O = \{\mathcal{V}^O, \mathcal{E}^O, \mathcal{T}^O\}$ (e.g., the green subgraph in Fig. 6.4c) contains generalized knowledge constructed only by the triples from the topic-level responses. Similarly, $\mathcal{E}^O = \{\mathcal{E}^{O,r_1}, \cdots, \mathcal{E}^{O,r_Q}\}$ and $\mathcal{E}^{O,r_q}$ represents the graph edges belonging to the relation of r_q.

Definition 6.3 (Hierarchical Knowledge Graph ($\mathbb{G}$)**)** the hierarchical knowledge graph $\mathbb{G} = \{\mathcal{V}, \mathcal{E}, \mathcal{T}, \mathcal{P}\}$ is constructed by all the triples from both the article-level and topic-level responses where $\mathcal{V} = \{\mathcal{V}^S, \mathcal{V}^O\}$, $\mathcal{E} = \{\mathcal{E}^R, \mathcal{E}^O\}$ and $\mathcal{T} = \{\mathcal{T}^S, \mathcal{T}^O\}$ represents the graph entities, graph relations and graph triples, respectively. $\mathcal{P}$ denotes a binary bipartite adjacent matrix that contains topics to connect triples in $\mathbb{G}^S$ with the triples in $\mathbb{G}^O$. If an expert worker proposes a generalized knowledge fact $\mathcal{T}_i^O \in \mathcal{T}^O$ that is related to the topic "Vaccine", then we set $\mathcal{P}_{ij} = 1$ for all $\mathcal{T}_j^S$ from the COVID-19 news articles that belong to the topic "Vaccine" in article-level responses. For example, the binary bipartite adjacent matrix $\mathcal{P} \in \mathbb{R}^{2\times 3}$ for Fig. 6.4c is $\mathcal{P}_{i,j} = 1, 1 \leq i \leq 2, 2 \leq j \leq 3$ and $\mathcal{P}_{i,j} = 0, 1 \leq i \leq 2, j = 1$.

6.2.1.2 Claim-Guided Specific Knowledge Propagator (CSKP)

In this subsection, we present CSKP in HC-COVID that propagates the encoded information of input claim to $\mathbb{G}^S$ for retrieving claim-related specific knowledge. CSKP consists of two specific components: (1) an input claim feature encoder, and (2) a multi-relational specific knowledge propagator. We define the two network architectures below.

Claim Feature Encoder

The input claim feature encoder aims to encode the input claim and extract high-level semantic features from the claim to propagate the feature of the claim into $\mathbb{G}^S$. We first design a *word-level* feature encoder that converts words in an input claim to high-dimensional vectors in order to integrate the semantic information from different words. Given an input claim $c_n = \{w_{n,1}, \cdots, w_{n,L}\}$, we convert all words in the claim to *one-hot* vectors and apply an embedding matrix to transform the vectors to a high-dimensional embedding. The embedding can be denoted as $\widetilde{c}_n = \{\widetilde{w}_{n,1}, \cdots, \widetilde{w}_{n,L}\}$ where each word denotes as $\widetilde{w}_{n,l} \in \mathbb{R}^d$.

Using the word embeddings from the word-level feature encoder, we design a bi-directional gated recurrent unit (biGRU) to encode the entire content of the claim. The biGRU strengthens the semantic connection between different words in a claim. In particular, given an embedded claim $\widetilde{c}_n$ with L word embeddings, the biGRU processes the embeddings from both directions of the claim. The forward biGRU $\overrightarrow{f}_{gru}$ reads from the first word embedding to the last one while the backward biGRU $\overleftarrow{f}_{gru}$ reads them reversely. The process can be formally denoted as:

$$
\begin{aligned}
\overrightarrow{h}_{n,l} &= \overrightarrow{f}_{gru}(\widetilde{w}_{n,l}), \; l \in \{1, \ldots, L\} \\
\overleftarrow{h}_{n,l} &= \overleftarrow{f}_{gru}(\widetilde{w}_{n,l}), \; l \in \{1, \ldots, L\}
\end{aligned}
\tag{6.1}
$$

where $\overrightarrow{h}_{n,l} \in \mathbb{R}^d$ and $\overleftarrow{h}_{n,l} \in \mathbb{R}^d$ are hidden states for the lth word of c_n. We then obtain the feature of each word by concatenating its forward and backward hidden states, i.e., $h_{n,l} = [\overrightarrow{h}_{n,l}, \overleftarrow{h}_{n,l}] \in \mathbb{R}^{2d}$. The aggregated feature of c_n can be denoted as $h_n \in \mathbb{R}^{L\times 2d}$. We perform the word-level average pooling operation to integrate

h_n into a single *claim-level* feature $H_n \in \mathbb{R}^{1\times 2d}$ that denotes the overall semantic representation of c_n.

Multi-Relational Specific Knowledge Propagator

Given the embedded claim-level feature H_n from Sect. 6.2.1.2, the multi-relational specific knowledge propagator aims to propagate the feature into $\mathbb{G}^S$ for retrieving claim-related knowledge facts from $\mathbb{G}^S$. In particular, we represent $\mathbb{G}^S$ as a multi-relational graph neural network (RGCN) for the aggregation of specific knowledge. RGCN is a specific type of graph convolutional network that contains multiple types of relations between different graph entities [33]. We model $\mathbb{G}^S$ as an RGCN because it can effectively represent different relations in $\mathbb{G}^S$ (e.g., a close relation to, no relation with) and aggregate specific knowledge with the information of the input claim. In particular, the entities $\mathcal{E}^S$ in $\mathbb{G}^S$ are represented as high-dimension entity embeddings $\widetilde{\mathcal{E}}^S \in \mathbb{R}^{E^S\times 2d}$ in RGCN where E^S is the number of unique entities in $\mathbb{G}^S$. Similarly, the relations $\mathcal{R}$ in $\mathbb{G}^S$ are represented as relation embeddings $\widetilde{\mathcal{R}} \in \mathbb{R}^{Q\times 2d}$. To learn the latent representations of the entities in $\mathbb{G}^S$, we develop a multi-relation information aggregation strategy defined as:

$$\widetilde{e}_i = \sigma\Big(\sum_{r\in\mathcal{R}} \sum_{(j,r,i)\in\mathcal{T}^*} \frac{1}{z_{i,r}} W^r_{i,j}\widetilde{e}_j A^r_{i,j}\Big) \tag{6.2}$$

where $\widetilde{e}_i \in \widetilde{\mathcal{E}}^S$ and $\widetilde{e}_j \in \widetilde{\mathcal{E}}^S$ are ith and jth graph entity embeddings in $\mathbb{G}^S$. σ stands for the non-linear activation ReLU function. $\mathcal{R}$ contains all available relations in $\mathbb{G}^S$ and $\mathcal{T}^* \in \mathcal{T}^S$ denotes the set of graph triples consisting of $\widetilde{e}_i$. $z_{i,r}$ is a normalization factor for $\widetilde{e}_i$ and $W^r_{i,j}$ is the learnable parameter. A^r is the adjacent matrix for the relation r and $A^r_{i,j}$ represents the scalar value for $\widetilde{e}_i$ and $\widetilde{e}_j$.

Unlike traditional graph neural network approaches that simply merge different features together to indicate the relation between the features (e.g., concatenating H_i with entity embeddings in $\mathbb{G}^S$), the CSKP encodes H_n as an additional adjacent matrix for $\mathbb{G}^S$ inRGCN to perform the claim guided graph convolution. The intuition is that the instance-specific knowledge propagation in the RGCN should match the semantic content in the input claim to detect incorrect information. For example, a claim that discusses the relation between the Pfizer vaccine and the human DNA can guide the RGCN to retrieve more Pfizer-related knowledge facts from $\mathbb{G}^S$ to check the truthfulness of the claim. Formally, given an embedded claim feature $H_n \in \mathbb{R}^{1\times 2d}$, the process for generating the adjacent matrix with relation r in RGCN can be denoted as:

$$A^r = \widetilde{\mathcal{E}}^S \cdot (H_n)^T + H_n \cdot (\widetilde{\mathcal{E}}^S)^T \tag{6.3}$$

where $A^r \in \mathbb{R}^{E^S \times E^S}$ is the result adjacent matrix corresponding to the relation $r \in \mathcal{R}$. The final output of the multi-relation information aggregation is the updated entity embeddings $\widetilde{e}_i \in \mathbb{R}^{2d}$ given the input graph entity $e_i \in \mathbb{G}^S$.

6.2.1.3 Topic-Based Generalized Knowledge Integrator (TGKI)

Previous knowledge graph-based methods for truth discovery mainly extract knowledge from general health-related documents that are not specific to COVID-19. More importantly, the direct knowledge extraction from the documents cannot identify *unseen* false information because the knowledge is limited to the content of the documents and not fully generalized. To address the above limitations, the TGKI designs a novel hierarchical co-attention mechanism to retrieve both specific knowledge facts and generalized knowledge facts from CHKG as explanations for the truth discovery results. We observe that retrieving accurate explanations from CHKG is determined by two correlation factors: (1) the correlation between the input claim and the specific knowledge from $\mathbb{G}^S$ and (2) the correlation between the specific knowledge from $\mathbb{G}^S$ and the generalized knowledge from $\mathbb{G}^O$. The first correlation determines whether the content of the input claim can be matched to any specific knowledge fact extracted from the news articles. For example, an incorrect input claim that makes up an unrealistic side effect (e.g., COVID-19 infection) caused by the Pfizer vaccine can be detected by Pfizer-specific knowledge (e.g., "Pfizer" $\xrightarrow{\text{not cause}}$ "COVID-19") from $\mathbb{G}^S$. The second correlation determines whether there exist generalized knowledge facts from $\mathbb{G}^O$ that can provide explanations for the input claim based on its topic connections with specific knowledge facts from $\mathbb{G}^S$. For example, if there is no matched Pfizer-specific knowledge fact from $\mathbb{G}^S$ for the input claim, TGKI detects the related specific knowledge facts (e.g., Moderna vaccine) and then retrieves their topic-wise connected generalized knowledge facts as explanations ("Vaccine" $\xrightarrow{\text{not cause}}$ "COVID-19").

To retrieve accurate and complementary explanations that explicitly consider the above correlation factors, we propose a novel dual hierarchical attention-based neural network for TGKI. The dual hierarchical attention-based neural network estimates the possibility of each knowledge fact from both $\mathbb{G}^S$ and $\mathbb{G}^O$ as the explanation for the truth discovery results. We first define the *triple-level* embedding below for the graph triples from both $\mathbb{G}^S$ and $\mathbb{G}^O$.

Definition 6.4 (Triple-Level Embedding) Triple-level embedding represents the semantic features of triples as the joint representations of graph entities and graph edges. Given an embedded triple $\widetilde{\mathcal{T}}_k = \{\widetilde{e}_i, \widetilde{r}_q, \widetilde{e}_j\}$ from CHKG, the triple-level embedding is denoted as $\psi_k = \widetilde{e}_i \odot \widetilde{r}_q \odot \widetilde{e}_j \in \mathbb{R}^{2d}$. For the embedded triples in $\mathbb{G}^S$ that are integrated with the input claims in the CSKP module, the triple-level embeddings are denoted as $\psi^S \in \mathbb{R}^{N^S \times 2d}$ where N^S is the number of triples.

Similarly, for the embedded triples in $\mathbb{G}^O$, the triple-level embeddings are denoted as $\psi^O \in \mathbb{R}^{N^O \times 2d}$ where N^O is the number of triples.

Given the triple-level embeddings ψ^S, the goal is to estimate the possibility of each triple in ψ^S being the explanation for the input claim. In particular, the dual hierarchical attention-based neural network generates the attention scores for ψ^S as $U^S = \text{Softmax}(\psi^S W^S)$ where $U^S \in \mathbb{R}^{N^S \times 1}$ are generated attention scores for all N^S triples from $\mathbb{G}^S$. The higher the score is, the more likely the corresponding triple is correlated with the input claim. In order to explore the complex correlation between ψ^S and ψ^O, the dual hierarchical attention-based neural network designs a co-attention mechanism to generate attention scores as:

$$M = \text{Softmax}_O(\tanh(\psi^S W_M (\psi^O)^T) \odot \mathcal{P}) \tag{6.4}$$

where $M \in \mathbb{R}^{N^S \times N^O}$ is the generated attention matrix and $M_{i,j}$ is the correlation score for ith triple from $\mathbb{G}^S$ with jth triple from $\mathbb{G}^O$. Softmax_O is the Softmax operation in the N^O dimension. To estimate the possibility for each triple from ψ^O of being the explanation for the input claim, the dual hierarchical attention-based network integrates U^S into M, which can be denoted as $U^O = \text{Softmax}(M^T U^S) \in \mathbb{R}^{N^O \times 1}$. We concatenate U^S and U^O as $U = [U^S, U^O]$ as the comprehensive explanations for the input claim. The higher the score is, the more likely the corresponding graph triple can reasonably explain the detection results of HC-COVID.

6.2.1.4 Joint Claim-Graph-Based Multi-relational Detector (CGMD)

Given the feature of the input claim from CSKP and triple-level embeddings from TGKI, the CGMD module aims to determine if the input claim is true or false by designing a binary neural network classifier. In particular, given an input claim c_n, we output the final prediction as:

$$\hat{y}_n = [H_n, \sum_{i=1}^{N^S} \psi_i^S \times U_i^S, \sum_{j=1}^{N^O} \psi_j^O \times U_j^O] W^b \tag{6.5}$$

where $[\cdot, \cdot, \cdot]$ denotes the concatenation operation to merge the features of the input claim with all triple-level embeddings from CHKG. $W^b \in \mathbb{R}^{5d \times 2}$ is the learnable parameter and $\hat{y}_n \in \mathbb{R}^2$ is the final prediction. Our loss function is the binary cross-entropy function that minimizes the loss between $\hat{y}_n$ and the ground-truth label y_n for each input claim c_n. The process is denoted as:

$$\mathcal{L} = \sum_{n=1}^{N} -y_n \log(\hat{y}_{n,2}) - (1 - y_n)\log(1 - \hat{y}_{n,1}) \tag{6.6}$$

where $\hat{y}_{n,1}$ and $\hat{y}_{n,2}$ are 1th and 2th scalar value in $\hat{y}_n$. The loss function measures the difference between two probability distributions (i.e., $\hat{y}_n$ and y_n) that is minimized by HC-COVID.

6.2.2 *DExFC: A Weakly Supervised Multimodal Approach*

The overview of the DExFC is shown in Fig. 6.5. It consists of four modules: (1) a Dual Graph Convolutional Feature Encoder (DGFE), (2) a Modality-Level Graph Refinement module (MGR) (3) a Multimodal Co-Attention module (MCA), and (4) a Modality-Level Discriminator (MLD). First, the DGFE module develops a set of feature encoding networks to encode the image, text, and comments of the post to high-dimensional features by aggregating them into a dual graph neural network structure. Second, the MGR module refines the adjacent matrix of the dual graph neural networks in the DGFE module by exploring the modality-level representations from the fauxtography posts in the constraint set. Third, the MCA module designs a multimodal co-attention network to integrate the encoded features and generate the attention scores that can be used for explainability. Finally, the MLD module determines whether a post is a fauxtography or not based on integrated features from the MCA module. For the detected fauxtography posts, MCA and MLD jointly output the content and comment explainability of the post.

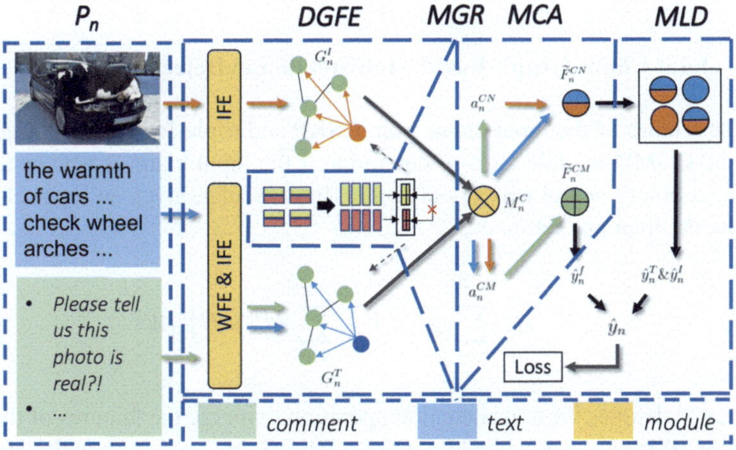

Fig. 6.5 The overview of the DExFC framework. P_n represents nth input multimodal social media post. The overview of each module in DExFC and their interactions are illustrated in Sect. 6.2.2. The orange node, blue node, and green nodes represent the visual feature, the text description feature, and the comment features, respectively. The yellow and red rectangles in the MGR module represent the contents of the posts in the constraint set with true and false labels, respectively

6.2.2.1 Dual Graph Convolutional Feature Encoder (DGFE)

In this subsection, we present the DGFE module in DExFC. The DGFE module consists of four deep learning architectures: a word feature encoder (WFE), a text feature encoder (TFE), an image feature encoder (IFE), and a dual graph convolutional network (DGCN). WFE linearly transforms all words into high-dimensional embeddings. The TFE encodes the text component of the post based on word embeddings to semantic features. The IFE encodes the image component of the post as the visual features with the same dimension. The DGCN connects and refines content and comment features by constructing a novel two-level multimodal graph structure. We first define the four network architectures below.

WFE is a word transformation network that transforms the text description and comments of a post to high-dimensional embeddings. In particular, we define $L_n = \{T_n, C_n^1, \ldots, C_n^M\}$ as a *text list* that contains both the text description and user comment components of a post P_n. The L_n^0 denotes T_n (i.e., text description component of the post) and M is the total number of comments. We convert all words in each element of L_n to one-hot vectors and build an embedding matrix W_D to transform the one-hot vectors to high-dimensional features as:

$$\widetilde{L_n^{i,j}} = L_n^{i,j} W_D, i \in \{0, \ldots, M\}, j \in \{1, \ldots, X\} \tag{6.7}$$

where i denotes the ith element in the text list and j represents the jth word in the ith element. $\widetilde{L_n^{i,j}} \in \mathbb{R}^d$ is the transformed word embeddings of d dimension.

We build the TFE as an attention bi-directional Gated Recurrent Unit (GRU) network [13, 20] to recurrently process word embeddings in each element of the text list and adaptively merge them to element-level features based on attention scores. In particular, we first construct a bi-directional GRU network to process word embedding sequences from both directions. The forward GRU $\overrightarrow{f}_{gru}$ reads from the first word embedding to the last one while the backward GRU $\overleftarrow{f}_{gru}$ reads them reversely. The bi-directional modeling process for the word embedding sequences of the post P_n can be denoted as:

$$\begin{aligned} \overrightarrow{h}_{n,x}^{i} &= \overrightarrow{f}_{gru}(\widetilde{L_{n,x}^{i}}),\ i \in \{0, \ldots, M\},\ x \in \{1, \ldots, X\} \\ \overleftarrow{h}_{n,x}^{i} &= \overleftarrow{f}_{gru}(\widetilde{L_{n,x}^{i}}),\ i \in \{0, \ldots, M\},\ x \in \{1, \ldots, X\} \end{aligned} \tag{6.8}$$

where $\overrightarrow{h}_{n,x}^{i} \in \mathbb{R}^d$ and $\overleftarrow{h}_{n,x}^{i} \in \mathbb{R}^d$ are hidden states for the xth word in the ith element of the text list, X is the total number of words in an element. For each word, we obtain its final feature by concatenating the forward and backward hidden states, i.e., $h_{n,x}^i = [\overrightarrow{h}_{n,x}^{i}, \overleftarrow{h}_{n,x}^{i}] \in \mathbb{R}^{2d}$. Therefore, the aggregated feature of an element in the text list is $h_n^i \in \mathbb{R}^{X \times 2d}$.

Given the aggregated features, we propose a word-level attention module to integrate word-level features into element-level features for each element in the text list. While the integration can be achieved by simply *averaging* or *max-pooling* the word features at the word level, those operations do not consider the semantic relations between adjacent words. Therefore, we leverage the attention scores from the attention module of the TFE to estimate the importance of each word in terms of their contributions to a higher-level semantic feature [17]. For the ith element in the text list of the post P_n, the above process can be characterized as:

$$u_n^i = \text{Softmax}(\tanh(W_u h_n^i + b_u)) \tag{6.9}$$

where $W_u \in \mathbb{R}^{2d\times 1}$ and $b_u \in \mathbb{R}$ are learnable parameters in the attention module and $u_n^i \in \mathbb{R}^{X\times 1}$ are attention scores for all words in h_n^i. The element-level feature is generated by the multiplication of u_n^i and h_n^i as follows:

$$S_n^i = \sum_{x=1}^{X} u_{n,x}^i * h_{n,x}^i \tag{6.10}$$

where X is the total number of word features. We denote the element-level feature of the text description T_n as $ST_n \in \mathbb{R}^{2d}$ and $SC_n^i \in \mathbb{R}^{2d}$ where $i \in \{1, \ldots M\}$.

We build IFE by constructing a deep convolutional neural network to extract visual features from the images of posts. The visual features provide abstract visual information for the framework to determine if the image part of a post contains incorrect content. We utilize the pre-trained ResNet [18] deep neural network as the encoder because it contains multiple residual convolutional blocks that can effectively extract visual features from the image. For the image I_n of the post P_n, the encoding process is:

$$EI_n = f_{res}(I_n) \tag{6.11}$$

where f_{res} is the encoder and $EI_n \in \mathbb{R}^{2d}$ is the generated visual feature.

Definition 6.5 (Dual Graph Neural Network (DGCN)) We define DGCN as a pair of graph convolution neural networks to explicitly connect the content and comment components of a post with a novel two-level content-comment graph structure. The output of DGCN will be utilized to generate the content and comment explanation of the fauxtography post, which we will elaborate in the following subsections.

Current fauxtography detection methods often encode the user comments of a post without explicitly considering the connection between comments [36, 47]. However, we observe that the "reply" connections between the user's comments can usually reflect the hidden relations between the user comments and the connection between the content and comments of a post. For example, if a user's comment on a post reports the post as incorrect and the comment is replied to by other comments with support, the post is likely to be fauxtography. Therefore, we model the comments and their interactions as a graph neural network structure to fully aggregate the useful information that helps to identify the fauxtography posts. In particular, the comments are modeled as graph nodes, and the "reply" relations are modeled as graph edges in the network. However, in many cases, only considering direct "reply" between user comments (e.g., ExFaux[26], FauxWard [35]) is insufficient because such direct "reply" is often either sparse (e.g., few discussions under the post) or long-chain (e.g., a long debate between two users) in reality [7]. One possible solution is to connect each comment with all other comments in the same thread of the given post as an indirect "reply". However, the solution ignores the dynamic correlation between different comments in a "reply-chain" that are of different depths from the head comment. For example, consider a "reply-chain" of comments $C = \{C_i\}, i \in [1, N]$ where comment C_i replies to its previous comment C_{i-1}. We define the correlation between the contents of C_i and C_j in the chain as $\text{Corr}(C_i, C_j), i, j \in N$. We empirically observe that the $\text{Corr}(C_i, C_j)$ decreases exponentially as the distance between the two comments (i.e., $|i - j|$) increases [9]. We observe that focusing on the highly correlated comments while ignoring the ones with low correlations in the comment graph network greatly facilitates the DExFC in accurately detecting and explaining fauxtography posts when the dataset is noisy. Therefore, we decide to only keep the connections between the pair of comments whose distance is less than or equal to 2. We propose a two-level graph neural network to fully explore both the direct and indirect interactions between user's comments.

We first formally define the two-level graph structure for the comments of the post P_n. In particular, we define the graph as $G_n = (V_n, E_n)$ where V_n is the set of user comments and E_n is the set of direct (i.e., first-level) replies between user comments. For example, an edge $e_{s,s'} \in E_n$ denotes that comment s' replies to comment s. We further extend the graph by adding more edges that connect comments with indirect (i.e., second-level) relations. For example, if there are three nodes s_1, s_2, s_3 in the comment graph and s_2 replies to s_1 while s_3 replies to s_2, we not only create edges e_{s_1,s_2} and e_{s_2,s_3}, but also connect s_1 and s_3 with e_{s_1,s_3}. Two examples of the two-level comment relations are shown in Fig. 6.6. We define the set of second-level indirect replies between user comments as E_n^*.

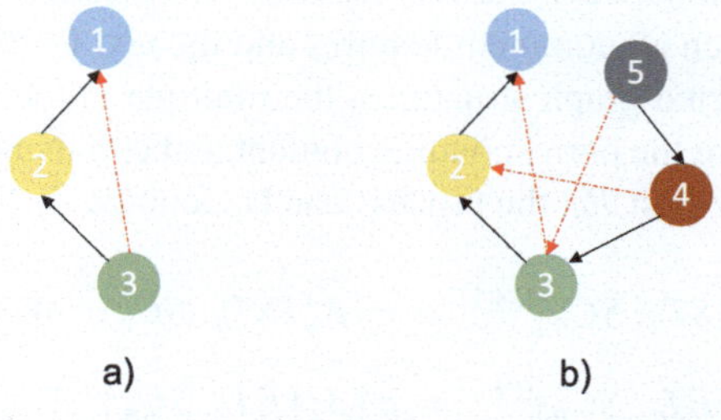

Fig. 6.6 Two-level graph based comment network. The nodes with different colors represent users' comments, the black solid arrows represent direct replies and the red dashed arrows represent second-level indirect connections. (**a**) Example 1. (**b**) Example 2

Based on the two-level graph comment network, we further develop a novel multimodal dual graph structure to integrate the text, image, and comment components of a post into a holistic structure. Unlike previous fauxtography detection methods that usually process the content and comments of the posts separately, the dual graph structure embeds the content as additional graph nodes for the graph comment network and connects all comments to the content nodes. Therefore, the dual graph structure is able to fully explore the hidden relations between the content and comments and identify the incorrect points in the post by aggregating the information between content and comments. Given the text feature ST_n from the text feature encoder and the image feature EI_n from the image feature encoder above, the process of building the new multimodal graphs is denoted as:

$$\begin{aligned} G_n^T &= (\{V_n, ST_n\}, \{E_n, E_n^*, e_{i,ST_n}\}),\ i \in \{1, \ldots, M\} \\ G_n^I &= (\{V_n, EI_n\}, \{E_n, E_n^*, e_{i,EI_n}\}),\ i \in \{1, \ldots, M\} \end{aligned} \tag{6.12}$$

where M is the total number of comments. $\{V_n, ST_n\}$ represents the union of features between the comment features and the text feature. Similarly, $\{V_n, EI_n\}$ represents the union of features between comment features and the image feature. e_{i,ST_n} denotes the edges between a comment feature and the text feature. e_{i,EI_n} denotes the edges between a comment feature and the image feature. G_n^T is the generated graph structure that contains the text and comments and G_n^I contains the image and comments. The edges in both G_n^T and G_n^I are further represented as adjacent matrices as below.

$$\begin{aligned} A_n^T &= \text{symmetric}(\{E_n, E_n^*, e_{i,ST_n}\}) + I_n \\ A_n^I &= \text{symmetric}(\{E_n, E_n^*, e_{i,EI_n}\}) + I_n \end{aligned} \tag{8}$$

where symmetric$(\cdot)$ represents adding edges to convert asymmetric directed graphs to symmetric undirected graphs and I_n denotes the identity matrix. Additionally, $A_n^T \in \mathbb{R}^{(M+1)\times(M+1)}$ and $A_n^I \in \mathbb{R}^{(M+1)\times(M+1)}$ are binary adjacent matrices where the value "1" denotes the connection between two features while "0" denotes no connection between the two features. For example, the values of $A_n^T \in \mathbb{R}^{(M+1)\times(M+1)}$ between all comment features and the text feature are "1".

Given the constructed graph structures, the multiple graph convolutional layers in the DGCN convolve the corresponding content and comment features with graph layer weights. For the post P_n, the process can be denoted as:

$$\begin{aligned} [ST_n, SC_n]^{(l+1)} &= \sigma(\widetilde{A_n^T}[ST_n, SC_n]^{(l)} W_l) \\ [EI_n, SC_n]^{(l+1)} &= \sigma(\widetilde{A_n^I}[EI_n, SC_n]^{(l)} W_l) \end{aligned} \tag{6.13}$$

where l is the layer index for DGCN ($l = 0$ for original $[*, SC_n]$), $\widetilde{A_n^*} = D^{\frac{1}{2}} A_n^* D^{\frac{1}{2}}$ is the normalized symmetric weight matrix with D as the degree of the matrix ($D_{ii} = \sum_j A_{ij}$), and $W_l \in \mathbb{R}^{2d \times 2d}$ denotes the learnable parameters, σ represents the non-linear functions *ReLU*. The comment features ${SC_n}^{(l+1)}$ are processed by *max-pooling* the comment features from the outputs $[ST_n, SC_n]^{(l+1)}$ and $[EI_n, SC_n]^{(l+1)}$ in the feature dimension.

6.2.2.2 Modality-Level Graph Refinement Module (MGR)

The MGR module aims to leverage the K fully annotated fauxtography posts in the constraint set $\mathbb{P}^G$ to improve both the detection and explanation performance of the DExFC. Given the non-trivial cost of obtaining modality-level labels of fauxtography posts, we limit the number of posts in $\mathbb{P}^G$ to be small. In particular, we divide the set into 4 subsets with equal size where each subset contains $K/4$ fauxtography posts with the same modality-level labels (e.g., the posts with true text and false images go to the same subset). However, it is difficult to leverage these subsets in a traditional gradient descent training process to optimize the DExFC due to the limited number of posts in the subsets. Therefore, the MGR module treats $\mathbb{P}^G$ as an internal constraint to the DExFC to further optimize the performance of the DGCN by adjusting its internal graph structure.

While various fauxtography posts contain totally different contents in both text and image components, the embedded incorrect information could be similar. For example, the texts of different fauxtography posts may include different terms (e.g., gigantic birds, finger elephants). However, they often deliver the same incorrect concept (e.g., exaggeration). Similarly, the visual contents in multiple photoshopped images are different but share the same type of pixel-level discrepancy (e.g., the inconsistency between the altered human face and its surrounding pixels [28]). Therefore, the goal of the MGR module is to retrieve the *meta-representations* of the fauxtography posts in $\mathbb{P}^G$ by performing a metric-based learning strategy. Metric learning is a machine learning task that learns a distance function to generate high-quality representations of input data samples [19]. In $\mathbb{P}^G$, for each modality of the posts in the constraint set (i.e., text or image), the modality-level contents annotated as *true* or *false* are expected to share the same true or false meta-representations. Moreover, we observe that the meta-representations related to true or false samples are often easier to distinguish from each other than the original contents of the post because they transfer low-level modality-specific descriptions into high-level representation concepts. With the above intuition, we design a novel metric-based loss function to generate meta-representations and utilize them as additional guidance to optimize the structure of the graph neural network in the DGCN.

In particular, the content of posts in $\mathbb{P}^G$ are first encoded as high-dimensional features by WFE, TFE and IFE described in Sect. 6.2.2.1. The encoded features are denoted as $F_{GT} \in \mathbb{R}^{K \times 2d}$ and $F_{GI} \in \mathbb{R}^{K \times 2d}$ for text and image part, respectively. Moreover, we define $F_{GT,T} \in \mathbb{R}^{K/2 \times 2d}$ and $F_{GT,F} \in \mathbb{R}^{K/2 \times 2d}$ as text related features of the posts with true and false labels in $\mathbb{P}^G$, respectively. Similarly, we define $F_{GI,T} \in \mathbb{R}^{K/2\times 2d}$ and $F_{GI,F} \in \mathbb{R}^{K/2\times 2d}$ as image related features of the posts with true and false labels in $\mathbb{P}^G$, respectively. With the above definitions, we derive the generation process for all meta-representations using the encoded features as follows:

$$\hat{F}_{GT,T} = \frac{1}{K/2}\sum_{i=0}^{K/2} F_{GT,T,i}, \qquad \hat{F}_{GT,F} = \frac{1}{K/2}\sum_{i=0}^{K/2} F_{GT,F,i}$$
$$\hat{F}_{GI,T} = \frac{1}{K/2}\sum_{i=0}^{K/2} F_{GI,T,i}, \qquad \hat{F}_{GI,F} = \frac{1}{K/2}\sum_{i=0}^{K/2} F_{GI,F,i} \tag{6.14}$$

where $\hat{F}_{GT,T} \in \mathbb{R}^{2d}$ and $\hat{F}_{GT,F} \in \mathbb{R}^{2d}$ are averaged text features with true and false labels, respectively. Similarly, $\hat{F}_{GI,T}$ and $\hat{F}_{GI,F}$ are averaged image features with true and false labels, respectively. The four generated representations (i.e., $\hat{F}_{GT,T}$, $\hat{F}_{GT,F}$, $\hat{F}_{GI,T}$, $\hat{F}_{GI,F}$) are the meta-representations for text/image component with true and false labels, respectively. We then design the metric-based loss function L_G to optimize all the concept representations, which can be denoted as:

$$L_{GT} = \frac{\sum_{i=0}^{K/2} \|\hat{F}_{GT,F} - F_{GT,F,i}\| + \|\hat{F}_{GT,T} - F_{GT,T,i}\|}{\|\hat{F}_{GT,F} - \hat{F}_{GT,T}\| + \epsilon}$$
$$L_{GI} = \frac{\sum_{i=0}^{K/2} \|\hat{F}_{GI,F} - F_{GT,F,i}\| + \|\hat{F}_{GI,T} - F_{GT,T,i}\|}{\|\hat{F}_{GI,F} - \hat{F}_{GI,T}\| + \epsilon} \tag{6.15}$$
$$L_G = L_{GT} + L_{GI}$$

where the sub-functions L_{GT} and L_{GI} denote the metric-based losses for the text and image modalities of the posts in $\mathbb{P}^G$, respectively.

Given an input multimodal post, the graph neural network in the DGCN connects content and comment features of the post via the graph structure. The generated meta-representations adjust the relations of the graph nodes (i.e., content and comment nodes) in the structure by updating the corresponding adjacent matrix. In particular, we first average the true and false meta-representations for both text and image to obtain the overall modality-level meta-representations, which are denoted as $\bar{F}_{GT} \in \mathbb{R}^{2d}$ and $\bar{F}_{GI} \in \mathbb{R}^{2d}$, respectively. For a given input post P_n with C comments, we first group the text and image representations with comment representations separately to construct joint features as $J_n^T = [ST_n, SC_n] \in \mathbb{R}^{(C+1)\times 2d}$ and $J_n^I = [EI_n, SC_n] \in \mathbb{R}^{(C+1)\times 2d}$. Then we calculate the correlation between the joint features of P_n and the meta-representations to estimate their correlations, which can be denoted as:

$$A_{n,i}^{G,T} = J_{n,i}^T \cdot \bar{F}_{GT}, \quad A_{n,i}^{G,I} = J_{n,i}^I \cdot \bar{F}_{GI} \tag{6.16}$$

where $A_{n,i}^{G,T}$ represents the ith correlation factor between the ith element in the text-related joint features (i.e., $J_{n,i}^{T}$) and the corresponding text meta-representation (i.e., $\bar{F}_{GT}$). Similarly, $A_{n,i}^{G,I}$ represents the ith correlation factor between the ith element in the image-related joint features (i.e., $J_{n,i}^{I}$) and the corresponding image meta-representation (i.e., $\bar{F}_{GI}$). We perform the matrix multiplication on $A_{n}^{G,T}$ and $A_{n}^{G,I}$ to construct a global adjacent matrix $A_{n}^{G} \in \mathbb{R}^{(C+1)\times(C+1)}$ that illustrates a new relation between content and comments from meta-representations. Finally, the adjacent matrices A_n^T and A_n^I in the DGCN are replaced with $A_n^T + A_n^G$ and $A_n^I + A_n^G$ as new adjacent matrices to perform graph convolution.

6.2.2.3 Multimodal Co-Attention Module (MCA)

In this subsection, we present the MCA module that integrates the encoded features from the DGFE and generates the attention scores that can be used for the explainability tasks. We observe that text and image components of a post may weigh differently in the user's judgment on a fauxtography post. For example, the post in Fig. 6.2a contains both false text and false image. However, people are more likely to determine the post as fauxtography based on the content of the image rather than the text. Similarly, we also observe that not all comments are equally important in determining and explaining a fauxtography post. For example, the first comment of the post in Fig. 6.2b is more convincing than others to explain that the text description of the post is incorrect. To accommodate the above observations, we develop the MCA module to estimate the relative importance of each content modality and each comment by generating corresponding attention scores. Using the features from the DGFE, we first concatenate ST_n and EI_n (i.e., text and image features from the DGCN) to create a content feature list $F_n^{con} = [ST_n, EI_n] \in \mathbb{R}^{2\times 2d}$. Then we compute the affinity matrix $M_n^C \in \mathbb{R}^{2\times M}$ for the post P_n to obtain the joint representations for content and comments as follows:

$$M_n^C = \tanh(F_n^{con} W_M (C_n)^T) \tag{6.17}$$

where T represents the transpose of a matrix, tanh is the activation function for the non-linear feature transformation, and $W_M \in \mathbb{R}^{2d\times 2d}$ represents the learnable parameters. Then we add the joint representations back to content and comment features and generate attention scores as follows:

$$\begin{aligned} a_n^{CN} &= (F_n^{con} + M_n^C C_n)W^{CN} \\ a_n^{CM} &= (C_n + (M_n^C)^T F_n^{con})W^{CM} \end{aligned} \tag{6.18}$$

where $W^{CN} \in \mathbb{R}^{2d\times 1}$ and $W^{CM} \in \mathbb{R}^{2d\times 1}$ are learnable parameters for transformation, $a_n^{CN} \in \mathbb{R}^{2\times 1}$ and $a_n^{CM} \in \mathbb{R}^{M\times 1}$ are generated attention scores that are further normalized to 1 by the *Softmax* operation. If the post P_n is determined as fauxtography, the two scores in a_n^{CN} estimate *what* component (i.e., text or image) is more likely to be false in post P_n. Furthermore, each score in a_n^{CM} indicates how likely a comment can explain the reason why a specific component is false in the fauxtography post.

Our next goal is to generate an integrated content-level feature and an integrated comment-level feature based on the attention scores to classify the fauxtography posts. The generation process is denoted as:

$$
\begin{aligned}
\widetilde{F}_n^{CN} &= (a_n^{CN})_0 * ST_n + (a_n^{CN})_1 * EI_n \\
\widetilde{F}_n^{CM} &= \sum_{i=1}^{M} C_{n,i} * a_{n,i}^{CM}
\end{aligned}
\tag{6.19}
$$

where $(a_n^{CN})_0$ and $(a_n^{CN})_1$ represent the first and second element in a_n^{CN}. $\widetilde{F}_n^{CN} \in \mathbb{R}^{2d}$ and $\widetilde{F}_n^{CM} \in \mathbb{R}^{2d}$ are the integrated content-level and comment-level features of P_n, respectively.

6.2.2.4 Modality-Level Discriminator (MLD)

In this subsection, we present the MLD module in DExFC. The module consists of two network architectures: (1) a dual modality-level false content discriminator (DMD) for the content explainability, and (2) a final fauxtography discriminator (FFD) based on the DMD and the generated text, image and comment features from the MCA module. First, the dual modality-level false content discriminators discriminate the text and image components of a post to provide content explainability. Second, the fauxtography discriminator concatenates all features and the modality-level predictions to determine if the post is fauxtography. We illustrate the two network architectures below.

While the scores in a_n^{CN} from the MCA module are able to indicate the importance of the text and image components of the post P_n, they are restricted by the *Softmax* operation that normalizes the sum of scores in a_n^{CN} to 1, which ignores the possibility that both text and image components can be true (i.e., both with low scores). To address this issue, we define the Dual Modality-Level False Content Discriminator (DMD) as a pair of binary neural network classifiers that discriminate the text and image features of a post. The results of DMD provide the content explainability to identify what component(s) (text or image or both) contain the incorrect information. We first concatenate the integrated content-level feature with the original text and image feature. The updated features are $\widehat{ST_n} = [ST_n, \widetilde{F}_n^{CN}] \in \mathbb{R}^{4d}$ and $\widehat{EI_n} = [EI_n, \widetilde{F}_n^{CN}] \in \mathbb{R}^{4d}$ for text and image components, respectively. After that, we derive the modality-level predictions from the refined features of the post P_n as:

$$\begin{aligned} \hat{y}_n^T &= (\widehat{ST_n})W_T + b_T \\ \hat{y}_n^I &= (\widehat{EI_n})W_I + b_I \end{aligned} \tag{6.20}$$

where $\hat{y}_n^T \in \mathbb{R}^2$ and $\hat{y}_n^I \in \mathbb{R}^2$ are predicted results for text and image components of a post, respectively.

We define the Final Fauxtography Discriminator (FFD) as a binary neural network classifier that considers the updated text and image features from the DMD and the integrated comment-level feature from the MCA module and makes the final decision to determine if a post is fauxtography. For a post P_n, we concatenate modality-level and comment-level features as:

$$F_n^{final} = [([\widehat{ST_n}, \widehat{EI_n}])W_p, \widetilde{F}_n^{CM}] \tag{6.21}$$

where $W_p \in \mathbb{R}^{8d \times 2d}$ are the learnable parameters and $F_n^{final} \in \mathbb{R}^{4d}$ is the overall feature vector. We apply the transformation on F_n^{final} to obtain the final prediction as:

$$\hat{y}_n^f = F_n^{final} W_f + b_f \tag{6.22}$$

where $W_f \in \mathbb{R}^{4d \times 2}$ are the learnable parameters. We fuse $\hat{y}_n^f$ with $\hat{y}_n^T$ and $\hat{y}_n^I$ for the computation of the final loss function as follows:

$$\hat{y}_n = \alpha \times \hat{y}_n^f + \hat{y}_n^T + \hat{y}_n^I \tag{6.23}$$

where $\hat{y}_n$ denotes the final prediction of the post and α is an adjustable factor to balance the optimization weights between the overall and modality-level predictions. The goal of the loss function is to minimize the cross-entropy loss. The above optimization process is denoted as follows:

$$\begin{aligned} \mathcal{L}_W &= \sum_{n=1}^{N} -y_n \log((\hat{y}_n)_1) - (1 - y_n)\log(1 - (\hat{y}_n)_0) \\ \mathcal{L} &= \mathcal{L}_W + \mathcal{L}_G \end{aligned} \tag{6.24}$$

6.3 Real-World Case Studies

We evaluate HC-COVID and DExFC using two real-world social intelligence case studies with multiple datasets. Specifically, we evaluate HC-COVID with a representative social intelligence application of explainable COVID-19 truth discovery and the goal is to jointly assess the truthfulness of COVID-19 news articles and explain the assessment results. We then evaluate DExFC through a case study of multimodal truth discovery that targets assessing multimodal social media information integrity, such as fauxtography, that contains both text and images.

6.3.1 Explainable COVID-19 News Truth Discovery

Explainable COVID-19 truth discovery aims to assess the truthfulness of news articles related to COVID-19 while simultaneously providing interpretable explanations for why each article is classified as true or false. Evaluation results on two real-world COVID-19 truth discovery datasets demonstrate that HC-COVID achieves superior performance in both truth discovery accuracy and explanation quality compared to state-of-the-art baselines.

6.3.1.1 Data

We use two public COVID-19 truth discovery datasets for the experiments. The first dataset is CoAID [10], a COVID-19 health truth discovery dataset that consists of *COVID-19 articles* and *COVID-19 claims*. The COVID-19 articles contain reliable COVID-19 medical news and fact-checking articles including both medical and non-medical concepts. The COVID-19 claims contain 1000 true COVID-19-related tweets and 1000 false COVID-19-related tweets as the dataset for evaluating the HC-COVID and state-of-the-art baselines. The second dataset CONSTRAINT [29] is a large-scale COVID-19 truth discovery dataset that consists of 10, 700 COVID-19 related tweets. In particular, the CONSTRAINT dataset is utilized for evaluating the truth discovery performance of HC-COVID where its hierarchical crowdsource knowledge graph is constructed from the COVID-19 articles in CoAID. For both datasets, we split the COVID-19 claims with 50% as training set, 20% as validation set, and 30% as testing set. The summary of the two datasets is shown in Table 6.1.

6.3.1.2 Crowdsourcing Platform

For each COVID-19 article in the article-level interface, we invite five independent Amazon Mechanical Turk (AMT) workers to participate in the construction of the article-level knowledge graph. For the topic-level interface, we select crowd workers

Table 6.1 Dataset summary

Dataset	Type	Count
CoAID [10]	COVID-19 articles	600
	True tweets	1632
	False tweets	544
CONSTRAINT [29]	True tweets	5600
	False tweets	5100

who are verified by AMT as "healthcare workers" and then develop a set of COVID-19 screening questions to select COVID-19 expert workers [3]. There are two types of potential biases in conducting both crowdsourcing tasks: (1) the *demographic bias* of various crowd workers and (2) the *opinion bias* of crowdsourcing responses. To mitigate the demographic bias of crowd workers, we follow the recruiting policy of AMT and provide an equal opportunity for each crowd worker. In particular, we design the crowdsourcing interfaces and upload the interfaces to the AMT website. The AMT displays the interfaces publicly and accepts the interested crowd workers regardless of their demographic attributes (e.g., race, gender, age). To mitigate the opinion bias, we adopt the majority voting mechanism to collect crowdsourcing responses from both article-level and topic-level interfaces. In particular, we accept a submitted article-level or topic-level response only if a submitted 3-tuple statement is the same in two or more responses. To ensure the quality of responses from workers, the workers are selected only if they have a 98% or higher Human Intelligence Task (HIT) rate.

We perform a COVID-19 relation selection pilot study to identify 11 relations as the relation pool. In particular, we randomly select 150 COVID-19 articles from the CoAID dataset [10] and assign 4 non-expert crowd workers and 1 expert worker for each article to summarize the knowledge triples. We allow crowd workers to use free texts to indicate the relations between entities when they accomplish the two crowdsourcing tasks developed in Section 4.1. We then identify the 11 most frequent relations that are used by 15 or more crowd responses. The relation-count summary is as follows: {*is*: 96, *cause*: 81, *close relation with*: 65, *no relation with*: 62, *have*: 49, *is good for*: 39, *no effect on*: 31, *is not*: 27, *is bad for*: 20, *not have*: 17, *prevent*: 15}. Similarly, we carried out a COVID-19 topic selection pilot study to identify 8 unique COVID-19 topics in the article-level interface for non-expert workers to select. In particular, we randomly select 100 COVID-19 articles from the CoAID dataset and asks three COVID-19 expert workers to propose possible COVID-19 topics for each article. We randomly select expert workers from AMT to reduce potential opinion bias from the workers. For each COVID-19 article, the selected expert worker needs to create three different COVID-19 topics that can cover the entire or most content of the article. After the study, we collect all proposed COVID-19 topics and select the 8 most frequent topics that are proposed more than 20 times by COVID-19 expert workers. The topic-count summary is: {*Prevention*: 71, *Virus Itself*: 52, *Cure*: 45, *Vaccine*: 44, *Spread*: 37, *Politics*: 32, *Influence*: 25, *Origin*: 21}.

We set the payment to all crowd workers well above the minimum requirement from AMT [2]. The average time to complete an article-level and a topic-level task by a crowd worker is 76 and 194 seconds, respectively. Finally, we collect 640 valid triples for the article-level knowledge graph (i.e., nearly 1 knowledge triple for each COVID-19 article) and 80 valid triples for the topic-level graph (nearly 10 knowledge triples for each COVID-19 topic).

6.3.1.3 Baseline Methods and Experimental Setting

Baseline Methods

We conduct experiments with state-of-the-art truth discovery models to evaluate the performance of HC-COVID.

- **HAN [45]:** HAN is a hierarchical attention network approach that applies both word-level and sentence-level mechanisms for document classification. We use COVID-19 claims in CoAID or CONSTRAINT as the input documents and train the model to classify incorrect claims from truthful claims.
- **PLAN [23]:** PLAN is a multi-head attention network approach to detect rumors in social media by constructing a conversation tree that models the various interactions between the original rumor and the corresponding user replies. In particular, we replace the false and true rumors in PLAN as true and false claims for the classification task, respectively.
- **MVAE [21]:** MVAE is a variational autoencoder neural network approach for truth discovery by learning a hidden representation from the content of social media posts.
- **dEFEND [36]:** dEFEND is a truth discovery model that applies a co-attention strategy to retrieve important sentences from both the textual news content and the user comments by analyzing the interaction between them.
- **DETERRENT [11]:** DETERRENT is a knowledge-guided graph attention network solution to detect false information in health-related articles by incorporating a medical knowledge graph and an article-entity bipartite graph. Specifically, we replace health-related articles in DETERRENT with COVID-19 claims and train the framework for the classification task.
- **COVID19-KG [14]:** COVID19-KG is a cause-and-effect knowledge model of COVID-19 pathophysiology. In particular, we replace the crowd knowledge graph in HC-COVID with the knowledge graph constructed by COVID19-KG to implement this baseline.
- **KMGCN [43]:** KMGCN is a knowledge-driven and graph-based model to assess the truthfulness of news in social media posts by exploring the background knowledge hidden in the text content of the posts. In particular, we retrieve the specific graph triples from the hierarchical knowledge graph as background knowledge if the graph triples contain the same word as the one used in the input COVID-19 claim.

Experimental Setting

In the experiments, we pre-select the COVID-19 claims as the independent *testing set* and perform 10-fold cross-validation on the *train-validation* set to estimate a more general performance of all schemes. For the implementation details of HC-COVID, the CIKP module holds 2 graph convolutional layers with each layer followed by the *ReLU* activation. We set the hidden state dimensions of the biGRU networks from CIKP as 128. We set the vocabulary size for the COVID-19 claims in the CoAID and CONSTRAINT datasets as 4500 and 6000, respectively. We set the total number of epochs as 40 and train HC-COVID with an initial learning rate of 0.001 and decay of 0.95 in each epoch. The optimizer is Adam with 5×10^{-4} weight decay. We run the experiments on Ubuntu 16.04 with two NVIDIA 1080Ti.

6.3.1.4 Detection Performance

First, we evaluate the truth discovery performance of HC-COVID and all the baselines on both the CoAID and CONSTRAINT datasets. The evaluation results are shown in Tables 6.2 and 6.3, respectively. We observe that HC-COVID consistently outperforms all the baseline methods on all evaluation metrics on both the CoAID

Table 6.2 Overall detection performance on CoAID

Methods	F1 score	Accuracy	Precision	Recall
HAN	0.653	0.807	0.664	0.642
PLAN	0.731	0.846	0.722	0.740
MVAE	0.688	0.823	0.685	0.691
dEFEND	0.745	0.855	0.742	0.748
DETERRENT	0.798	0.885	0.792	0.805
COVID19-KG	0.761	0.871	0.802	0.724
KMGCN	0.797	0.887	0.814	0.780
HC-COVID	**0.820**	**0.899**	**0.826**	**0.813**

The bold values indicate the best performing results in each evaluation metric

Table 6.3 Overall detection performance on CONSTRAINT

Methods	F1 score	Accuracy	Precision	Recall
HAN	0.750	0.769	0.788	0.716
PLAN	0.895	0.898	0.892	0.897
MVAE	0.827	0.830	0.817	0.838
dEFEND	0.868	0.875	0.887	0.851
DETERRENT	0.911	0.915	0.923	0.899
COVID19-KG	0.883	0.886	0.880	0.887
KMGCN	0.910	0.913	0.912	0.907
HC-COVID	**0.938**	**0.939**	**0.925**	**0.951**

The bold values indicate the best performing results in each evaluation metric

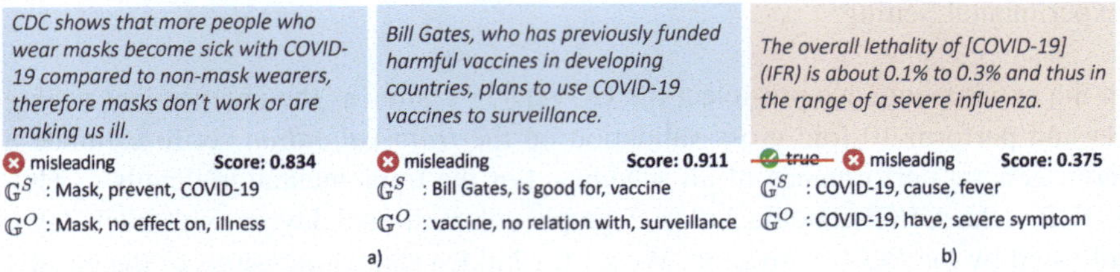

Fig. 6.7 Case study of COVID-19 truth discovery. (**a**) Successful truth discovery by HC-COVID over other baselines. (**b**) Failure case

and CONSTRAINT datasets. In particular, HC-COVID achieves performance gains of 2.2 and 2.7% in terms of F1 score compared to the best-performing baseline (i.e., DETERRENT) on the CoAID and CONSTRAINT datasets, respectively. Such a performance gain can be attributed to the incorporation of the COVID-19 generalized knowledge facts in the hierarchical knowledge graph that can effectively infer the truthfulness of an unseen COVID-19 claim. Moreover, we observe that the medical knowledge graph based baselines (i.e., DETERRENT, COVID19-KG, KMGCN) perform better than other baselines that do not utilize professional medical knowledge. Such an observation further verifies the effectiveness of leveraging medical knowledge facts for the detection of COVID-19 false information. However, HC-COVID outperforms these medical knowledge graph based baselines because it develops a crowdsourcing approach to abstract both specific and generalized knowledge facts from COVID-19 articles.

We further visualize several testing cases in Fig. 6.7 to evaluate the detection performance of HC-COVID. The score in each case is the prediction probability that represents the confidence level of HC-COVID. Figure 6.7a shows two testing cases that are correctly identified as false by HC-COVID but misclassified by other baselines. The explanations from the hierarchical knowledge graph demonstrate that HC-COVID can accurately detect and explain the COVID-19 false information based on both specific (e.g., "Bill Gates" $\xrightarrow{\text{is good for}}$ "COVID-19") and generalized knowledge facts (e.g., "Mask" $\xrightarrow{\text{no effect on}}$ "illness"). Moreover, we show one testing case in Fig. 6.7b that all methods fail to detect the false information in it. The reason for the post being false is the actual IFR of COVID-19 is more than 0.65% which cannot be classified as any common influenza. However, the detection of manipulation on real numbers is difficult because it requires the algorithms to understand the definition of the numbers (e.g., the definition of IFR) and have the ability to infer the truthfulness of the number associated with the specific concepts (e.g., the possible IFR of COVID-19). We will further explore it in future works.

6.3.1.5 Explainability Performance

We study the explainability performance of the proposed HC-COVID through multiple real-world user studies. In particular, we compare the explainability performance of HC-COVID with the COVID19-KG and DETERRENT baselines which are the only baselines that involve knowledge graphs that can output attention weights to explain the detection results. In the user study, we carry out two sets of experiments using AMT. In particular, we randomly select 25 COVID-19 false claims and 25 COVID-19 true claims from the testing set to perform explainability evaluation.

In the first subset of experiments, we study the explainability performance by comparing the quality of the explanations generated from HC-COVID with other schemes. In particular, we define *explainability ranked list* as a list of graph triples retrieved from the knowledge graph based on their attention scores in descending order. For each compared scheme and each COVID-19 claim, we create Top-1, Top-3, and Top-5 explainability ranked list to fully evaluate the explainability performance of each scheme. For each type of explainability ranked list (e.g., Top-1, Top-3, Top-5), we recruit 5 AMT workers and ask them to select one scheme from all the three compared schemes that can best explain the detection results of each input COVID-19 claim. The explainability performance is evaluated using the following two metrics that are commonly used for quantifying the quality of explanation [36].

- **Percentage of Posts** (% of Posts): the percentage of posts whose explanation is picked by the majority of workers as their preferred ones belonging to each scheme. For example, given an input COVID-19 claims, if three or more crowd workers believe that the claim is best explained by the knowledge triples from the COVID19-KG scheme. Then we assign COVID19-KG as the best explainable scheme to the claim. If there are totally 10 claims with COVID19-KG, the % of Posts for COVID19-KG is $\frac{10}{50} \times 100\% = 20\%$.
- **Percentage of Workers** (% of Workers): the percentage of workers who select their preferred explanation from the explainability ranked list predicted by each scheme. For example, given an input COVID-19 claim, if there are 3 crowd workers choosing HC-COVID as the best explainable scheme for the claim and 2 crowd workers choosing DETERRENT, we record the number of crowd workers for each scheme. If HC-COVID is finally chosen by 100 crowd works from all 50 claims, the % of Workers for HC-COVID is $\frac{100}{50\times5} = 40\%$.

The above two metrics evaluate the explainability performance of compared schemes from *claim-level* and *worker-level*, respectively (Fig. 6.8). The results are summarized in Fig. 6.9. We observe that HC-COVID significantly outperforms the compared baseline schemes in terms of both metrics. The performance gains demonstrate HC-COVID's capability of generating relevant and accurate explanations by the TGKI module.

In the second subset of experiments, we evaluate the explainability performance by investigating the efficiency of the explanations generated by each compared

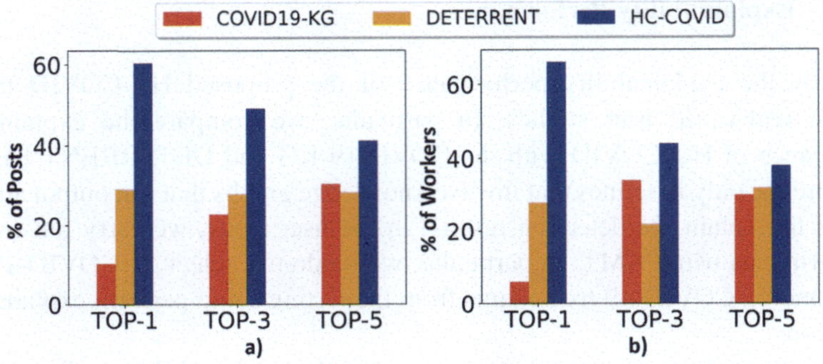

Fig. 6.8 Explainability evaluation on CoAID. (**a**) Claim level. (**b**) Worker level

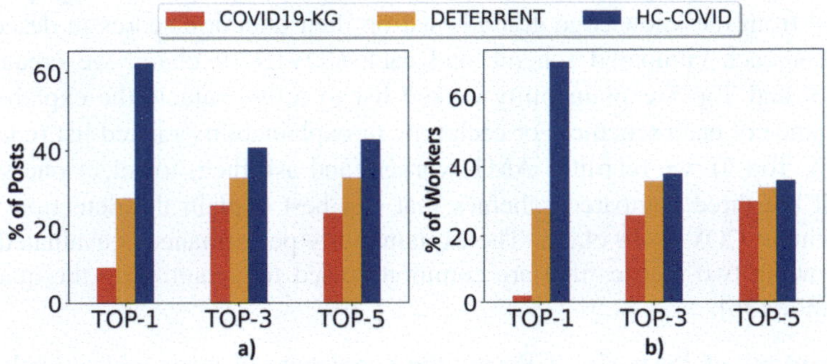

Fig. 6.9 Explainability evaluation on CONSTRAINT. (**a**) Claim level. (**b**) Worker level

scheme. In particular, we ask 5 AMT workers to first read through Top-5 explainability ranked list from the first one with the highest attention weights, and stop when a worker thinks the cumulative explanation triples are sufficient to convince the worker about the detection result. The number of explanation triples a worker has read for each post is recorded and is denoted as the *minimum reading index (MRI)*. We then measure the explanation efficiency using the following metrics with respect to MRI:

- **Average Minimum Reading Index** (AvgMRI): The average value of MRI for each compared scheme.
- **Percentage of Posts** (% of Posts): The percentage of posts on which each compared scheme achieves the lowest MRI.

We present the results in Table 6.4. We observe that HC-COVID achieves the lowest average MRI on both the CoAID and CONSTRAINT datasets compared to the COVID19-KG and DETERRENT schemes. In addition, HC-COVID also explains most of the detection results (i.e., 58% on the CoAID dataset and 52% on the DETERRENT dataset) with the lowest number of explanation triples.

Table 6.4 Evaluation for minimum reading index

Dataset	Metric	COVID19-KG	DETERRENT	HC-COVID
CoAID	AvgMRI	3.32	2.93	**2.25**
	% of Posts	10.0	32.0	**58.0**
CONSTRAINT	AvgMRI	2.94	2.99	**2.48**
	% of Posts	26.0	22.0	**52.0**

The bold values indicate the best performing results in each evaluation metric

Table 6.5 Ablation study for variants of HC-COVID on CONSTRAINT

	F1 score	Accuracy	Precision	Recall
HC-COVID	**0.938**	**0.939**	**0.925**	**0.951**
HC-COVID\C	0.920	0.921	0.903	0.938
HC-COVID\T	0.916	0.918	0.905	0.928
HC-COVID\G	0.896	0.895	0.862	0.933

The bold values indicate the best performing results in each evaluation metric

6.3.1.6 Ablation Study

We carry out an ablation study to further investigate the importance of each component in the HC-COVID framework. In particular, we consider three ablations of the HC-COVID framework: (1) *HC-COVID\C* that excludes the encoding of claim-level feature into CHKG by replacing the claim guided adjacency matrix in Eq. (6.3) with binary adjacency matrix; (2) *HC-COVID\T* that excludes the TGKI module from HC-COVID by considering COVID-19 specific and COVID-19 generalized knowledge facts as a homogeneous set of knowledge facts; (3) *HC-COVID\G* that excludes the COVID-19 generalized knowledge facts from the hierarchical knowledge graph. We reported the results of the ablation study in Table 6.5. We note that HC-COVID achieves the best performance when incorporating all components. In particular, we observe that the COVID-19 generalized knowledge facts significantly contribute to the detection performance of HC-COVID. The reason is that COVID-19 generalized knowledge facts not only contain the summarized knowledge facts about COVID-19 from COVID-19 articles but also allow HC-COVID to identify incorrect content that has not appeared in existing COVID-19 articles.

6.3.2 Explainable Fauxtography Detection

We conduct extensive experiments on a real-world dataset to study the performance of DExFC and compare it with state-of-the-art solutions. Evaluation results show that DExFC not only achieves significant performance gains in the accuracy of fauxtography detection but also generates more relevant and coherent cross-modal explanations, demonstrating the effectiveness of its modality-aware dual explanation mechanism with constrained supervision.

Table 6.6 Dataset summary

Type	Claim	Image	Post	Comment
Non-fauxtography	True	True	150	27,125
Fauxtography	False	False	32	3395
	True	False	38	4835
	False	True	62	7045
	True	True	21	1826
	ALL	ALL	153	17,101

6.3.2.1 Data

We create a real-world dataset by collecting social media posts from Twitter and Reddit, both of which are widely used online social platforms that contain a good amount of fauxtography posts [47]. In particular, we first collect a set of social media posts from three independent fact-checking websites (i.e., snopes.com, factcheck.org, truthorfiction.com). We then assign three different annotators to manually verify the labels from the fact-checking websites. We also utilize Google Vision API[1] for reverse search on the image of the post to obtain the corresponding URLs of the images. If a URL points to a post on Twitter or Reddit, we crawl the text description, image, and comments of the post using a crawler script we developed. For each post in the collected dataset, we ask the annotators to further check if the text description and the image components are false and record their decisions (1 for false and 0 for true). We use majority voting on the annotations to decide the final labels of all components of the post [46]. The social media posts in the new dataset are crawled from different social media platforms (e.g., Twitter, Reddit). It covers all types of fauxtography posts in Fig. 6.2 to ensure the trained model is capable of identifying various incorrect information embedded in the fauxtography posts across different social media platforms. Moreover, the newly added social media posts are all recent ones posted in 2020, which demonstrates the capability of the model in terms of identifying the recent fauxtography posts. The summary of the dataset is shown in Table 6.6.

6.3.2.2 Baseline Methods and Experimental Setting

Baseline Methods

We compare the performance of DExFC with the following state-of-the-art baselines.

- **FxBuster** [47]: FxBuster is a fauxtography detection tool that detects the fauxtography posts by exploring the comments from readers of the posts.

[1] https://cloud.google.com/vision.

- **FCMF** [50]: FCMF is a fauxtography detector that identifies fauxtography posts by exploring the image URLs and hand-crafted text features of the posts.
- **ExFaux** [26]: ExFaux is an explainable fauxtography detection method. Compared to DExFC with an adjustable constraint set to perform both content and comment explainability, the ExFaux can only work with an empty constraint set (i.e., weakly supervised) and provide only the content explainability.
- **AIFN** [44]: AIFN develops a gated neural network for truth discovery by fusing text and comments based on a multi-head attention mechanism.
- **EANN** [42]: EANN is a recent truth discovery scheme that handles multi-modal content with convolution filters and applies an adversarial loss function to make the model event-invariant.
- **DEAN** [16]: DEAN leverages both text content and comments to distinguish truthful news from the false ones by employing two independent recurrent neural networks and a fully connected layer for the truth discovery task.
- **HAN** [45]: HAN constructs a hierarchical attention neural network from word level to sentence level to assess the truthfulness of news. It can not only accomplish the truth assessment of news but also explain why a news post is fake by pointing out relevant sentences in the news.
- **MVAE** [22]: MVAE develops a variational autoencoder neural network for truth discovery by learning a shared representation of multimodal content of posts.
- **HPA** [17]: HPA segments user engagements (e.g., user comments) in social media to different levels and constructs an attention neural network to detect rumors. The generated attention scores can help to explain why a post is a rumor by indicating rumor-related comments.
- **dEFEND** [36]: dEFEND assesses the truthfulness of news by applying a co-attention strategy to retrieve relevant sentences from both text content and comments that offer the potential reasons for the detection.

We adapt the above baselines to solve the problem in a way that ensures all schemes take the same inputs for a fair comparison. For the methods that utilize only text content, such as HAN, DEAN, DEFEND, and AIFN, we let them treat the image in the dataset as a new feature in addition to the text in their models. For EANN, we remove the adversarial loss function because it needs additional annotations that the dataset does not contain. We strictly follow the parameters and configurations of all schemes as documented in their papers.

Experimental Setting

In the experiments, the dataset is split into a *train-val set* and a *test set*. The *train-val* set contains 80% data samples and the *test set* contains the other 20%. We perform 10-fold cross-validation on *train-val* set to tune the network parameters of all schemes and evaluate them on the *test set*. For the implementation details of DExFC, the GCN network in the DGCN holds 2 layers with each layer followed by *ReLU* activation. We empirically set the size (i.e., K) of the constraint set $\mathbb{P}^G$ as 8 and tune K in the evaluation. We resize the input images to 256×256 and randomly crop them to 224×224 to prevent the overfitting issue for training. For testing, we directly resize images to 224×224. We set the total number of epochs as 40 and train the model with an initial learning rate of 0.001 and decay of 0.95 in each epoch. The optimizer is Adam with 5×10^{-4} weight decay. We run the experiments on Ubuntu 16.04 with two NVIDIA 1080Ti.

To evaluate DExFC and the state-of-the-art schemes, we conduct several experiment tasks with different evaluation metrics. We first evaluate the fauxtography detection performance of all compared schemes by leveraging four classic evaluation metrics: *F1-Score*, *Accuracy*, *Precision* and *Recall*. Then, we evaluate the explainability performance of the compared schemes in terms of explaining *which* component of a detected fauxtography post is false by using *Accuracy* metric. Additionally, we evaluate the compared schemes by explaining *why* the detected post is fauxtography by using the *list-wise* comparison [36] and *minimum read index*. Finally, we carry out ablation studies to investigate the contribution of different modules in DExFC by applying *F1-Score* and *Accuracy* as evaluation metrics. We elaborate on the above experiments in detail below.

6.3.2.3 Fauxtography Detection

In the first set of experiments, we focus on the overall performance of all schemes in terms of fauxtography detection. We use the classic evaluation metrics for binary-class classification: *F1-Score*, *Accuracy*, *Precision*, and *Recall*. The results are reported in Table 6.7. We observe that DExFC significantly outperforms all baselines. For example, DExFC is able to achieve an 11.1% higher F-1 score than dEDEND, one of the state-of-the-art explainable truth discovery approaches. The reason is that the dual graph convolutional network design in the DGCN effectively refines the representations of both content and comments of the input

Table 6.7 Fauxtography detection performance

Methods	F1 score	Accuracy	Precision	Recall
FxBuster	0.739	0.721	0.686	0.800
FCMF	0.667	0.705	0.750	0.600
HAN	0.714	0.738	0.769	0.667
HPA	0.737	0.754	0.778	0.700
EANN	0.767	0.721	0.651	0.933
DEAN	0.789	0.754	0.683	0.933
dEFEND	0.781	0.771	0.735	0.833
AIFN	0.772	0.787	0.815	0.733
MVAE	0.708	0.689	0.657	0.767
ExFaux	0.794	0.771	0.711	0.900
DExFC	**0.892**	**0.885**	**0.829**	**0.967**

The bold values indicate the best performing results in each evaluation metric

Table 6.8 Content explainability of fauxtography detection

Methods	Overall	Text only	Image only
HAN	0.600	0.367	0.400
dEFEND	0.567	0.500	0.200
ExFaux	0.633	0.333	0.500
DExFC	**0.767**	**0.500**	**0.533**

The bold values indicate the best performing results in each evaluation metric

post by connecting all of them with a novel tow-level multimodal graph structure. More importantly, we also observe that DExFC is superior to ExFaux.For example, DExFC outperforms ExFaux on F1-score and Accuracy by 9.8 and 11.4%, respectively. This is because the DExFC scheme develops a metric-based optimization strategy in the MGR module to generate meta-representations from posts in the constrained set, which improves the effectiveness of fauxtography identification. Moreover, unlike the traditional attention mechanism used in ExFaux that only considers the content component of the input post, we develop a multimodal co-attention module in DExFC to fully explore the internal relations between content and comments of a post, which also improves its performance of fauxtography detection.

6.3.2.4 Content Explainability

In the second experiment, we study the performance of DExFC in terms of identifying false component(s) in the detected fauxtography posts (i.e., content explainability). In this experiment, we select HAN, dEFEND, and ExFaux for comparison because they are the only baselines that can generate attention scores for the content of posts, which can be used for explanations. The evaluation results are presented in Table 6.8. In Table 6.8, the *Overall* metric evaluates if a scheme can at least determine the truthfulness of either the text or image component of the fauxtography posts correctly. The *Text Only* metric evaluates if a scheme can correctly determine the truthfulness of the text component. Similarly, the *Image Only* metric evaluates if a scheme can correctly determine the truthfulness of the image component. We observe that DExFC outperforms all baselines in identifying the false component(s) of a fauxtography post. For example, DExFC achieves 13.4, 16.7, and 20.0% higher overall accuracy than ExFaux, HAN, and dEFEND on the overall metric, respectively. The above results validate the hypothesis that the MCA module of the design can provide better representations for content features, which significantly improves the content explainability accuracy of the DExFC framework. The visualization of explainable results of DExFC is shown in Fig. 6.10.

Fig. 6.10 Visualization of explanation results of DExFC. For content explainability, the DExFC identifies the false component(s): the cross mark indicates the corresponding component is false and the check mark indicates it is true. For comment explainability, the DExFC ranks the users' comments based on their likelihood to explain the false component(s) of a post. We show the top three comments identified by DExFC in each post in this example. (**a**) False Text and False Image (**b**) False Text and True Image (**c**) True Text and False Image (**d**) True Text and True Image

6.3.2.5 Comment Explainability

In the third experiment, we study how effectively the DExFC can retrieve the relevant user comments to explain why the identified component(s) of a post is false (i.e., comment explainability). In particular, we carry out a real-world user study using AMT. In the experiment, we recruited AMT workers with an approval rate > 0.95. We set the payment to workers well above the minimum requirement from AMT [2]. We select a test set that contains the fauxtography posts with different fauxtography types for the experiment. For each testing post, we compare the results of DExFC with two other baselines (i.e., DEFEND and HPA) because they are the only baselines that are capable of providing comment explanations on their results. We collect the attention scores from all compared schemes and then rank the user comments on the post based on the scores in descending order. For example, the comments in the posts of Fig. 6.10 are ranked by the attention scores from DExFC. The higher a comment ranks, the more likely it can explain why the post is fauxtography.

We design several AMT tasks to evaluate the comment explainability of all compared schemes. In particular, we first perform a *list-wise* comparison [36] to evaluate the explainability quality of the comment lists ranked by different schemes. For each testing post, each compared scheme generates three types of comment lists that contain Top-1, Top-3, and Top-5 comments from all the comments sorted by the corresponding attention scores. Given each type of the generated comment lists by all compared schemes, we ask four AMT crowd workers to pick the best comment list that they believe can explain why the post is identified as fauxtography. If there exists more than one highest vote, we ask more workers to vote on it until only one comment list receives the highest votes. We adopt two evaluation metrics from dEFEND [36] to study the performance of DExFC and the baselines as below.

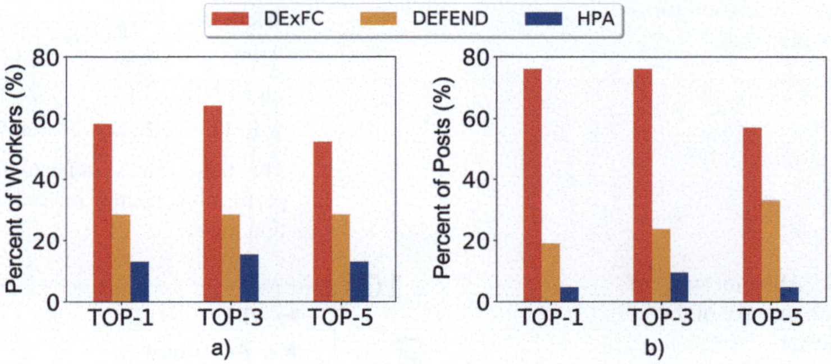

Fig. 6.11 Listwise comment explainability evaluation. (**a**) Worker level listwise evaluation. (**b**) Post level listwise evaluation

- **Worker Level Evaluation**: the worker level evaluation denotes the percentage of workers who select their preferred comment list generated by each scheme. For example, given 10 fauxtography posts, if there are totally 25 crowd workers choosing DExFC as the best explainable scheme for the post, the percentage of Workers for DExFC is $\frac{25}{10\times4} = 62.5\%$.
- **Post Level Evaluation**: the post level evaluation denotes the percentage of posts whose comment list is picked by the majority of workers as their preferred ones belonging to each scheme. For example, given an input fauxtography post, if three or more crowd workers believe that the post is best explained by the comment list from the DEFEND scheme, we assign DEFEND as the best explainable scheme to the post."

The results are shown in Fig. 6.11. We observe that DExFC outperforms the compared baselines on both evaluation metrics. We attribute the significant performance gains of the DExFC framework to its dual multimodal graph convolutional networks and co-attention module design that explicitly explores both direct and indirect relations hidden in the user's comments.

To further investigate the efficiency of the comment explainability of DExFC, we did an additional experiment to study how many top comments in the ranked list a user has to read before she/he decides the post is fauxtography. In particular, we ask each AMT worker to read the user comment list of a post ranked by a scheme from the top to end and stop reading if the worker feels comfortable to make a decision on whether the post is fauxtography. We then ask the worker to document the number of comments she/he reads in order to make the decision. We define this recorded number as the *minimum read index (MRI)*. We focus on two evaluation metrics as below.

- **Average Minimum Reading Index** (AvgMRI): The average value of MRI for each compared scheme.

Table 6.9 Evaluation for minimum read index

Methods	AvgMRI	% of posts
HPA	3.46	13.0
dEFEND	3.13	26.1
DExFC	**2.54**	**60.9**

The bold values indicate the best performing results in each evaluation metric

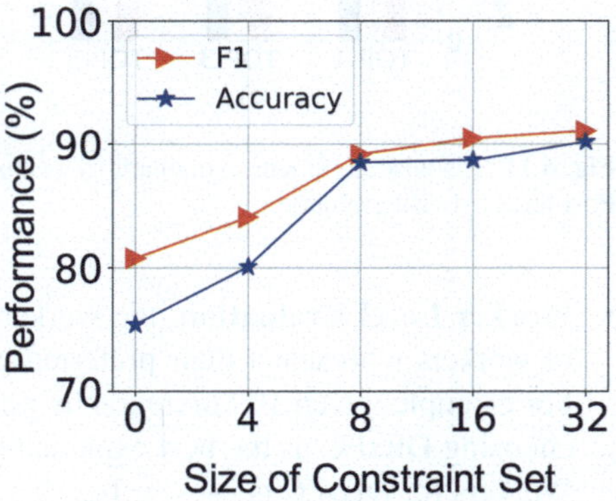

Fig. 6.12 Ablation study of DExFC on the size of the constraint set

- **Percentage of Posts** (% of Posts): The percentage of posts on which each compared scheme achieves the lowest MRI.

The results are reported in Table 6.9. We observe that DExFC outperforms the compared baselines on both evaluation metrics. In particular, the users of DExFC only have to read less than 3 comments on average to detect a fauxtography post and more than 60% of the posts can be detected by DExFC with the smallest AvgMRI.

6.3.2.6 Ablation Study

Finally, we perform a comprehensive *ablation study* to study the contribution of each important component of DExFC. In particular, we first investigate the effect of the size of the constraint set on the performance of DExFC. The results are shown in Fig. 6.12. We observe that the non-empty constraint set can clearly help to improve the performance of the DExFC framework and the performance gain stabilizes when the size of the constrained set reaches 8, which indicates a very affordable labeling cost of the solution (i.e., only 8 posts with modality-level labels are needed for DExFC to reach its optimized performance).

We then create different variants of the DExFC framework by removing its key components: (1) DEx-base: we remove the dual graph neural networks and modality-level discriminators; (2) DEx-graph-1v: we remove the modality-level discriminators and also change the dual graph to one-level (i.e., only use the direct replies in comments), and (3) DEx-graph-2v: we only remove the modality-level

Table 6.10 Ablation study of DExFC on overall detection

Methods	F1 score	Accuracy	Precision	Recall
DEx-base	0.746	0.721	0.676	0.833
DEx-graph-1v	0.806	0.787	0.730	0.900
DEx-graph-2v	0.844	0.836	0.794	0.900
DExFC	**0.892**	**0.885**	**0.829**	**0.967**

The bold values indicate the best performing results in each evaluation metric

discriminators. The fauxtography detection results are shown in Table 6.10. We observe that, by adding the one-level graph neural networks, DExFC is able to increase its F-1 score and Accuracy score by 6.0 and 6.6%, respectively. This result illustrates the importance of connecting content and comments with the dual graph structures. The two-level design that involves indirect comment connections also contributes to 3.8 and 4.9% in F-1 score and accuracy score, respectively. Furthermore, we also found the modality-level discriminators are helpful, which yield 4.8 and 4.9% higher F-1 score and Accuracy score improvement, respectively.

6.4 Discussion

This chapter presented two novel frameworks for explainable AI in social intelligence applications: HC-COVID and DExFC. These frameworks address fundamental challenges in developing explainable social intelligence systems, including the varied knowledge fact quality for explanation, lack of modality-level annotation, and diverse cross-modal explanation. Extensive experiments on principle social intelligence case studies, such as uni-modal truth discovery classification and multi-modal fauxtography detection, demonstrate how combining structured knowledge, crowdsourced human intelligence, and advanced neural network architectures can advance both the accuracy and explainability of AI systems in social intelligence.

While the case studies primarily focus on the detection and explanation of uni-modal and multimodal false information, we envision the generalizability of the proposed frameworks to broader social intelligence applications where explainability is crucial. For example, various COVID-19-related applications can leverage the knowledge facts in the hierarchical knowledge graph of HC-COVID to improve their application-specific performance. In particular, the machine learning-based COVID-19 diagnosis approaches [1, 12, 51] can utilize hierarchical knowledge graphs to boost their diagnosis accuracy. The COVID-19 diagnosis approaches usually consider the COVID-19 symptoms (e.g., "fever", "cough") as important features to determine COVID-19 infection of participants. However, it is difficult for the approaches to estimate the complex relations between various COVID-19 symptoms and the COVID-19 infection, especially when the data samples are insufficient. HC-COVID can address the problem by explicitly retrieving COVID-19 knowledge facts from the hierarchical knowledge graph that are relevant to COVID-19 symptoms (e.g., "fever" $\xrightarrow{\text{close relation to}}$ "COVID-19", "cough" $\xrightarrow{\text{cause}}$ "COVID-19"). The COVID-19 symptoms and the corresponding COVID-19 knowledge facts can be integrated into more informative features for more accurate COVID-19 diagnosis.

Moreover, the overall framework of HC-COVID can be generalized to address different classification problems that require professional knowledge to perform classification and explanation tasks. For example, William *et al.* [6] designed a human-machine system to classify human heart records by assigning expert crowd workers and non-expert workers together to perform the classification task. However, assigning expert workers the same classification task as the non-expert workers is not always effective due to either the lack of available expert workers or the lack of professional medical knowledge of non-expert workers. HC-COVID can address such a problem by tasking the expert workers to propose generalized medical knowledge facts that are specific to this application (e.g., the characteristics of abnormal heart records) and tasking non-expert workers to identify the abnormal heart records that satisfy the proposed characteristics by the expert workers. A human heart-related knowledge graph constructed using input from expert workers can effectively guide non-expert workers in identifying abnormal heart records and provide explicit explanations for the classification results.

Similarly, DExFC's modality-aware explanation mechanism can be extended to various multimodal social intelligence applications beyond fauxtography detection. For instance, in a disaster response system that analyzes both satellite imagery data and social media feeds, DExFC's dual graph structure can effectively model the relationship between visual evidence of damage and textual descriptions from affected communities. The framework's ability to work with limited modality-level annotations is particularly valuable in time-sensitive disaster scenarios where obtaining detailed annotations is impractical. Furthermore, DExFC's approach to generating cross-modal explanations could enhance social recommendation systems that leverage both user-generated content and visual information. For example, in e-commerce recommendation systems, the framework could explain product recommendations by highlighting relevant visual features and connecting them to user reviews and comments, while requiring minimal supervised modality-level training data.

With the recent advancement of large language and vision models, we highlight several opportunities to further enhance XAI in social intelligence. For example, large language models could be helpful in the initial construction and maintenance of knowledge graphs by suggesting potential entities and their relations that could be further validated by expert workers. Similarly, the advanced visual and textual understanding capabilities of large language vision models could be integrated with DExFC or other multimodal explainable social intelligence frameworks to improve the multimodal feature extraction process which often requires extensive pre-training on domain-specific datasets. We envision that the integration of large language and vision models with explainable social intelligence frameworks could lead to more robust and adaptable solutions while maintaining interpretability.

References

1. N. Alballa and I. Al-Turaiki. Machine learning approaches in covid-19 diagnosis, mortality, and severity risk prediction: A review. *Informatics in Medicine Unlocked*, page 100564, 2021.
2. Amazon. Pricing of amazon mechanical turk, 2022.
3. AMT, https://www.mturk.com/.
4. P. P. Angelov, E. A. Soares, R. Jiang, N. I. Arnold, and P. M. Atkinson. Explainable artificial intelligence: an analytical review. *Wiley Interdisciplinary Reviews: Data Mining and Knowledge Discovery*, 11(5):e1424, 2021.
5. M. Azmy, P. Shi, J. Lin, and I. F. Ilyas. Matching entities across different knowledge graphs with graph embeddings. *arXiv preprint arXiv:1903.06607*, 2019.
6. W. Callaghan, J. Goh, M. Mohareb, A. Lim, and E. Law. Mechanicalheart: A human-machine framework for the classification of phonocardiograms. *Proceedings of the ACM on Human-Computer Interaction*, 2(CSCW):1–17, 2018.
7. S. Chandra, L. Khan, and F. B. Muhaya. Estimating twitter user location using social interactions–a content based approach. In *2011 IEEE Third International Conference on Privacy, Security, Risk and Trust and 2011 IEEE Third International Conference on Social Computing*, pages 838–843, 2011.
8. J. C. Chang, S. Amershi, and E. Kamar. Revolt: Collaborative crowdsourcing for labeling machine learning datasets. In *Proceedings of the 2017 CHI Conference on Human Factors in Computing Systems*, pages 2334–2346, 2017.
9. L.-A. Cougnon, J. Coppin, and V. G. Figueroa. A mixed quantitative-qualitative approach to disagreement in online news comments on social networking sites. *Social Media Corpora for the Humanities (CMC-Corpora2019)*, 31–35, 2019.
10. L. Cui and D. Lee. Coaid: Covid-19 healthcare misinformation dataset, 2020.
11. L. Cui, H. Seo, M. Tabar, F. Ma, S. Wang, and D. Lee. Deterrent: Knowledge guided graph attention network for detecting healthcare misinformation. In *Proceedings of the 26th ACM SIGKDD International Conference on Knowledge Discovery & Data Mining*, pages 492–502, 2020.
12. A. F. de Moraes Batista, J. L. Miraglia, T. H. R. Donato, and A. D. P. Chiavegatto Filho. Covid-19 diagnosis prediction in emergency care patients: a machine learning approach. *medRxiv*, 2020.
13. R. Dey and F. M. Salem. Gate-variants of gated recurrent unit (gru) neural networks. In *2017 IEEE 60th international midwest symposium on circuits and systems (MWSCAS)*, pages 1597–1600. IEEE, 2017.
14. D. Domingo-Fernández, S. Baksi, B. Schultz, Y. Gadiya, R. Karki, T. Raschka, C. Ebeling, M. Hofmann-Apitius, et al. Covid-19 knowledge graph: a computable, multi-modal, cause-and-effect knowledge model of covid-19 pathophysiology. *BioRxiv*, 2020.
15. A. Founta, C. Djouvas, D. Chatzakou, I. Leontiadis, J. Blackburn, G. Stringhini, A. Vakali, M. Sirivianos, and N. Kourtellis. Large scale crowdsourcing and characterization of twitter abusive behavior. In *Proceedings of the International AAAI Conference on Web and Social Media*, volume 12, 2018.
16. C. Guo, J. Cao, X. Zhang, K. Shu, and H. Liu. Dean: Learning dual emotion for fake news detection on social media. *arXiv e-prints*, pages arXiv–1903, 2019.
17. H. Guo, J. Cao, Y. Zhang, J. Guo, and J. Li. Rumor detection with hierarchical social attention network. In *Proceedings of the 27th ACM International Conference on Information and Knowledge Management*, CIKM '18, pages 943–951, New York, NY, USA, 2018. Association for Computing Machinery.
18. K. He, X. Zhang, S. Ren, and J. Sun. Deep residual learning for image recognition. *CoRR*, abs/1512.03385, 2015.
19. E. Hoffer and N. Ailon. Deep metric learning using triplet network. In *International workshop on similarity-based pattern recognition*, pages 84–92. Springer, 2015.

20. S. A. Khan, S. M. D. Khalid, M. A. Shahzad, and F. Shafait. Table structure extraction with bi-directional gated recurrent unit networks. In *2019 International Conference on Document Analysis and Recognition (ICDAR)*, pages 1366–1371. IEEE, 2019.
21. D. Khattar, J. S. Goud, M. Gupta, and V. Varma. Mvae: Multimodal variational autoencoder for fake news detection. In *The world wide web conference*, pages 2915–2921, New York, NY, USA, 2019. ACM.
22. D. Khattar, J. S. Goud, M. Gupta, and V. Varma. Mvae: Multimodal variational autoencoder for fake news detection. In *The World Wide Web Conference*, WWW '19, pages 2915–2921, New York, NY, USA, 2019. Association for Computing Machinery.
23. L. M. S. Khoo, H. L. Chieu, Z. Qian, and J. Jiang. Interpretable rumor detection in microblogs by attending to user interactions. In *Proceedings of the AAAI Conference on Artificial Intelligence*, volume 34, pages 8783–8790, 2020.
24. Z. Kou, L. Shang, Y. Zhang, and D. Wang. Hc-covid: A hierarchical crowdsource knowledge graph approach to explainable covid-19 misinformation detection. *Proceedings of the ACM on Human-Computer Interaction*, 6(GROUP):1–25, 2022. https://doi.org/10.1145/3492855.
25. Z. Kou, D. Zhang, L. Shang, and D. Wang. What and why? towards duo explainable fauxtography detection under constrained supervision. *IEEE Transactions on Big Data*, 9(1):133–146, 2023, https://doi.org/10.1109/TBDATA.2021.3130165.
26. Z. Kou, D. Y. Zhang, L. Shang, and D. Wang. Exfaux: A weakly supervised approach to explainable fauxtography detection. In *Proceedings of IEEE BigData 2020*, 2020.
27. P. Lara-Navarra, H. Falciani, E. A. Sánchez-Pérez, and A. Ferrer-Sapena. Information management in healthcare and environment: Towards an automatic system for fake news detection. *International journal of environmental research and public health*, 17(3):1066, 2020.
28. Y. Nirkin, L. Wolf, Y. Keller, and T. Hassner. Deepfake detection based on the discrepancy between the face and its context. *arXiv e-prints*, pages arXiv–2008, 2020.
29. P. Patwa, M. Bhardwaj, V. Guptha, G. Kumari, S. Sharma, S. PYKL, A. Das, A. Ekbal, S. Akhtar, and T. Chakraborty. Overview of constraint 2021 shared tasks: Detecting english covid-19 fake news and hindi hostile posts. In *Proceedings of the First Workshop on Combating Online Hostile Posts in Regional Languages during Emergency Situation (CONSTRAINT)*. Springer, 2021.
30. V. Pérez-Rosas, B. Kleinberg, A. Lefevre, and R. Mihalcea. Automatic detection of fake news. *arXiv preprint arXiv:1708.07104*, 2017.
31. R. Pierrard, J.-P. Poli, and C. Hudelot. A new approach for explainable multiple organ annotation with few data. In *IJCAI 2019 Workshop on Explainable Artificial Intelligence (XAI)*, 2019.
32. R. Ramanath, F. Schaub, S. Wilson, F. Liu, N. Sadeh, and N. Smith. Identifying relevant text fragments to help crowdsource privacy policy annotations. In *Proceedings of the AAAI Conference on Human Computation and Crowdsourcing*, volume 2, 2014.
33. M. Schlichtkrull, T. N. Kipf, P. Bloem, R. van den Berg, I. Titov, and M. Welling. Modeling relational data with graph convolutional networks, 2017.
34. L. See, A. Comber, C. Salk, S. Fritz, M. Van Der Velde, C. Perger, C. Schill, I. McCallum, F. Kraxner, and M. Obersteiner. Comparing the quality of crowdsourced data contributed by expert and non-experts. *PloS one*, 8(7):e69958, 2013.
35. L. Shang, Y. Zhang, D. Zhang, and D. Wang. Fauxward: a graph neural network approach to fauxtography detection using social media comments. *Social Network Analysis and Mining*, 10:1–16, 2020.
36. K. Shu, L. Cui, S. Wang, D. Lee, and H. Liu. defend: Explainable fake news detection. In *Proceedings of the 25th ACM SIGKDD international conference on knowledge discovery & data mining*, pages 395–405, 2019.
37. K. Shu, D. Mahudeswaran, S. Wang, and H. Liu. Hierarchical propagation networks for fake news detection: Investigation and exploitation. In *Proceedings of the International AAAI Conference on Web and Social Media*, volume 14, pages 626–637, 2020.

38. K. Shu, S. Wang, and H. Liu. Beyond news contents: The role of social context for fake news detection. In *Proceedings of the twelfth ACM international conference on web search and data mining*, 2019.
39. M. Someswar and A. Bhattacharya. Minear: using crowd knowledge for mining association rules in the health domain. In *Proceedings of the ACM India Joint International Conference on Data Science and Management of Data*, pages 108–117, 2018.
40. D. Wang, T. Abdelzaher, and L. Kaplan. *Social sensing: building reliable systems on unreliable data*. Morgan Kaufmann, 2015.
41. D. Wang, T. Abdelzaher, L. Kaplan, and C. C. Aggarwal. Recursive fact-finding: A streaming approach to truth estimation in crowdsourcing applications. In *2013 IEEE 33rd international conference on distributed computing systems*, pages 530–539. IEEE, 2013.
42. Y. Wang, F. Ma, Z. Jin, Y. Yuan, G. Xun, K. Jha, L. Su, and J. Gao. Eann: Event adversarial neural networks for multi-modal fake news detection. In *Proceedings of the 24th ACM SIGKDD International Conference on Knowledge Discovery & Data Mining*, KDD '18, pages 849–857, New York, NY, USA, 2018.
43. Y. Wang, S. Qian, J. Hu, Q. Fang, and C. Xu. Fake news detection via knowledge-driven multimodal graph convolutional networks. In *Proceedings of the 2020 International Conference on Multimedia Retrieval*, pages 540–547, 2020.
44. L. Wu and Y. Rao. Adaptive interaction fusion networks for fake news detection. In *ECAI 2020*, pages 2220–2227. IOS Press, 2020.
45. Z. Yang, D. Yang, C. Dyer, X. He, A. Smola, and E. Hovy. Hierarchical attention networks for document classification. In *Proceedings of the 2016 conference of the North American chapter of the association for computational linguistics: human language technologies*, pages 1480–1489, 2016.
46. D. Zhang, T. Rashid, X. Li, N. Vance, and D. Wang. Heteroedge: taming the heterogeneity of edge computing system in social sensing. In *Proceedings of the International Conference on Internet of Things Design and Implementation*, pages 37–48, 2019.
47. D. Zhang, L. Shang, B. Geng, S. Lai, K. Li, H. Zhu, T. Amin, and D. Wang. Fauxbuster: A content-free fauxtography detector using social media comments. In *Proceedings of IEEE BigData 2018*, 2018.
48. D. Y. Zhang, Y. Huang, Y. Zhang, and D. Wang. Crowd-assisted disaster scene assessment with human-ai interactive attention. In *Proceedings of the AAAI Conference on Artificial Intelligence*, volume 34, pages 2717–2724, 2020.
49. D. Y. Zhang, L. Shang, B. Geng, S. Lai, K. Li, H. Zhu, M. T. Amin, and D. Wang. Fauxbuster: A content-free fauxtography detector using social media comments. In *2018 IEEE international conference on big data (big data)*, pages 891–900. IEEE, 2018.
50. D. Zlatkova, P. Nakov, and I. Koychev. Fact-checking meets fauxtography: Verifying claims about images. In *Proceedings of the 2019 Conference on Empirical Methods in Natural Language Processing and the 9th International Joint Conference on Natural Language Processing (EMNLP-IJCNLP)*, pages 2099–2108, Hong Kong, China, Nov. 2019. Association for Computational Linguistics.
51. Y. Zoabi, S. Deri-Rozov, and N. Shomron. Machine learning-based prediction of covid-19 diagnosis based on symptoms. *npj digital medicine*, 4(1):1–5, 2021.

Chapter 7
Fusing Crowd Wisdom and AI

Abstract Human-AI collaboration is a transformative approach in advancing AI-driven applications, combining artificial intelligence and human expertise to address complex problems. This chapter presents collaborative frameworks that enable the integration of human intelligence from crowdsourcing systems into the AI process, overcoming critical challenges such as large design search spaces and managing imperfect crowd-sourced data. Specifically, we present two case studies: (1) *CrowdNAS*, a crowd-guided neural architecture search framework for disaster damage assessment, which uses crowd inputs to identify optimal network architectures for accurate damage severity estimation, and (2) *CrowdOptim*, a crowd-driven hyperparameter optimization framework for AI-based smart urban sensing applications, which leverages crowdsourced feedback to enhance model performance in assessing urban environments. These frameworks and case studies demonstrate the power of collaborative frameworks in guiding AI optimization and neural architecture discovery, showing how crowd-AI systems can achieve high accuracy while reducing computational demands, paving the way for robust human-centered AI applications across dynamic and data-intensive environments.

Keywords Crowd-AI · Human-AI collaboration · Neural architecture search · Hyperparameter optimization · Crowdsourcing · Disaster response · Urban sensing

7.1 Challenges in Human-AI Collaboration for Architecture Search and Model Optimization

AI systems are primarily designed and optimized through two primary approaches: neural architecture search (NAS) and hyperparameter optimization (HPO). NAS automates the selection of efficient neural network (NN) structures and HPO optimizes parameters such as learning rates or epoch numbers to boost the model performance. Such methods are essential for the development of AI models but are computationally intensive and limited by manual effort and expertise [31]. The challenges in balancing computational costs, scalability, and optimal performance have led to increasing interest in combining human intuition and expertise with

D. Wang et al., *Social Intelligence*, https://doi.org/10.1007/978-3-031-90080-8_7

machine-driven processes. Human-AI synergy opens novel avenues for overcoming these problems in NAS and HPO. In particular, human inputs can help refine search spaces, incorporate domain-specific knowledge, and guide the prioritization of promising architectures or parameter configurations, which may not be immediately evident to automated methods. By leveraging human insights, NAS and HPO processes can become more efficient, adaptive, and better aligned with real-world constraints. The choice of an effective neural network (NN) architecture, along with the tuning of hyperparameters such as learning rate or epoch count, can significantly impact model performance. Despite the importance of NAS and HPO, many current methods still depend on manual tuning by AI specialists, which is a time-intensive and error-prone process [16]. This chapter presents human-AI collaborative frameworks that automate the configurations of neural architecture and hyperparameters, minimizing the need for expert intervention while achieving optimized performance across diverse applications. By integrating crowd-sourced human intelligence with AI-driven NAS and HPO approaches, this chapter focuses on presenting SI collaborative frameworks in guiding AI optimization and neural architecture discovery [47, 48]. This chapter addresses three core challenges in fusing crowd intelligence with AI to enable scalable and efficient model design and optimization across varied application domains. We discuss these challenges in detail below.

Crowd-manageable Design Space

The first challenge lies in effectively translating the highly complex tasks of both NAS and HPO in AI into simplified problems that can be managed by crowd workers without extensive AI expertise. Unlike AI specialists, who can provide insights into setting optimal values for each hyperparameter and architecture component in an AI model, crowd workers are typically limited to simpler annotation tasks (e.g., assessing the physical status of urban environments in assigned images)[27]. A straightforward approach to address the combined NAS and HPO problem might involve exhaustively seeking feedback from crowd workers on every possible configuration of both the architecture and hyperparameters for the AI model on each image to identify the optimal setup. However, this method is costly and time-intensive due to the massive search space, which could potentially exceed 100 million configurations for hyperparameters alone in deep convolutional networks applied to social intelligence applications[8]. Current solutions in both NAS and HPO often rely on heuristic search strategies to explore this vast space efficiently [20]. While effective, these strategies are computationally intensive [11], and the learned configurations risk overfitting to the validation set, resulting in non-negligible performance loss when applied to new test data [26]. Therefore, a key question remains: how can we design a search space that is manageable for crowd workers but still likely to contain the optimal configurations for both NAS and HPO in social intelligence applications?

Black-box NAS and HPO

The second challenge lies in how to effectively identify the optimal combination of neural network architecture and hyperparameter configuration within a crowd-manageable search space, given the black-box nature of AI models. Specifically, the limited interpretability of outputs generated by different architectures and hyper-parameter configurations in social intelligence applications makes it challenging to accurately pinpoint the best setup in the absence of ground-truth labels [10]. This challenge arises because, without ground-truth labels, it is very challenging to objectively evaluate and compare the performance of different configurations, making it difficult to determine whether variations in performance are caused by differences in model effectiveness, noise in the data, or stochastic variability. Recent advancements in crowd-AI collaborative systems have attempted to address this black-box issue by focusing on selecting complex imagery data (e.g., images with intricate color distributions or densely packed objects) for crowd labeling, based on the assumption that AI models are more prone to errors with such challenging data [33, 45]. By analyzing the discrepancies between AI predictions and human-generated labels on these challenging samples, the current approaches identify specific failure modes and enhance interpretability by linking errors to particular model behaviors or data characteristics [13]. Crowd-sourced labels on features like the physical condition of urban environments (e.g., levels of infrastructure damage) are then used to retrain AI models or to replace their outputs, thereby optimizing the overall model performance. Therefore, the black-box nature of AI models presents a critical challenge to crowd-driven optimization of both NAS and HPO in social intelligence applications.

Crowd-guided NAS and HPO

The third challenge lies in leveraging potentially imperfect crowd intelligence to address both crowd-guided NAS and HPO in social intelligence applications. Unlike AI experts, who can directly offer guidance on designing effective neural network architectures (e.g., by suggesting layer modifications) and fine-tuning hyperparameters, crowd workers are often limited to providing simpler annotations, such as damage severity assessment labels for disaster-related images. A key question in the system design is how to translate these crowd-sourced labels into meaningful decisions for both optimizing neural network architecture and setting hyperparameters within a social intelligence application. Furthermore, unlike labels annotated by domain specialists, crowd-generated labels are often imperfect-subject to bias, noise, and even internal conflict [15]. These imperfections can significantly hinder the optimization for both NAS and HPO, as noisy crowd inputs may be recursively amplified during the optimization process, potentially resulting in suboptimal architecture and parameter choices [51]. Therefore, a critical challenge remains: how can we effectively leverage imperfect crowd intelligence to reliably identify the optimal neural network architecture and hyperparameter configuration in social intelligence applications?

To address the above challenges, this chapter introduces two SI frameworks: CrowdNAS, a crowd-guided NAS approach, and CrowdOptim, a crowd-driven HPO system. Both frameworks leverage crowd wisdom to enhance AI systems' scalability (e.g., handling large-scale false information across platforms) and adaptability (e.g., adjusting to dynamic conditions in disaster damage assessment). By combining design space transformations, robust learning frameworks, and crowd-driven knowledge transfer, these systems illustrate the potential for human-AI collaboration to optimize models and architectures in real-world, high-stakes human-centered AI applications. In the rest of this chapter, we will review the design of the crowd-AI solutions and the real-world case studies to evaluate the performance of these solutions. We will conclude this chapter with a discussion on the implications of the reviewed crowd-AI solutions and future work to address their limitations.

7.2 A Crowd-AI Co-Design: CrowdNAS and CrowdOptim

In this section, we present two novel crowd-AI collaborative frameworks, CrowdNAS (Crowd-guided Neural Network Architecture Search) [47] and CrowdOptim (Crowd-driven Neural Network Hyperparameter Optimization) [48], designed to address the challenges of integrating human intelligence into AI model optimization and architecture search. Specifically, CrowdNAS employs a crowd-guided neural architecture search approach that harnesses crowd input to identify optimal neural network architectures for effective disaster damage assessment. CrowdOptim introduces a crowd-driven hyperparameter optimization strategy that leverages crowd feedback to refine neural network configurations in smart urban sensing applications. Together, these frameworks exemplify innovative approaches to utilizing crowd intelligence for enhancing model performance across diverse real-world scenarios.

7.2.1 CrowdNAS: A Crowd-Guided Neural Architecture Searching Approach

CrowdNAS is a crowd-guided NAS framework that carefully explores crowd intelligence to identify the optimal neural network architecture in social intelligence applications. Our principled design of CrowdNAS integrates interdisciplinary techniques from NAS, crowdsourcing, and estimation theory into an end-to-end novel crowd-AI collaborative learning framework to address the crowd-guided NAS problem. The key novelty of CrowdNAS is twofold: (1) it designs a principled crowd-manageable neural network search space that significantly reduces the search space of the NAS problem while maximizing the likelihood of including the optimal

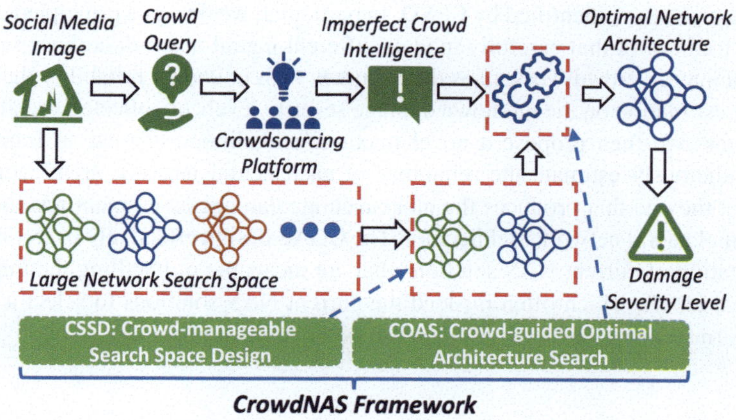

Fig. 7.1 Overview of CrowdNAS framework

neural network architecture in the reduced search space; and (2) it develops a novel crowd-AI integration model that leverages the imperfect crowd intelligence to effectively identify the optimal neural network architecture in the crowd-manageable search space. The overview of the CrowdNAS is shown in Fig. 7.1. The CrowdNAS consists of two core modules, (1) *Crowd-manageable Search Space Design (CSSD)* and (2) *Crowd-guided Optimal Architecture Search (COAS)*. The two modules work collaboratively to transfer the imperfect crowd intelligence to the optimal neural network architecture selection for desirable social intelligence performance. In particular, we have:

- *Crowd-manageable Search Space Design (CSSD)*: The CSSD module designs a set of sequential neural network search sub-spaces on top of a pre-trained damage assessment network to effectively reduce the search space for the crowd-guided NAS problem. Our design allows the CrowdNAS framework to effectively search for an optimal damage assessment network architecture by focusing the search on the essential network layers (e.g., pre-trained CNN layers, convolutional layers, dense layers) that are required as the key network components of a social intelligence solution. The search space design contains two key advantages. First, the sequential search space is significantly smaller than a regular NAS search space so that it is more manageable to the crowd intelligence. Second, the search space is explicitly generalized from a pre-trained damage assessment network so that the search space has a high likelihood of including the optimal neural network architecture for social intelligence applications. Our design addresses the key limitation of existing NAS solutions that work on a large search space and depend on a large-scale high-quality training dataset to fully explore the large NAS search space.
- *Crowd-guided Optimal Architecture Search (COAS)*: The COAS module develops a principled crowd-AI integration model to incorporate the imperfect crowd response to guide the selection of the optimal neural network architecture from

the search space identified by CSSD. In particular, we design a principled estimation framework that carefully models different neural network architectures and participating crowd workers as data sources with unknown reliability that make their estimation on the unknown damage severity levels of collected social media images. We then propose a novel maximum likelihood estimation framework to judiciously estimate the reliability of each neural network architecture and select the one that produces the most accurate damage assessment results as the optimal neural network architecture. The COAS design effectively overcomes the limitation of current NAS solutions that are incapable of handling the imperfect crowd labels, which often mislead the current NAS solutions to select a poorly performed neural network architecture as the optimal one.

7.2.1.1 Crowd-Manageable Search Space Design (CSSD)

In this subsection, we present the crowd-manageable neural network search space design that effectively reduces the search space for the Crowd-guided NAS problem. In particular, current NAS solutions often work on a large search space [25]. For example, the search space of a standard NAS solution in an image classification application often includes more than 423,000 candidate convolutional architectures in its search space [6]. To fully explore such a large search space, the current NAS solutions also need a massive amount of high-quality training data (e.g., 100,000 well-labeled image data in the image classification application) to train their NAS models in order to identify the optimal neural network architecture. However, such a large training dataset is not always available in the social intelligence applications due to the high labeling cost and unpredictability of many disaster events. Therefore, the current social intelligence solutions often invite AI experts to hand-pick a neural network architecture to be used in their solutions. However, such a manual process is known to be both costly and suboptimal.

To address the above problems, we design a CSSD module that identifies a reduced search space which (1) is orders of magnitude smaller than a regular NAS search space and (2) has a high likelihood to include the optimal neural network architecture for the application. In particular, the CSSD module focuses on designing a set of sequential sub-search spaces that aim to search for the optimal neural network architecture for the key network components of a social intelligence solution. The overall architecture of the CSSD design is shown in Fig. 7.2. The *feature extraction sub-search space* (FS) contains a set of candidate pre-trained CNN layers to provide a sub-search space to discover the optimal pre-trained CNN layers required to extract deep visual features from the input image. The *convolutional operation sub-search space* (CS) contains a set of candidate convolutional layers to provide a sub-search space to identify the optimal number of required convolutional layers to further process the extracted deep visual features from FS. Finally, the *dense layer sub-search space* (DS) contains a set of candidate dense layers to provide a sub-search space to discover the optimal number of required dense layers to estimate the damage severity level of the input image using

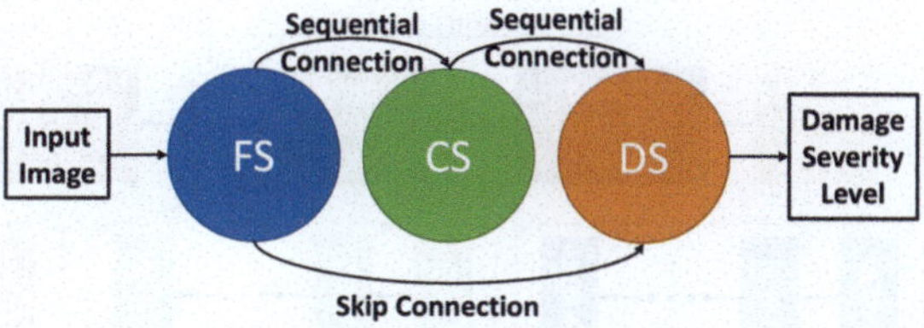

Fig. 7.2 Overall of crowd-manageable search space design

the processed deep visual features from CS. In addition, the CSSD design includes an option that allows the solution to skip *CS* if the system decides convolutional operations are not needed in the identified optimal neural network architecture. Such a design provides a flexible option for the CrowdNAS framework to establish a damage assessment network architecture where the deep visual features extracted from the FS are sufficient for DS to infer the damage severity level for each input image without requiring any additional convolutional operation by CS. In such a case, the skip connection design could keep the extracted disaster-related deep visual features from being mistakenly filtered out by the non-necessary convolutional process in CS. As a result, the design could prevent DS from generating inaccurate social intelligence results using incomplete deep visual features. In particular, the COAS module will decide whether the damage assessment network architecture using the skip connection is the optimal neural network architecture or not via a principled estimation framework, which will be discussed in the next subsection. We formally define *FS*, *CS*, and *DS* as follows:

Definition 7.1 (Feature Extraction Sub-search Space (*FS*)) We define *FS* as the first network search sub-search space for the framework to discover the optimal pre-trained CNN layers for deep visual feature extraction as:

$$VF^X = FS(X) \tag{7.1}$$

where VF^X represents the extracted deep visual features. We show the design of FS in (A) of Fig. 7.3. Instead of exhaustively searching all possible network architectures for deep feature extraction, the FS focuses on examining the deep features extracted by different layers of a pre-trained CNN (e.g., VGG) to identify the best layer for the given social intelligence task in order to effectively reduce the search space.

Definition 7.2 (Convolutional Operation Sub-search Space (*CS*)) We define *CS* as the second network sub-search space for the framework to decide the optimal number of convolutional layers needed in social intelligence solutions as:

$$DF^X = CS(VF^X) \tag{7.2}$$

where DF^X represents the damage-related visual features extracted from VF^X. We show the design of CS in (B) of Fig. 7.3. In CS, we focus on searching for the number of convolutional layers to achieve the optimal network depth for the

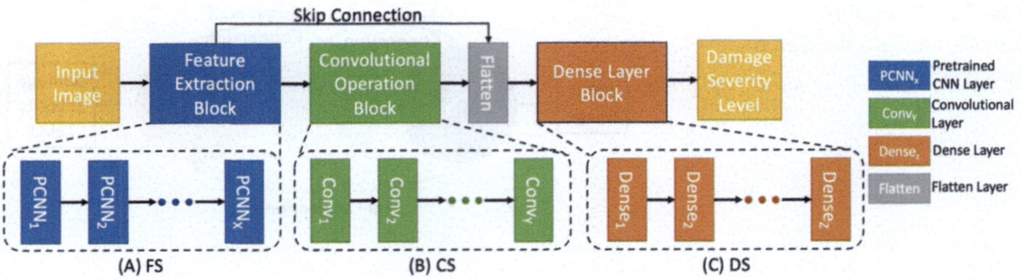

Fig. 7.3 Illustrations of design for crowd-manageable search space

given social intelligence task. In particular, the CS transfers the layer-wise parameter settings (e.g., kernel size) from convolutional layers in the pre-trained CNN to the candidate convolutional layers in CS to effectively reduce the search space.

Definition 7.3 (Dense Layer Sub-search Space (*DS*)) We define DS as the last network search sub-search space for the framework to identify the optimal number of dense layers required for damage assessment as:

$$\widehat{Y^S} = DS(DF^X) \tag{7.3}$$

where $\widehat{Y^S}$ is the estimated damage severity level for all studied social media images. We show the design of DS in (C) of Fig. 7.3. Similar to FS and CS, to reduce the search space, the DS focuses on identifying the optimal number of dense layers to accurately estimate the damage severity level instead of exploring different types of dense layer combinations.

Given the network search sub-search space defined above, we can construct a neural network architecture S_b in S for social intelligence applications by selecting a specific number of layers from each of FS, CS, and DS. In addition, each neural network architecture S_b in S is further supervised by a damage assessment loss function to maximize its disaster damage assessment performance so that the COAS module discussed next can identify the optimal neural network architecture S^* with the best social intelligence performance accordingly:

$$\mathcal{L}_{S_b} : \mathcal{L}_{Cross-Entropy}(S_b(X), Y) \tag{7.4}$$

where $\mathcal{L}_{S_b}$ represents the damage assessment loss function for S_b. $\mathcal{L}_{Cross-Entropy}$ represents the cross-entropy loss that measures the difference between the actual and estimated disaster damage severity levels reported in the images.

7.2.1.2 Crowd-Guided Optimal Architecture Search (COAS)

In this subsection, we develop a principled crowd-AI integration model to transfer the imperfect crowd intelligence to discover the optimal neural network architecture from the crowd-manageable search space defined in the CSSD module. In particular, a straightforward approach to leverage the crowd intelligence for NAS is to directly ask the crowd workers to label all image samples and use annotated labels as ground truth to evaluate the performance of all candidate network architectures and identify the optimal one. However, two critical problems exist in such a solution: (1) it is not practical to send all data samples for the crowd to label due to budget and time constraints, which is especially challenging in the context of social intelligence applications with massive social media data inputs; (2) unlike labels annotated by domain experts in disaster damage management, the labels from crowd workers are often imperfect (e.g., biased, noisy, and even conflicting with each other) [15].

To address the above problems, the COAS module first designs an entropy-driven query set selection mechanism to identify the subset of images for crowd query. In particular, we choose the images in the query set to be the ones that different candidate neural network architectures are less likely to reach a consensus on. The collected crowd labels for queried images are then used to identify the optimal neural network architecture in the search space.

Definition 7.4 (Estimation Entropy (E)**)** We define the estimation entropy E given a set of different deep architectures as follows:

$$E_a = -\sum_{i=1}^{I} P_i \times \log(P_i) \tag{7.5}$$

where E_a indicates the estimation entropy for the image X_a. I indicates the number of different damage severity levels in a disaster damage assessment application. P_i indicates the percentage of neural network architectures in the search space S that estimate the damage severity level in X_a to be i.

Intuitively, a higher E_a value indicates that different neural network architectures in S have a higher degree of disagreement with each other about the damage severity level in X_a. We then sort the estimation entropy of all images X and select the top $\alpha \cdot A$ ranked images into the crowd query Q, where α refers to the crowd query ratio and A is the total number of studied images.

To address the imperfect crowd label challenge, the COAS module designs a crowd-AI integration model to accurately identify the optimal neural network architecture. The design integrates the estimations of different neural network architectures and the imperfect crowd responses into a principled estimation framework to estimate the performance of each neural network architecture S_b in S. In particular, we observe that every neural network architecture S_b in S and every participated crowd worker C_m in a crowd query Q generate their own assessments on damage severity levels for the images in Q. Therefore, we can treat both S_b and C_m as data sources with unknown reliability that makes their estimations on the variables of unknown labels (i.e., images of unknown damage severity levels). We first formulate a crowd-AI committee as follows:

Definition 7.5 (Crowd-AI Committee (CA)) We define CA as a committee that includes both different neural network architectures in S and the crowd workers who participate in the crowd query Q in the social intelligence application as follows:

$$CA = \{S_1, S_2, \ldots, S_B, C_1, C_2, \ldots, C_M\} \tag{7.6}$$

where S_b is the bth neural network architecture in S and C_m is the mth crowd worker in Q. In particular, we define CA_n to be the nth member in CA, and a total of N (i.e., $N = B + M$) members are included in the crowd-AI committee.

Definition 7.6 (Crowd-AI Reliability (R)) We define R_{CA_n} to represent the reliability of a member CA_n in CA, which is used to indicate the probability that the estimation from CA_n is correct (i.e., the estimation of CA_n matches the ground-truth damage severity level of an image).

Given the above definitions, the goal of the COAS module is to select the neural network architecture in CA with the highest reliability as the optimal neural network architecture for the problem. To that end, we further define $P^T_{CA_n,i}$ and $P^F_{CA_n,i}$ to represent the *unknown* probability that a member CA_n estimates the damage severity level of a given image to be the ith level correctly and the level other than ith level incorrectly when the actual damage severity of image X_a is ith level, respectively. Formally, we define $P^T_{CA_n,i}$ and $P^F_{CA_n,i}$ as follows:

$$\begin{aligned} P^T_{CA_n,i} &= \Pr(\widehat{Y_a^{CA_n}} = i | Y_a = i) \\ P^F_{CA_n,i} &= \sum_{\bar{i} \neq i}^{I} \Pr(\widehat{Y_a^{CA_n}} = \bar{i} | Y_a = i) \end{aligned} \tag{7.7}$$

where $\widehat{Y_a^{CA_n}}$ indicates the damage severity level of an image X_a estimated by a member CA_n. Y_a is the ground-truth damage severity level for X_a. We can further apply the Bayesian theorem to establish the connection between $P^T_{CA_n,i}$, $P^F_{CA_n,i}$ and R_{CA_n} as follows:

$$\begin{aligned} P^T_{CA_n,i} &= \frac{Q_{CA_n,i} \times R_{CA_n}}{D_i} \\ P^F_{CA_n,i} &= \frac{Q_{CA_n,\bar{i}} \times (1 - R_{CA_n})}{D_i} \end{aligned} \tag{7.8}$$

where $Q_{CA_n,i}$ and $Q_{CA_n,\bar{i}}$ represent the probability that a member CA_n reports the damage severity level of the image X_a to be the ith level and the value other than ith level, respectively. D_i indicates the prior probability that an arbitrary image is of damage severity level i. We observe that we can learn the reliability R_{CA_n} for CA_n if we can learn the accurate values for other parameters in the above equations.

To that end, the problem of learning the reliability R_{CA_n} of each member in CA can be nicely formulated as a maximum likelihood estimation (MLE) problem as follows:

$$\Pr\left((\widehat{Y^{S_1}}, \widehat{Y^{S_2}}, \ldots, \widehat{Y^{S_B}}, \widehat{Y^{C_1}}, \widehat{Y^{C_2}}, \ldots, \widehat{Y^{C_M}})|\Phi\right) \tag{7.9}$$

where $(\widehat{Y^{S_1}}, \widehat{Y^{S_2}}, \ldots, \widehat{Y^{S_B}}, \widehat{Y^{C_1}}, \widehat{Y^{C_2}}, \ldots, \widehat{Y^{C_M}})$ indicates the observed variable of the MLE problem. $\widehat{Y^{S_b}}$ represents the damage severity level estimated by a deep architecture S_b. $\widehat{Y^{C_m}}$ represents the damage severity level labeled by a crowd worker C_m in the crowd query Q. Φ indicates the estimation parameter of the above MLE problem, where $\Phi = \{P^T_{CA_1,i}, P^T_{CA_2,i}, \ldots, P^T_{CA_N,i}; P^F_{CA_1,i}, P^F_{CA_2,i}, \ldots, P^F_{CA_N,i}, D\}\ for\ i = 1, 2 \ldots, I$. The goal is to learn the source reliability R_{CA_n} for each member CA_n in CA from the estimation parameter Φ using Eq. (7.8). To that end, we define a likelihood function $\mathbb{L}(\Phi; \Delta, Z)$ of the problem as follows:

$$\begin{aligned}
&\mathbb{L}(\Phi; \Delta, Z) \\
&= \mathbb{L}(\Phi; (\widehat{Y^{S_1}}, \widehat{Y^{S_2}}, \ldots, \widehat{Y^{S_B}}, \widehat{Y^{C_1}}, \widehat{Y^{C_2}}, \ldots, \widehat{Y^{C_M}}), \overline{Y}) \\
&= \prod_{a=1}^{A}\left(\sum_{i=1}^{I}(\prod_{n=1}^{B+M} P^{T}_{S_b,i}{}^{U^i_{n,a}} \times P^{F}_{S_b,i}{}^{U^{\bar{i}}_{n,a}}\right. \\
&\left.\times (1 - P^T_{S_b,i} - P^F_{S_b,i})^{(1-U^i_{n,a}-U^{\bar{i}}_{n,a})} \times D_i \times Z_{a,i})\right)
\end{aligned} \tag{7.10}$$

The above likelihood function represents the likelihood of the observed data Δ (i.e., damage severity levels estimated by different deep architectures and crowd workers) and the values of hidden variables Z (i.e., the actual damage severity level of an image) given the estimated parameter Φ. The detailed explanations of the above parameters of the likelihood function are summarized in Table 7.1.

In particular, the formulated problem can be solved using a constrained expectation maximization (EM) algorithm [40, 41]. Finally, we can derive R_{CA_n} for each CA_n by plugging Φ to Eq. (7.8). After obtaining the reliability score for each neural network architecture (i.e., each neural network architecture comes with different layers from the designed crowd-manageable search space and with or without the skip connection option), we select the neural network architecture CA_n with the highest reliability score R_{CA_n} as the optimal neural network architecture S^* for the disaster damage assessment as follows:

$$\begin{aligned}
&\arg\max_{CA_n} R_{CA_n}, \text{ where } CA_n \in \{S_1, S_2, \ldots, S_B\} \\
&\text{set } CA_n \text{ as } S^*
\end{aligned} \tag{7.11}$$

Table 7.1 Notations in crowd-guided architecture searching

Notations	Definitions/Explanations
A	Number of collected social media images
I	Number of damage severity levels
B	Number of neural network architectures
M	Number of crowd workers in a crowd query
$U^i_{n,a}$	Indicator variable that is set to be 1 when a member CA_n estimates the damage severity of a given image x_a to be the ith level and is set to be 0 otherwise.
$U^{\bar{i}}_{n,a}$	Indicator variable that is set to be 1 when a member CA_n estimates the damage severity of a given image x_a to be the value other than ith level and is set to be 0
$Z_{a,i}$	Probability that the damage severity of a given image x_a to be ith level.
Δ	Observed variable of the model, where $\Delta = (\widehat{Y^{S_1}}, \widehat{Y^{S_2}}, \ldots, \widehat{Y^{S_B}}, \widehat{Y^{C_1}}, \widehat{Y^{C_2}}, \ldots, \widehat{Y^{C_M}})$
Z	Latent variable of the model, which indicates the damage severity Y for each image

Finally, the estimated damage severity $\widehat{Y^{S^*}}$ from the optimal neural network architecture S^* is taken as the final output of the CrowdNAS framework.

7.2.2 *CrowdOptim: A Crowd-Driven Neural Network Hyperparameter Optimization Approach*

CrowdOptim is a crowd-driven NN hyperparameter optimization approach that explicitly utilizes crowd intelligence to guide the search for the optimal hyperparameter configuration in social intelligence applications. The overview of the CrowdOptim is shown in Fig. 7.4. In particular, it consists of two main modules:

- *Crowd-Manageable Hyperparameter Space Transformation (CHST)*: the CHST module designs a crowd-manageable hyperparameter space transformation model that effectively reduces the hyperparameter search space to a crowd-manageable one through a novel resource constraint multi-armed bandit learning model design.
- *Crowd-driven Optimal Hyperparameter Identification (COHI)*: the COHI module develops a principled crowd-AI collaborative estimation model to leverage the imperfect crowd intelligence to guide the selection of the optimal hyperparameter configuration from the crowd-manageable search space identified by CHST. The identified hyperparameter configuration is then used to generate class label estimation for the studied social intelligence application.

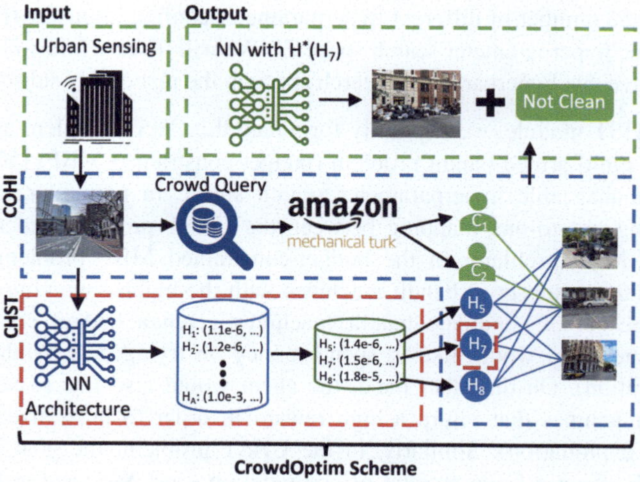

Fig. 7.4 Overview of CrowdOptim framework

7.2.2.1 Crowd-Manageable Hyperparameter Space Transformation (CHST)

In the first subsection, we study the crowd-manageable hyperparameter space transformation problem where the goal is to (1) effectively reduce the large hyperparameter search space of an AI model to be crowd-manageable, and (2) ensure that the identified crowd-manageable search space has a high likelihood to include the optimal hyperparameter configuration. We observe that the heuristic search strategies used in current hyperparameter optimization solutions can be computationally expensive and the learned hyperparameters could be overfitting to the images in the validation set and cause non-negligible performance loss when applied to the images in the testing set [20]. The CHST module is designed to effectively generate the crowd-manageable hyperparameter space to address the above problem.

In particular, we first formally define the crowd-manageable hyperparameter space in the CrowdOptim framework as follows:

Definition 7.7 (Crowd-manageable Hyperparameter Search Space ($\boldsymbol{H^R}$)) We define $\boldsymbol{H^R}$ to be a crowd-manageable hyperparameter search space that is significantly smaller than the original hyperparameter search space $\boldsymbol{H}$ and has a high likelihood to include the optimal hyperparameter configuration H^* as follows:

$$\boldsymbol{H^R} \subset \boldsymbol{H} \text{ , where } D << A \text{ and } \arg\max_{H^R} \Pr(H^* \in \boldsymbol{H^R}) \tag{7.12}$$

where D is the number of different hyperparameter configurations in $\boldsymbol{H}^R$ and A is the size of the hyperparameter search space $\boldsymbol{H}$. We will discuss how to learn such a crowd-manageable hyperparameter search space in the rest of this subsection.

In the CHST module, we explicitly formulate the CHST problem as a budget-constrained multi-armed bandit problem (budget-constrained MBP) [50] to derive the crowd-manageable hyperparameter search space. In particular, we observe an interesting one-to-one mapping between the CHST problem and the budget-constrained MBP problem. In the budget-constrained MBP problem, an agent aims to identify a subset of bandit machines with the highest winning probability from a large set of candidate bandit machines given a budget constraint. On one hand, the agent would like to spend money on trying new bandit machines (i.e., exploration). On the other hand, the agent would also like to keep playing the bandit machines that return a high reward in order to maximize the overall profit (i.e., exploitation). Similarly, in the CHST problem, the goal is to select $\boldsymbol{H}^R$ from $\boldsymbol{H}$ given a finite amount of computation time. We have to balance the exploration of new hyperparameter configurations and the exploitation of tuning the selected hyperparameter configuration with the best social intelligence application performance. We first start with a few key definitions in the CHST problem formulation (Fig. 7.5).

Definition 7.8 (Budget (γ)**)** We define the budget in the CHST problem to be the amount of computational time that is needed to train different hyperparameter configurations to find the optimal one. In particular, a straightforward solution to find the optimal hyperparameter configuration is to train and test the performance of all possible hyperparameter configurations if computational time is unlimited. However, in real-world applications, there is always a finite amount of computational time for the hyperparameter optimization task. Hence, we take the computational

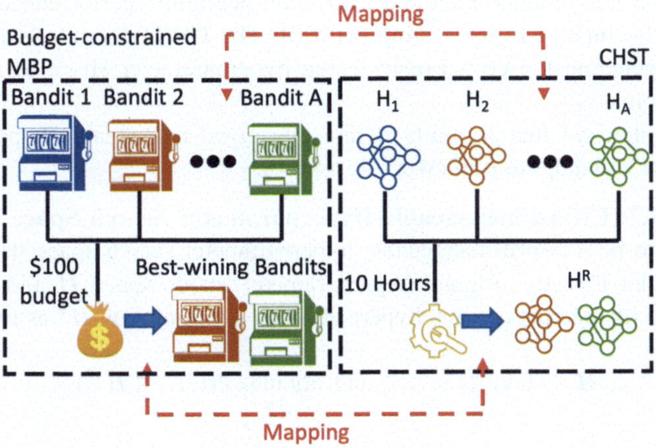

Fig. 7.5 One-to-one mapping between CHST and budget-constrained MBP

time available for the hyperparameter optimization task as the budget in the CHST problem.

Definition 7.9 (Action (α)) Similar to the budget-constrained MBP problem where we can take actions to try different bandit machines under a given budget, we define the action in the CHST problem to be training different hyperparameter configurations given a certain amount of computational time.

Definition 7.10 (Reward (ϕ)) In the budget-constrained MBP problem, we expect to receive a reward after trying a bandit machine. The reward on each trial could help us find the machines that are more likely to return the high rewards. In the CHST problem, we leverage a validation dataset that is randomly sampled from the training dataset to evaluate the performance of a hyperparameter configuration after taking an action. We define the reward in the CHST problem as the estimation accuracy of a hyperparameter configuration in the validation dataset, which indicates whether the configuration is likely to perform well or not on the testing dataset.

Given the above definitions, we can solve the CHST problem by exploring the trade-off between the exploitation and exploration in the budget-constrained MBP problem [10]. On one hand, similar to the budget-constrained MBP problem where we keep exploiting bandit machines that return a high reward, the CHST module keeps allocating the computational time to keep tuning the same hyperparameter configuration with the high estimation accuracy on the validation set. On the other hand, like the budget-constrained MBP problem also explores new bandit machines to avoid missing other high-reward machines, the CHST module takes actions to try new hyperparameter configurations to prevent itself from being trapped into a local optimal hyperparameter configuration. Such a learning process could help effectively explore the large hyperparameter search space and identify the optimal hyperparameter configuration.

After performing the budget-constrained MBP learning process, one straightforward solution is to use the hyperparameter with the highest reward as the optimal hyperparameter configuration. However, the learned hyperparameter could be overfitting to the images in the validation set and cause non-negligible performance loss when applied to the studied images in the testing set [28]. In particular, the application-specific visual features (e.g., color distributions and object layouts and patterns) in the validation set might not exactly match the features in the testing set. As a result, the hyperparameter configuration with the highest reward is not always guaranteed to be the optimal configuration for the testing set. To address this issue, the CHST module not only exploits the hyperparameter configurations with the highest reward but also explores other candidate hyperparameter configurations as a part of the crowd-manageable search space to regularize the CHST from being overfitted to the validation set by leveraging the trade-off between the exploitation and exploration in the budget-constrained MBP problem. Such a design achieves a reasonable trade-off between the size of the crowd-manageable search space and the likelihood of including the optimal hyperparameter configuration in the identified search space. The CrowdOptim then leverages crowd intelligence to effectively identify the hyperparameter configuration that achieves the best social intelligence application performance on the studied images from the crowd-manageable search space, which will be discussed next.

7.2.2.2 Crowd-Driven Optimal Hyperparameter Identification (COHI)

In this subsection, we propose a novel crowd-driven hyperparameter optimization model to effectively leverage the imperfect crowd intelligence to identify the optimal hyperparameter configuration from the crowd-manageable hyperparameter search space generated by the CHST module. The COHI module focuses on addressing two key challenges in leveraging crowd intelligence to guide the hyperparameter optimization task. First, it is not practical to send all imagery data for crowd query due to resource and time constraints. Second, the collected labels from crowd workers can be noisy, biased, and inconsistent due to the lack of domain knowledge of the studied social intelligence applications [12].

To address the above challenges, the COHI module first introduces a crowd query set identification mechanism to select the subset of images that will be sent to the crowd workers for their annotations on the class label. In particular, the design focuses on selecting the images where the different hyperparameter configurations generate inconsistent results on the estimated class labels. The collected crowd labels can then be used to effectively guide the identification of the optimal hyperparameter configuration to ensure desirable social intelligence application performance.

Definition 7.11 (Assessment Entropy (ω)) We define the assessment entropy ω for a set of different hyperparameter configurations as $\omega_i = -\sum_{j=1}^{J} d_j \times \log(d_j)$, where ω_i represents the assessment entropy of the image X_i. J is the number of different classes in a studied social intelligence application. d_j represents the percentage of hyperparameter configurations in the crowd-manageable search space that estimate the class label for X_i to be j. Intuitively, a higher ω_i represents the fact that different hyperparameter configurations are less likely to reach a consensus on the class label in X_i.

Using the assessment entropy, the top $I \cdot \sigma$ ranked images are added to the crowd query to collect the crowd labels where I is the number of studied images and σ is the crowd query ratio. We observe that the labels returned by the crowd query are often imperfect (e.g., noisy, biased, and even conflicting with each other). To address such a challenge, the COHI module introduces a principled CI & AI collaboration framework to accurately identify the optimal hyperparameter configuration using imperfect crowd intelligence. In the model, we consider both hyperparameter configurations and crowd workers as data sources with unknown optimality that make their estimations on the images of unknown class labels. We first define the concept of CI&AI Collaboration Group as follows:

Definition 7.12 (CI&AI Collaboration Group (G)) we define $\boldsymbol{G} = \{G_1, \ldots, G_B\}$ as a CI&AI Collaboration Group that includes all D different hyperparameter configurations in $\boldsymbol{H^R}$ and all K different crowd workers $\boldsymbol{C}$ in an social intelligence application as follows:

$$\boldsymbol{G} = \boldsymbol{H^R} \cup \boldsymbol{C}, \text{ and } B = D + K \tag{7.13}$$

where B is the number of members in $\boldsymbol{G}$. We further define R_{G_b} to represent the *unknown* likelihood of each member G_b in making accurate class label estimations. Such likelihood of G_b in $\boldsymbol{H^R}$ indicates the optimality of the corresponding hyperparameter configuration.

The goal of the COHI module is to identify the optimal hyperparameter configuration from the crowd-manageable search space. Hence, we select the hyperparameter configuration in $\boldsymbol{H^R}$ with the highest optimality R_{G_b} as the optimal hyperparameter configuration. In particular, we can obtain the optimality of each member in $\boldsymbol{G}$ using the Bayesian theorem as follows:

$$\begin{aligned} R_{G_b} &= \Pr(Y_i = j | \widehat{Y_i^{G_b}} = j) = \frac{U_{G_b,j,+} \times V_j}{W_{G_b,j}} \\ 1 - R_{G_b} &= \Pr(Y_i = \overline{j} | \widehat{Y_i^{G_b}} = j) = \frac{U_{G_b,j,-} \times V_j}{W_{G_b,\overline{j}}} \end{aligned} \tag{7.14}$$

where Y_i and $\widehat{Y_i^{G_b}}$ are the ground-truth label and estimated label by G_b for an image X_i, respectively. $U_{G_b,j,+}$ and $U_{G_b,j,-}$ indicate the probability that G_b estimates the class label to be j and the label other than j given the ground-truth label is j, respectively. $W_{G_b,j}$ and $W_{G_b,\overline{j}}$ represent the probability G_b that estimates the label for a given image to be j and the label other than j, respectively. V_j is the probability that the label of a random given image is j. Given the above equation, the next step is to derive the accurate value for each unknown variable in the equation in order to derive the R_{G_b} for each hyperparameter configuration in $\boldsymbol{H^R}$. To that end, we design a maximum likelihood estimation (MLE) framework to solve the above problem as follows:

$$\begin{aligned} \Pr\Big((\widehat{Y^{G_1}}, \widehat{Y^{G_2}}, \ldots, \widehat{Y^{G_B}}) | (U_{G_1,1,+/-}, U_{G_2,1,+/-}, \ldots, U_{G_B,1,+/-}), \\ (U_{G_1,2,+/-}, U_{G_2,2,+/-}, \ldots, U_{G_B,2,+/-}), \\ (U_{G_1,J,+/-}, U_{G_2,J,+/-}, \ldots, U_{G_B,J,+/-}), (V_1, V_2, \ldots, V_J)\Big) \end{aligned} \tag{7.15}$$

where $(\widehat{Y^{G_1}}, \widehat{Y^{G_2}}, \ldots, \widehat{Y^{G_B}})$ are the observed data of the MLE problem. $(U_{G_1,j,+/-}, U_{G_2,j,+/-}, \ldots, U_{G_B,j,+/-})$ for all j in $\{1, 2, .., J\}$ and $(V_1, V_2, \ldots, V_J)$ are the estimation parameters of the model. In the MLE problem, we define the likelihood function to learn the estimation parameter in order to learn the optimality of each hyperparameter configuration as follows:

$$
\begin{aligned}
&\mathbb{L}(\Omega;\Phi,Z) = \\
&\prod_{i=1}^{I}\Big(\sum_{j=1}^{J}\Big(\prod_{d=1}^{D}\big(U_{H_d^R,j,+}{}^{\delta_{i,j,d}} \times U_{H_d^R,j,-}{}^{\delta_{i,\bar{j},d}} \\
&\quad \times (1-U_{H_d^R,j,+}-U_{H_d^R,j,-})^{(1-\delta_{i,j,d}-\delta_{i,\bar{j},d})} \times V_j \times z_{i,j}\big) \\
&\quad \times \beta \times \prod_{k=1}^{K}\big(U_{C_k,j,+}{}^{\delta_{i,j,k}} \times U_{C_k,j,-}{}^{\delta_{i,\bar{j},k}} \\
&\quad \times (1-U_{C_k,j,+}-U_{C_k,j,-})^{(1-\delta_{i,j,k}-\delta_{i,\bar{j},k})} \times V_j \times z_{i,j}\big)\Big)\Big)
\end{aligned}
\tag{7.16}
$$

where the detailed explanations of the notations in the above equation are summarized in Table 7.2. In particular, such a likelihood function design indicates the likelihood of the observed data Φ (the class label estimated by different hyperparameter configurations and annotated by different crowd workers) and the value of the hidden variables Z given the estimation parameter Ω.

Our formulated MLE problem can be solved using the expectation maximization algorithm [42]. Given the learned estimation parameter Ω, we can obtain the R_{G_b} for each G_b by plugging the learned Ω into Eq. (7.14). We then use the

Table 7.2 Notations in crowd-driven Hyperparameter optimization

Notations	Explanations
$U_{H_d^R/C_k,j,+}$ & $U_{H_d^R/C_k,j,-}$	Probability that H_d^R or C_k estimates the class label to be j and the label other than j given the ground-truth label is j, respectively
$\delta_{i,j,d}$ & $\delta_{i,j,k}$	Binary variable that is set to be 1 when a member H_d^R or C_k estimates the class label of a given image x_i to be the j and is set to be 0 otherwise.
$\delta_{i,\bar{j},d}$ & $\delta_{i,\bar{j},k}$	Binary variable that is set to be 1 when a member H_d^R or C_k estimates the class label of a given image x_i to be the value other than j and is set to be 0 otherwise.
β	Weighting factor that balances the trade-off between the inputs of crowd workers and hyperparameter configurations
$z_{i,j}$	Probability for the class label of a image x_i to be j.
Ω	Estimation parameter of the MLE model with $(U_{G_1,j,+/-},\ldots,U_{G_B,j,+/-})$ for all j in $\{1, 2, .., J\}$ and $(V_1, V_2, \ldots, V_J)$
Φ	Observed variable of the MLE model with $\Phi = (\widehat{Y^{G_1}}, \widehat{Y^{G_2}}, \ldots, \widehat{Y^{G_B}})$
Z	Latent variable of the MLE model that includes all $z_{i,j}$ for all possible i and j

learned optimality R_{G_b} to select the hyperparameter configuration with the highest optimality value as the optimal hyperparameter configuration H^* for the studied social intelligence application. Finally, the class labels estimated by the optimal hyperparameter configuration are used as the output of the CrowdOptim framework.

Our COHI module can effectively leverage imperfect crowd intelligence to guide the discovery of the optimal hyperparameter configuration for two reasons. First, a straightforward solution to solve the hyperparameter optimization problem is to exhaustively collect crowd labels on all studied images to evaluate the performance of each hyperparameter configuration in order to identify the optimal one. However, it is not practical to send all imagery data for crowd query due to the resource and time constraints [46]. Therefore, the COHI module introduces a principled assessment entropy design that effectively identifies a subset of studied images for crowd query, where different hyperparameter configurations are less likely to reach a consensus on the class labels. The collected labels are then used by the COHI module to identify the optimal hyperparameter configuration. Second, the labels returned by the crowd query are often imperfect (e.g., noisy, biased, and even conflicting with each other), which could mislead us to select the poorly performed hyperparameter configuration as the optimal one. To address this challenge, the COHI module explicitly considers both hyperparameter configurations and crowd workers as data sources with unknown optimality that make their estimations on the images of unknown class labels. The COHI module then introduces a principled MLE framework (Eqs. (7.15) and (7.16)) to derive the unknown optimality score of each hyperparameter configuration to identify the optimal hyperparameter configuration.

In addition, we note that there exist several limitations of the COHI design. First, the assessment entropy design could identify the wrong image for crowd query when all hyperparameter configurations in the crowd-manageable search space happen to make similar mistakes on the same image. To address such a problem, one possible solution is to leverage the epsilon-greedy algorithm from reinforcement learning [37] to occasionally include the images with low assessment entropy for crowd query by exploring the trade-off between exploitation and exploration in crowd query data selection. Second, while the COHI module can effectively identify the optimal hyperparameter configuration that achieves the overall optimal social intelligence application performance across all classes, it does not guarantee that the identified optimal hyperparameter optimization can achieve the best performance across every single class in the studied application [36]. To address this challenge, instead of focusing on identifying a single optimal hyperparameter configuration that achieves the best overall performance, we can further extend the crowd-AI collaborative MLE framework to learn the class-wise optimality score for each class. The learned optimality scores are then used to determine a vector of class-wise optimal hyperparameter configurations, where the hyperparameter configuration with the highest class-wise optimality score for a specific class is used to estimate the class label for that class.

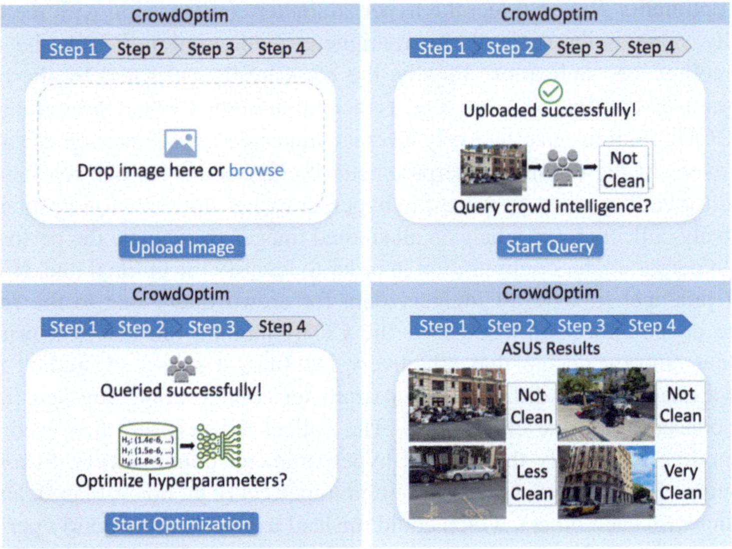

Fig. 7.6 A walkthrough of CrowdOptim framework for practical users

7.2.2.3 Summary of CrowdOptim Framework

In this subsection, we first present an overview on how practical users without extensive AI backgrounds can use CrowdOptim in a real-world social intelligence application (e.g., urban environment cleanliness assessment (UECA)) in Fig. 7.6. In particular, a practical user can use CrowdOptim to perform social intelligence tasks in four steps. First, the user can choose to upload urban sensing images of interest to CrowdOptim. Second, the user can start the crowd query to acquire crowd intelligence to guide the search for the optimal hyperparameter configuration. Third, the user can then start the hyperparameter optimization process, where CrowdOptim leverages the acquired crowd labels to identify the optimal hyperparameter configuration for social intelligence tasks. Finally, CrowdOptim generates the estimated class label for each uploaded image using the identified optimal hyperparameter configuration.

In addition, we also present a detailed elaboration for more advanced users (e.g., AI researchers) to better understand the insights of how CrowdOptim works in four main phases and discuss how such advanced users can interact with (e.g., tuning) CrowdOptim at each phase in Fig. 7.7 as follows:

- *Phase (a): Generating Crowd-Manageable Hyperparameter Space.* The objective of phase (a) is to use the CHST module to generate a crowd-manageable hyperparameter space that has a high likelihood of including the optimal hyperparameter configuration for social intelligence tasks. The inputs to this phase are the state-of-the-art deep convolutional network architecture N selected

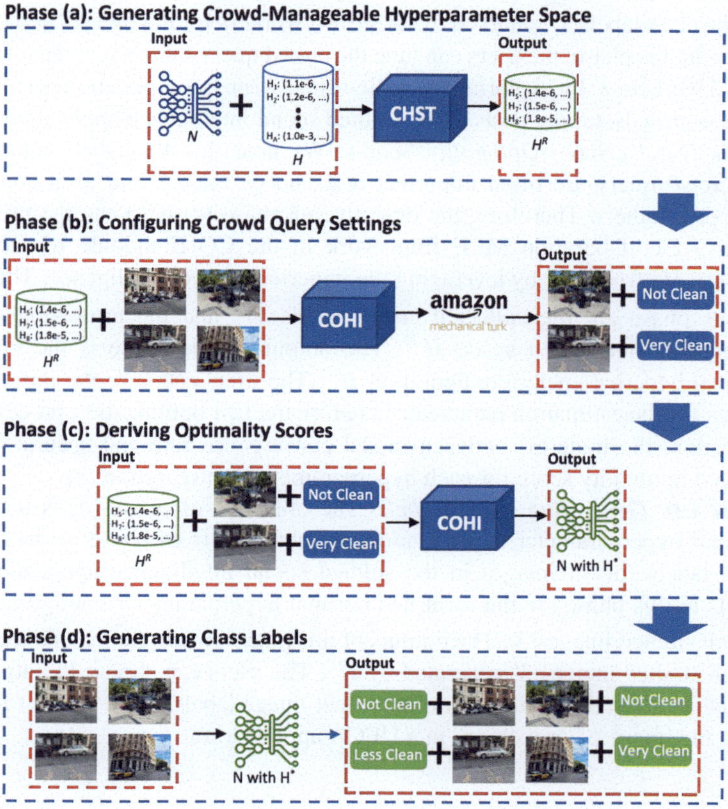

Fig. 7.7 Elaboration of CrowdOptim framework for advanced users

for a given social intelligence task and the associated hyperparameter search space $\boldsymbol{H}$ for N. The output is the crowd-manageable hyperparameter search space $\boldsymbol{H}^{\boldsymbol{R}}$. We note that CrowdOptim is capable of performing hyperparameter optimization for *different* neural network architectures for social intelligence tasks. In this phase, the users can choose the convolutional network architecture N (e.g., VGG, ResNet, DenseNet) for the studied social intelligence application of interests by leveraging existing neural architecture search solutions [23].

- *Phase (b): Configuring Crowd Query Settings.* The objective of phase (b) is to apply the assessment entropy estimation in COHI module to identify a subset of $I \cdot \sigma$ studied images (I is the number of studied images and σ is the crowd query ratio) where different hyperparameter configurations in $\boldsymbol{H}^{\boldsymbol{R}}$ are less likely to reach a consensus on the class labels. The COHI module then forwards the identified subset of images to the crowd workers to collect their labels, which are used to help determine the optimal hyperparameter configuration H^* from $\boldsymbol{H}^{\boldsymbol{R}}$. The inputs to this phase are the crowd-manageable hyperparameter search space $\boldsymbol{H}^{\boldsymbol{R}}$ and application-specific crowd query ratio σ. The outputs of this phase are the class labels $\widehat{\boldsymbol{Y^C}}$ marked by the crowd workers for the images in the crowd query. In this phase, the users can tune the crowd query ratio σ and the number of crowd workers K by exploring the trade-off between the application performance and the crowdsourcing costs in the studied social intelligence application.

- *Phase (c): Deriving Optimality Scores.* We note that the labels returned by the crowd query are often imperfect (e.g., noisy, biased, and even conflicting with each other). Therefore, the objective of phase (c) is to use the principled CI & AI collaboration MLE framework in the COHI module to accurately identify H^* from $\boldsymbol{H^R}$ by leveraging the imperfect crowd intelligence. The inputs to this phase are the collected crowd labels $\widehat{\boldsymbol{Y^C}}$ and the crowd-manageable hyperparameter search space $\boldsymbol{H^R}$. The output of this phase is the identified optimal hyperparameter configuration H^*. The users can vary the initialization values for the estimation parameter Ω before the EM optimization process starts to explore the trade-off between model convergence rate and accuracy of the derived optimality score for each hyperparameter configuration [3].
- *Phase (d): Generating Class Labels.* The objective of phase (d) is to use the optimal hyperparameter configuration H^* obtained from phase (c) to estimate class labels for all images in the studied social intelligence application. The inputs to this phase are the identified optimal hyperparameter configuration H^* and all studied images $\boldsymbol{X}$. The outputs of this phase are the estimated labels $\widehat{\boldsymbol{Y^{H^*}}}$ for all studied images $\boldsymbol{X}$ generated by H^*. The users can choose to output class labels for all studied images or only output image labels of the class of interests (e.g., the image of "not clean" in a UECA application).

7.3 Real-World Case Studies

We evaluate the effectiveness of CrowdNAS and CrowdOptim through two real-world case studies across multiple datasets. Specifically, we evaluate CrowdNAS in the context of disaster damage assessment, where the objective is to identify the severity of damage in affected areas by leveraging crowd input to guide neural architecture selection. To assess CrowdOptim, we use the application scenario of smart urban sensing, aiming to optimize neural network hyperparameters with crowd feedback to enhance model performance in monitoring urban environments. These case studies demonstrate the potential of crowd-AI collaborative frameworks to improve accuracy and efficiency in diverse, high-impact applications.

7.3.1 Disaster Damage Assessment (DDA)

In this subsection, we conduct extensive experiments on two real-world DDA applications from Typhoon Hagupit and California Wildfires to answer the following research questions:

- Q1: Can CrowdNAS achieve a better DDA accuracy by selecting the optimal network architecture than state-of-the-art baselines?
- Q2: Is the performance gain achieved by CrowdNAS robust across different crowdsourcing settings?
- Q3: How does each module of CrowdNAS contribute to its overall performance?

7.3.1.1 Dataset and Crowdsourcing Platform

Disaster Damage Assessment Datasets In the evaluation, we use two real-world datasets on disaster damage assessment collected by [29].[1] In particular, the datasets consist of social media images collected from two different disaster events: Typhoon Hagupit in the Philippines (2014) and the California wildfires in the US (2017). The two datasets have different damage characteristics (e.g., damage types, object layouts, and color distributions) as shown in Fig. 7.8. In the datasets, the ground-truth damage severity level of each social media image is manually classified by domain experts in disaster damage management into three categories (i.e., severe damage, mild damage, and no damage). The statistics of the two datasets are summarized in Table 7.3. In addition, we keep the ratio of training to testing data as 3:1, the same as [29]. The training dataset is used to train all compared AI models for disaster damage assessment.

Fig. 7.8 Examples of studied disaster events

[1] https://crisisnlp.qcri.org/.

Table 7.3 Statistics of disaster damage assessment datasets

	Typhoon Hagupit	California Wildfires
Number of images	661	592
Percentage of severe damage	11.2%	41.2%
Percentage of mild damage	42.2%	8.1%
Percentage of no damage	46.6%	50.7%

Amazon Mechanical Turk Platform To obtain the crowd intelligence, we utilize the Amazon Mechanical Turk (AMT) [1]. In each crowdsourcing task, we ask the crowd workers to label the damage severity level of the image in the query. To ensure the crowd label quality, we select the crowd workers who have an overall task approval rate greater than 95% and have completed at least 1000 approved tasks to participate in the crowdsourcing tasks. We pay $0.20 to each worker per image in the experiment. In the evaluation, we study a diversified set of crowd query settings to create a challenging evaluation scenario for the CrowdNAS framework. In particular, we vary the crowd query ratio from 10 to 20% in the experiments. We also vary the number of crowd workers who respond to each queried image from 3, 5 to 7. In particular, we observe that an average of 72.7% of the images are correctly labeled by the crowd workers, which matches the observation that the crowd intelligence is imperfect.

7.3.1.2 Baselines and Experiment Settings

We compare CrowdNAS with a set of representative AI, crowd-AI, and NAS baselines from the literature in the DDA applications.

- **AI-Only Baselines:**
  1. **InceptionNet** [39]: InceptionNet is a widely used deep neural network approach that utilizes convolution factorization to accelerate the learning process of the damage severity assessment.
  2. **DenseNet** [14]: DenseNet is a popular deep learning model that leverages the feed-forwarding mechanism to achieve dense connections among different network layers for desirable damage assessment accuracy.
  3. **VGG** [22]: VGG is a state-of-the-art deep learning framework that is widely adopted in disaster damage assessment, which leverages a stack of deep convolutional operations to boost the classification accuracy.
- **Crowd-AI Hybrid Baselines:**
  1. **CrowdLearn** [45]: CrowdLearn is a recent crowd-AI framework that explores the crowd intelligence and AI by combining crowd labels with AI outputs to improve the accuracy of the estimated damage severity level.

2. **Deep Active** [33]: Deep Active is a state-of-the-art deep active learning-based crowd-AI system that proposed a core-set selection mechanism to select the representative images for crowd labeling and the crowd labels are used for model retraining to optimize the DDA performance.
3. **Hybrid Para** [17]: Hybrid Para is an elastic crowd-AI learning architecture that forwards the images with complex image property (e.g., color distributions) to seek crowd labels to improve the assessment accuracy in DDA applications.

- **NAS Baselines:**

1. **NASNetLarge** [51]: NASNetLarge is a state-of-the-art NAS approach that proposes a scheduled drop path mechanism to effectively refine the neural network architecture during the NAS process.
2. **NASNetMobile** [32]: NASNetMobile is a lightweight NAS framework that conducts network searching on cell-based architectural building blocks to ensure the desirable NAS performance.
3. **Darts** [25]: Darts is a representative NAS framework that leverages a differentiable architecture representation to achieve an effective NAS process through a gradient descent.
4. **ProxylessNAS** [4]: ProxylessNAS is a lightweight NAS framework that conducts network searching on cell-based architectural building blocks to ensure the desirable NAS performance.
5. **UnNAS** [24]: UnNAS is a representative NAS framework that leverages a differentiable architecture representation to achieve an effective NAS process through a gradient descent.

To ensure a fair comparison, the inputs to all compared schemes are set to be the same, which include: (1) the input social media images, (2) the ground-truth labels of images in the training dataset, and (3) the labeled images from crowd workers. In particular, we retrain the AI only and NAS baselines using the labels returned by the crowd for a fair comparison. In addition, we also consider the *random* baseline, which estimates the damage severity for each image by randomly selecting a damage severity level from the possible categories. In the experiments, we implement the CrowdNAS model using Tensorflow 2.0 libraries[2] and train the model using the NVIDIA Quadro RTX 6000 GPUs. In the experiments, all hyper-parameters are optimized using the Adam optimizer [19]. In particular, we set the learning rate to be 10^{-6}. We also set the batch size to be 20 and the model is trained over 300 epochs. In addition, we directly use layers from ImageNet pre-trained VGG19 [35] as the pre-trained CNN layers in the model.

To evaluate the performance of all compared schemes, we adopt three representative metrics that are widely used to evaluate the performance of multi-class image classification tasks in image processing: (1) *F1-score*, (2) *Cohen's kappa Score*

[2] https://www.tensorflow.org/.

($\mathcal{K}$-Score) [2], and *Matthews Correlation Coefficient (MCC)* [18]. In particular, we use $\mathcal{K}$-Score and MCC in the evaluation because we have an imbalance evaluation dataset, where $\mathcal{K}$-Score and MCC have been proven to be reliable evaluation metrics for imbalanced data [5]. Intuitively, higher F1-score, $\mathcal{K}$-Score, and MCC indicate a better disaster damage assessment performance.

7.3.1.3 Evaluation Results

Q1: Performance Comparison between CrowdNAS and Baselines.

We first evaluate the accuracy of all compared schemes in terms of classification accuracy in the studied DDA application. In this experiment, we select three representative values of crowd query ratio α (the percentage of images sent to the AMT crowd workers) as 10, 15, and 20%. We will also study the robustness of the CrowdNAS over a wider range of α in the robustness study of Q2 below. In addition, we set the number of crowd workers for each queried image (M) to 5. The results are presented in Tables 7.4 and 7.5. We observe that the CrowdNAS scheme consistently outperforms all compared baselines when the crowd query ratio changes. In particular, the performance gains of CrowdNAS over the AI-only and crowd-AI baselines mainly come from the fact that we developed a crowd-guided NAS system to effectively identify the optimal neural network architecture in the design space to reduce the bias and errors compared to the baselines designed by AI-experts. In addition, we observe that NAS baselines perform worse compared to the crowd-AI baselines. This is because the current NAS baselines are often noise-sensitive [9]. In particular, the noises introduced by crowd inputs are recursively amplified during the NAS process and eventually lead to inaccurate neural network architecture selections.

Additionally, we further evaluate the performance of all compared schemes by varying the number of crowd workers (M) to label each image from 3 to 7. We set the crowd query ratio α to be 20% in this experiment. The evaluation results are shown in Tables 7.6 and 7.7. We observe that CrowdNAS continuously outperforms all compared baselines when the number of crowd workers changes. For example, the performance gains of CrowdNAS compared to the best-performing baseline (i.e., Deep Active) for the Typhoon Hagupit dataset when the crowd query number $M = 5$ on F1-Score, $\mathcal{K}$-Score, and MCC are 5.59, 7.68, and 8.31%, respectively. In this case, the optimal network architecture identified by CrowdNAS includes 19 PCNN layers, 1 Conv layer, and 3 dense layers. In general, the consistent performance gains over various crowd query settings demonstrate the effectiveness of the COAS design. We also observe that the performance of CrowdNAS remains the same when M increases from 5 to 7. This is because CrowdNAS is able to identify the optimal network architecture (i.e., 19 PCNN layers, 1 Conv layer, and 3 dense layers) with the responses from 5 crowd workers. When we further increase the number of crowd workers to 7, CrowdNAS also consistently identifies the same optimal network architecture that achieves the same optimal DDA performance.

Table 7.4 Performance comparisons on typhoon Hagupit Dataset (varying crowd query ratios)

		$\alpha = 10\%$			$\alpha = 15\%$			$\alpha = 20\%$		
Category	Algorithm	F1-score	$\mathcal{K}$-score	MCC	F1-score	$\mathcal{K}$-score	MCC	F1-score	$\mathcal{K}$-score	MCC
Random	Random	0.3105	0.0020	0.0022	0.3850	0.0501	0.0519	0.3950	0.0621	0.0650
AI Only	InceptionNet	0.6709	0.4492	0.4692	0.6211	0.3403	0.3604	0.6521	0.4018	0.4186
	DenseNet	0.6707	0.4644	0.4682	0.6645	0.4355	0.4425	0.6894	0.4805	0.4808
	VGG	0.6708	0.4407	0.4656	0.6335	0.3382	0.4022	0.6211	0.3252	0.3883
Crowd-AI	CrowdLearn	0.6460	0.4046	0.4170	0.6024	0.2995	0.3223	0.5590	0.2318	0.2466
	Deep active	0.6459	0.4226	0.4268	0.7018	0.5063	0.5079	0.6956	0.4886	0.4892
	Hybrid Para	0.6956	0.4752	0.4788	0.6770	0.4428	0.4457	0.6521	0.4010	0.4058
NAS	NASNetLarge	0.6211	0.3661	0.3948	0.6273	0.3524	0.3956	0.6397	0.3734	0.4251
	NASNetMobile	0.6149	0.3422	0.4095	0.6086	0.3161	0.3677	0.6521	0.3909	0.4434
	DARTS	0.4596	0.1644	0.1750	0.5403	0.1873	0.2014	0.5155	0.1994	0.2057
	ProxylessNAS	0.6583	0.3948	0.4338	0.6583	0.3900	0.4333	0.6708	0.4193	0.4560
	UnNAS	0.5403	0.2009	0.2271	0.5031	0.0961	0.1394	0.5652	0.2419	0.2711
Our model	**CrowdNAS**	**0.7142**	**0.5149**	**0.5197**	**0.7329**	**0.5375**	**0.5412**	**0.7515**	**0.5654**	**0.5723**

The bold values indicate the best performing results in each evaluation metric

Table 7.5 Performance comparisons on California Wildfires dataset (varying crowd query ratios)

Category	Algorithm	$\alpha = 10\%$			$\alpha = 15\%$			$\alpha = 20\%$		
		F1-score	$\mathcal{K}$-score	MCC	F1-score	$\mathcal{K}$-score	MCC	F1-score	$\mathcal{K}$-score	MCC
Random	Random	0.3221	0.0084	0.0094	0.3959	0.0801	0.0862	0.3691	0.0433	0.0467
AI Only	InceptionNet	0.6174	0.3464	0.3996	0.6107	0.2960	0.3630	0.6174	0.3013	0.3719
	DenseNet	0.6107	0.3473	0.3792	0.6241	0.3271	0.3767	0.6241	0.3237	0.3819
	VGG	0.7382	0.5483	0.5548	0.7449	0.5672	0.5773	0.7114	0.5079	0.5178
Crowd-AI	CrowdLearn	0.7046	0.4995	0.5051	0.6912	0.4899	0.5064	0.6845	0.4693	0.4841
	Deep active	0.7516	0.5340	0.5455	0.7315	0.5009	0.5264	0.6778	0.3945	0.4407
	Hybrid para	0.7114	0.4820	0.4864	0.7046	0.4749	0.4820	0.6912	0.4587	0.4664
NAS	NASNetLarge	0.6107	0.3388	0.3551	0.6644	0.3971	0.4163	0.6711	0.4062	0.4271
	NASNetMobile	0.6107	0.3814	0.4041	0.6442	0.3929	0.4170	0.6174	0.3470	0.3700
	DARTS	0.6644	0.3917	0.3980	0.6375	0.3854	0.3886	0.5369	0.2638	0.2833
	ProxylessNAS	0.7181	0.5103	0.5219	0.7449	0.5351	0.5613	0.7583	0.5465	0.5641
	UnNAS	0.4899	0.2260	0.2458	0.5436	0.2685	0.2836	0.5771	0.3012	0.3136
Our model	**CrowdNAS**	**0.7651**	**0.5726**	**0.5733**	**0.7718**	**0.5806**	**0.5823**	**0.7785**	**0.5967**	**0.6007**

The bold values indicate the best performing results in each evaluation metric

Table 7.6 Performance comparisons on typhoon Hagupit dataset (varying crowd worker numbers)

Category	Algorithm	M = 3			M = 5			M = 7		
		F1-score	$\mathcal{K}$-score	MCC	F1-score	$\mathcal{K}$-score	MCC	F1-score	$\mathcal{K}$-score	MCC
Random	Random	0.3291	0.0061	0.0065	0.3105	0.0020	0.0022	0.3291	0.0247	0.0272
AI Only	InceptionNet	0.6832	0.4646	0.4996	0.6521	0.4018	0.4186	0.6708	0.4274	0.4644
	DenseNet	0.6024	0.3809	0.3917	0.6894	0.4805	0.4808	0.7080	0.5126	0.5130
	VGG	0.6832	0.4578	0.4860	0.6211	0.3252	0.3883	0.7018	0.4753	0.5043
Crowd-AI	CrowdLearn	0.6024	0.3327	0.3394	0.5590	0.2318	0.2466	0.6521	0.4057	0.4085
	Deep active	0.6894	0.4711	0.4816	0.6956	0.4886	0.4892	0.6832	0.4755	0.4794
	Hybrid para	0.6397	0.3814	0.3848	0.6521	0.4010	0.4058	0.6583	0.4164	0.4221
NAS	NASNetLarge	0.6521	0.4226	0.4389	0.6397	0.3734	0.4251	0.7018	0.4853	0.5068
	NASNetMobile	0.6770	0.4613	0.4829	0.6521	0.3909	0.4434	0.7018	0.4824	0.5137
	DARTS	0.5962	0.3096	0.3178	0.5155	0.1994	0.2057	0.5465	0.2343	0.2426
	ProxylessNAS	0.6708	0.4265	0.4537	0.6708	0.4193	0.4560	0.7080	0.4850	0.5275
	UnNAS	0.5838	0.2873	0.2976	0.5652	0.2419	0.2711	0.6086	0.3216	0.3381
Our model	**CrowdNAS**	**0.7391**	**0.5434**	**0.5569**	**0.7515**	**0.5654**	**0.5723**	**0.7515**	**0.5654**	**0.5723**

The bold values indicate the best performing results in each evaluation metric

Table 7.7 Performance comparisons on California Wildfires dataset (varying crowd worker numbers)

		M = 3			M = 5			M = 7		
Category	Algorithm	F1-score	$\mathcal{K}$-score	MCC	F1-score	$\mathcal{K}$-score	MCC	F1-score	$\mathcal{K}$-score	MCC
Random	Random	0.3557	0.0384	0.0422	0.3355	0.0034	0.0038	0.3758	0.0493	0.0531
AI Only	InceptionNet	0.6174	0.2908	0.3752	0.6174	0.3013	0.3719	0.6107	0.2673	0.3591
	DenseNet	0.5973	0.2571	0.3370	0.6241	0.3237	0.3819	0.6174	0.2800	0.3704
	VGG	0.7449	0.5528	0.5647	0.7114	0.5079	0.5178	0.7382	0.5276	0.5424
Crowd-AI	CrowdLearn	0.6979	0.4849	0.5002	0.6845	0.4693	0.4841	0.7046	0.4844	0.5018
	Deep active	0.6845	0.4101	0.4552	0.6778	0.3945	0.4407	0.6644	0.3689	0.4371
	Hybrid para	0.6711	0.4262	0.4314	0.6912	0.4587	0.4664	0.6845	0.4495	0.4578
NAS	NASNetLarge	0.6510	0.3570	0.3945	0.6711	0.4062	0.4271	0.6711	0.3880	0.4340
	NASNetMobile	0.6442	0.3506	0.4109	0.6174	0.3470	0.3700	0.6442	0.3308	0.4093
	DARTS	0.4832	0.2059	0.2228	0.5369	0.2638	0.2833	0.6510	0.3714	0.3722
	ProxylessNAS	0.7046	0.4449	0.5045	0.7583	0.5465	0.5641	0.7181	0.4702	0.5253
	UnNAS	0.6107	0.3264	0.3450	0.5771	0.3012	0.3136	0.6107	0.2863	0.3168
Our model	**CrowdNAS**	**0.7718**	**0.5806**	**0.5823**	**0.7785**	**0.5967**	**0.6007**	**0.7785**	**0.5967**	**0.6007**

The bold values indicate the best performing results in each evaluation metric

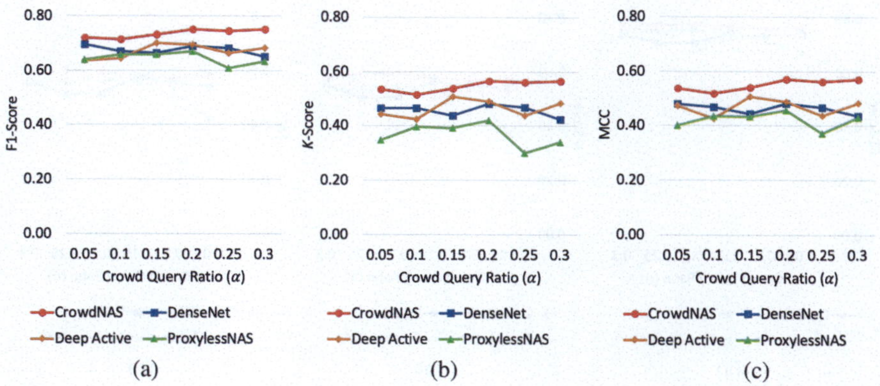

Fig. 7.9 Robustness study of CrowdNAS with different crowd query ratios (Typhoon Hagupit Dataset). **(a)** F1-score. **(b)** $\mathcal{K}$-score. **(c)** MCC

Such a performance indicates the capability of CrowdNAS to identify the optimal neural network architecture from a small number of crowd workers.

Q2: Robustness Study of CrowdNAS Scheme

In the second set of experiments, we study the robustness of the CrowdNAS scheme by evaluating its performance over the settings of two key crowdsourcing parameters (i.e., crowd query ratio α and crowd worker number M).[3] We compare the performance of the CrowdNAS with the best-performing baselines from all three different categories (i.e., DenseNet from the AI Only baselines, Hybrid Para from the crowd-AI baselines, and NASNetLarge from the NAS baselines). The results are shown in Figs. 7.9, 7.10, 7.11, and 7.12. We observe that the performance of the CrowdNAS scheme is relatively stable as both the crowd query ratio α and the crowd worker number M change. We also observe that CrowdNAS consistently outperforms the best-performing baselines on different evaluation metrics. The above results further demonstrate the robustness and effectiveness of the scheme to leverage the imperfect crowd knowledge to identify the optimal neural network architecture in accurately assessing the damage severity in DDA applications.

Q3: Ablation Study of CrowdNAS Scheme

In the third set of experiments, we perform an ablation study to understand the contribution of each module of CrowdNAS to its overall performance. In particular,

[3] Note that we stop at $\alpha = 30\%$ because it is not feasible to send a large number of images for crowd query due to the budget constraints.

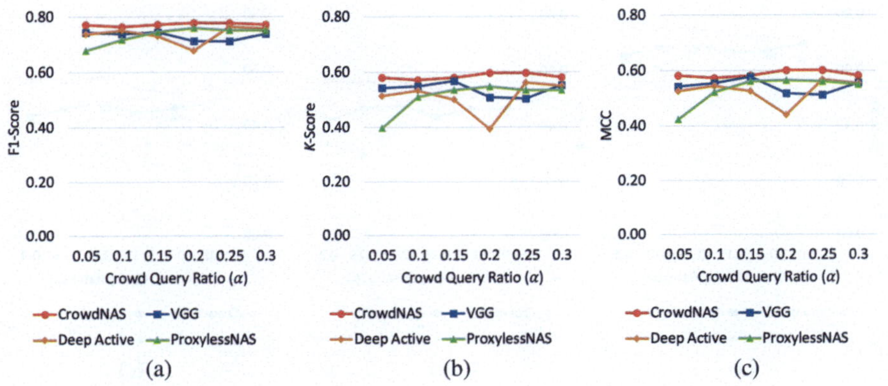

Fig. 7.10 Robustness study of CrowdNAS with different crowd query ratios (California Wildfires Dataset). (**a**) F1-score. (**b**) $\mathcal{K}$-score. (**c**) MCC

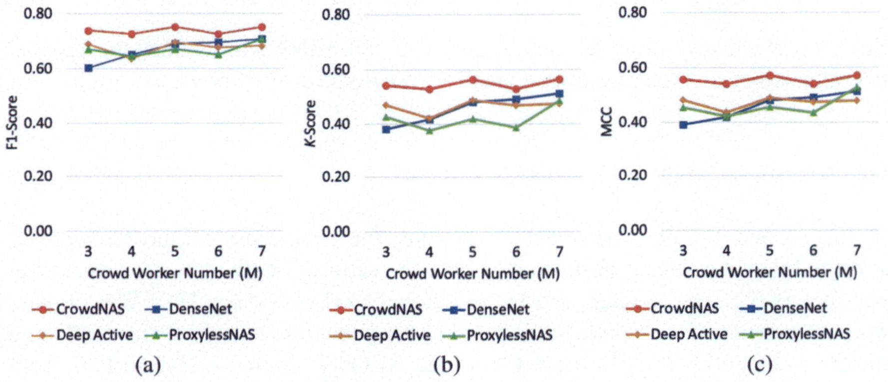

Fig. 7.11 Robustness study of CrowdNAS with different crowd worker numbers (Typhoon Hagupit Dataset). (**a**) F1-score. (**b**) $\mathcal{K}$-score. (**c**) MCC

we present the DDA classification results by removing each of the key modules in CrowdNAS (i.e., CSSD module in Sect. 7.2.1.1 and COAS module in Sect. 7.2.1.2). The results are shown in Figs. 7.13, 7.14, 7.15, and 7.16. We observe that both the CSSD and COAS modules make non-trivial contributions in improving the performance of the CrowdNAS framework. For example, the performance gains of CrowdNAS compared to w/o CSSD for the Typhoon Hagupit dataset when $\alpha = 20\%$ and $M = 5$ (Fig. 7.13c) on F1-Score, $\mathcal{K}$-Score, and MCC are 13.04, 24.01, and 18.3%, respectively. Such performance gains validate the effectiveness of the CSSD module in designing a crowd-manageable searching space that has a high likelihood of incorporating the optimal neural network architecture for DDA applications. Similarly, the performance gains of CrowdNAS compared to w/o COAS for the Typhoon Hagupit dataset when $\alpha = 20\%$ and $M = 5$ on F1-Score, $\mathcal{K}$-Score, and MCC are 5.60, 8.79, and 9.39%, respectively. The results

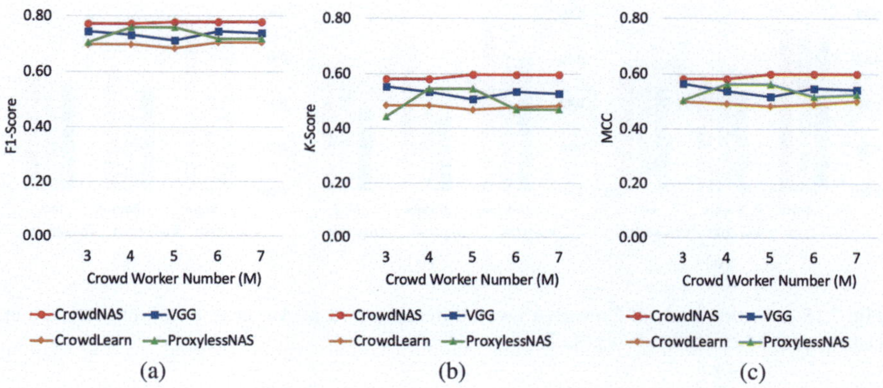

Fig. 7.12 Robustness study of CrowdNAS with different crowd worker numbers (California Wildfires Dataset). (**a**) F1-score. (**b**) $\mathcal{K}$-score. (**c**) MCC

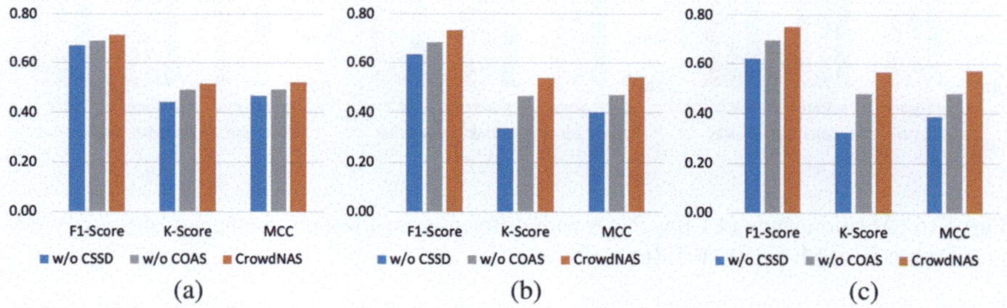

Fig. 7.13 Ablation study of CrowdNAS with different crowd query ratios (Typhoon Hagupit Dataset). (**a**) $\alpha = 10\%$. (**b**) $\alpha = 15\%$. (**c**) $\alpha = 20\%$

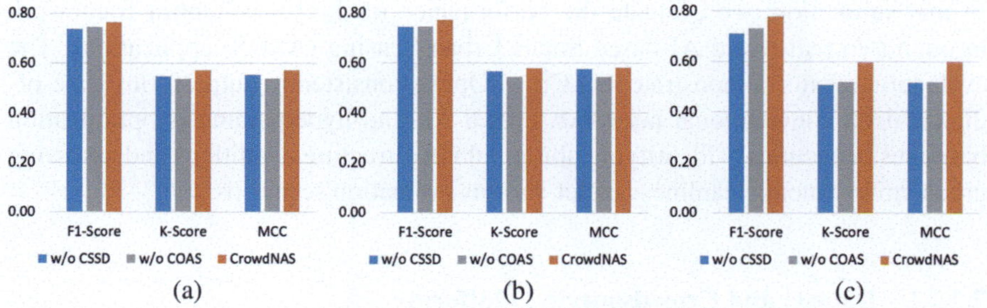

Fig. 7.14 Ablation study of CrowdNAS with different crowd query ratios (California Wildfires Dataset). (**a**) $\alpha = 10\%$. (**b**) $\alpha = 15\%$. (**c**) $\alpha = 20\%$

demonstrate the effectiveness of the COAS module in transferring the imperfect crowd intelligence to identify the optimal neural network architecture from the search space identified by CSSD.

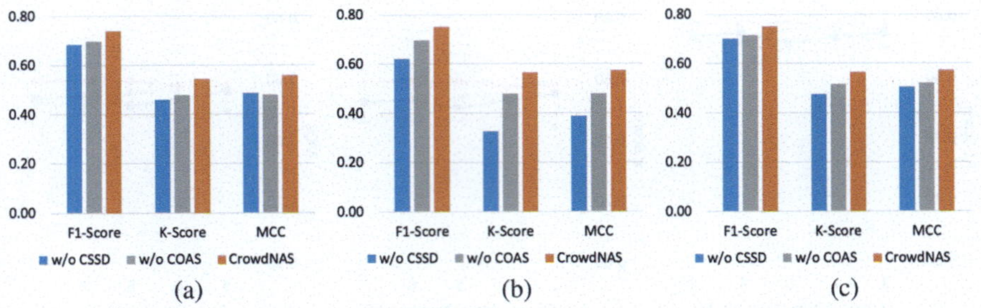

Fig. 7.15 Ablation study of CrowdNAS with different crowd worker numbers (Typhoon Hagupit Dataset). (**a**) M=3. (**b**) M=5. (**c**) M=7

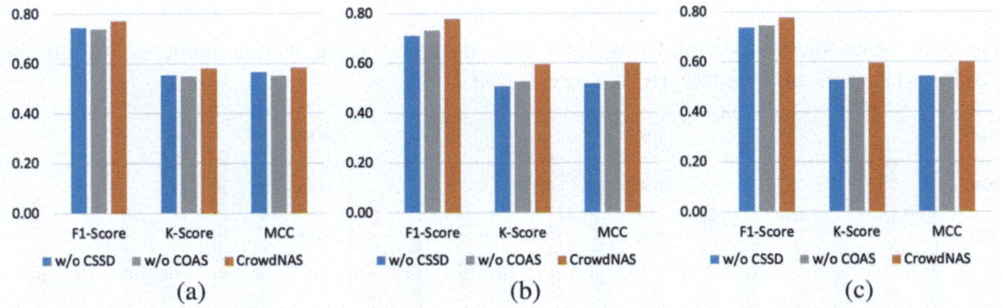

Fig. 7.16 Ablation study of CrowdNAS with different crowd worker numbers (California Wildfires Dataset). (**a**) M=3. (**b**) M=5. (**c**) M=7

7.3.2 Smart Urban Sensing

In this subsection, we evaluate the performance of the CrowdOptim framework through two real-world AI-based Smart Urban Sensing (ASUS) applications. The evaluation results demonstrate that CrowdOptim consistently outperforms state-of-the-art deep convolutional networks, crowd-AI, and hyperparameter optimization baselines in accurately identifying abnormal infrastructure conditions and assessing urban environment cleanliness under various evaluation scenarios.

7.3.2.1 Dataset and Crowdsourcing Platform

Smart Urban Sensing Datasets

In the experiments, we evaluate the performance of the CrowdOptim framework through two real-world ASUS datasets collected from online social media (i.e., Twitter) using Twitter API v2:[4] (1) smart city infrastructure monitoring (SCIM)

[4] https://developer.twitter.com/en/docs/twitter-api.

Fig. 7.17 Examples of studied ASUS datasets. (**a**) Smart city infrastructure monitoring (SCIM). (**b**) Urban environment cleanliness assessment (UECA)

Table 7.8 Statistics of two ASUS datasets

	SCIM	UECA
Number of images	1153	665
Percentage of class 1	Severe damage: 13.9%	Not clean: 33.1%
Percentage of class 2	Moderate damage: 39.7%	Less clean: 27.1%
Percentage of class 3	No or minor damage: 46.4%	Very clean: 39.8%

and (2) urban environment cleanliness assessment (UECA). Following a standard practice in SCIM applications [29], the ground-truth labels (i.e., the infrastructure damage severity label for each image) are annotated by trained annotators into three categories (i.e., severe damage, moderate damage, no or minor damage as shown in Fig. 7.17a). Similarly, the street cleanliness level of the urban environment reported in each image is manually classified by trained annotators into three different classes (i.e., very clean, less clean, and not clean as shown in Fig. 7.17b). Moreover, to ensure the quality of the ground-truth labels, each image is labeled by three independent annotators for both datasets. In particular, we observe that three annotators have the consensus of their labels of an image in 79.8% of the studied images, and two of the three annotators share the same labels of an image on the remaining 20.2% of the studied images. We apply majority voting on the collected labels to generate the ground-truth labels for each image in the evaluation. The statistics of the two datasets are summarized in Table 7.8. In addition, we set the ratio of training to testing data to be 7:3. In particular, we use the training sets to train all compared baselines for both the SCIM and UECA tasks.

Crowdsourcing Platform

We use Amazon Mechanical Turk (AMT) to obtain crowd intelligence. AMT is one of the largest crowdsourcing platforms that provides 24/7 crowdsourcing service with a large amount of crowd workers worldwide. In the crowdsourcing task, we recruit the crowd workers with an overall task approval rate above 95% and have finished at least 1000 approved tasks to ensure the crowd label quality. We pay $0.05 to each worker per image in the experiment. We follow the IRB protocol approved for this project. In the experiment, we study a diversified set of crowd query settings, where we vary the crowd query ratio from 5 to 20% and vary the number of crowd workers per task from 3 to 7.

7.3.2.2 Baseline and Evaluation Settings

In the evaluation, we compare CrowdOptim with a set of representative deep convolutional networks, crowd-AI, and hyperparameter optimization schemes for ASUS tasks. We elaborate on the baselines below.

Deep Convolutional Networks:

- **ResNet** [38]: ResNet is a widely used convolutional neural network architecture that leverages residual block design to extract the application-specific visual features for ASUS tasks.
- **DenseNet** [14]: DenseNet is a convolutional neural network based model where the network layers are connected via dense connections to perform ASUS tasks with strengthened visual feature propagation.
- **VGG** [22]: VGG is a very deep convolutional network architecture that can effectively learn the visual representations from images for ASUS tasks.

Crowd-AI:

- **Hybrid Para** [17]: Hybrid Para is a crowdsourcing-based elasticity framework that adaptively optimizes the hybrid utilization of crowd and machine intelligence to boost the performance of the ASUS model.
- **Deep Active** [33]: Deep Active is a deep active learning approach that jointly models crowd and AI efforts to efficiently select a core set of images to be labeled by crowd workers and the labeled images are utilized to improve the ASUS performance.
- **CrowdLearn** [45]: CrowdLearn is a crowd-AI hybrid approach that incorporates crowdsourcing intelligence to troubleshoot deep learning algorithms for improving the performance of deep learning-based ASUS models.

Hyperparameter Optimization:

- **HyperBand** [20]: HyperBand is a representative hyperparameter optimization approach that utilizes a non-stochastic infinite-armed bandit-based mechanism to ensure an effective neural network optimization process.

- **BOHB** [8]: BOHB is a popular hyperparameter optimization framework that introduces Bayesian and bandit-based hybrid optimization design to ensure desirable hyperparameter optimization performance at scale.
- **ASHA** [21]: ASHA is a recent hyperparameter optimization scheme with an aggressive early-stopping design to effectively explore additional hyperparameter spaces given the limited computational resource.

In the experiments, we keep the same inputs to all compared schemes for a fair comparison. In particular, the inputs to a scheme include: (1) the studied smart urban sensing images, (2) the infrastructure damage severity labels for images in the training data set, and (3) the labeled images returned by the crowd workers. In particular, we retrain the deep convolutional network and hyperparameter optimization baselines using the crowd labels to make sure all baselines have the same inputs. We also include a *random* baseline that performs the ASUS tasks by randomly selecting an infrastructure damage severity label from all possible candidates. In the experiment, the CrowdOptim model is implemented using PyTorch 1.1.0 libraries [5] and is trained on the NVIDIA Quadro RTX 6000 GPUs. Following a standard hyperparameter search space design [20], we set the hyperparameter search space in the experiments as follows: we set the learning rate to be between 10^{-6} and 10^{-3} and set the weight decay to be between 0 and 10^{-3}. We also consider three optimizer candidates in the experiments: SGD, RMSprop, and ADAM. We further set the SGD momentum to be between 0.8 and 1.0, and the RMSprop alpha to be between 0.8 and 1.0. We also set the beta1 for ADAM optimizer to be between 0.8 and 1.0 and the beta2 for ADAM optimizer to be between 0.9 and 1.0. In addition, we set the epochs in the experiments to be between 30 and 150 in the experiments.

To evaluate the performance of all compared schemes, we use three metrics that are widely adopted to evaluate the performance of multi-class image classification tasks in image processing: (1) *F1-score*, (2) *Cohen's kappa Score ($\mathcal{K}$-Score)* [2], and (3) *Matthews Correlation Coefficient (MCC)* [18]. We use $\mathcal{K}$-Score and MCC in the evaluation since the datasets are imbalanced and those two metrics have been proven to be reliable for imbalanced data [5]. The higher values of these metrics indicate better SCIM and UECA performance.

7.3.2.3 Evaluation Results

Performance Comparisons on Different Crowd Query Ratio

We first compare the performance of all schemes in terms of classification accuracy in the studied SCIM and UECA applications. In this experiment, we vary the crowd query ratio σ from 5 to 20%, which provides a good balance between the amount of crowd responses and the crowdsourcing cost. In addition, we set the number

[5] https://pytorch.org.

of crowd workers to be 5 in this experiment. The evaluation results are shown in Tables 7.9 and 7.10. We observe that the CrowdOptim clearly outperforms all compared baselines in all evaluation settings for both applications. For example, the performance gains of CrowdOptim compared to the best-performing baseline (i.e., BOHB) when $\sigma = 5\%$ in the SCIM dataset on F1-Score, $\mathcal{K}$-Score, and MCC are 5.79, 6.43, and 4.62%, respectively. The performance gains of CrowdOptim are mainly achieved by the effective crowd-driven hyperparameter optimization design that addresses the bias and inefficiency of the manual NN hyperparameter configuration process by exploring the collective wisdom of the crowd and AI. In particular, the performance gains of CrowdOptim over the deep convolutional network baselines mainly come from the fact that CrowdOptim develops a crowd-driven hyperparameter configuration framework to automatically identify the optimal hyperparameter configuration from the large hyperparameter search space. In contrast, the hyperparameter configurations of current deep convolutional network solutions are often manually configured by the AI specialists, which is known to be error-prone and suboptimal due to the lack of interpretability of the hyperparameter optimization in the absence of the ground-truth labels [16]. In addition, CrowdOptim outperforms the crowd-AI baselines because it designs an effective crowd-driven hyperparameter optimization scheme, which models different NN hyperparameter configurations and crowd inputs under a collaborative estimation framework to accurately estimate the optimality of each hyperparameter configuration. In contrast, current crowd-AI approaches often leverage the collected crowd labels to retrain AI models or replace their outputs to optimize the overall model performance. However, those solutions primarily focus on optimizing the performance of AI models with manually pre-selected hyperparameter configurations and imperfect crowd labels. As a result, their performance could still be undesirable due to the bias and constraints of the manual hyperparameter selection process and potential model collapse during the AI model training process [10]. Finally, CrowdOptim outperforms the hyperparameter optimization baselines because CrowdOptim designs a principled maximum likelihood estimation framework that can effectively leverage imperfect crowd intelligence to guide the selection of the optimal hyperparameter configuration. In contrast, current hyperparameter optimization solutions do not work well with the imperfect crowd labels, where the noises introduced by crowd inputs could mislead the current hyperparameter optimization solutions to select the poorly performed hyperparameter configuration as the optimal one. In addition, CrowdOptim achieves consistent performance gains in both SCIM and UECA datasets, which demonstrate the effectiveness of the principled estimation framework design in CrowdOptim that carefully estimates the optimality of each hyperparameter configuration to identify the optimal one in different ASUS tasks with diversified and excessive visual features.

Table 7.9 Performance comparisons on SCIM classification accuracy

	$\sigma = 5\%$			$\sigma = 10\%$			$\sigma = 15\%$			$\sigma = 20\%$		
Algorithm	F1-score	$\mathcal{K}$-score	MCC	F1-score	$\mathcal{K}$-score	MCC	F1-score	$\mathcal{K}$-score	MCC	F1-score	$\mathcal{K}$-score	MCC
Random	0.3433	0.0031	0.0033	0.3769	0.0279	0.0288	0.3702	0.0185	0.0192	0.3797	0.0475	0.0500
ResNet	0.4292	0.1764	0.2602	0.6387	0.4394	0.4497	0.6563	0.4580	0.4662	0.6372	0.4220	0.4258
DenseNet	0.5158	0.3305	0.4071	0.6852	0.5092	0.5266	0.6352	0.4394	0.4616	0.7041	0.5248	0.5289
VGG	0.5339	0.3060	0.3749	0.5544	0.2937	0.2966	0.6548	0.4401	0.4492	0.6197	0.3989	0.4131
Hybrid para	0.6445	0.4347	0.4440	0.6586	0.4529	0.4604	0.6545	0.4437	0.4487	0.6634	0.4592	0.4638
Deep active	0.6125	0.3708	0.3894	0.6545	0.4398	0.4406	0.6082	0.3563	0.3709	0.5795	0.3484	0.3604
CrowdLearn	0.6595	0.4455	0.4519	0.6190	0.4203	0.4554	0.6740	0.4929	0.5070	0.6159	0.4153	0.4333
HyperBand	0.6938	0.5028	0.5256	0.7058	0.5314	0.5457	0.6838	0.4977	0.5125	0.7222	0.5565	0.5657
BOHB	0.6325	0.4192	0.4573	0.7092	0.5400	0.5532	0.6874	0.5164	0.5363	0.7174	0.5490	0.5552
ASHA	0.6372	0.4313	0.4804	0.7174	0.5484	0.5546	0.6621	0.4764	0.4937	0.7006	0.5253	0.5335
CrowdOptim	**0.7157**	**0.5351**	**0.5415**	**0.7416**	**0.5692**	**0.5708**	**0.7453**	**0.5807**	**0.5825**	**0.7572**	**0.5983**	**0.6006**

The bold values indicate the best performing results in each evaluation metric

Table 7.10 Performance comparisons on UECA classification accuracy

	$\sigma = 5\%$			$\sigma = 10\%$			$\sigma = 15\%$			$\sigma = 20\%$		
Algorithm	F1-score	$\mathcal{K}$-score	MCC	F1-sore	$\mathcal{K}$-score	MCC	F1-score	$\mathcal{K}$-score	MCC	F1-score	$\mathcal{K}$-score	MCC
Random	0.3359	0.0032	0.0030	0.3373	0.0031	0.0029	0.3457	0.0196	0.0198	0.3412	0.0116	0.0118
ResNet	0.3948	0.2029	0.2522	0.5107	0.3043	0.3195	0.5774	0.3872	0.4028	0.5983	0.3931	0.3978
DenseNet	0.4368	0.2382	0.2648	0.6515	0.4833	0.4885	0.5629	0.3549	0.3576	0.6360	0.4548	0.4565
VGG	0.3234	0.0681	0.0770	0.4328	0.2573	0.3144	0.5150	0.3317	0.3476	0.5216	0.3100	0.3252
Hybrid para	0.6115	0.4601	0.4871	0.6183	0.4674	0.4919	0.6370	0.4899	0.5140	0.6621	0.5264	0.5511
Deep active	0.5351	0.3755	0.4271	0.6091	0.4321	0.4428	0.5184	0.3711	0.4173	0.5650	0.4196	0.4470
CrowdLearn	0.4091	0.2117	0.2582	0.5335	0.3335	0.3480	0.5902	0.4104	0.4272	0.6270	0.4381	0.4425
HyperBand	0.6837	0.5415	0.5593	0.6427	0.5022	0.5325	0.6799	0.5522	0.5679	0.6807	0.5377	0.5448
BOHB	0.4425	0.2415	0.2754	0.5843	0.4109	0.4278	0.5746	0.3657	0.3759	0.5468	0.3386	0.3598
ASHA	0.5780	0.3826	0.4150	0.6552	0.5221	0.5815	0.7044	0.5520	0.5567	0.7077	0.5585	0.5666
CrowdOptim	**0.7064**	**0.5732**	**0.5901**	**0.7176**	**0.5823**	**0.5910**	**0.7212**	**0.5897**	**0.5995**	**0.7399**	**0.6189**	**0.6372**

The bold values indicate the best performing results in each evaluation metric

The Effect of Number of Crowd Workers

In the second set of experiments, we evaluate the performance of the CrowdOptim scheme on SCIM and UECA datasets over different numbers of crowd workers. In the experiment, we vary the number of crowd workers from 3 to 7 and set the crowd query ratio to be 15%. In the experiments, we compare the performance of CrowdOptim with the best-performing baselines in each category (i.e., RestNet for deep convolutional network baselines in both SCIM and UECA dataset, CrowdLearn and Hybrid Para for crowd-AI baselines in SCIM and UECA datasets, respectively, and BOHB and ASHA for hyperparameter optimization baselines in SCIM and UECA datasets, respectively). The evaluation results are shown in Figs. 7.18 and 7.19. We observe that the performance of CrowdOptim is relatively stable and consistently outperforms the best-performing baselines as the number of crowd workers changes in both SCIM and UECA datasets. The above results demonstrate the robustness and effectiveness of the CrowdOptim scheme in effectively leveraging the imperfect crowd intelligence from different numbers of crowd workers to guide the identification of the optimal hyperparameter configuration. We also observe that the performance of compared baselines drop when we increase the number of crowd workers from 5 to 7 in the SCIM dataset.

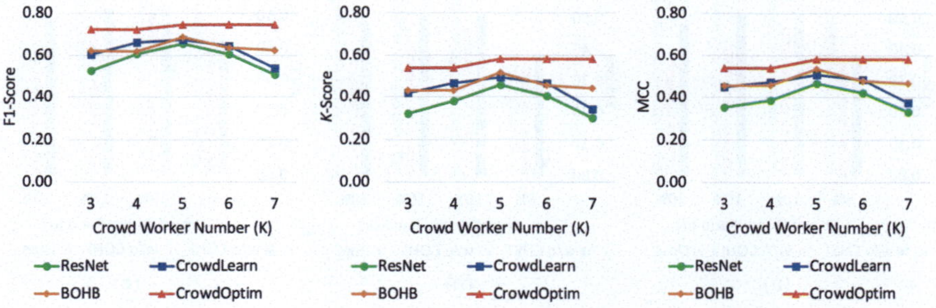

(a) (b) (c)

Fig. 7.18 The effect of number of crowd workers (SCIM). (**a**) F1-score. (**b**) $\mathcal{K}$-Score. (**c**) MCC

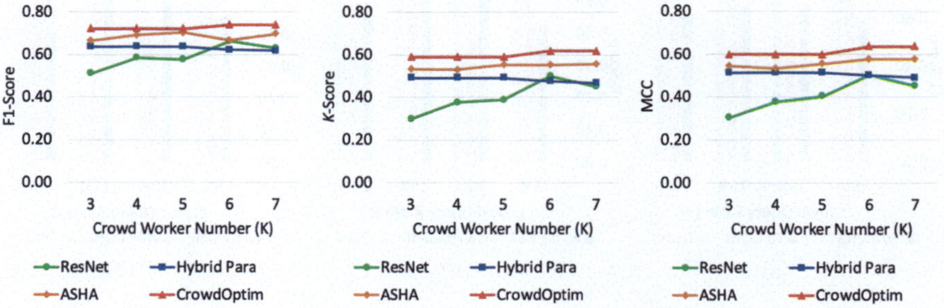

(a) (b) (c)

Fig. 7.19 The effect of number of crowd workers (UECA). (**a**) F1-score. (**b**) $\mathcal{K}$-Score. (**c**) MCC

This is because the training labels returned by crowd workers can be biased and inconsistent, which could lead to the model collapse during the training process for the compared baselines and a decrease in their ASUS performance.

Ablation Study of CrowdOptim Scheme

In the last set of experiments, we conduct an ablation study to learn the contribution of each core module design in CrowdOptim to its overall performance. In the experiments, we present the SCIM and UECA classification results by removing each of the core modules in CrowdOptim (i.e., CHST and COHI). In particular, we uniformly sample the hyperparameter configurations from the search space to replace the CHST model to generate the crowd-manageable search space. We randomly select one hyperparameter in the crowd-manageable hyperparameter search space as the optimal hyperparameter configuration to replace the COHI module. The evaluation results are shown in Figs. 7.20 and 7.21. We observe that both core modules in the CrowdOptim framework make important contributions to the performance of the CrowdOptim framework over the two ASUS applications.

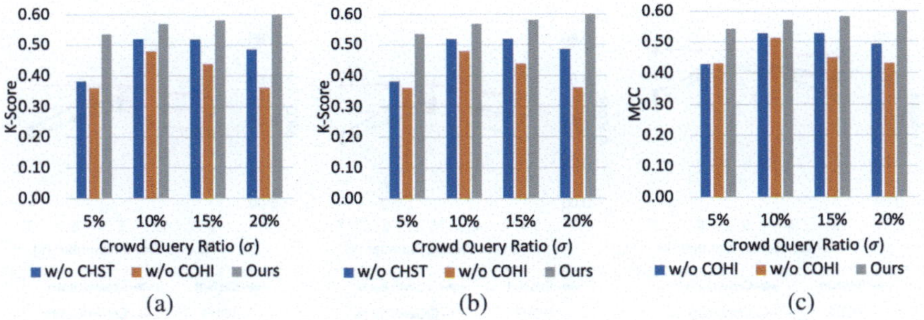

Fig. 7.20 Ablation study of CrowdOptim scheme (SCIM). (**a**) F1-score. (**b**) $\mathcal{K}$-Score. (**c**) MCC

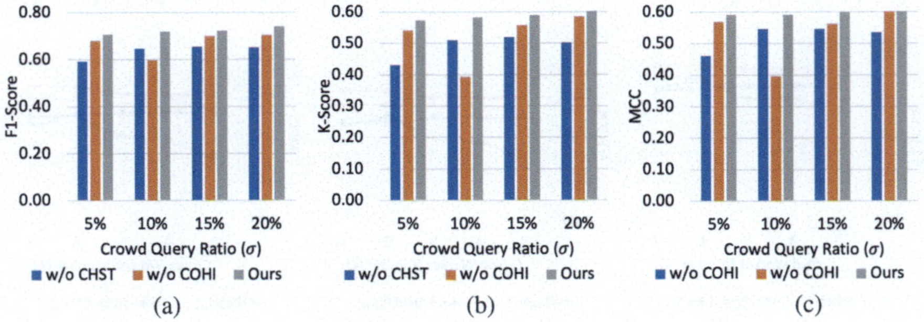

Fig. 7.21 Ablation study of CrowdOptim scheme (UECA). (**a**) F1-score. (**b**) $\mathcal{K}$-Score. (**c**) MCC

7.4 Discussion

This section provides further discussions on the impact and limitations of the presented human-AI collaboration frameworks to address the challenging NAS and HPO problem in social intelligence applications. First, the results show that CrowdNAS consistently surpasses all baseline models, achieving the highest DDA accuracy and the lowest computational cost. This performance improvement stems from the unique approach of leveraging human intelligence from public crowdsourcing platforms rather than relying on input from AI experts. CrowdNAS addresses the primary limitations of existing DDA and NAS solutions, which often depend on large volumes of high-quality training data or extensive expert input. Additionally, CrowdNAS demonstrates consistent performance gains across two distinct disaster scenarios—Typhoon Hagupit and California wildfires– highlighting its robustness and adaptability to various disaster contexts (e.g., flooding vs. fire damage, urban vs. rural damage). Similarly, the CrowdOptim model outperforms state-of-the-art baselines, achieving the highest accuracy in both SCIM and UECA applications. This suggests that CrowdOptim can effectively support local and federal agencies in implementing timely actions and countermeasures to enhance public safety and health in urban areas, such as preventing incidents like the 2021 Florida condominium collapse or reducing mosquito breeding to curb malaria. Furthermore, CrowdOptim consistently performs well across diverse social intelligence applications, specifically SCIM and UECA. These applications both involve using social media images to monitor urban environments, yet have distinct objectives—detecting abnormal infrastructure conditions vs. assessing urban cleanliness—and utilize images with varied visual characteristics (e.g., color distributions, object layouts, and patterns). The strong performance of CrowdOptim across these applications suggests its potential for broader use in other image-driven social intelligence applications with varied goals.

The integration of crowdsource human intelligence with AI, as shown by the examples of CrowdNAS and CrowdOptim, represents a new intelligence paradigm in addressing complex social intelligence challenges. By leveraging the diversity and flexibility of crowdsourcing, the collaborative systems eliminate dependence on massive labeled data and inputs from domain experts, which enables AI solutions to be more flexible and accessible. The crowdsource human intelligence introduces diverse, context-specific insights (e.g., local knowledge of disaster-affected areas), enabling robust performance across varied domains, such as disaster response [47], urban monitoring [48], and public safety [7]. In contrast, AI models deliver computational efficiency, scalability, and reasonable precision but rely on pre-defined data quality and may be incapable of contextual understanding and nuances without human inputs [30]. Combining the best of both—the flexibility of crowdsourced human intelligence and the scalability of AI—these frameworks address limitations inherent in each approach. This synergy positions crowd-AI systems as powerful tools for social intelligence applications, from truth discovery [34], to recommender systems [44] and public health monitoring [49].

There are also a few limitations of the introduced human-AI collaboration frameworks, which can potentially be addressed in future work. First, the CrowdNAS and CrowdOptim frameworks are currently designed to work with social intelligence applications where the studied physical status of disaster damage or urban environments can be categorized. However, it is noted that there exist also social intelligence applications where the physical status is represented by a numerical variable (e.g., air quality index, population density, traffic volume). To address this limitation, the CrowdNAS and CrowdOptim framework can be extended by focusing on optimizing neural network architectures and hyperparameter configurations for deep regression models, which are commonly used to estimate numerical variables. Specifically, one potential solution is to introduce a principled hidden Markov model that effectively models the numerical physical status as a hidden variable. Then, the next step is to derive a closed-form expectation-maximization solution to estimate the optimality of each neural network architecture and hyperparameter configuration for the deep regression model, identifying the optimal configuration for the desired social intelligence application performance.

Second, the neural architecture search and hyperparameter optimization process in CrowdNAS and CrowdOptim is currently performed in a batch manner, where the discussed models identify an optimal network architecture and hyperparameter configuration for all studied imagery data within a social intelligence application. However, this design may not perform well in streaming social intelligence applications (e.g., real-time disaster damage assessment, dynamic traffic flow monitoring), which aim to provide on-the-fly social intelligence services using real-time social intelligence data. In these cases, the optimal network architecture and hyperparameter configuration may change over time. To address this challenge, the CrowdNAS and CrowdOptim frameworks can be extended to streaming, crowd-driven neural architecture and hyperparameter optimization approaches that recursively update the estimation of the optimal neural architecture and hyperparameter configuration on-the-fly, using a novel recursive maximum likelihood estimation model.

Third, the incentive mechanism for crowd query tasks could be further optimized. Currently, the crowd query design in CrowdNAS and CrowdOptim assigns a uniform incentive for all images in the query, but it is noted that images with complex visual features often require additional incentives to recruit more crowd workers to cross-validate the collected labels, ensuring high-quality results. To address this challenge, one possible solution is to develop a quality-aware incentive policy that balances crowd label quality and crowdsourcing cost. Specifically, the first step is to quantify the complexity of each labeling task by leveraging a recent crowdsourcing task complexity prediction algorithm [43], which estimates complexity by quantifying the divergence in visual features (e.g., color distributions and object layouts) extracted from each image. The next step is to dynamically adjust incentives to recruit crowd workers based on the quantified complexity of the input image. The objective of this design is to ensure that the crowd-AI collaborative framework achieves a high likelihood of collecting accurate labels from the crowd while maintaining costs within the application's budget.

References

1. AMT, https://www.mturk.com/.
2. R. Artstein and M. Poesio. Inter-coder agreement for computational linguistics. *Computational Linguistics*, 34(4), 2008.
3. C. Biernacki, G. Celeux, and G. Govaert. Choosing starting values for the em algorithm for getting the highest likelihood in multivariate gaussian mixture models. *Computational Statistics & Data Analysis*, 41(3-4):561–575, 2003.
4. H. Cai, L. Zhu, and S. Han. Proxylessnas: Direct neural architecture search on target task and hardware. In *International Conference on Learning Representations*, 2018.
5. D. Chicco and G. Jurman. The advantages of the matthews correlation coefficient (mcc) over f1 score and accuracy in binary classification evaluation. *BMC genomics*, 21(1):6, 2020.
6. T. Elsken, J. H. Metzen, F. Hutter, et al. Neural architecture search: A survey. *J. Mach. Learn. Res.*, 20(55):1–21, 2019.
7. E. Estellés-Arolas. Using crowdsourcing for a safer society: When the crowd rules. *European Journal of Criminology*, 19(4):692–711, 2022.
8. S. Falkner, A. Klein, and F. Hutter. Bohb: Robust and efficient hyperparameter optimization at scale. In *International Conference on Machine Learning*, pages 1437–1446. PMLR, 2018.
9. N. Fayyazifar. An accurate cnn architecture for atrial fibrillation detection using neural architecture search. In *2020 28th European Signal Processing Conference (EUSIPCO)*, pages 1135–1139. IEEE, 2020.
10. M. Feurer and F. Hutter. Hyperparameter optimization. In *Automated Machine Learning*, pages 3–33. Springer, 2019.
11. M. Feurer, J. Springenberg, and F. Hutter. Initializing bayesian hyperparameter optimization via meta-learning. In *Proceedings of the AAAI Conference on Artificial Intelligence*, volume 29, 2015.
12. K. Hansson and T. Ludwig. Crowd dynamics: Conflicts, contradictions, and community in crowdsourcing. *Computer Supported Cooperative Work (CSCW)*, 28(5):791–794, 2019.
13. V. Hassija, V. Chamola, A. Mahapatra, A. Singal, D. Goel, K. Huang, S. Scardapane, I. Spinelli, M. Mahmud, and A. Hussain. Interpreting black-box models: a review on explainable artificial intelligence. *Cognitive Computation*, 16(1):45–74, 2024.
14. G. Huang, Z. Liu, L. Van Der Maaten, and K. Q. Weinberger. Densely connected convolutional networks. In *CVPR*, page 3, 2017.
15. N. Q. V. Hung, N. T. Tam, L. N. Tran, and K. Aberer. An evaluation of aggregation techniques in crowdsourcing. In *International Conference on Web Information Systems Engineering*, pages 1–15. Springer, 2013.
16. F. Hutter, J. Lücke, and L. Schmidt-Thieme. Beyond manual tuning of hyperparameters. *KI-Künstliche Intelligenz*, 29(4):329–337, 2015.
17. J. Jarrett, I. Saleh, M. B. Blake, R. Malcolm, S. Thorpe, and T. Grandison. Combining human and machine computing elements for analysis via crowdsourcing. In *10th IEEE International Conference on Collaborative Computing: Networking, Applications and Worksharing*, pages 312–321. IEEE, 2014.
18. G. Jurman, S. Riccadonna, and C. Furlanello. A comparison of mcc and cen error measures in multi-class prediction. *PloS one*, 7(8):e41882, 2012.
19. D. P. Kingma and J. Ba. Adam: A method for stochastic optimization. *arXiv preprint arXiv:1412.6980*, 2014.
20. L. Li, K. Jamieson, G. DeSalvo, A. Rostamizadeh, and A. Talwalkar. Hyperband: A novel bandit-based approach to hyperparameter optimization. *Journal of Machine Learning Research*, 18(185):1–52, 2018.
21. L. Li, K. Jamieson, A. Rostamizadeh, E. Gonina, J. Ben-tzur, M. Hardt, B. Recht, and A. Talwalkar. A system for massively parallel hyperparameter tuning. *Proceedings of Machine Learning and Systems*, 2:230–246, 2020.

22. X. Li, D. Caragea, H. Zhang, and M. Imran. Localizing and quantifying damage in social media images. In *2018 IEEE/ACM International Conference on Advances in Social Networks Analysis and Mining (ASONAM)*, pages 194–201. IEEE, 2018.
23. C. Liu, L.-C. Chen, F. Schroff, H. Adam, W. Hua, A. L. Yuille, and L. Fei-Fei. Auto-deeplab: Hierarchical neural architecture search for semantic image segmentation. In *Proceedings of the IEEE conference on computer vision and pattern recognition*, pages 82–92, 2019.
24. C. Liu, P. Dollár, K. He, R. Girshick, A. Yuille, and S. Xie. Are labels necessary for neural architecture search? In *European Conference on Computer Vision*, pages 798–813. Springer, 2020.
25. H. Liu, K. Simonyan, and Y. Yang. Darts: Differentiable architecture search. In *International Conference on Learning Representations*, 2018.
26. J. Lorraine, P. Vicol, and D. Duvenaud. Optimizing millions of hyperparameters by implicit differentiation. In *International Conference on Artificial Intelligence and Statistics*, pages 1540–1552. PMLR, 2020.
27. D. McDuffie. Using amazon's mechanical turk: benefits, drawbacks, and suggestions. *APS Observer*, 32(2), 2019.
28. A. Y. Ng et al. Preventing" overfitting" of cross-validation data. In *ICML*, volume 97, pages 245–253. Citeseer, 1997.
29. D. T. Nguyen, F. Ofli, M. Imran, and P. Mitra. Damage assessment from social media imagery data during disasters. In *Proceedings of the 2017 IEEE/ACM International Conference on Advances in Social Networks Analysis and Mining 2017*, pages 569–576, 2017.
30. K. Nikolenko. Artificial intelligence and society: Pros and cons of the present, future prospects. *Futurity Philosophy*, 1(2):54–67, 2022.
31. P. Ren, Y. Xiao, X. Chang, P.-Y. Huang, Z. Li, X. Chen, and X. Wang. A comprehensive survey of neural architecture search: Challenges and solutions. *ACM Computing Surveys (CSUR)*, 54(4):1–34, 2021.
32. F. Saxen, P. Werner, S. Handrich, E. Othman, L. Dinges, and A. Al-Hamadi. Face attribute detection with mobilenetv2 and nasnet-mobile. In *2019 11th International Symposium on Image and Signal Processing and Analysis (ISPA)*, pages 176–180. IEEE, 2019.
33. O. Sener and S. Savarese. Active learning for convolutional neural networks: A core-set approach. In *International Conference on Learning Representations*, 2018.
34. L. Shang, Y. Zhang, Z. Yue, Y. Choi, H. Zeng, and D. Wang. A domain adaptive graph learning framework to early detection of emergent healthcare misinformation on social media. In *Proceedings of the International AAAI Conference on Web and Social Media*, volume 18, pages 1408–1421, 2024, https://doi.org/10.1609/icwsm.v18i1.31398.
35. K. Simonyan and A. Zisserman. Very deep convolutional networks for large-scale image recognition. *arXiv preprint arXiv:1409.1556*, 2014.
36. S. Sinha, H. Ohashi, and K. Nakamura. Class-wise difficulty-balanced loss for solving class-imbalance. In *Proceedings of the Asian Conference on Computer Vision*, 2020.
37. R. S. Sutton and A. G. Barto. *Reinforcement learning: An introduction.* MIT press, 2018.
38. S. Targ, D. Almeida, and K. Lyman. Resnet in resnet: Generalizing residual architectures. *arXiv preprint arXiv:1603.08029*, 2016.
39. C. Wang, D. Chen, L. Hao, X. Liu, Y. Zeng, J. Chen, and G. Zhang. Pulmonary image classification based on inception-v3 transfer learning model. *IEEE Access*, 7:146533–146541, 2019.
40. D. Wang, L. Kaplan, T. Abdelzaher, and C. C. Aggarwal. On credibility estimation tradeoffs in assured social sensing. *IEEE Journal on Selected Areas in Communications*, 31(6):1026–1037, 2013.
41. D. Wang, L. Kaplan, and T. F. Abdelzaher. Maximum likelihood analysis of conflicting observations in social sensing. *ACM Transactions on Sensor Networks (ToSN)*, 10(2):1–27, 2014.
42. D. Wang, L. Kaplan, H. Le, and T. Abdelzaher. On truth discovery in social sensing: A maximum likelihood estimation approach. In *Information Processing in Sensor Networks (IPSN), 2012 ACM/IEEE 11th International Conference on*, pages 233–244. IEEE, 2012.

43. J. Yang, J. Redi, G. Demartini, and A. Bozzon. Modeling task complexity in crowdsourcing. In *Fourth AAAI Conference on human computation and crowdsourcing*, 2016.
44. Z. Yue, H. Zeng, Y. Zhang, J. McAuley, and D. Wang. Transferable sequential recommendation via vector quantized meta learning. *arXiv preprint arXiv:2411.01785*, 2024.
45. D. Zhang, Y. Zhang, Q. Li, T. Plummer, and D. Wang. Crowdlearn: A crowd-ai hybrid system for deep learning-based damage assessment applications. In *2019 IEEE 39th International Conference on Distributed Computing Systems (ICDCS)*, pages 1221–1232. IEEE, 2019.
46. Q. Zhang, Y. Wen, X. Tian, X. Gan, and X. Wang. Incentivize crowd labeling under budget constraint. In *2015 IEEE Conference on Computer Communications (INFOCOM)*, pages 2812–2820. IEEE, 2015.
47. Y. Zhang, R. Zong, Z. Kou, L. Shang, and D. Wang. Crowdnas: A crowd-guided neural architecture searching approach to disaster damage assessment. *Proceedings of the ACM on Human-Computer Interaction*, 6(CSCW2):1–29, 2022. https://doi.org/10.1145/3555179.
48. Y. Zhang, R. Zong, L. Shang, Z. Kou, H. Zeng, and D. Wang. Crowdoptim: A crowd-driven neural network hyperparameter optimization approach to ai-based smart urban sensing. *Proceedings of the ACM on Human-Computer Interaction*, 6(CSCW2):1–27, 2022. https://doi.org/10.1145/3555536.
49. Y. Zhang, R. Zong, L. Shang, Z. Yue, H. Zeng, Y. Liu, and D. Wang. Tripartite intelligence: Synergizing deep neural network, large language model, and human intelligence for public health misinformation detection (archival full paper). In *Proceedings of the ACM Collective Intelligence Conference*, pages 63–75, 2024.
50. D. Zhou and C. Tomlin. Budget-constrained multi-armed bandits with multiple plays. In *Proceedings of the AAAI Conference on Artificial Intelligence*, volume 32, 2018.
51. B. Zoph, V. Vasudevan, J. Shlens, and Q. V. Le. Learning transferable architectures for scalable image recognition. In *Proceedings of the IEEE conference on computer vision and pattern recognition*, pages 8697–8710, 2018.

Chapter 8
Fairness and Bias Issues

Abstract Fairness and bias are critical concerns in modern AI and social intelligence systems. This chapter first introduces the fundamental issues of demographic bias in data-driven social intelligence applications, such as facial analysis and educational assessment. We present two novel frameworks, FairCrowd and DebiasEdu to address these critical concerns. In particular, FairCrowd is a fair crowdsourcing-based data sampling framework that leverages crowd intelligence to infer demographic labels and achieve balanced dataset representation without requiring extensive manual annotations. DebiasEdu is a crowd-AI collaborative framework that combines gradient-based bias identification with crowd-guided bias calibration to achieve fair and accurate student performance prediction. Through comprehensive case studies on human face data sampling and student performance prediction, we demonstrate the effectiveness of these approaches to address fairness and bias issues in social intelligence and show the potential of integrating human intelligence with AI systems to create more equitable and effective social intelligence applications.

Keywords Fairness · Bias · Crowdsourcing · AI for education · Face recognition

8.1 Fairness and Bias in Social Intelligence

With the proliferation of big data and the collective power of crowdsourced human intelligence, social intelligence has become a paradigm for addressing complex societal challenges and improving decision-making processes in human communities. However, it also presents critical issues that may lead to undesirable discrimination and amplify societal disparities. In particular, fairness and bias emerge as fundamental concerns that require careful consideration in both data curation and algorithm design. For example, human face images have been widely adopted by various social intelligence applications, such as face recognition, face generation, and face attribute prediction [42]. However, these applications usually suffer from a non-trivial performance bias toward certain demographic groups caused by the well-known data imbalance issue. A recent study from IBM has found

D. Wang et al., *Social Intelligence*, https://doi.org/10.1007/978-3-031-90080-8_8

that current commercial facial recognition services have much higher error rates for images that involve dark-skinned women than for light-skinned men [5]. More importantly, data-driven social intelligence solutions trained on such imbalanced datasets could also encode the underlying data biases into the automated decision-making process and lead to discriminatory outcomes in critical applications such as face recognition and student performance assessment.

Several initial efforts have been made to address the fairness issue in social intelligence [1, 4, 6, 23, 24, 46]. Those solutions often require pre-annotated demographic labels of data samples to identify fairer sub-datasets by balancing the number of samples from different demographic groups. However, many large-scale human-centered datasets do not contain such demographic labels due to the high cost of data annotations [11]. While some demographic label prediction methods (e.g., gender recognition, age classification) can be leveraged to predict demographic labels, the prediction accuracy is affected by many factors (e.g., face angle, face covering, facial expression) and the incorrect demographic labels will significantly degrade the fairness of the sampled dataset [18]. From the algorithm perspective, existing solutions primarily address the bias issue by increasing the weights of underrepresented samples during training (e.g., sample re-weighting) [24] or integrating fairness regularization into the training objective (e.g., fairness constraints and adversarial learning) [23, 49]. However, these solutions often achieve results with improved fairness at the cost of reduced overall accuracy due to the trade-off between fairness and accuracy of data-driven models [7]. Therefore, to comprehensively tackle the problem of bias and ensure fairness in social intelligence, it is essential to holistically address the bias issue at both data and algorithm levels to maintain high accuracy while promoting fairness across all demographic groups [25, 56]. However, several challenges remain to be addressed.

Crowdsourcing-Based Demographic Label Inference

Crowdsourcing is an effective solution to address demographic bias by incorporating the common sense knowledge and experience of crowd workers. For example, a possible crowdsourcing strategy for obtaining demographic labels of face images in the dataset pool is to assign crowd workers to annotate demographic labels for *all* images in the pool. However, such a strategy is both time-consuming and expensive when the scale of the dataset pool is large [11]. An alternative approach is to select a reasonably sized set of face images from the dataset pool and assign crowd workers to annotate them with demographic labels. The fair dataset is then constructed by taking the same number of annotated images from different demographic groups. However, the limitation of this approach is that it only considers the images with annotated labels from the crowd but ignores a large number of informative images that are not selected for annotations. Moreover, the crowd workers will have to annotate each selected image with multiple demographic labels in case the bias of the dataset is associated with more than one demographic attribute (e.g., both age and gender in Fig. 8.1). Thus, it is challenging to sample a fair sub-dataset from the dataset pool by using crowdsourcing effectively without prior knowledge of demographic labels of images.

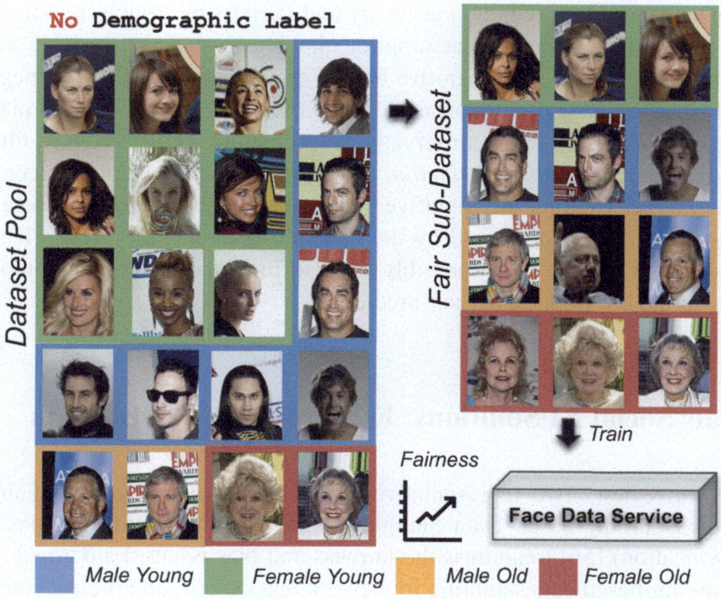

Fig. 8.1 Fair dataset sampling problem

Trade-Off between Fairness and Accuracy

It is not sufficient to achieve a desirable dataset if only the fairness aspect is considered. For example, a data service that generates equally poor prediction results for all demographic groups is perfectly fair but of little practical value [51]. It is observed that training the human face data models on a fair sub-dataset could sometimes cause a significant performance drop on accuracy compared to the case where the models are trained on a randomly sampled sub-dataset [30]. The main reason is that there exists an inherent trade-off between fairness and accuracy objectives in the data sampling process: some images in the dataset pool may contribute more to the fairness objective (e.g., images from a minority group), while other images may contribute more to the accuracy objective (e.g., images from majority group). This challenge is particularly important when selecting a subset of samples where social intelligence models are likely to make inaccurate predictions due to the lack of training data and different behavioral patterns in underrepresented groups.

Potential Bias of Crowd Intelligence

While crowdsourced human intelligence could be incorporated to reduce demographic bias in social intelligence data, the inherent biases in human judgment may potentially pose significant challenges to achieving fair outcomes in social intelligence algorithms. Recent efforts in crowd–AI collaboration [38, 48, 54] have been made to address this challenge. These approaches often utilize crowd intelligence to improve prediction accuracy and fairness by troubleshooting failure cases of AI models under the assumption that the crowd can provide accurate and fair responses. However, cognitive bias of crowd workers [17] may negatively impact their annotation performance [22]. For example, crowd workers may have the confirmation bias of being conservative in predicting a *Distinction* result due to their preexisting beliefs that *Distinction* is assigned to a really small percentage of students. Another example of cognitive bias is the anchoring effect, where crowd workers can be overly influenced by the first few examples they see. Hence, the generated crowd feedback can possibly mislead the social intelligence models to learn inaccurate information in their predictions.

8.2 Fair Social AI Solutions: FairCrowd and DebiasEdu

This section reviews two representative social intelligence solutions, FairCrowd (Fair Crowdsourcing-based Data Sampling) [25] and DebiasEdu (Debias AI for Online Education) [56] to address the fairness and bias issues. FairCrowd is a fair crowdsourcing-based data sampling framework that designs an efficient batch-level demographic label inference model and a joint fair-accuracy-aware data shuffling method to ensure fairness in sampled social intelligence data. DebiasEdu is a crowd-AI collaborative debias framework that melds AI and crowd intelligence through a novel gradient-based bias identification mechanism and a bias calibration crowdsourcing design to achieve an optimal trade-off between accuracy and fairness.

8.2.1 *FairCrowd: A Bias Inference Approach to Fair Data Sampling*

The overview of FairCrowd is shown in Fig. 8.2. FairCrowd consists of four modules: (1) a Service-Specific Batch Data Sampler (SBDS), (2) a Crowdsourcing Batch Bias Estimator (CBBE), (3) a Similarity-Based Demographic Label Predictor (SDLP), and (4) an Accuracy-Fairness-Aware Dataset Balancer (AFDB). First, the SBDS module trains an application-specific model (e.g., a face attractiveness prediction (FAP) model) on the randomly sampled dataset $\mathcal{X}$ from the dataset pool $\mathcal{D}$ and generates data batches from $\mathcal{X}$ for the crowdsourcing tasks. Second, the CBBE module designs a crowdsourcing scheme that tasks crowd workers to infer the demographic bias of $\mathcal{X}$ by estimating the bias of data batches output by the SBDS module. Third, the SDLP predicts the demographic labels of all face images in $\mathcal{X}$ and $\mathcal{D}$ by leveraging the demographic bias inferred by CBBE. Finally, the AFDB shuffles the images between $\mathcal{X}$ and $\mathcal{D}$ to generate FairCrowd sampled dataset $\widetilde{\mathcal{X}}$ to improve both accuracy and fairness of the FAP service trained on $\widetilde{\mathcal{X}}$. We discuss the above modules in detail below.

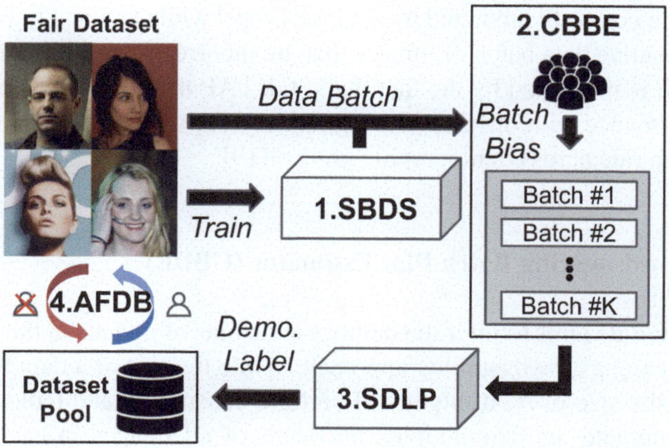

Fig. 8.2 Overview of FairCrowd

8.2.1.1 Service Specific Batch Data Sampler (SBDS)

The SBDS module consists of two components: (1) a FAP model and (2) a random batch image sampler. The FAP model is designed to perform face attribute prediction on a given dataset. Given the FAP model as $\mathcal{M}$ and the ith input face image X_i from $\mathcal{X}$, the attribute prediction result $\hat{y}_i$ (e.g., predicted face attribute) of X_i can be represented as $\hat{y}_i = \mathcal{M}(X_i)$.

We train the FAP model on $\mathcal{X}$ with the ground-truth labels $\mathcal{Y} = \{y_1, \ldots, y_M\}$ and generate the prediction results of all images in $\mathcal{X}$ as $\hat{\mathcal{Y}} = \{\hat{y}_1, \ldots, \hat{y}_M\}$. By comparing $\mathcal{Y}$ and $\widetilde{\mathcal{Y}}$, we can identify face images in $\mathcal{X}$ that are correctly and incorrectly predicted by $\mathcal{M}$ respectively, which is critical to generate data batches from $\mathcal{X}$. Due to the imbalanced data distribution of $\mathcal{X}$ across different demographic attributes, the accuracy performance of the FAP model could be biased towards some specific demographic groups (e.g., young females in Fig. 8.1). It is difficult to detect such performance bias because the images in $\mathcal{X}$ contain no demographic labels. We design the random batch image sampler component to address this issue. We first define *data batch* below.

Definition 8.1 (Data Batch) We define a *data batch* as a set of items randomly sampled from a combination list $\mathcal{T} = \{\mathcal{X}, \mathcal{Y}, \widetilde{\mathcal{Y}}\}$ where the mth combination item is denoted as $\mathcal{T}_m = \{X_m, y_m, \hat{y}_m\}$. We further denote a set of data batches as $\Omega = \{\Omega_1, \ldots, \Omega_K\}$ where $\Omega_k = \{T_{k,1}, \ldots, T_{k,P}\}$ is kth data batch in Ω, K is the total number of batches in the set and P is the number of images in a batch.

We choose random sampling in generating the data batches to ensure the demographic distribution of images in a batch can reasonably approximate that in $\mathcal{X}$. Therefore, we can infer the bias of $\mathcal{X}$ by estimating the performance bias of the FAP model on the data batches. For a data batch Ω_k, we further split it into two groups $\Omega_k = \{\Omega_k^+, \Omega_k^-\}$ where $\Omega_k^+ = \{T_{k,1}, \ldots, T_{k,P^+}\}$ denotes the positive data batch of images that are correctly predicted by the FAP model while $\Omega_k^- = \{T_{k,1}, \ldots, T_{k,P^-}\}$ denote the negative data batch of images that are incorrectly predicted. Such split of the data batch is motivated by the fact that a fair FAP model is expected to achieve similar performance with different demographic groups on both prediction rate and mis-prediction rate across demographic groups [19].

8.2.1.2 Crowdsourcing Batch Bias Estimator (CBBE)

The CBBE module aims to infer the demographic bias of images in the data batches from SBDS using a crowdsourcing approach. While the size of a data batch is often smaller than the size of $\mathcal{X}$, it might still be time-consuming and tedious for crowd workers to annotate the demographic attributes of all images in each batch. The CBBE module designs a novel batch-level bias estimation scheme that only asks crowd workers to estimate the *overall* bias of each data batch (e.g., more female than male in the batch) instead of providing the demographic attribute annotation for each image in the batch. An example of the crowdsourcing task for a data batch is shown in Fig. 8.3. In the task, we ask crowd workers to answer a set of questions about the demographic attributes of images in the batch. For example, a crowd worker can often quickly determine the bias of the data batch towards young people and estimate the degree of bias in the task shown in Fig. 8.3.

After receiving the responses from all the crowd workers, we estimate the bias of the data batch by applying the majority voting scheme on the crowd response to overcome the potential noise from the crowd. We denote the bias of all data

1. Are there more females or males in this group of faces?
a) Female b) Male c) Equal
2. How much more faces are females(males) than males(females)?
a) Slightly b) Much c) Very Much
3. Are there more young or old in this group of faces?
a) Old b) Young c) Equal
4. How much more faces are young(old) than old(young)?
a) Slightly b) Much c) Very Much

Fig. 8.3 Crowdsourcing interface

batches as a bias list $\mathcal{B} = \{B_1, \ldots, B_K\}$ where $B_k = \{B_{k,1}, \ldots, B_{k,C}\}$ represents the bias of kth data batch with C demographic attributes of interests. For example, the answer to the gender bias of the data batch in Fig. 8.3 should be "female". Similarly, we define the bias degree list for all data batches as $\mathcal{S} = \{S_1, \ldots, S_K\}$ where $S_k = \{S_{k,1}, \ldots, S_{k,C}\}$ represents the bias degree for all demographic bias in B_k. For example, the degree of gender bias in the data batch in Fig. 8.3 could be "much".

8.2.1.3 Similarity-Based Batch Label Propagator (SDLP)

Given the estimated batch-level bias $\mathcal{B}$ and $\mathcal{S}$ from CBBE, SDLP aims to predict demographic labels for all images in $\mathcal{D}$. The predicted labels are critical to the FairCrowd scheme in order to shuffle images between $\mathcal{X}$ and $\mathcal{D}$ to improve the data fairness of the sampled dataset. The SDLP module consists of two different components: a face similarity calculator and a demographic label predictor. For each face image in $\mathcal{D}$, the face similarity calculator computes the face similarity scores between the image of interest and the images in the data batch from SBDS. The demographic label predictor then leverages the computed face similarity scores and the bias of data batches from CBBE to infer the demographic label of the image. We describe these components in detail below.

Face similarity indicates the overall relevance of two human faces based on the facial characteristics including various demographic attributes (e.g., age, gender, race). The face similarity calculator aims to measure the similarity between the face images in $\mathcal{D}$ and the images in data batches Ω. We first define the image-batch face similarity as below.

Definition 8.2 (Image-Batch Face Similarity) Given an image D_n from $\mathcal{D}$ and a data batch Ω_k from CBBE, the image-batch face similarity is computed by averaging the face similarity between D_n with each face image in Ω_k. The calculation process can be denoted as $M_{i,k} = \frac{1}{P}\sum_{i=1}^{P} \cos(\mathcal{F}(D_n), \mathcal{F}(\mathcal{T}_{k,i}))$, where $\cos(\cdot)$ denotes the cosine similarity function, $\mathcal{F}$ is the face representation extractor that is usually a pre-trained deep face representation learning model (e.g., FaceNet [37]), $M_{i,k}$ is the image-batch face similarity. We further denote the image-batch face similarity between D_n and all data batches in Ω as a similarity list $M(D_n) = \{M_{i,1}, \ldots, M_{i,K}\}$ where K is the total number of data batches.

Leveraging the image-batch face similarity and the estimated bias of data batches from CBBE, the demographic label predictor infers demographic labels of all face images in $\mathcal{D}$. The intuition of the solution is: if a face image has a high image-batch face similarity with a data batch and the data batch has a high bias degree score, the face image has a high likelihood of belonging to the majority demographic group of the data batch. In particular, given a face image D_n from $\mathcal{D}$, the bias list $\mathcal{B}$, the bias degree list $\mathcal{S}$, and the demographic attribute of interest a_c, the demographic label predictor infers the demographic label for D_n on attribute a_c as $\widetilde{\mathcal{A}}(D_n, a_c) =$

$\sum_{i=1}^{K} \mathcal{B}_{i,a_c}^{*} \times M_{n,i} \times S_{i,a_c}$ where $\mathcal{B}_{i,a_c}$ is the bias of data batch Ω_i towards the demographic attribute a_c, $M_{n,i}$ is the face-batch similarity between D_n and Ω_i, S_{i,a_c} is the bias degree for $\mathcal{B}_{i,a_c}$. $\mathcal{B}_{i,a_c}^{*}$ is a binary variable whose value is decided by $\mathcal{B}_{i,a_c}$. In particular, $\mathcal{B}_{i,a_c}^{*} = 1$ if $\mathcal{B}_{i,a_c}$ is a_c^{+} (e.g., male) or $\mathcal{B}_{i,a_c}^{*} = -1$ otherwise. The higher $\widetilde{\mathcal{A}}(D_n, a_c)$ is, the more likely D_n belongs to a_c^{+}. We segment $\widetilde{\mathcal{A}}(D_n, a_c)$ for all D_n in D across all demographic a_c via pre-defined thresholds and convert segmented $\widetilde{\mathcal{A}}(D_n, a_c)$ to the estimated demographic label of D_n. The demographic labels are leveraged to shuffle face images between $\mathcal{X}$ and $\mathcal{D}$ to improve the fairness of $\mathcal{X}$ in the next subsection.

8.2.1.4 Accuracy-Fairness-Aware Dataset Balancer (AFDB)

After estimating the demographic labels of all face images in $\mathcal{D}$, the AFDB aims to shuffle the images between $\mathcal{X}$ and $\mathcal{D}$. The shuffling process iteratively converts $\mathcal{X}$ to the FairCrowd sampled dataset $\widetilde{\mathcal{X}}$ with improved dataset fairness. The shuffling operations include removing existing images from $\mathcal{X}$ and adding additional images from $\mathcal{D}$ to $\mathcal{X}$. However, there exists an inherent trade-off between fairness and accuracy in the image shuffling process. In particular, some images contribute more to the fairness of the sampled dataset while other images contribute more to the accuracy of the FAP model. It is not a trivial task to decide which images to remove and add during the image shuffling process to achieve a desirable trade-off between fairness and accuracy. Therefore, the AFDB designs two components to solve the problem: the image contribution estimator and the balanced image shuffler. The image contribution estimator estimates the contribution of an image to the FAP model accuracy on both $\mathcal{X}$ and $\mathcal{D}$. The balanced image shuffler considers both the fairness of the sampled dataset and the accuracy of the FAP model when performing data shuffling operations. We describe these components in detail below.

We choose the Max Entropy [40] score as the metric to measure the contribution of an image to the FAP model accuracy. A high Max Entropy score of an image indicates the FAP model trained with the image is likely to achieve better accuracy performance [40]. The image contribution estimator computes Max Entropy scores for all images in both $\mathcal{X}$ and $\mathcal{D}$ to estimate their contributions to improve the FAP model accuracy. Given the Max Entropy scores, the balanced image shuffler aims to shuffle the face images between $\mathcal{X}$ and $\mathcal{D}$ to generate a less biased dataset $\widetilde{\mathcal{X}}$ (the FairCrowd sampled dataset). We first define the demographic combination set.

Definition 8.3 (Demographic Combination) We define the demographic combination as a set of combinations with different demographic attributes. For example, the combination set of two demographic attributes a_1 and a_2 (e.g., age, gender) is denoted as $O(a_1, a_2) = \{a_1^{+}a_2^{+}, a_1^{+}a_2^{-}, a_1^{-}a_2^{+}, a_1^{-}a_2^{-}\}$ (e.g., young male, young female, old male, old female).

The number of combinations is 2^C where C is the number of demographic attributes of interest. We further define the *combination score* of a face image as the summation of the absolute value of estimated demographic label scores from SDLP over the demographic combinations in $\mathcal{A}$. For example, given a face image D_n from $\mathcal{D}$ with estimated demographic label scores $\{\widetilde{\mathcal{A}}(D_n, a_1), \widetilde{\mathcal{A}}(D_n, a_2)\}$ from SDLP, its combination score is $\mathcal{A}(D_n) = |\widetilde{\mathcal{A}}(D_n, a_1)| + |\widetilde{\mathcal{A}}(D_n, a_2)\}|$. The combination score of an image indicates the likelihood that the demographic attribute label of the image is correct.

We divide the images from $\mathcal{X}$ into 2^C groups based on the estimated demographic labels from SDLP to estimate the number of images in each demographic combination of a fair sampled dataset. If $\mathcal{X}$ is perfectly balanced across all demographic combinations, the number of face images belonging to each combination should be exactly $M_C = M/2^C$. Therefore, the balanced image shuffler removes the images from a demographic combination in $\mathcal{X}$ whose size is larger than M_C and adds images from $\mathcal{D}$ to a demographic combination whose size is smaller than M_C. To decide the exact set of images that should be removed or added, the balanced image shuffler leverages the Max Entropy scores and the combination scores of all images in $\mathcal{X}$ and $\mathcal{D}$. In particular, a face image in $\mathcal{X}$ is removed if it has a low Max Entropy score and a high combination score. Alternately, a face image in $\mathcal{D}$ is added to $\mathcal{X}$ if it has a high Max Entropy score and a high combination score. With such a data shuffling strategy, the AFDB transforms $\mathcal{X}$ to $\widetilde{\mathcal{X}}$ by achieving a more desirable trade-off between the fairness and accuracy in $\widetilde{\mathcal{X}}$.

The FairCrowd repeats the process of the above four modules iteratively to predict more accurate demographic labels for face images and improve the fairness of the sampled dataset. To define the termination condition of the iterative process, we derive the overall demographic bias score $\widetilde{\Omega} = \sum_{i=1}^{K} \sum_{j=1}^{C} S_{k,c}$. We stop the iteration if $\widetilde{\Omega}$ reaches a threshold $\widetilde{\Omega}^*$ pre-defined by the application, which indicates the bias of the sampled dataset has met the requirement from the application.

8.2.2 *DebiasEdu: A Bias-Aware Crowd-AI Collaborative Approach*

DebiasEdu is a bias-aware crowd-AI collaborative approach that integrates AI and crowd intelligence to achieve accurate and fair student performance prediction. The overview of DebiasEdu is presented in Fig. 8.4. In particular, the DebiasEdu consists of two key modules: (1) a *Gradient-based Bias Identification (GBI)* module that analyzes the variation in gradients of training samples to identify biased AI results from different demographic groups, and (2) a *Crowd-Guided Bias Calibration (CBC)* module that creates a bias-aware crowdsourcing interface design and a crowd-guided calibration model to address the demographic bias of AI and the cognitive bias of the crowd.

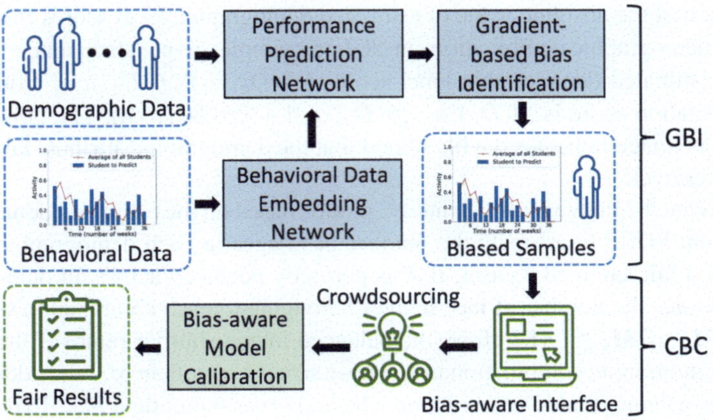

Fig. 8.4 Overview of the DebiasEdu framework

8.2.2.1 Gradient-Based Bias Identification (GBI)

To effectively predict student final performance $\boldsymbol{L}$ using inputs of behavioral data $\boldsymbol{X^B}$ and demographic attributes $\boldsymbol{X^D}$, we first design two key networks as follows.

To extract useful information from the behavioral data $\boldsymbol{X^B}$ for student performance prediction (e.g., consistent hard work, extra hard work before the final), we design a *behavioral data embedding network* $f(\cdot)$ as follows:

$$E_k^B = f(X_k^B), \quad \forall 1 \le k \le K \tag{8.1}$$

where E_k^B represents the generated embedding of the behavioral data X_k^B for the kth student. K is the total number of students in the training set. In particular, we utilize the long short-term memory (LSTM) model as the behavioral data embedding network $f(\cdot)$ in the setting, which has been shown to be effective in extracting information from sequential data [21, 27].

After feature embedding, we build a student *performance prediction network* $g(\cdot, \cdot)$ that leverages the generated behavioral embedding and the demographic information to predict a student's final result as:

$$\widehat{L_k^{AI}} = g(E_k^B, X_k^D), \quad \forall 1 \le k \le K \tag{8.2}$$

where $\widehat{L_k^{AI}}$ is the *AI prediction* for the kth student's final performance. In particular, the performance prediction network $g(\cdot, \cdot)$ is a multilayer perceptron consisting of a sequence of fully connected feedforward neural network layers to predict a student's performance by comprehensively examining the embedded behavioral data.

To guide the behavioral data embedding network $f(\cdot)$ to effectively capture useful behavior pattern information (e.g., consistent work throughout the semester) and train the performance prediction network $g(\cdot, \cdot)$ to accurately predict a student's final performance result, we define the objective function $\mathcal{L}_{AI}$ for the AI model as follows:

$$\mathcal{L}_{AI} = \mathcal{L}_{\mathrm{CE}}\left(g\left(f(X_k^B), X_k^D\right), L_k\right), \quad \forall 1 \leq k \leq K \tag{8.3}$$

where $\mathcal{L}_{\mathrm{CE}}$ is the cross entropy loss to measure classification accuracy. L_k is the ground-truth label of the kth student's final performance on the training set.

Given the designed AI model, the key focus of the GBI module is identifying biased AI results from the testing set for crowd intelligence to improve framework prediction fairness. We first define the set of these AI results as follows:

Definition 8.4 (Crowdsourcing Subset (S)) We select a subset of students on the testing set where the AI model is likely to generate inaccurate predictions for crowd workers to improve. We focus particularly on selecting from underrepresented groups $\boldsymbol{U}$ since these students are more likely to receive incorrect predictions due to the lack of training data and differences in behavioral patterns (e.g., older students often need to complete more activities to achieve the same result compared to younger students). We formally define the crowdsourcing subset to include the behavioral and demographic data for the selected J students as $\boldsymbol{S} = \{\{X_1^B, X_1^D\}, \ldots, \{X_J^B, X_J^D\}\}$, where $J = \alpha I$.

We refer to the demographic data and behavioral data of students as *samples* in the rest of the solution. It is observed that the AI prediction network is more likely to predict incorrectly for the samples with gradients varying significantly during the training process [35]. These samples exhibiting more variant gradients are more likely to belong to underrepresented groups. This is because underrepresented samples, with different input data characteristics (e.g., behavioral patterns) compared to the non-underrepresented samples, pose greater challenges for deep neural networks to learn to predict accurately [35]. Therefore, we define these samples whose gradients vary significantly during training as the *biased training samples*. The objective is to identify biased training samples from different demographic groups inversely proportional to the number of students in each group (e.g., more samples from worse-performing underrepresented groups).

To identify biased training samples using gradient variation, we first define the *training sample gradient* $\nabla = \{\nabla_1, \nabla_2, \ldots, \nabla_K\}$ to be the gradients of training samples with respect to the objective function $\mathcal{L}_{AI}$ as follows:

$$\nabla_k = \mathrm{E}\left[\frac{\partial \mathcal{L}_{AI}}{\partial \{X_k^B, X_k^D\}}\right], \quad \forall 1 \leq k \leq K \tag{8.4}$$

where $\mathrm{E}[\cdot]$ denotes the expectation and ∂ denotes the partial derivative. The training sample gradient can be computed by the chain rule using derivatives of each neural network layer.

Definition 8.5 (Gradient Variance (V)) We define $V = \{V_1, V_2, \ldots, V_K\}$ to be the variance of sample gradient ∇:

$$V_k = \mathrm{Var}\left[\frac{\partial \mathcal{L}_{AI}}{\partial \{X_k^B, X_k^D\}}\right], \quad \forall 1 \leq k \leq K \tag{8.5}$$

where Var[·] denotes the variance. In particular, the variance of sample gradient can be approximated by the average gradient in different epochs [12], where the first several epochs are eliminated due to unstable performance at the beginning of training.

We select a subset of training samples with the top α largest gradient variances in the training set (i.e., *variant gradient subset*), where α is selected empirically based on the trade-off between the algorithmic fairness and the crowdsourcing budget. However, it remains challenging to identify a subset of samples with gradients varying significantly from the *testing* set since there are no ground-truth annotations available to even train a model and compute gradients. Therefore, we select the testing samples that share a similar behavioral pattern as the training samples in the selected variant gradient subset. This idea is motivated by the fact that an AI model generates similar predictions and gradients for input samples with similar characteristics (e.g., behavioral patterns) [13]. We introduce the measurement to identify the crowdsourcing subset S of demographically biased testing samples as follows:

Definition 8.6 (Bias Measurement (B)) We define $B = \{B_1, B_2, \ldots, B_I\}$ to be the bias measurements of all studied testing samples. In particular, the bias measurement B_i for the ith student is formally defined as follows:

$$B_i = \sum_{k=1}^{K} \left(\left\| X_k^B - X_i^B \right\|_2 + \left\| X_k^D - X_i^D \right\|_2 \right), \forall 1 \leq i \leq I \tag{8.6}$$

where $\| \cdot \|_2$ denotes the L2-norm of a vector. In particular, a lower value of the bias measurement B_i indicates a larger bias (i.e., a higher similarity with the variant gradient subset) for the ith student in the testing set.

Based on the bias measurement for all testing samples, we then select the samples with top α lowest B_i from the testing set to generate the crowdsourcing subset S that primarily contains underrepresented students who are likely to receive inaccurate AI predictions. In the next subsection, we discuss how to use crowd intelligence to address the identified bias.

8.2.2.2 Crowd-Guided Bias Calibration (CBC)

Given the selected crowdsourcing subset $\boldsymbol{S}$ from the GBI module discussed above, we then design a crowdsourcing interface and a model calibration mechanism to address the identified demographic bias while mitigating the negative impact of cognitive bias from crowd workers. In particular, we leverage crowd intelligence to work on the student performance prediction task and mitigate demographic bias. For an in-depth effectiveness analysis of using the crowd in student performance prediction.

We first design the visualization of behavioral data since student performance prediction based on behavioral data is not a trivial task for crowd workers. In particular, humans are often not good at analyzing the raw data (e.g., dozens or hundreds of numbers) compared to AI models, which motivates the design of a clear visualization of the high-level behavioral patterns (e.g., the general trend of activities and consistent hard work) to the crowd workers. The behavioral data X_i^B for the ith student are their activities on the online learning platform *per day* during the semester, which is shown in Fig. 8.5a. However, crowd workers often do not need such detailed information to predict student performance accurately. In particular, we observe that even those students who achieve *Distinction* results in many classes do not spend time on every course every day, highlighting the fact that accumulative activities within a certain time period can be more informative to help crowd workers to predict accurately. Therefore, we present the accumulative activities on a *bi-weekly* basis of a student to crowd workers using the blue bars shown in Fig. 8.5b. In addition to the bar plot of the behavioral data, we also add the *average activities* of all students in a course to help crowd workers make their predictions.

However, crowd workers are observed to have cognitive bias [17], which can lead to inaccurate crowd prediction in student performance prediction [22]. Therefore, the next question is how to design a crowdsourcing interface to address the cognitive

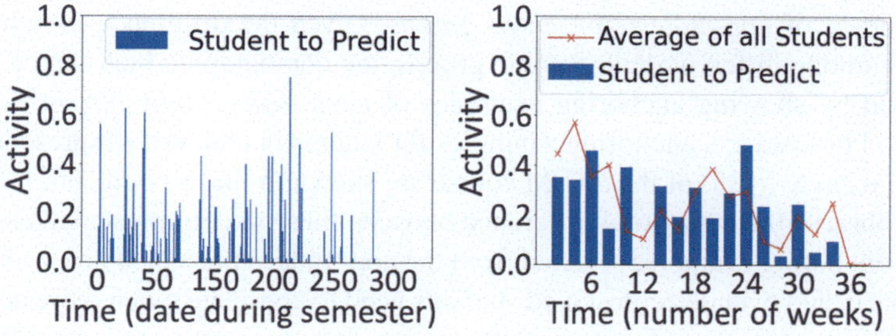

(a) (b)

Fig. 8.5 Examples of the original behavioral data and the behavioral data visualization design. (**a**) Visualization of the original per-day behavioral data. (**b**) Behavioral data visualization design for the crowd

bias of the crowd. In particular, confirmation bias is a key cognitive bias of humans observed in prediction tasks [2, 17]. We define it as follows:

Definition 8.7 (Confirmation Bias) Confirmation bias of the crowd refers to the fact that crowd workers can be overly influenced by their preexisting beliefs. For example, crowd workers can be conservative in predicting a *Distinction* result if they believe *Distinction* is assigned to a really small percentage of students. The confirmation bias is more obvious when a crowd worker is only presented with the behavioral data visualization of a specific student since they need to predict completely based on their preexisting beliefs if no additional information (e.g., annotation examples provided by the task administrator as reference) is provided to the crowd workers regarding the labeling tasks.

We design an approach to address the confirmation bias of the crowd by leveraging the anchoring effect of human cognition. We first define the anchoring effect as follows:

Definition 8.8 (Anchoring Effect) Anchoring effect refers to the fact that crowd workers can be influenced by the first few examples they see and then use these examples as the anchor for the subsequent prediction.

We can leverage this cognitive characteristic of the crowd to train the crowd workers to calibrate their preexisting prediction criteria with only a few *anchoring examples* for each student performance category (e.g., *Fail*, *Pass*, and *Distinction*). For instance, anchoring examples selected from the training set of a STEM course are shown in Fig. 8.6a, c, and e. Note that we cannot simply train the AI model with such anchoring examples since AI models often rely on a large number of data samples for effective predictions. Even the few-shot learning methods still depend on large-scale datasets to pre-train data representations, which are not available in the problem setting.

In addition, while crowd workers achieve better overall accuracy and fairness compared to the AI model on the selected crowdsourcing subset S (Definition 8.4), the crowd prediction accuracy of *underrepresented groups* can still be worse than the accuracy of *non-underrepresented groups*. Given the difference in behavioral patterns among different demographic groups, the demographic bias can be further addressed by showing anchoring examples of *each demographic group* to crowd workers. For instance, anchoring examples for students in the underrepresented age group (i.e., age ≥ 35) of the STEM course are shown in Fig. 8.6b, d, and f. We can clearly observe the behavioral difference between these underrepresented examples and the anchoring examples selected from the non-underrepresented group shown in Fig. 8.6a, c, and e: underrepresented students need to complete much more activities to achieve the same result compared to non-underrepresented students. Observed behavioral difference demonstrates that the crowd prediction accuracy and fairness can be further enhanced by presenting accurate anchoring examples from each demographic group to help crowd workers form accurate performance criteria. The pilot studies show an 18.9% performance improvement when using the anchoring

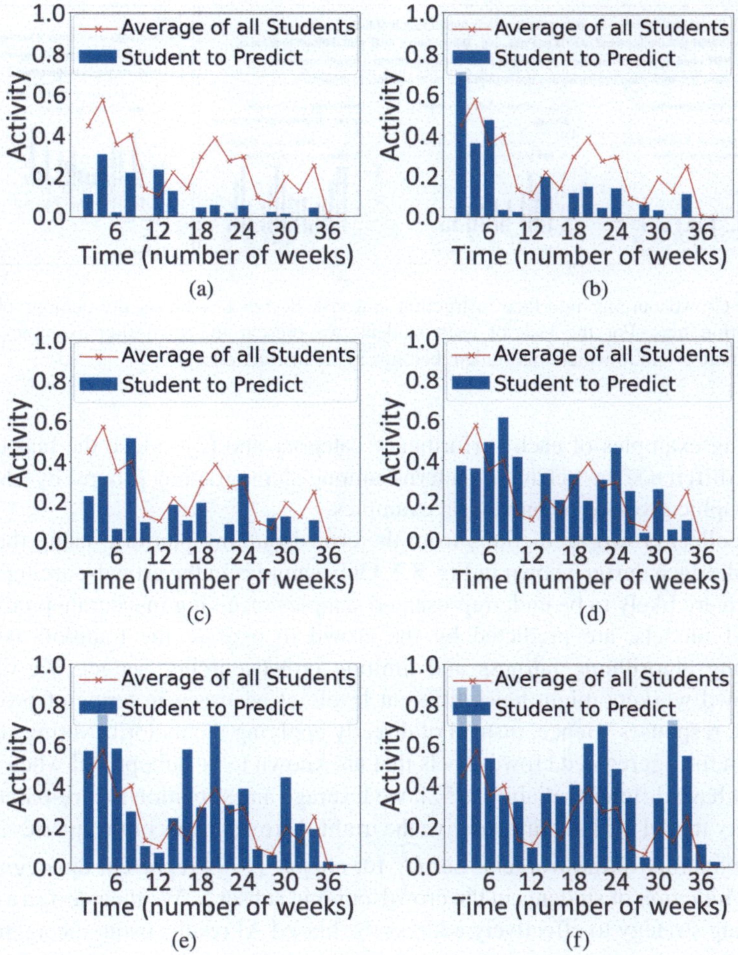

Fig. 8.6 Anchoring examples for students in the non-underrepresented and underrepresented age group. (**a**) *Fail* (non-underrepresented). (**b**) *Fail* (underrepresented). (**c**) *Pass* (non-underrepresented). (**d**) *Pass* (underrepresented). (**e**) *Distinct* (non-underrepresented). (**f**) *Distinct* (underrepresented)

examples from each demographic group compared to not using such anchoring examples.

We present the crowdsourcing interface design for student performance prediction in Fig. 8.7. For the prediction task of each student, we present the anchoring examples and corresponding descriptions of the demographic group this student belongs to. For instance, in Fig. 8.7, since the sample student in the prediction task belongs to the underrepresented age group, the interface also presents the anchoring examples for this group (Fig. 8.6b, d, and f) in the instructions. The objective of this interface design is to (1) address the confirmation bias by presenting

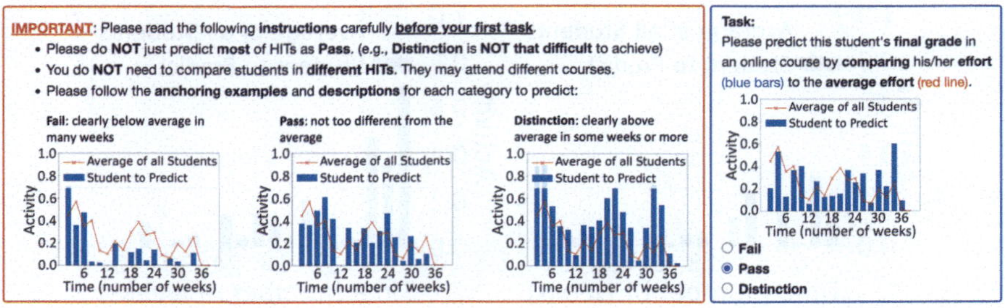

Fig. 8.7 Crowdsourcing interface instruction and task design to address the demographic and confirmation bias. For the task of each student, we present the anchoring examples of the demographic group to which this student belongs in the instructions

anchoring examples of each performance category and (2) reduce the bias caused by the difference in behavior patterns among demographic groups by showing demographic group-wise anchoring examples.

We collect crowd predictions from the crowdsourcing platform using the bias-aware interface design shown in Fig. 8.7. Only samples in the crowdsourcing subset S, which are likely to be underrepresented samples receiving inaccurate predictions from AI models, are predicted by the crowd to explore the trade-off between improving algorithmic fairness and limiting crowdsourcing budget. We observe that crowd workers might have different levels of accuracy in terms of providing accurate responses. Hence, instead of directly applying the majority voting strategy to obtain the aggregated crowd labels that are known to be suboptimal when crowd workers have different reliability [52], we leverage an estimation theory-based truth discovery model [45] to jointly derive the truthful crowd labels of the queries as well as the reliability of the workers. Let $\widehat{L_j^C}$ for all $j \in [1, J]$ represent the *aggregated crowd prediction* of students in the crowdsourcing subset S. We then design a crowd offloading strategy to effectively address the biased AI results using the aggregated crowd labels. In the strategy, for all J students, the truthful labels $\widehat{L_j^C}$ derived from the crowd are used to replace the AI predictions $\widehat{L_j^{AI}}$ of the testing samples in the crowdsourcing subset S to generate the final framework prediction $\widehat{\boldsymbol{L}}$.

8.3 Real-World Case Studies

We evaluate the performance of the FairCrowd and DebiasEdu using two real-world case studies. Specifically, we evaluate the effectiveness of FairCrowd in sampling a fair human face dataset which is often prone to demographic bias. To evaluate DebiasEdu, we show a case study of online student performance prediction that demonstrates its ability to mitigate demographic bias while maintaining prediction accuracy.

8.3.1 *Fair Human Face Data Sampling*

Fair human face data sampling is a fundamental application in social intelligence, which is essential for the training and evaluation of many downstream tasks, such as face recognition, face attribute prediction, and facial expression analysis.

8.3.1.1 Data

We use a large-scale human face dataset CelebA [28] as the dataset pool for the experiments. The selected dataset contains hundreds of thousands of human face images that are biased toward certain demographic groups. Moreover, CelebA consists of several demographic labels (e.g., gender, age, race) of the face images, which can be used to thoroughly evaluate the performance of FairCrowd. We perform the face attractiveness prediction as the FAP task on the dataset, which comes with ground-truth binary face attractiveness labels (i.e., 1 for attractive and 0 for non-attractive). We also note that the face attractiveness prediction is related to various demographic attributes (e.g., age, gender), and the prediction performance can be biased towards a majority demographic group if the training dataset is imbalanced. The summary of the dataset pool is shown in Table 8.1.

8.3.1.2 Baseline Methods

We conduct experiments with the state-of-the-art FAP models to evaluate the performance of FairCrowd.

- **VGGFace2** [11]: VGGFace2 is a face recognition framework trained on a large-scale face dataset with millions of face images that do not contain demographic labels.
- **LightCNN** [47]: LightCNN is a face recognition framework that consists of a light convolutional neural network to learn compact embeddings of human faces.
- **FMTNet** [55]: FMTNet is a FAP framework that learns from labeled facial attributes and transfers the knowledge to predict unlabeled attributes.
- **Slim-CNN** [41]: Slim-CNN is a light-weighted FAP scheme that designs a computationally-efficient CNN module to tackle the large variations of face images in pose, background, and illumination.

Table 8.1 Dataset summary

Dataset	Demo. attributes	Sample
CelebA	Male & Young	53,447
	Female & Young	103,287
	Male & Old	30,987
	Female & Old	14,878

- **CascadeCNN** [16]: CascadeCNN is a FAP scheme that automatically detects face regions specific to different demographic attributes to classify the face attributes.
- **PSMC** [10]: PSMC is a face attribute representation learning framework that considers face similarity between people to generate feature representations for specific face attributes (e.g., attractiveness).

For VGGFace2 and LightCNN, we first extract high-dimensional face image features from the pre-trained networks and then construct a deep neural network classifier for attractiveness prediction. For FMTNet, we remove the knowledge transfer module because we have face attractiveness labels in the training data of the problem and do not need to transfer the learned knowledge from other face attributes. We strictly follow the parameters and configurations of all schemes as documented in their papers.

8.3.1.3 Experimental Setting

In the experiments, the randomly sampled dataset and the FairCrowd sampled dataset are both *training sets* that are used to train the FAP models. For the *testing set*, we randomly select a subset from the dataset pool $\mathcal{D}$. The size of the training set and testing set are both 10% of the dataset pool. We set the number of data batches as $K = 50$ and the number of images in each batch as 32. We select the gender (i.e., male or female) and age (i.e., young or old) as two demographic attributes of interest in FairCrowd as the dataset pool is heavily biased on both attributes (i.e., more young than old, more female than male as shown in Table 8.1). For each data batch, we assign five crowd workers to perform the batch-level bias estimation task from the CBBE module. We set the payment to crowd workers well above the requirement from Amazon Mechanical Turk (AMT) [3]. We set the size of input face images as 218×178 and align all face images using similarity transformation according to the eye locations in order to unify the angles of faces. We set the total number of training epochs as 40 and train the model with an initial learning rate of 0.001 and decay of 0.95 in each epoch. The optimizer is Adam with 5×10^{-4} weight decay. We run the experiments on Ubuntu 16.04 with two NVIDIA 1080Ti.

8.3.1.4 Performance of FairCrowd Sampled Dataset

In the first set of experiments, we focus on the overall performance of all schemes trained on the FairCrowd sampled dataset in terms of fairness, prediction accuracy, and overall training time. For fairness, we use four widely used metrics to evaluate the performance discrimination of a scheme between different demographic groups: *Demographic Parity* [20], *True Positive Parity* [29], *False Positive Parity* [29], and *Equalized Odds* [19]. The lower values of the above metrics indicate a better fairness performance of a model. The results are reported in Table 8.2. We observe

Table 8.2 Overall fairness performance

Model	Demographic parity	T.P. parity	F.P. parity	Equalized odds
Randomly sampled dataset				
VGGFace2	0.264	0.175	0.105	0.280
LightCNN	0.446	0.282	0.217	0.499
FMTNet	0.426	0.253	0.191	0.444
SlimCNN	0.501	0.276	0.275	0.552
CascadeCNN	0.481	0.239	0.265	0.505
PSMC	0.462	0.235	0.236	0.475
FairCrowd sampled dataset				
VGGFace2	**0.242**	**0.042**	**0.099**	**0.141**
LightCNN	**0.344**	**0.055**	**0.152**	**0.207**
FMTNet	**0.326**	**0.081**	**0.160**	**0.242**
SlimCNN	**0.390**	**0.087**	**0.213**	**0.300**
CascadeCNN	**0.400**	**0.129**	**0.197**	**0.327**
PSMC	**0.345**	**0.085**	**0.165**	**0.250**

The bold values indicate the best performing results in each evaluation metric

all compared FAP schemes achieve significantly better fairness performance on the FairCrowd sampled dataset than the randomly sampled dataset. For example, LightCNN, one of the state-of-the-art face recognition approaches, is able to achieve 0.102 lower Demographic Parity and 0.292 lower Equalized Odds on the FairCrowd sampled dataset than the randomly sampled dataset. The performance gains are mainly due to the fact that the FairCrowd scheme estimates demographic attribute labels of images in the dataset pool and shuffles face images between the sampled dataset and the dataset pool to make the sampled dataset more balanced across different demographic groups.

To evaluate the performance of the attractiveness prediction task, we use the classic metrics for binary-class classification: *F1-Score*, *Accuracy*, *Precision*, and *Recall*. The results are shown in Table 8.3. We observe that the compared schemes achieve accuracy improvements on most of the evaluation metrics on the FairCrowd sampled dataset compared to the randomly sampled dataset. For example, the face attribute prediction model FMTNet is able to achieve 1.3% higher F1-score and 2.2% higher accuracy on the FairCrowd sampled dataset than the randomly sampled dataset. The reason is that the AFDB module in FairCrowd shuffles the images between the randomly sampled dataset and the dataset pool by explicitly considering both the fairness and prediction accuracy of the FAP model trained on the sampled dataset.

Finally, we compare the training time of all FAP schemes on the FairCrowd sampled dataset with that on the randomly sampled dataset. The results are shown in Table 8.4. We observe that the total training time for all compared schemes on the FairCrowd sampled dataset is significantly shorter than that on the randomly sampled dataset. The reason is that the randomly sampled dataset is heavily biased towards a majority demographic group and the AFDB module in FairCrowd tends to

Table 8.3 Overall detection performance

Method	F1 score	Accuracy	Precision	Recall
Randomly sampled dataset				
VGGFace2	0.662	0.670	0.757	0.513
LightCNN	0.774	0.774	**0.792**	0.751
FMTNet	0.780	0.781	0.798	0.759
SlimCNN	0.801	0.802	**0.783**	0.841
CascadeCNN	0.798	0.798	0.777	**0.844**
PSMC	0.793	0.794	0.784	**0.818**
FairCrowd sampled dataset				
VGGFace2	**0.692**	**0.738**	**0.818**	**0.600**
LightCNN	**0.794**	**0.787**	0.758	**0.833**
FMTNet	**0.793**	**0.803**	**0.821**	**0.767**
SlimCNN	**0.824**	**0.803**	0.737	**0.933**
CascadeCNN	**0.807**	**0.803**	**0.781**	0.833
PSMC	**0.807**	**0.820**	**0.852**	0.767

The bold values indicate the best performing results in each evaluation metric

Table 8.4 Overall training time (minute:second)

Methods	Randomly sampled dataset	FairCrowd sampled dataset
VGGFace2	5 : 37	**4:18**
LightCNN	7 : 20	**5:49**
FMTNet	52 : 20	**46:10**
SlimCNN	30 : 09	**24:25**
CascadeCNN	75 : 03	**61:48**
PSMC	154 : 39	**128:20**

The bold values indicate the best performing results in each evaluation metric

remove more images in the majority demographic group from the randomly sampled dataset than adding images in alternative demographic groups from the dataset pool. This often results in a smaller data size of the FairCrowd sampled dataset compared to the randomly sampled dataset.

8.3.1.5 Convergence of Bias on FairCrowd Sampled Dataset and Demographic Label Prediction Accuracy

In the second set of experiments, we study the convergence of the bias on the FairCrowd sampled dataset and the accuracy of the demographic label prediction with respect to the image shuffling iterations of FairCrowd. We first study the data distribution of the FairCrowd sampled dataset across different demographic groups. The results are shown in Fig. 8.8. We observe that the FairCrowd sampled dataset becomes more balanced across different demographic groups as the number of data shuffling iterations increases. The reason is that FairCrowd continually adds new images in minority demographic groups from the dataset pool to the FairCrowd sampled dataset and removes images in the majority demographic group from the

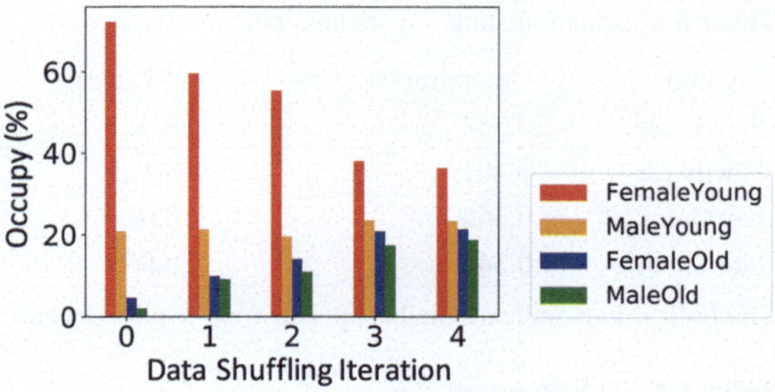

Fig. 8.8 FairCrowd sampled dataset distribution convergence

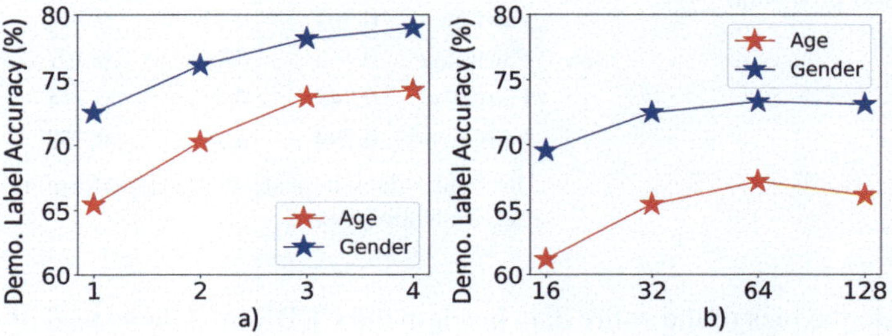

Fig. 8.9 Demographic label prediction accuracy. (**a**) Data shuffling iteration. (**b**) Batch size

FairCrowd sampled dataset based on predicted demographic labels from the AFDB module in FairCrowd.

We conduct further experiments to study the demographic label prediction accuracy of FairCrowd. The results are shown in Fig. 8.9. In Fig. 8.9a, we observe that the prediction accuracy of demographic labels (i.e., gender, age) of the images increases as the number of data shuffling iterations increases. The reason is that the predicted demographic labels become more accurate and stable as the combination scores in the SDLP module are estimated and improved iteratively. In Fig. 8.9b, we observe that the prediction accuracy of FairCrowd improves as the batch size increases. The reason is the data distribution of images in a data batch becomes closer to the data distribution of the FairCrowd sampled dataset as the batch size increases, which helps crowd workers to better estimate the bias of the sampled dataset. However, we also observe the prediction accuracy drops a bit when the batch size further increases. The reason could be that too many images displayed in the crowdsourcing interface may overwhelm the crowd workers and prevent them from working effectively.

8.3.1.6 Ablation Study

Finally, we perform a comprehensive *ablation study* to understand the contributions of important components of FairCrowd. We create different variants of FairCrowd by changing its key components: (1) FairBatch: we directly assign crowd workers

Table 8.5 Ablation study on fairness performance

Method	Demographic parity	T.P. parity	F.P. parity	Equalized odds
FairBatch	0.354	0.071	0.158	0.229
FairImage	0.401	0.125	0.179	0.304
FairOnly	0.366	0.066	0.191	0.257
FairCrowd	**0.344**	**0.055**	**0.152**	**0.207**

The bold values indicate the best performing results in each evaluation metric

Table 8.6 Ablation study on attractiveness prediction

Method	F1 score	Accuracy	Precision	Recall
FairBatch	0.767	0.774	0.742	0.793
FairImage	0.765	0.765	0.707	0.833
FairOnly	0.748	0.711	0.744	0.753
FairCrowd	**0.794**	**0.787**	**0.758**	**0.833**

The bold values indicate the best performing results in each evaluation metric

to estimate the bias of the entire data batch in the CBBE module instead of splitting the batch based on the correctness of prediction results; (2) FairImage: we replace the deep face recognition model in the SBLP module that computes the similarity between deep face representations with a function to directly compare pixel-level similarity between raw face images; and (3) FairOnly: we only consider the predicted demographic labels in the AFDB module and do not apply the estimation of Max Entropy scores on the images. We select LightCNN as the underlying FAP scheme for the ablation study because it is a widely adopted deep learning scheme for FAP applications. The results are shown in Tables 8.5 and 8.6. In Table 8.5. We observe that, by splitting the data batches based on the FAP prediction results, FairCrowd achieves better fairness and accuracy performance on all evaluation metrics, indicating the importance of data batch splitting in the CBBE module. Moreover, FairCrowd also outperforms FairImage and FairOnly on both fairness and accuracy, which demonstrates the necessity of the deep face recognition model for computing face similarity and the image shuffling design in FairCrowd.

8.3.2 *Student Performance Prediction*

Social intelligence can be applied to address fairness and bias in student performance prediction for online education which aims to predict a student's final performance result in a course (e.g., *Fail*, *Pass*, and *Distinction*) based on the behavioral data of students. The prediction results can provide feedback to improve a student's metacognitive ability [8] and assist educational institutions in designing effective mechanisms to improve academic outcomes and avoid dropout [34].

8.3.2.1 Data

To evaluate the accuracy and fairness of the DebiasEdu framework, we leverage the demographic, behavioral, and performance data collected from the online learning platform Open University [26]. In particular, we take the age of students as the demographic attribute in the evaluation since potential disadvantages have been observed for underrepresented older students in online education [26]. Following the common practice in fairness applications [19], we categorize the age attribute into two demographic groups (i.e., age less than 35 and age greater than or equal to 35). The behavioral data is measured by the activities (i.e., clickstream data) on different web pages (e.g., course material, course quizzes, topic forums, and collaborative activities) on the online learning platform per day for each student. The ground-truth label of a student's final performance is assigned by the course instructors into three different levels (i.e., *Fail*, *Pass*, and *Distinction*). We use two datasets for different types of courses to comprehensively evaluate the DebiasEdu framework. In particular, the first dataset is collected from a STEM course, and the second dataset is collected from a Social Science course. Statistics of the two datasets are shown in Table 8.7.

8.3.2.2 Crowdsourcing Setting and Pilot Study

We deploy the interface design shown in Fig. 8.7 to collect the crowd prediction from Amazon Mechanical Turk (AMT), one of the largest crowdsourcing platforms that provides access to a massive number of online crowd workers worldwide with reasonable costs. To ensure the crowdsourcing quality, we set the qualification requirement as follows: the crowd workers must have completed over 10,000 approved tasks with an overall approval rate greater than 95% before starting to work on the task. The inter-worker agreements of different crowd workers are 0.664 and 0.637 in terms of Cohen's Kappa score (Kappa) on the STEM course dataset and the Social Science course dataset, respectively. A Kappa score greater than 0.6 typically indicates good agreement [15]. We pay $0.05 to a crowd worker for each prediction task. We follow the Institutional Review Board protocol approved for this project. In the evaluation, we set the percentage α of crowdsourcing samples as 15% and the number of crowd workers as 5.

Table 8.7 Student performance prediction dataset statistics

	STEM	Social science
Total number of students	1938	1767
Percent of *fail*	34.0%	36.4%
Percent of *pass*	58.2%	51.3%
Percent of *distinction*	7.8%	12.3%
Percent of $age < 35$	75.6%	67.6%
Percent of $age \geq 35$	24.4%	32.4%

We first demonstrate the effectiveness of utilizing general crowd workers without educational domain knowledge in the student performance prediction task using both quantitative and qualitative analysis. In particular, we conduct a pilot study using the crowdsourcing subset (Definition 8.4) on the STEM course that includes 50 sample students, which are predicted by crowd workers in the experiments. We recruit both general crowd workers and educational practitioners (i.e., crowd workers who engage in educational activities as job responsibilities) to predict the final grades of these students using the same crowdsourcing task design (Fig. 8.7). The objective is to study if educational domain knowledge is required to conduct this task by comparing the crowdsourcing performance of general crowd workers and educational workers. The educational workers are selected on AMT using the premium qualification of job function [3]. We set the number of crowd workers per student to be 5. The crowdsourcing experiments involved the participation of 69 educational workers and 113 general workers. The difference in the number of crowd workers is related to the fact that there are more general crowd workers available on AMT compared to educational workers. The collected predictions from educational workers are aggregated by the estimation theory-based truth discovery model for each student. We utilize the same estimation theory-based aggregation model for general crowd workers in this study to ensure a fair comparison. By comparing the aggregated prediction results, we observe that general crowd workers and educational workers achieve an agreement of 0.746 in terms of the Kappa score. The notable consensus demonstrates that the student performance prediction task can be completed by general crowd workers without educational domain knowledge. In addition, for the recruited educational practitioners, we further ask them the following question: "Based on your work experience in education, do you think completing this task requires educational domain knowledge? If you think it is required, please provide explanations of what domain knowledge is required." Collected results indicate that 95.7% of educational workers involved in the study believe that no educational domain knowledge is required to effectively conduct the student performance prediction task. Specifically, some educational workers justify their conclusions by acknowledging the clarity of the prediction task, such as "I don't think it is required as the graphical representation makes it easy to predict". To conclude, the quantitative prediction comparison and qualitative inquiry results consistently demonstrate the effectiveness of recruiting general crowd workers to work on the student performance prediction task.

To further verify the effectiveness of the crowdsourcing task design, we formulate the following question to ask the recruited educational workers after they finish the prediction tasks: "Based on your work experience in education, do you feel comfortable predicting a student's final grade in an online course based on online activities (e.g., measured by clickstream data)?" A noteworthy 87.0% of educational practitioners felt comfortable conducting this task. This substantial percentage serves as evidence of the effectiveness of the task design since it is important to note that no measurements can 100% effectively predict a student's final grade except for the final grade itself. Particularly, we receive responses from educational workers who endorse the task design based on their professional domain experience, such as "I feel comfortable to predict a student's final grade because I do this work in my current job." The inquiry results confirm the effectiveness of the crowdsourcing task design in predicting a student's performance.

8.3.2.3 Baseline Methods and Experimental Setting

In the evaluation, we compare the DebiasEdu with a rich set of state-of-the-art AI, fair AI, and crowd-AI baselines.

AI Baselines:

- **ANN** [44] utilizes a deep neural network to predict a student's performance based on a set of handcrafted features (e.g., clicks in a course, clicks on the assignment web page).
- **BCEP** [33] classifies and fuses different types of online behavior (e.g., consistent hard work) to predict a student's performance.
- **SPDN** [27] utilizes an LSTM-based feature extraction network and a convolutional feature fusion network to predict a student's performance from online learning records.

Fair AI Baselines:

- **JMLR19** [49] integrates fairness measurements (e.g., false positive parity) as constraints during training to achieve fair performance prediction.
- **NeurIPS21** [6] utilizes data re-weighting and fairness constraints (e.g., equal opportunity) to achieve robust fairness in student performance prediction.
- **VS** [24] is a vector-scaling-based optimization approach that utilizes multiplicative and logit adjustments for fair group-sensitive classification.

Crowd-AI Baselines:

- **StreamCollab** [53] is a crowd-AI system that leverages uncertainty quantification and crowd knowledge fusion for effective student performance prediction.
- **DeepActive** [38] is a deep active learning framework that identifies a core set of samples and integrates the crowd on them to improve prediction accuracy.
- **LearningLoss** [43] is a crowd-AI framework that leverages a task-agnostic loss design to efficiently integrate AI and the crowd for accurate student performance prediction.

For a fair comparison, we use the same inputs for all compared schemes: (1) the demographic attribute of age for all students, (2) the behavioral data of online activities per day for all students, and (3) the crowd prediction collected from the crowdsourcing platform for students in the crowdsourcing subset. The DebiasEdu and all baselines are implemented using PyTorch libraries and trained on NVIDIA RTX 6000 GPUs. We use the Adam optimizer with a learning rate of 1×10^{-3} to train all compared models. We set the batch size to 20 and trained the models for over 200 epochs.

To evaluate the model accuracy, we leverage four representative metrics for multi-class classification [32]: (1) Accuracy, (2) F1-Score, (3) Cohen's Kappa Score (Kappa), and (4) Matthews Correlation Coefficient (MCC). We include Kappa and MCC since the datasets are imbalanced as shown in Table 8.7 and these metrics have been demonstrated to be reliable in evaluating prediction accuracy given imbalanced data [14]. Higher values of these accuracy metrics indicate better performance. To evaluate the model fairness, we utilize four commonly used fairness metrics [19, 50]: (1) True Positive Parity (T.P. Parity) (i.e., Equal Opportunity), (2) False Positive Parity (F.P. Parity), (3) Equalized Odds (Eq. Odds), and (4) Accuracy Parity (Acc. Parity). Lower values of the fairness metrics indicate less bias and better fairness.

8.3.2.4 Accuracy

First, we evaluate the accuracy of all compared approaches in student performance prediction on the STEM course and Social Science course datasets. Evaluation results are shown in Table 8.8. We observe that the DebiasEdu consistently outperforms all baselines on all accuracy metrics. For example, on the STEM course dataset, the performance gains of the DebiasEdu compared to the best-performing baseline DeepActive on Accuracy, F1-Score, Kappa, and MCC are 12.3, 14.6, 35.2, and 34.6%, respectively. Such performance gains can be attributed to the fact that the DebiasEdu framework develops a novel gradient-based module to identify the demographic bias of AI and designs a bias-driven crowd-AI collaboration module to address the identified bias and improve the overall student performance prediction accuracy.

8.3.2.5 Fairness

Second, we compare the fairness of DebiasEdu and the compared baselines on the two datasets. The evaluation results are presented in Table 8.9. We note that the DebiasEdu achieves consistent performance gains compared to all baselines on both datasets by reaching the lowest prediction bias. For instance, on the Social Science course dataset, the decreases in T.P. Parity, F.P. Parity, Eq. Odds, and Acc. The parity of DebiasEdu compared to the best-performing baseline BCEP are 55.2, 75.3, 68.3, and 50.8%, respectively. The significant improvements in fairness demonstrate that the DebiaEdu approach successfully identifies and addresses the demographic bias in student performance prediction by carefully modeling the AI bias by gradient variation and designing a novel crowdsourcing interface to reduce the crowd cognitive bias.

Table 8.8 Evaluation results of student performance prediction *Accuracy* on the STEM and social science course datasets

Category	Algorithm	STEM course				Social science course			
		Accuracy	F1	Kappa	MCC	Accuracy	F1	Kappa	MCC
AI	ANN	0.6059	0.6177	0.3142	0.3164	0.5500	0.5567	0.2230	0.2238
	BCEP	0.7322	0.7039	0.4733	0.4786	0.7086	0.6659	0.4405	0.4600
	SPDN	0.7118	0.7162	0.5011	0.5083	0.7059	0.6864	0.4430	0.4691
Fair AI	JMLR19	0.6500	0.6706	0.4282	0.4432	0.6588	0.6734	0.4122	0.4183
	NeurIPS21	0.7000	0.7179	0.4870	0.4927	0.6882	0.6959	0.4516	0.4586
	VS	0.6676	0.6833	0.4424	0.4514	0.5265	0.5727	0.3059	0.3392
Crowd-AI	StreamCollab	0.7147	0.7169	0.4949	0.4981	0.6824	0.6868	0.4418	0.4482
	DeepActive	0.7382	0.7228	0.5063	0.5089	0.6324	0.6468	0.3593	0.3692
	LearningLoss	0.6882	0.6717	0.4144	0.4352	0.6882	0.6717	0.4144	0.4352
Ours	**DebiasEdu**	**0.8294**	**0.8283**	**0.6844**	**0.6850**	**0.7647**	**0.7556**	**0.5676**	**0.5818**

The bold values indicate the best performing results in each evaluation metric

Table 8.9 Evaluation results of student performance prediction *Fairness* on the STEM and social science course datasets

		STEM course				Social science course			
Category	Algorithm	T.P. parity	F.P. parity	Eq. odds	Acc. parity	T.P. parity	F.P. parity	Eq. odds	Acc. parity
AI	ANN	0.2150	0.2056	0.2103	0.2129	0.2150	0.2824	0.2487	0.2158
	BCEP	0.1400	0.3253	0.2301	0.1377	0.1450	0.2720	0.2085	0.1453
	SPDN	0.1550	0.3714	0.2607	0.1520	0.1800	0.3259	0.2529	0.1795
Fair AI	JMLR19	0.1500	0.2526	0.2013	0.1470	0.1950	0.3675	0.2813	0.1973
	NeurIPS21	0.1700	0.1786	0.1743	0.1611	0.2850	0.1919	0.2385	0.2833
	VS	0.1350	0.2316	0.1833	0.1388	0.2300	0.3629	0.2965	0.2277
Crowd-AI	StreamCollab	0.1450	0.4909	0.3130	0.1347	0.2350	0.1290	0.1820	0.2339
	DeepActive	0.1250	0.2678	0.1964	0.1334	0.1750	0.2720	0.2235	0.1719
	LearningLoss	0.1050	0.2717	0.1884	0.1096	0.1600	0.3324	0.2462	0.1648
Ours	**DebiasEdu**	**0.0400**	**0.1635**	**0.1017**	**0.0451**	**0.0650**	**0.0672**	**0.0661**	**0.0716**

The bold values indicate the best performing results in each evaluation metric

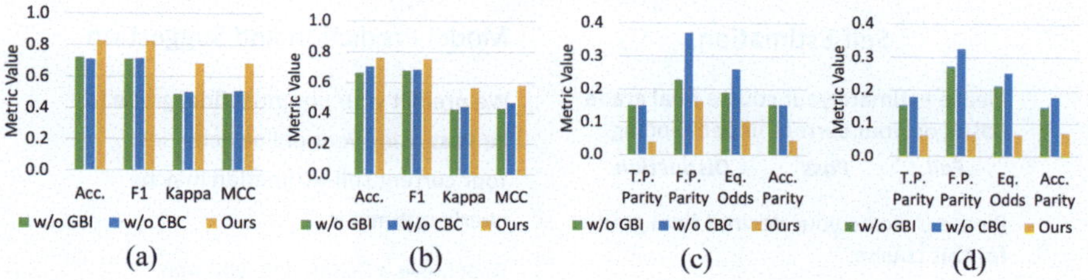

Fig. 8.10 Ablation study on the two datasets. (**a**) Accuracy on STEM. (**b**) Accuracy on social science. (**c**) Fairness on STEM. (**d**) Fairness on social science

8.3.2.6 Ablation Study

Next, we conduct an ablation study to evaluate the contribution of the two key modules (i.e., GBI and CBC) of the DebiasEdu framework. We present the accuracy and fairness evaluation results when removing each of the two modules in DebiasEdu. In particular, to remove the GBI module, we randomly select 15% of samples from the testing set for crowd prediction and model calibration. The sampling rate is the same as the one used in the framework to ensure a fair comparison in terms of crowdsourcing budget. To remove the CBC module, we utilize the crowd prediction on the crowdsourcing subset to retrain the AI model. The accuracy and fairness evaluation results on two datasets are shown in Fig. 8.10. The evaluation results demonstrate that both the GBI and CBC modules make critical contributions to the DebiasEdu framework in terms of both prediction accuracy and fairness.

8.3.2.7 Discussion of Benefits for Students

The accurate and fair student performance prediction results can be utilized to provide feedback to students, thereby enhancing their metacognitive abilities [8]. Figure 8.11 shows the sample feedback design for students in the pilot testing. First, we incorporate a self-estimation page where students are prompted to estimate their final grades and specify their desired grades. Second, we design a model prediction and suggestion page that offers (1) predicted final grades from the framework and (2) suggestions to help students refine their self-estimation and achieve the desired final grades given current completed activities. Qualitative results from initial pilot testing suggest that self-estimation of learning performance relative to an accurate AI prediction leads to students thinking critically about their own knowledge. Specifically, the results involve participants trying to decipher why their self-estimation differs from AI predictions by assessing their own knowledge.

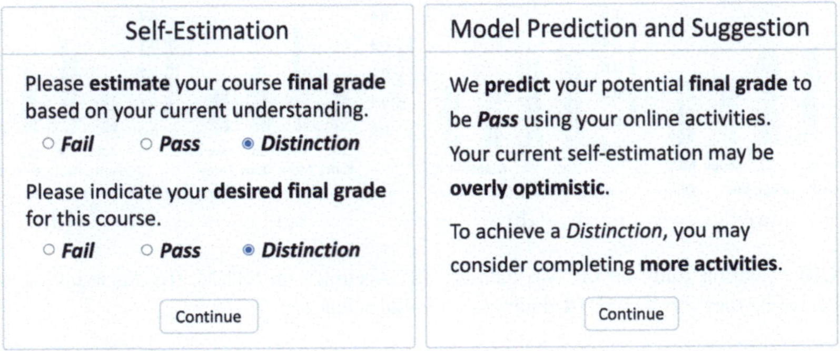

Fig. 8.11 Sample feedback design for students in an online course based on the prediction results

8.4 Discussion

This chapter has examined the critical challenges of fairness and bias in social intelligence systems. We present two novel social intelligence approaches, FairCrowd and DebiasEdu, that leverage crowd-AI collaboration to address these challenges. In particular, FairCrowd tackles the fairness and bias issues from the data curation perspective by sampling a balanced dataset. Additionally, DebiasEdu attempts to enhance fairness and reduce bias from algorithm design that incorporates human judgment to calibrate bias in model predictions. Both solutions demonstrate how carefully designed human-AI interaction can help mitigate demographic biases while maintaining or improving system performance across different social intelligence application domains.

Despite the promising results, a few limitations and challenges remain as ongoing research topics that need to be further explored. First, these frameworks face challenges in handling demographic complexity. The current implementations primarily focus on binary demographic attributes such as young/old and male/female classifications. However, real-world applications often involve intersectional demographic factors that create more complex fairness considerations. The frameworks would need substantial adaptation to handle continuous demographic attributes or multiple overlapping demographic categories that better reflect the complexity of real-world demographic variations. A potential solution is to develop a hierarchical crowdsourcing design that can capture both demographic categories and their intersections. This could be combined with adaptive sampling strategies [9] that progressively refine demographic representations based on discovered subgroups and their interactions. Additionally, incorporating techniques from multiclass classification [39] could also help extend these frameworks beyond binary categorizations.

Cognitive bias mitigation presents another significant challenge. While the bias calibration strategy in DebiasEdu shows promise in reducing human cognitive bias, other forms of cognitive bias may still influence crowd workers' judgments. The effectiveness of bias mitigation strategies may vary significantly across different cultural contexts and worker populations. For example, availability bias [36] may cause workers to overemphasize recent examples they have seen, and stereotype bias [31] could affect their judgments when assessing students from different backgrounds. There is also concern that long-term exposure to certain patterns in the data might create new forms of bias in crowd workers, which may potentially affect the quality and reliability of their annotations over time. To address such limitations, several approaches could be explored. For example, dynamic worker rotation strategies could be adopted to prevent stereotype bias. Designing adaptive interface elements could help detect and mitigate emerging biases. As the bias varies from application to application, application- or domain-specific bias mitigation strategies need to be carefully designed and evaluated to ensure the effectiveness of bias mitigation.

References

1. J. Abernethy, P. Awasthi, M. Kleindessner, J. Morgenstern, and J. Zhang. Adaptive sampling to reduce disparate performance, 2020.
2. A. Abrahamyan, L. L. Silva, S. C. Dakin, M. Carandini, and J. L. Gardner. Adaptable history biases in human perceptual decisions. *Proceedings of the National Academy of Sciences*, 113(25):E3548–E3557, 2016.
3. Amazon. Pricing of amazon mechanical turk, 2022.
4. H. Anahideh and A. Asudeh. Fair active learning. *CoRR*, abs/2001.01796, 2020.
5. R. K. Bellamy, K. Dey, M. Hind, S. C. Hoffman, S. Houde, K. Kannan, P. Lohia, J. Martino, S. Mehta, A. Mojsilovic, et al. Ai fairness 360: An extensible toolkit for detecting, understanding, and mitigating unwanted algorithmic bias. *arXiv preprint arXiv:1810.01943*, 2018.
6. H. C. Bendekgey and E. Sudderth. Scalable and stable surrogates for flexible classifiers with fairness constraints. *Advances in Neural Information Processing Systems*, 34:30023–30036, 2021.
7. R. Berk, H. Heidari, S. Jabbari, M. Joseph, M. Kearns, J. Morgenstern, S. Neel, and A. Roth. A convex framework for fair regression. *arXiv preprint arXiv:1706.02409*, 2017.
8. D. Boud, R. Lawson, and D. G. Thompson. The calibration of student judgement through self-assessment: disruptive effects of assessment patterns. *Higher education research & development*, 34(1):45–59, 2015.
9. W. Cai, R. Encarnacion, B. Chern, S. Corbett-Davies, M. Bogen, S. Bergman, and S. Goel. Adaptive sampling strategies to construct equitable training datasets. In *Proceedings of the 2022 ACM Conference on Fairness, Accountability, and Transparency*, pages 1467–1478, 2022.
10. J. Cao, Y. Li, and Z. Zhang. Partially shared multi-task convolutional neural network with local constraint for face attribute learning. In *Proceedings of the IEEE Conference on Computer Vision and Pattern Recognition (CVPR)*, June 2018.
11. Q. Cao, L. Shen, W. Xie, O. M. Parkhi, and A. Zisserman. Vggface2: A dataset for recognising faces across pose and age. *CoRR*, abs/1710.08092, 2017.
12. H.-S. Chang, E. Learned-Miller, and A. McCallum. Active bias: Training more accurate neural networks by emphasizing high variance samples. *Advances in Neural Information Processing Systems*, 30, 2017.
13. G. Charpiat, N. Girard, L. Felardos, and Y. Tarabalka. Input similarity from the neural network perspective. *Advances in Neural Information Processing Systems*, 32, 2019.

14. D. Chicco and G. Jurman. The advantages of the matthews correlation coefficient (mcc) over f1 score and accuracy in binary classification evaluation. *BMC genomics*, 21(1):6, 2020.
15. J. Cohen. A coefficient of agreement for nominal scales. *Educational and Psychological Measurement*, 20:37–46, 1960.
16. H. Ding, H. Zhou, S. K. Zhou, and R. Chellappa. A deep cascade network for unaligned face attribute classification. *CoRR*, abs/1709.03851, 2017.
17. T. Draws, A. Rieger, O. Inel, U. Gadiraju, and N. Tintarev. A checklist to combat cognitive biases in crowdsourcing. In *Proceedings of the AAAI Conference on Human Computation and Crowdsourcing*, volume 9, pages 48–59, 2021.
18. W. Gao and H. Ai. Face gender classification on consumer images in a multiethnic environment. In *International Conference on Biometrics*, pages 169–178. Springer, 2009.
19. M. Hardt, E. Price, and N. Srebro. Equality of opportunity in supervised learning. *Advances in neural information processing systems*, 29, 2016.
20. M. Hardt, E. Price, and N. Srebro. Equality of opportunity in supervised learning. *CoRR*, abs/1610.02413, 2016.
21. S.-U. Hassan, H. Waheed, N. R. Aljohani, M. Ali, S. Ventura, and F. Herrera. Virtual learning environment to predict withdrawal by leveraging deep learning. *International Journal of Intelligent Systems*, 34(8):1935–1952, 2019.
22. D. Hettiachchi, N. Van Berkel, V. Kostakos, and J. Goncalves. Crowdcog: A cognitive skill based system for heterogeneous task assignment and recommendation in crowdsourcing. *Proceedings of the ACM on Human-Computer Interaction*, 4(CSCW2):1–22, 2020.
23. W. Jiang and Z. A. Pardos. Towards equity and algorithmic fairness in student grade prediction. In *Proceedings of the 2021 AAAI/ACM Conference on AI, Ethics, and Society*, pages 608–617, 2021.
24. G. R. Kini, O. Paraskevas, S. Oymak, and C. Thrampoulidis. Label-imbalanced and group-sensitive classification under overparameterization. *Advances in Neural Information Processing Systems*, 34:18970–18983, 2021.
25. Z. Kou, Y. Zhang, L. Shang, and D. Wang. Faircrowd: Fair human face dataset sampling via batch-level crowdsourcing bias inference. In *2021 IEEE/ACM 29th International Symposium on Quality of Service (IWQOS)*, pages 1–10. IEEE, 2021, DOI:10.0.4.85/IWQOS52092.2021.9521312, Reprinted with permission from IEEE.
26. J. Kuzilek, M. Hlosta, and Z. Zdrahal. Open university learning analytics dataset. *Scientific data*, 4(1):1–8, 2017.
27. X. Li, X. Zhu, X. Zhu, Y. Ji, and X. Tang. Student academic performance prediction using deep multi-source behavior sequential network. In *Pacific-Asia Conference on Knowledge Discovery and Data Mining*, pages 567–579. Springer, 2020.
28. Z. Liu, P. Luo, X. Wang, and X. Tang. Deep learning face attributes in the wild. In *Proceedings of International Conference on Computer Vision (ICCV)*, December 2015.
29. R. Long. Fairness in machine learning: against false positive rate equality as a measure of fairness, 2020.
30. A. K. Menon and R. C. Williamson. The cost of fairness in binary classification. In S. A. Friedler and C. Wilson, editors, *Proceedings of the 1st Conference on Fairness, Accountability and Transparency*, volume 81 of *Proceedings of Machine Learning Research*, pages 107–118, New York, NY, USA, 23–24 Feb 2018. PMLR.
31. A. Omrani, A. Salkhordeh_Ziabari, C. Yu, P. Golazizian, B. Kennedy, M. Atari, H. Ji, and M. Dehghani. Social-group-agnostic bias mitigation via the stereotype content model. In *Proceedings of the 61st Annual Meeting of the Association for Computational Linguistics (Volume 1: Long Papers)*. Association for Computational Linguistics, 2023.
32. C. Parker. An analysis of performance measures for binary classifiers. In *2011 IEEE 11th International Conference on Data Mining*, pages 517–526. IEEE, 2011.
33. F. Qiu, G. Zhang, X. Sheng, L. Jiang, L. Zhu, Q. Xiang, B. Jiang, and P.-k. Chen. Predicting students' performance in e-learning using learning process and behaviour data. *Scientific Reports*, 12(1):1–15, 2022.

34. J. L. Rastrollo-Guerrero, J. A. Gómez-Pulido, and A. Durán-Domínguez. Analyzing and predicting students' performance by means of machine learning: A review. *Applied sciences*, 10(3):1042, 2020.
35. M. Ren, W. Zeng, B. Yang, and R. Urtasun. Learning to reweight examples for robust deep learning. In *International conference on machine learning*, pages 4334–4343. PMLR, 2018.
36. M. Salman, B. Khan, S. Z. Khan, and R. U. Khan. The impact of heuristic availability bias on investment decision-making: Moderated mediation model. *Business Strategy & Development*, 4(3):246–257, 2021.
37. F. Schroff, D. Kalenichenko, and J. Philbin. Facenet: A unified embedding for face recognition and clustering. *CoRR*, abs/1503.03832, 2015.
38. O. Sener and S. Savarese. Active learning for convolutional neural networks: A core-set approach. In *International Conference on Learning Representations*, 2018.
39. L. Shang, Y. Zhang, B. Chen, R. Zong, Z. Yue, H. Zeng, N. Wei, and D. Wang. Mmadapt: A knowledge-guided multi-source multi-class domain adaptive framework for early health misinformation detection. In *Proceedings of the ACM on Web Conference 2024*, pages 4653–4663, 2024.
40. C. E. Shannon. A mathematical theory of communication. *The Bell system technical journal*, 27(3):379–423, 1948.
41. A. K. Sharma and H. Foroosh. Slim-cnn: A light-weight CNN for face attribute prediction. *CoRR*, abs/1907.02157, 2019.
42. S. Shen, R. Furuta, T. Yamasaki, and K. Aizawa. Fooling neural networks in face attractiveness evaluation: Adversarial examples with high attractiveness score but low subjective score. In *2017 IEEE Third International Conference on Multimedia Big Data (BigMM)*, pages 66–69. IEEE, 2017.
43. M. Shukla and S. Ahmed. A mathematical analysis of learning loss for active learning in regression. In *Proceedings of the IEEE/CVF Conference on Computer Vision and Pattern Recognition*, pages 3320–3328, 2021.
44. H. Waheed, S.-U. Hassan, N. R. Aljohani, J. Hardman, S. Alelyani, and R. Nawaz. Predicting academic performance of students from vle big data using deep learning models. *Computers in Human behavior*, 104:106189, 2020.
45. D. Wang, L. Kaplan, H. Le, and T. Abdelzaher. On truth discovery in social sensing: A maximum likelihood estimation approach. In *Information Processing in Sensor Networks (IPSN), 2012 ACM/IEEE 11th International Conference on*, pages 233–244. IEEE, 2012.
46. Y. Wang, S. Inguva, and B. Adsumilli. Youtube ugc dataset for video compression research. In *2019 IEEE 21st International Workshop on Multimedia Signal Processing (MMSP)*, pages 1–5. IEEE, 2019.
47. X. Wu, R. He, and Z. Sun. A lightened CNN for deep face representation. *CoRR*, abs/1511.02683, 2015.
48. D. Yoo and I. S. Kweon. Learning loss for active learning. In *Proceedings of the IEEE/CVF conference on computer vision and pattern recognition*, pages 93–102, 2019.
49. M. B. Zafar, I. Valera, M. Gomez-Rodriguez, and K. P. Gummadi. Fairness constraints: A flexible approach for fair classification. *The Journal of Machine Learning Research*, 20(1):2737–2778, 2019.
50. M. B. Zafar, I. Valera, M. Rodriguez, K. Gummadi, and A. Weller. From parity to preference-based notions of fairness in classification. *Advances in Neural Information Processing Systems*, 30, 2017.
51. D. Y. Zhang, R. Han, D. Wang, and C. Huang. On robust truth discovery in sparse social media sensing. In *Big Data (Big Data), 2016 IEEE International Conference on*, pages 1076–1081. IEEE, 2016.
52. X. Zhang, Y. Wu, L. Huang, H. Ji, and G. Cao. Expertise-aware truth analysis and task allocation in mobile crowdsourcing. *IEEE Transactions on Mobile Computing*, 20(3):1001–1016, 2019.

53. Y. Zhang, L. Shang, R. Zong, Z. Wang, Z. Kou, and D. Wang. Streamcollab: A streaming crowd-ai collaborative system to smart urban infrastructure monitoring in social sensing. In *Proceedings of the AAAI Conference on Human Computation and Crowdsourcing*, volume 9, pages 179–190, 2021.
54. Y. Zhang, R. Zong, Z. Kou, L. Shang, and D. Wang. Crowdnas: A crowd-guided neural architecture searching approach to disaster damage assessment. *Proceedings of the ACM on Human-Computer Interaction*, 6(CSCW2):1–29, 2022. https://doi.org/10.1145/3555179.
55. N. Zhuang, Y. Yan, S. Chen, H. Wang, and C. Shen. Multi-label learning based deep transfer neural network for facial attribute classification. *CoRR*, abs/1805.01282, 2018.
56. R. Zong, Y. Zhang, F. Stinar, L. Shang, H. Zeng, N. Bosch, and D. Wang. A crowd–ai collaborative approach to address demographic bias for student performance prediction in online education. In *Proceedings of the AAAI Conference on Human Computation and Crowdsourcing*, volume 11, pages 198–210, 2023. https://doi.org/10.1609/hcomp.v11i1.27560.

Chapter 9
Privacy Issue

Abstract This chapter discusses critical privacy challenges in social intelligence systems when the collective social intelligence data meets privacy constraints. We examine how the collection and integration of sensitive personal information across platforms raise significant privacy concerns which potentially limit the effectiveness of social intelligence solutions. To address these challenges, we present two novel solutions: CoviDKG and FaceCrowd. CoviDKG is a distributed knowledge graph framework that constructs a set of knowledge graphs from individual sources/platforms and exchanges the privacy-aware information across different sources/platforms to effectively detect online false information. FaceCrowd is a web crowdsourcing-based face partition approach that aims to improve the performance of current face recognition models in social intelligence by designing a novel crowdsourced partial face graph generated from privacy-preserved social media face images. Through extensive experiments on real-world datasets and user studies, we demonstrate that both frameworks successfully balance privacy protection with superior performance.

Keywords Privacy · Crowd-AI · Distributed knowledge graph · Social media · Crowdsourcing · Face recognition

9.1 Understanding Privacy in Social Intelligence

Social intelligence is built upon the collective intelligence of individuals who share and contribute their observations, knowledge, and experiences. However, such a valuable resource of human insights raises critical privacy concerns since the data that makes social intelligence meaningful often contains sensitive personal information, such as face recognition, social relationships, and location data. For example, a study shows 80% of social media users are concerned about businesses and advertisers accessing and using their social media posts [39]. Major social media and online platforms often enforce strict policies and access controls that prohibit unauthorized data collection and analysis beyond the individual platform that owns the data. Such privacy constraints prevent cross-platform information integration and comprehensive data analysis, which greatly reduce the applicability

D. Wang et al., *Social Intelligence*, https://doi.org/10.1007/978-3-031-90080-8_9

and benefits of social intelligence. For example, important health advice/clues shared on Facebook may not be accessible by a truth discovery solution to identify related false claims on other platforms. Therefore, to alleviate the privacy concern, the design of social intelligence systems also requires privacy-preserving mechanisms that enable collaborative analysis while protecting individual user data.

Many efforts have been made to address the privacy issue in machine learning and cryptography, such as federated learning [42], differential privacy [15], and multi-party computation [20]. However, these solutions primarily focus on collaboratively developing a shared global model or analyzing a shared database. They are insufficient for social intelligence applications which often require user- or domain-specific analysis while preserving privacy. For example, in face recognition, a typical pipeline is to collect public face images of celebrities, manually annotate them via crowdsourcing, and train face recognition models on this public dataset (Fig. 9.1 with black arrows). In particular, the crowd workers annotate the identity of the public celebrity face images with blue frames and provide the annotations to ML/AI researchers to train face recognition models. However, the face recognition models trained on public images usually do not perform well on personal face images (e.g., the images shared within an individual's network) due to the significant image domain discrepancy (e.g., facial expression, shooting environment) between the public and personal face images [26]. Similarly, certain unified truth discovery models often focus on utilizing social media data from multiple platforms to train a uniform truth discovery classifier [41]. While these solutions explore the social media posts on different platforms, they directly aggregate the posts from different platforms to construct a centralized dataset. Thus, they largely ignore the growing

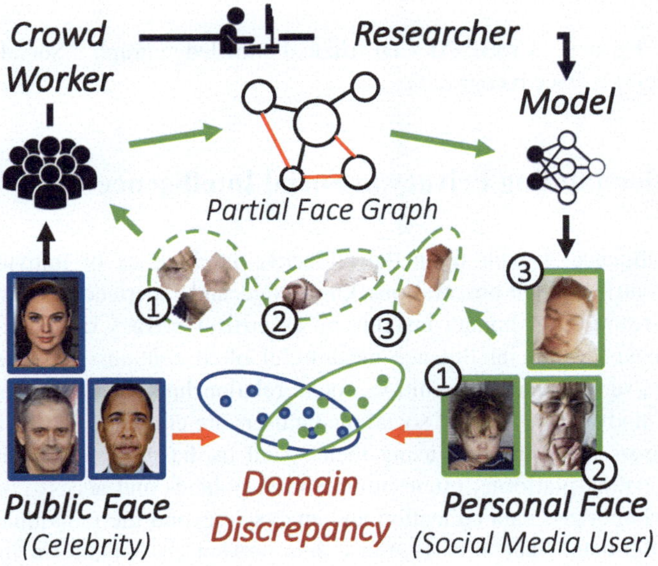

Fig. 9.1 The problem of privacy-aware face recognition

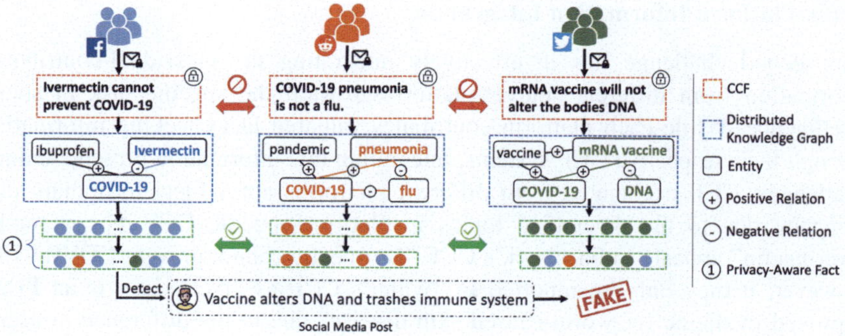

Fig. 9.2 Truth discovery with CCF

concerns of privacy and fail to capture platform-specific characteristics and user behaviors that are crucial for effective truth discovery in social intelligence. However, it is a non-trivial task to collaboratively leverage the rich social intelligence from diverse sources while preserving privacy [21, 34]. We elaborate on the key challenges below.

Privacy-Aware Representation Learning

The first challenge lies in learning privacy-aware representation from the content obtained from diverse sources/platforms. Let us consider an example of leveraging community-contributed facts (CCF) to detect false information (Fig. 9.2). CCF refers to the fact-checking reports submitted to different social media platforms by their users and partnered professionals. For example, Twitter's Birdwatch is a community-based fact-checking portal for authorized Twitter users to submit fact-checking reports of incorrect Tweets [31]. Similarly, Facebook partners with independent professionals to review and submit fact-checking articles about COVID-19 false information [46]. A possible strategy to incorporate CCF from diverse sources/platforms is to construct a centralized knowledge graph by aggregating the available CCF from all platforms [14]. However, such a strategy largely ignores the privacy constraints of CCF. For example, some Twitter users may not want the reported information to be publicly shared with other Twitter users or other platforms (e.g., Facebook, Reddit) due to privacy concerns [47]. Moreover, social media platforms are also unwilling to share CCF with the public or other platforms since CCF usually contains reports that debunk the incorrect posts on their platform which may raise sensitive public criticism or legal issues about content censorship against free speech [1]. Therefore, it remains challenging to learn privacy-aware representation from the platform-specific social intelligence data (e.g., CCF) while avoiding the privacy leakage of sharing the raw data.

Cross-Platform Information Integration

The second challenge lies in effectively integrating the individual-contributed information from different sources/platforms toward the specific task in social intelligence. While each platform contributes valuable fact-checking information through their respective CCF systems, integrating this information presents unique challenges. CCF exchanged from different platforms are subject to domain discrepancy due to the diversified topics in platform-specific CCF. For example, "Ivermectin" appears in Facebook's CCF "Ivermectin cannot prevent COVID-19". However, it may only be reported in Twitter's CCF as "Ivermectin is an FDA-approved medicine for worm-caused skin disease" due to the difference in users' interests on the two platforms [36]. As a result, the fact of "Ivermectin" learned from Facebook's CCF (e.g., "false treatment of COVID-19") is different from the one learned from Twitter's CCF (e.g., "skin disease medicine"). Thus, the fact of "Ivermectin" learned from Facebook cannot be directly transferred to detect false information on Twitter due to the domain discrepancy. This phenomenon poses significant challenges in leveraging cross-platform CCF for social intelligence tasks, as the contextual differences and platform-specific characteristics can lead to misaligned or incomplete information integration. Therefore, developing robust methods to bridge these domain gaps and integrate cross-platform information while preserving platform-specific information integrity remains a critical research challenge in social intelligence applications.

Partial Information Utilization

The third challenge lies in incorporating privacy-preserved information from different sources. In the problem of privacy-aware face recognition, to protect the privacy of individuals who contributed their personal face images, only partial information (e.g., face image partitions as shown in the dotted circle in Fig. 9.1) is typically shared instead of raw images. Since the partial face images often have no ground-truth identity labels, it is not feasible to use the partial face images as the same training data as the public face images for face recognition. Recent facial applications improve their face recognition performance by reconstructing the unlabeled face images in an encoder-decoder manner to pre-train the model before training with public face images [26, 32]. However, such approaches require the labeled and unlabeled images to be in the same feature space (e.g., images with full faces), which is not applicable to the privacy-preserved face recognition problem with partial face images. This mismatch in feature representations between complete and partial faces poses fundamental challenges for leveraging existing pre-training and reconstruction techniques. It is necessary to develop an effective social intelligence solution that can bridge the gap between partial and complete facial information while maintaining privacy guarantees.

9.2 Privacy-Aware Crowd-AI Approach: CoviDKG and FaceCrowd

In this section, we present two novel privacy-aware social intelligence solutions, CoviDKG (COVID-19 Distributed Knowledge Graph) [34] and FaceCrowd (Face Partition based on Crowdsourcing) [21], that effectively address privacy constraints in modeling privacy-sensitive social intelligence data. First, the CoviDKG framework introduces a privacy-aware distributed knowledge graph approach that effectively integrates CCF from various platforms to jointly detect false information across different platforms while preserving the privacy of both individual users and platform-specific fact-checking content. Second, the FaceCrowd scheme is a privacy-aware face recognition framework that constructs a crowdsourcing-based partial face graph that contains privacy-preserved partial face images from online social media users to effectively optimize the performance of face recognition models in social intelligence.

9.2.1 *CoviDKG: A Distributed Crowd-AI Approach*

Figure 9.3 shows an overview of the CoviDKG framework. In particular, CoviDKG consists of three modules: (1) a *Distributed Knowledge Graph Constructor (DKGC)* that constructs a set of distributed knowledge graphs to effectively extract the knowledge facts from the platform-specific CCF data, (2) a *Privacy-aware Knowledge Generator (PAKG)* that is designed to accurately learn the privacy-aware latent COVID-19 knowledge representations from the distributed knowledge graphs constructed by DKGC, (3) a *Domain-aware Knowledge Integrator (DAKI)* that aims

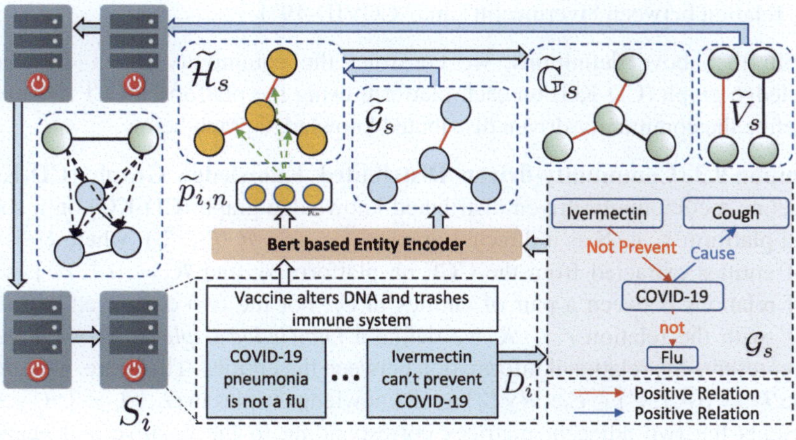

Fig. 9.3 An overview of the CoviDKG framework

at efficiently integrating the distributed knowledge graph with the latent COVID-19 knowledge facts obtained from other social media platforms. We discuss the details of each module below.

9.2.1.1 Distributed Knowledge Graph Constructor (DKGC)

The distributed knowledge graph constructor is designed to construct a knowledge graph to explicitly model the relational information of COVID-19 knowledge from the unstructured platform-specific CCF of each platform. We observe that CCF contains meaningful COVID-19 knowledge facts (i.e., COVID-19 entities and their relations) for detecting incorrect COVID-19 posts. In particular, noun-based entities often serve as the key vehicles to carry the incorrect information related to COVID-19. For example, the COVID-19 fact "Ivermectin" $\xrightarrow{\text{not prevent}}$ "COVID-19" in the CCF shown in Fig. 9.3 can help identify the incorrect posts that claim "Ivermectin can prevent or treat COVID-19." Therefore, we focus on the noun-based entities (i.e., a single-word noun or multiple-word noun phrase) and their relations to obtain COVID-19 knowledge in the CCF. Formally, we define the COVID-19 entity and relation as follows.

Definition 9.1 (Entity (e)) We define an entity e as the single-word noun ("Ivermectin") or multiple-word noun phrase ("mRNA vaccine") in CCF. In particular, we extract all entities from the CCF on each platform $s_i \in \mathcal{S}$ using the advanced part-of-speech tagging tool [9]. The set of M_i entities extracted from the CCF on platform s_i is denoted as $\mathcal{E}_i = \{e_{i,1}, \ldots, e_{i,M_i}\}$.

Definition 9.2 (Relation (r)) We define the semantic relation between a pair of entities in CCF. In particular, we focus on the binary relations between a pair of entities: i) *positive* relation r^+ (e.g., the "prevent" relation between "COVID-19 vaccine" and "COVID-19 pneumonia"); and ii) *negative* relation r^- (e.g., the "not cure" relation between "Ivermectin" and "COVID-19").

With the above definitions, we construct the community-driven distributed knowledge graph (CD-KG) on each platform using the platform's CCF. Formally, we define the community-driven distributed knowledge graph below.

Definition 9.3 (Community-driven Distributed Knowledge Graph (CD-KG)) We define a community-driven distributed knowledge graph (CD-KG) on a social media platform $s_i \in \mathcal{S}$ as a directed graph $\mathcal{G}_i = (\mathcal{E}_i, \mathcal{R}, \mathcal{T}_i, \mathcal{A}_i)$, where $\mathcal{E}_i$ is the set of entities extracted from the CCF on platform s_i, and $\mathcal{R} = \{r^+, r^-\}$ is the set of relations between a pair of entities in $\mathcal{E}_i$. For the two connected entities e and e' with the relation $r \in \mathcal{R}$, we define a *knowledge triple* as $T = \{e, r, e'\}$ that represents the relational information between the entities. Therefore, we further define $\mathcal{T}_i = \{(e, r, e') \in \mathcal{E}_i \times \mathcal{R} \times \mathcal{E}_i\}$ as all knowledge triples in $\mathcal{G}_i$. $\mathcal{A}_i = \{\mathcal{A}_i^+, \mathcal{A}_i^-\}$ represents the two adjacent matrices corresponding to the positive and negative relations from $\mathcal{R}$. Each adjacent matrix from $\mathcal{A}_i$ denotes an $M_i \times M_i$ matrix that contains binary values to denote whether two entities from $\mathcal{G}_i$ are connected (i.e., value is 1) or not (i.e., value is 0).

In addition, DKGC also aims to extract the high-level semantic information from the text-based entities (i.e., nouns or noun phrases) to effectively propagate COVID-19 knowledge information between entities in each distributed knowledge graph. To this end, DKGC designs a BERT-based entity encoder to accurately transform the text-based entities with different numbers of words to the high-dimensional latent embeddings in the same vector space. In particular, let $e = [w_1, w_2, \cdots, w_n]$ be an entity in $\mathcal{E}_i$ where w_i for $1 \leq i \leq n$ represents the ith word in entity e. We then convert w_i to the pre-trained BERT word embedding [13] as $\widetilde{w}_i \in \mathbb{R}^d$ where d is the dimension of the embedding. Given all the word embeddings from e, we apply the max-pooling and average-pooling operations on the embeddings to effectively extract the representative semantic information of e and concatenate the generated embedding as $\widetilde{e} \in \mathbb{R}^{2d}$. We apply the BERT-based entity encoder to encode all entities $\mathcal{E}_i$ in each platform s_i and denote the encoded knowledge graph as $\widetilde{\mathcal{G}}_i = (\widetilde{\mathcal{E}}_i, \mathcal{R}, \widetilde{\mathcal{T}}_i, \mathcal{A}_i)$.

9.2.1.2 Privacy-Aware Knowledge Generator (PAKG)

Given the CD-KG of each platform s_i, the privacy-aware knowledge generator (PAKG) generates the privacy-aware knowledge facts from $\mathcal{G}_i$ by retrieving discriminative knowledge triples and protecting the semantic information of the triples from being attacked by malicious users from other platforms. In particular, PAKG consists of two components: (1) the variational knowledge autoencoder and (2) the post-guided knowledge triple extractor. We illustrate the details of each component below.

While the graph entities from $\mathcal{G}_i$ are transformed to high-dimensional embeddings in DKGC, the direct exchange of such entity embeddings is still subject to high privacy risk because the target platform (i.e., the platform that receives the entity embeddings) can recover the semantic words of the exchanged embeddings by applying the BERT-based entity encoder to encode all English words and discovering the words with the same embedding values as the exchanged embeddings [13]. One possible solution for protecting the privacy of the entity embeddings from each platform is to design a platform-specific encoder network that encodes the entity embeddings into the latent entity features that are unknown to other platforms. However, a major limitation of such an encoding method is that the encoded entity features cannot be effectively integrated because the learnable parameters of the encoder networks from different platforms are independent of each other. Therefore, the entity embeddings from different platforms are encoded to different vector spaces.

To address the above limitation, we develop the variational knowledge autoencoder (VKAE) for each platform s_i to explicitly encode the entity embeddings into privacy-preserved entity embeddings. In particular, VKAE consists of an encoder and a decoder network that take the entity embeddings from $\mathcal{G}_i$ as inputs and generate new entity embeddings with the same dimensions as the original embeddings. The generated entity embeddings contain similar semantic information as the original entity embeddings. However, they also contain variations (i.e., noisy values) that are generated from VKAE by sampling the hidden distribution of the original entity embeddings. Therefore, the entity embeddings generated from one platform cannot be attacked by other platforms because of the variations that are specific to the original platform. Formally, given an entity embedding $\widetilde{e}$, we define the encoding and decoding processes as follows.

$$\widetilde{h} = \mathcal{F}_{encoder}(\widetilde{e}) \text{ and } \widetilde{v} = \mathcal{F}_{decoder}(\mathbb{Z}(\mu(\widetilde{h}), \sigma(\widetilde{h}))) \quad (9.1)$$

where $\mathcal{F}_{encoder}$ represents the sequential linear parameter matrix that encodes $\widetilde{e}$ to the latent entity feature $\widetilde{h} \in \mathbb{R}^{d'}$, $d' < 2d$. $\mathbb{Z}$ is the sampling distribution with the $\mu \in \mathbb{R}^{d'}$ and $\sigma \in \mathbb{R}^{d'}$ parameters transformed from $\widetilde{h}$. $\widetilde{v} \in \mathbb{R}^{2d}$ denotes the decoded entity embedding with variations sampled from $\mathbb{Z}$. We further define the set of encoded entities from $\widetilde{\mathcal{E}}_i$ as $\widetilde{\mathcal{H}}_i$ and the decoded embeddings as $\widetilde{\mathcal{V}}_i$.

Given the encoded latent entity features $\widetilde{\mathcal{H}}_i$ from the platform s_i, the post-guided knowledge triple extractor aims to identify the discriminative knowledge triples from $\mathcal{G}_i$. We first formally define the discriminative knowledge triple below.

Definition 9.4 (Discriminative Knowledge Triple (T^*)**)** Given the platform s_i and the constructed knowledge graph $\mathcal{G}_i$, we define a knowledge triple T^* from $\mathcal{G}_i$ as discriminative if it is used to correctly classify more than δ COVID-19 posts where δ is pre-defined as a hyper-parameter. Similarly, a knowledge triple is defined as *non-discriminative* if it fails to correctly classify more than δ COVID-19 posts.

Each platform is expected to exchange its discriminative knowledge triples with other platforms because such knowledge triples are more likely to improve the detection performance of the knowledge graphs from other platforms compared to non-discriminative knowledge triples. In order to identify the discriminative knowledge triples from $\mathcal{G}_i$ of the platform s_i, we leverage the attention mechanism to explore the importance degree of each knowledge triple in identifying incorrect COVID-19 posts. In particular, we design an attention-based knowledge graph convolutional network that leverages the knowledge triples from $\mathcal{G}_i$ to classify the COVID-19 posts and extracts specific knowledge triples with high attention scores as discriminative knowledge triples. In particular, we represent $\mathcal{G}_i$ as a multi-relational graph convolutional network (RGCN). RGCN is a specific type of graph convolutional network that contains multiple types of relations between different graph entities [33]. The multi-relation knowledge aggregation strategy is formally defined as:

$$\widetilde{h}_m = \sigma(\sum_{r \in \mathcal{R}} \sum_{(m,r,n) \in \mathcal{T}^+} \frac{1}{z_{n,r}} W^r_{i,m,n} \widetilde{h}_n \widetilde{A}^r_{i,m,n}) \quad (9.2)$$

where $\widetilde{h}_m$ and $\widetilde{h}_n$ are mth and nth encoded entities from $\widetilde{\mathcal{G}}_i$. σ represents the non-linear activation ReLU function. $\mathcal{R}$ contains both positive and negative relations in $\mathcal{G}_i$ and $\mathcal{T}^+ \in \mathcal{T}$ denotes the set of graph triples consisting of $\widetilde{v}_m$. $z_{n,r}$ is a normalization factor for $\widetilde{v}_n$ with relation r and $W^r_{i,m,n}$ is the learnable parameter. $\widetilde{A}^r_i$ is the matrix that is transformed from the adjacent matrix $A^r_i \in \mathcal{A}_i$ for the relation r by applying the softmax operation on the last dimension. In particular, the adjacent matrix $\widetilde{A}^r_i$ is derived by jointly aggregating the semantic information from the input COVID-19 posts $p_{i,n}$ and A^r_i. The intuition of such aggregation is that the knowledge aggregation in the RGCN should match the semantic content in the input COVID-19 post to determine if the post contains incorrect information. For example, a COVID-19 post that discusses the relation between the COVID-19 vaccine and human DNA can guide the RGCN to retrieve more COVID-19 vaccine-related knowledge facts from the knowledge graph to check the truthfulness of the post. Formally, given the feature of a COVID post $p_{i,n}$ that is embedded by the BERT-based entity encoder as $\widetilde{p}_{i,n} \in \mathbb{R}^{1\times 2d}$, the process for generating the adjacent matrix $\widetilde{A}^r_i$ with relation $r \in \mathcal{R}$ can be denoted as:

$$\widetilde{A}^r_i = \text{Softmax}((\widetilde{\mathcal{E}}_i \cdot (\widetilde{p}_{i,n})^T + \widetilde{p}_{i,n} \cdot (\widetilde{\mathcal{E}}_i)^T) \odot \mathcal{A}^r_i) \tag{9.3}$$

where $\widetilde{A}^r_i \in \mathbb{R}^{M_i \times M_i}$ is the result adjacent matrix. We define $\widetilde{\mathcal{A}}_i = \{\widetilde{A}^+_i, \widetilde{A}^-_i\}$ as the two adjacent matrices to represent the positive and negative relations from $\mathcal{R}$. After the knowledge aggregation process in Eq. (9.2), we aggregate all encoded entities $\widetilde{\mathcal{H}}_i$ for each knowledge graph $\widetilde{\mathcal{G}}_i$ by concatenation and classify the concatenated feature with the cross entropy loss. After optimizing the knowledge graph with all COVID-19 posts in each platform s_i, we aggregate the attention scores from $\widetilde{A}_i$ for the knowledge triples and extract the top Ω triples with highest attention scores as discriminative knowledge triples $\mathcal{T}^*_i = \{T^*_1, \ldots, T^*_\Omega\}$ of s_i. Similarly, we denote the embedded discriminative knowledge triples as $\widetilde{\mathcal{T}}^*_i = \{\widetilde{T}^*_1, \ldots, \widetilde{T}^*_\Omega\}$. We denote the decoded entities of the discriminative knowledge triples by VKAE as $\widetilde{V}^*_i = \{\widetilde{v}^*_1, \ldots, \widetilde{v}^*_\omega\}$ where ω is the total number of entities.

9.2.1.3 Domain-Aware Knowledge Integrator (DAKI)

After each platform generates the platform-specific discriminative knowledge triples, the domain-aware knowledge integrator (DAKI) models the platforms $\mathcal{S}$ as a fully connected graph and exchanges the knowledge triples between each two platforms. In particular, given a total of I platforms from $\mathcal{S}$, DAKI assigns each platform s_i to exchange the decoded discriminative knowledge triples $\widetilde{\mathcal{T}}^*_i$ generated by the PAKG with all other platforms $s_j \in \{S|s_i \neq s_j\}$ simultaneously. After the exchange process, each platform s_i receives the decoded discriminative knowledge triples from all other platforms with the entities denoted as $\widetilde{\mathcal{V}}_i = \{\widetilde{V}_1, \ldots, \widetilde{V}_I \setminus \widetilde{V}_i\} \in \mathbb{R}^{(I-1)\omega \times 2d}$.

For each platform s_i, DAKI is then expected to integrate the exchanged knowledge triples $\widetilde{\mathcal{V}}_i$ with the original knowledge graph $\mathcal{G}_i$ to generate a new knowledge graph that contains more diversified COVID-19 knowledge facts to accurately detect COVID-19 false information. A possible strategy for the knowledge integration is to directly connect the entities from $\widetilde{\mathcal{V}}_i$ with all entities from $\mathcal{G}_i$ with uniform relation values (i.e., value 1 for both positive and negative relations). However, such a one-size-fits-all integration method largely ignores the knowledge domain discrepancy between different platforms. The topics of CCF vary on different social media platforms due to the different demographic distributions of those platforms with varied interests in COVID-19 topics (e.g., Facebook users are more interested in COVID-19 cures than Twitter users).

To solve the above problem, we design a distribution-weighted knowledge integration strategy that explicitly considers the domain discrepancy between the COVID-19 knowledge facts from $\mathcal{G}_i$ and the exchanged knowledge triples from $\widetilde{\mathcal{T}}_i^*$. In particular, we denote the new adjacent matrix sets for the integrated knowledge as $\mathbb{A}_i = \{\mathbb{A}_i^+, \mathbb{A}_i^-\}$ where $\mathbb{A}_i^+$ and $\mathbb{A}_i^-$ are both $(M_i + (I-1)\omega) \times (M_i + (I-1)\omega)$ matrices. For each adjacent matrix, the $M_i \times M_i$ sub-matrix is the same as the original adjacent matrix with total M_i entities. For the entities of the exchanged discriminative knowledge triples $\widetilde{V}_i$ from the platform s_i, the relations between the entities in $\widetilde{V}_i$ are recorded in the sub-matrix $\mathbb{A}_i$ with the value equaling to 1. For the entities that are not from the same platform (e.g., $\widetilde{v}_{i,m}$ from $\widetilde{V}_i$ and $\widetilde{v}_{j,n}$ from the original platform s_j), we measure the positive relation between them by applying the Bhattacharyya distance [7] as follows.

$$\mathbb{A}_{i,m,n}^+ = \sqrt{(\mu_m - \mu_n)^T (\frac{\sigma_m + \sigma_n}{2})^{-1} (\mu_m - \mu_n)} \tag{9.4}$$

The reason of choosing Bhattacharyya distance is to quantitatively estimate the distance between the exchanged entities from $\widetilde{V}_i$ and the original entities from s_j. If the embedding space of $\widetilde{v}_{i,m}$ is far from the embedding space of $\widetilde{v}_{j,n}$ based on the positive relation (i.e., low $\mathbb{A}_{i,m,n}^+$), the domain discrepancy of topics of CCF between the two platforms is large. Therefore, the exchanged knowledge facts from the platform s_i is less discriminative on detecting COVID-19 false information on the platform s_j. Similarly, we apply the Bhattacharyya distance to measure the negative relations between entities from different platforms.

After generating the new adjacent matrices for each platform, we perform the multi-relation knowledge aggregation strategy from the PAKG again to classify the COVID-19 false information on each individual platform. In particular, we denote the new COVID-19 knowledge graph from each platform s_i as $\mathbb{G}_i = (\mathbb{E}_i, \mathcal{R}, \mathbb{T}_i, \mathbb{A}_i)$ and the embedded knowledge graph as $\widetilde{\mathbb{G}}_i = (\widetilde{\mathbb{E}}_i, \mathcal{R}, \widetilde{\mathbb{T}}_i, \mathbb{A}_i)$. The PAKG on each platform s_i then generates new attention scores for the embedded graph entities $\widetilde{\mathbb{E}}_i$ and leverages the scores to retrieve new discriminative knowledge triples. In particular, if the attention score of an entity is lower than φ where φ is a predefined hyper-parameter, we remove the entity and the connected relations from $\mathbb{A}_i$ in order to reduce the ineffective exchanged knowledge. We repeat the optimization process

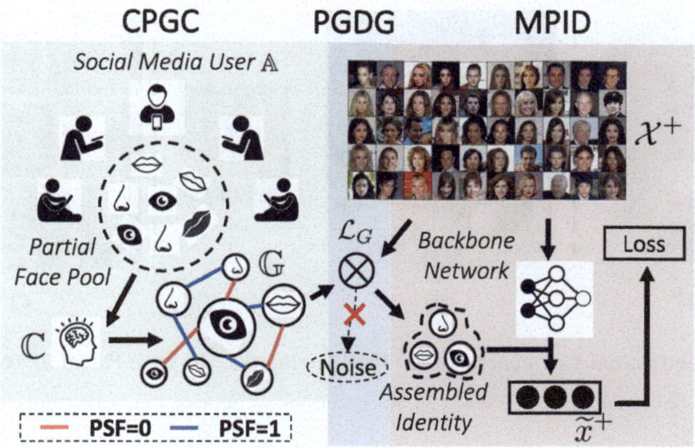

Fig. 9.4 The pipeline of FaceCrowd

of the PAKG and the DAKI until the accuracy performance of COVID-19 truth discovery does not increase anymore.

9.2.2 *FaceCrowd: A Crowdsourcing-Based Partition Approach*

The FaceCrowd consists of three different modules: (1) a crowdsource partial graph constructor (CPGC), (2) a partial graph denoising generator (PGDG), and (3) a metric-based partial identity discriminator (MPID). The overview of FaceCrowd is shown in Fig. 9.4. We elaborate on each module below.

9.2.2.1 Crowdsource Partial Graph Constructor

The crowdsource partial graph constructor (CPGC) aims to construct a bi-relational partial face graph (bPFG) that contains partial face images shared by social media users from the user-end devices (e.g., phones, smart cameras). In particular, bPFG considers partial face images as graph nodes, and crowdsourced binary face similarity annotation (i.e., low or high) as edges. The CPGC module consists of two components: (1) a user-end partial face generator, and (2) a server-end crowdsource face matching estimator.

The user-end partial face generator can be deployed on the local devices of social media users to generate and share their partial face images. The design of sharing on user-end devices effectively protects the identity information of the users by preventing access from other people (e.g., crowd workers, ML/AI researchers) to users' personal face images. We show the generation process and generated partial face examples in Fig. 9.5. In particular, the generator firstly detects the facial landmarks [4] of the personal face images as a set of 2-dimensional points (e.g., the

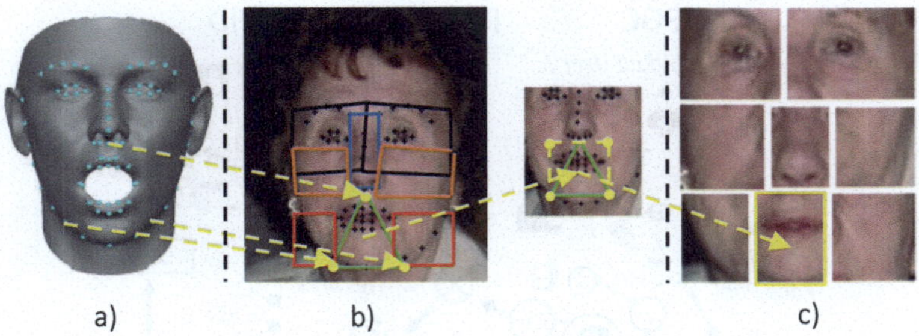

Fig. 9.5 User-end partial face generator. (**a**) Face landmarks. (**b**) Face Partition. (**c**) Partial faces

blue points in Fig. 9.5a) in order to specify key facial positions for creating partial face images [48]. If the generator cannot detect facial landmarks of an image, it skips the image and does not use it in the following process of FaceCrowd. Given the facial landmarks of a face image, we formally define *landmark-based partial face* as follows.

Definition 9.5 (Landmark-based Partial Face (r)**)** A rectangular face image region (e.g., a piece of face region in Fig. 9.5c) that is partitioned from the full human face image according to a set of selected facial landmarks.

The generator allows social media users to select different facial landmarks to generate and share partial face images of their interest. We observe that partial face images significantly protect the identity information in the original face images as each partial face contains only a small part of the facial components (e.g., the nose) that is not enough for other people (e.g., the crowd workers or ML/AI researchers) to accurately determine the unique identity of the social media users. The generator in each user-end device shares partial face images to the center server of FaceCrowd and aggregates them into a joint set of partial face images, denoted as *partial face pool*. The images in the partial face pool *cannot* be tracked back to the corresponding user-end devices because we do not record ID information of the devices on the backend server, which further protects the identity of social media users [30]

Given the partial face pool, the server-end crowdsource face-matching estimator asks crowd workers from online crowdsourcing websites [2] to identify the partial face pairs from the pool based on *potential face similarity* defined as follows.

Definition 9.6 (Potential Face Similarity (PFS)) A binary value (i.e., 0 or 1) that indicates if two partial face images belong to the same identity or not. We expect online crowd workers to estimate PFS based on the similarity of three different factors in partial face images: (1) demographic information (e.g., wrinkle, beard); (2) facial expression (e.g., surprised, calm) and (3) shot environment (e.g., profile, frontal). Therefore, the more similar the two partial face images are, the more likely a crowd worker pairs them with the same identity (i.e., PFS=1).

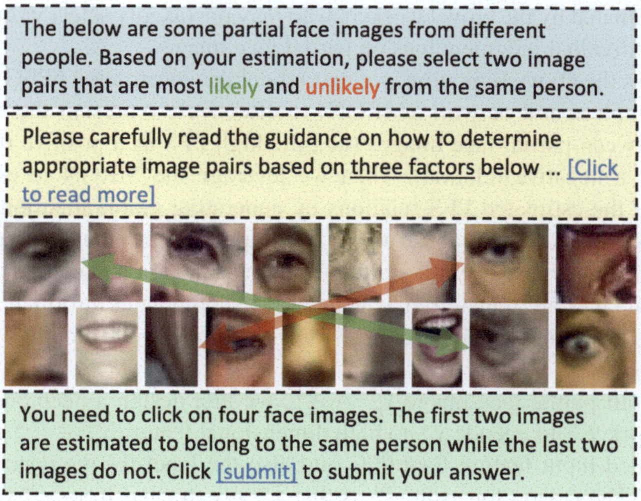

Fig. 9.6 The partial face matching interface

We define a novel partial face-matching interface in Fig. 9.6. In each crowdsourcing task, we randomly select a set of face images from the partial face pool as a candidate *partial face group* (e.g., the images in Fig. 9.6) and instruct a crowd worker to estimate PFS of image pairs. Unlike traditional face-related crowdsourcing tasks that grant the crowd workers access to full face images and assign them simple annotation tasks (e.g., face identity annotation [8]), our task limits the crowd workers' access to only the partial face images to protect the identities of users and leverage the intelligence of the crowd workers to infer the PFS of partial faces. For example, a crowd worker may select the partial face pair with the green arrow in Fig. 9.6 with PFS equal to 1 because the selected partial faces both look like old male faces with similar eye shapes. Similarly, the crowd worker may select the partial face images with the red arrow with PFS equal to 0 because the two partial faces have potentially different face shapes based on facial color and texture.

After collecting the responses from all crowd workers, we construct the bi-relational partial face graph (bPFG) based on the responses. In particular, we denote bPFG as a graph structure $\mathbb{G} = \{\mathcal{V}, \mathcal{E}\}$ where $\mathcal{V} = \{v_1, \ldots, v_K\}$ denotes the total K partial face images $\mathcal{P}^-$ as graph nodes. $\mathcal{E} = \{\mathcal{E}_0, \mathcal{E}_1\}$ represents the set of negative and positive PFS relations of $\mathcal{V}$ as graph edges.

9.2.2.2 Partial Graph Denoising Generator

Given the constructed partial face graph bPFG from the CPGC module, the partial graph denoising generator (PGDG) is designed to denoise the unreliable PFS relations estimated by the crowd workers who may mistakenly select wrong answers or contain individual judgment bias on partial face images.

To address the above limitation, we first model the constructed bPFG as a multi-relational graph neural network (MRGN) to effectively represent the binary PFS relations between partial face images (i.e., the high PFS as a positive relation and low PFS as a negative relation). Then we leverage the MRGN to estimate the reliability of the estimated PFS relations by generating graph attention scores for the relations based on the reconstruction of the public face images in an encoder-decoder manner. In this way, the common human facial characteristics from the public face images are transferred as general face component information to refine the relations of partial face images in MRGN. We show the structure of PGDG in Fig. 9.7 below.

Given a full public face image $x_n^+ \in \mathcal{X}^+$, we first design a deep convolutional neural network $\mathcal{F}^+$ to encode x_n^+ to high dimensional feature $\widetilde{x}_n^+ \in \mathbb{R}^{2d}$ that is used as the encoded input feature for bPFG and also the label for the decoded feature from bPFG. The reason for using $\widetilde{x}_n^+$ is that $\widetilde{x}_n^+$ is extracted from x_n^+ with higher-level identity information and less pixel-level noise, which identifies more reliable PFS relations in bPFG compared to the raw face image x_n^+. Similarly, we encode the partial face images in bPFG by another network $\mathcal{F}^-$ to the same feature dimension as $\widetilde{x}_n^+$ in order to aggregate the facial information across different features. We denote the encoded partial face images as $\widetilde{\mathcal{V}} = \{\widetilde{v}_1, \ldots, \widetilde{v}_K\}$. After the encoding process, the PGDG aggregates the information in both $\widetilde{x}_n^+$ and $\widetilde{\mathcal{V}}$ by concatenating the corresponding features of $\widetilde{x}_n^+$ and each $\widetilde{v}_k \in \widetilde{\mathcal{V}}$. To estimate the reliability of PFS relations between different partial face images, we generate the attention score for each PFS relation edge in the partial face graph by developing a partial graph-based reliability propagation strategy to decode $\widetilde{x}_n^+$ based on $\widetilde{\mathcal{V}}$ as follows.

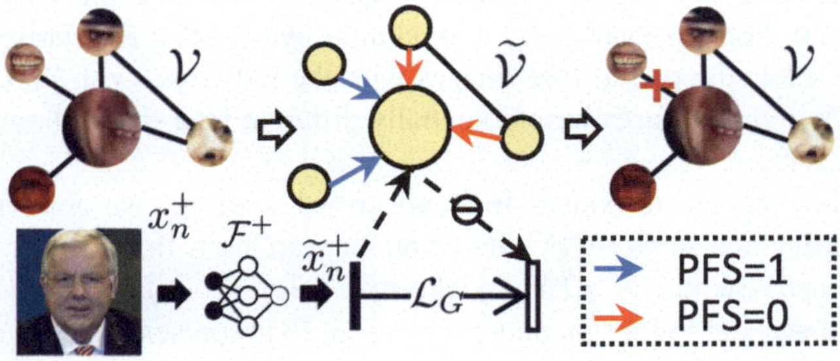

Fig. 9.7 Partial graph denoising generator

$$pos_{n,k}^{(l)} = \sigma(W_1[\widetilde{x}_n^{+}, \widetilde{v}_k^{(l-1)}] + \sum_{j \in \mathcal{V}_k^{pos}} \alpha_{k,j} W_2^{pos} \Delta_{k,j}^{(l-1)})$$

$$neg_{n,k}^{(l)} = \sigma(W_1[\widetilde{x}_n^{+}, \widetilde{v}_k^{(l-1)}] + \sum_{j \in \mathcal{V}_k^{neg}} \alpha_{k,j} W_2^{neg} \Delta_{k,j}^{(l-1)}) \quad (2)$$

$$\min \mathcal{L}_G = \sum_{n=1}^{N} \| \sum_{k \in \mathcal{V}} (pos_{n,k}^{(l)} - neg_{n,k}^{(l)}) - \widetilde{x}_n^{+} \|$$

where $\widetilde{v}_k^{(l-1)} \in \mathbb{R}^{2d}$ is kth encoded partial face image in $(l-1)$th MRGN graph layer and $\widetilde{x}_n^{+} \in \mathbb{R}^{2d}$ is nth encoded public face image. $\mathcal{V}_k^{pos}$ and $\mathcal{V}_k^{neg}$ denotes the set of encoded partial face images that have positive and negative relations with $\widetilde{v}_k^{(l-1)}$. $\Delta_{k,j}^{(l-1)} = \widetilde{v}_k^{(l-1)} - \widetilde{v}_j^{(l-1)}$ is the feature difference between the kth and jth encoded partial face image. $pos_{n,k}^{(l)} \in \mathbb{R}^d$ and $neg_{n,k}^{(l)} \in \mathbb{R}^d$ are aggregated partial face embeddings based on positive and negative relations of $\mathbb{G}$. $W_2^{pos} \in \mathbb{R}^{2d \times 2d}$ and $W_2^{pos} \in \mathbb{R}^{2d \times 2d}$ are learnable parameter matrices that learn discriminative features to represent positive and negative relations. $\mathcal{L}_G$ is the reconstruction loss of the encoded public face images based on the aggregated embeddings from all partial face images in MRGN. $\alpha_{k,j} \in [0, 1]$ is the normalized attention score between kth and jth partial face embeddings. The normalization process of $\alpha_{k,j}$ is defined as $\alpha_{k,j} = \frac{\exp(\sigma(a^T W_2^{pos/neg} \Delta_{k,j}^{(l-1)}))}{\sum_{j \in \mathcal{V}_k} \exp(\sigma(a^T W_2^{pos/neg} \Delta_{k,j}^{(l-1)}))}$ where $a \in \mathbb{R}^{2d}$ is the attention vector that estimates the importance of each neighbor partial face $\widetilde{v}_j$ to $\widetilde{v}_k$. After the training of PGDG, we remove the positive and negative relations of partial face pairs if the absolute value of the corresponding attention score is lower than the predefined threshold in order to reduce the potential annotation noise from crowd workers.

9.2.2.3 Metric-Based Partial Discriminator (MPID)

Given a denoised partial face graph from the PGDG module, the metric-based partial discriminator (MPID) aims to leverage the partial face images in $\mathbb{G}$ to optimize face recognition models that generate more discriminative face features across different identities for full input face images. Current face recognition models usually contain a backbone neural network module [17, 35] to embed input training images to high-dimensional features for classifying their identity labels. However, it is insufficient for the models trained only on the public celebrity face images to generate discriminative face features for personal face images from social media users due to the image domain discrepancy (e.g., face expression, shooting environment) [26]. Therefore, we model the denoised partial face graph from PGDG as a feature-level regularization that adapts the face features from the face recognition models to be more discriminative on both public and personal face images.

Given an embedded public face image $\widetilde{x}^+$ as input, we first define a representative partial face retrieval strategy to retrieve the partial face image that contains similar identity information as $\widetilde{x}^+$ from the MRGN module. The process is formally denoted as $\widetilde{V}^* = \arg\max_{\widetilde{v}_1,\ldots,\widetilde{v}_{K^*}} \max((\widetilde{x}_n^+ \circledast \widetilde{v}_k)W_c), \forall v_k \in \mathcal{V}$. where $\circledast$ represents the circular convolution operation [28] that periodically convolves $\widetilde{x}^+$ by $\widetilde{v}_k$ to estimate the similarity of two features based on each possible feature aggregation position. W_c transforms the convolved features to single values and $\max(\cdot)$ calculates the maximal value. We denote the retrieved partial face images as $\widetilde{V}^* = \{\widetilde{v}_1, \ldots, \widetilde{v}_{K^*}\}$

Since each encoded partial face image $\widetilde{v}_{k^*} \in \widetilde{V}^*$ only contains a small component of a personal human face and cannot be directly aggregated with the full public face image $\widetilde{x}^+$, we design a graph-based partial face assembling method that retrieves $v_k \in \mathcal{V}$ that are connected to $\widetilde{v}_{k^*}$ with positive PFS from CPGC module and high attention scores from the PGDG module. The retrieved partial faces contain different facial components (e.g., the facial components in Fig. 9.5c) that an assembled full personal face image shares similar identity information. The MPID encodes all retrieved partial face images by $\mathcal{F}^-$ and aggregates the encoded face features with $\widetilde{x}^+$ to generate more discriminative face features for both the public and potential personal face images. The process is denoted as $\widetilde{x}^+ := \widetilde{x}^+ + \sum_{k=1}^{K^*}(\widetilde{v}_k + \sum_{j=1}^{K} \widetilde{v}_j \cdot \mathbb{1}[(PFS_{k,j} = 1)\&(\alpha_{k,j} > \eta]))$

$$\widetilde{x}^+ := \widetilde{x}^+ + \sum_{k=1}^{K^*}(\widetilde{v}_k + \sum_{j=1}^{K} \widetilde{v}_j \cdot \mathbb{1}[(PFS_{k,j} = 1)\&(\alpha_{k,j} > \eta])) \tag{9.5}$$

where $PFS_{k,j}$ represents the PFS relation between the partial face image v_k and v_j. η is the predefined threshold value for $\alpha_{k,j}$. After the adaptation of $\hat{x}^+$, the face recognition model continues to utilize $\hat{x}^+$ to classify face identity labels. Therefore, FaceCrowd is generalized enough as a plug-in regularization module to optimize a broad set of data-driven face recognition models. We evaluate the performance of FaceCrowd in the next section.

9.3 Real-World Case Studies

9.3.1 Truth Discovery with Distributed Knowledge Graph

We evaluate the detection performance of CoviDKG using two real-world social media post datasets collected from Twitter and Facebook. Evaluation results show that CoviDKG achieves significant performance gains compared to state-of-the-art baselines by accurately detecting incorrect COVID-19 posts on social media.

Table 9.1 Data summary of CCF

Data trace	Statistics
Average number of documents	163
Average number of entities	474
Average number of triples	1979

9.3.1.1 Data

First, we describe the platforms-specific CCF and COVID-19 posts datasets we used in the experiments.

Platform-specific CCF

In light of the privacy concern of CCF, we focus on the platform-specific CCF whose source is publicly available for research purposes. In particular, we consider two types of CCF: (1) *professional fact-checking articles* that are published by fact-checking journalists and health professionals on major fact-checking websites (e.g., politifact.com, factcheck.org), and (2) *fact-checking community reports* that are posted by volunteer online users on online fact-checking communities (e.g., Birdwatch[1]). In the study, we collect CCF from 5 major social media platforms (i.e., Twitter, Facebook, Instagram, Reddit, Snapchat) to construct the community-driven distributed knowledge graph (CD-KG) in CoviDKG. A summary of the CCF in the study is presented in Table 9.1.

COVID-19 Posts

To evaluate the detection performance of classifying incorrect COVID-19 posts, we collect two real-world datasets of COVID-19 posts from the mainstream social media platforms: Twitter and Facebook. In particular, we leverage the public COVID-19 false information dataset, CoAID [10] to collect the social media posts from Twitter and Facebook. In particular, we retrieved the COVID-19 posts from each social media platform based on the post id identified in CoAID. To preserve the user privacy, we only crawl the post content (i.e., the text of each post) using the official Twitter API and Facebook's CrowdTangle tool [38]. In this study, we primarily focus on social media posts in English and remove any non-English posts. We use the ground-truth labels provided in the original datasets, which are validated by medical experts and professional journalists. We finally obtain 684 incorrect and 2510 correct posts from Twitter, and 581 incorrect and 2218 correct posts from Facebook (Table 9.2).

[1] https://twitter.com/i/birdwatch.

Table 9.2 Data summary of COVID-19 posts

	Data trace	Statistics
Twitter	Number of incorrect posts	684
	Number of correct posts	2510
Facebook	Number of incorrect posts	581
	Number of correct posts	2218

9.3.1.2 Baseline Methods and Experimental Setting

We compare the model with several state-of-the-art baseline methods that leverage knowledge graphs to detect false information on social media.

- **GUpdater [37]:** GUpdater is a graph neural network framework that leverages a text-based attention mechanism to guide the information propagation in knowledge graph. In particular, we replace the decoder module of GUpdater with a fully connected layer to classify incorrect social media posts.
- **DETERRENT [11]:** DETERRENT is a knowledge-driven healthcare misinformation detection framework that utilizes a graph attention network to learn useful knowledge information from the biomedical and health knowledge base in life sciences to detect incorrect healthcare news. In particular, we replace the healthcare news in DETERRENT with social media posts to perform the classification task.
- **COVID-BKM [14]:** COVID-BKM is a COVID-19 biomedical knowledge miner that incorporates the cause-and-effect information network learned from scientific literature of COVID-19 pathophysiology. We adapt COVID-BKM to detect incorrect COVID-19 social media posts by replacing the distributed knowledge graph nodes in CoviDKG with the information network constructed in COVID-BKM.
- **FedE [6]:** FedE is a federated learning based framework that jointly learns the entity embeddings in different knowledge graphs for classification tasks (e.g., truth discovery). In particular, we adapt FedE to learn the entity embeddings in CD-KG of different social media platforms and the learned entity embeddings are input to PAKG to classify incorrect COVID-19 posts.

For the implementation details of CoviDKG, the PAKG module holds 2 graph convolutional layers with each layer followed by the *ReLU* activation. We set the embedding dimensions of the BERT-based entity encoder as 768. We set the total number of epochs as 40 and train CoviDKG with an initial learning rate of 0.001 and decay of 0.95 in each epoch. The optimizer is Adam with 5×10^{-4} weight decay. We run the experiments on Ubuntu 20.04 with four NVIDIA A40.

To ensure a fair comparison, we use the same input of social media posts to all the baseline methods for training and testing the classification models. In the experiments, we use 80% of each dataset as the training set, and the remaining 20% of each dataset as the testing set. For GUpdater, DETERRENT, and FedE, we use the same CCF to construct the knowledge graph. For COVID-BKM, since it is a pathophysiology-based cause-and-effect knowledge graph of COVID-19, we use the knowledge graph constructed in COVID-BKM to learn COVID-19 knowledge for detecting incorrect COVID-19 posts. We strictly follow the configurations of all baselines as documented in the original papers, and carefully tune the hyperparameters for the best results.

9.3.1.3 Detection Performance

In the first set of experiments, we evaluate the classification performance of all compared methods in detecting incorrect COVID-19 social media posts. We adopt the evaluation metrics that are commonly used to evaluate classification performance, including *Accuracy*, *Precision*, *Recall*, and *F1 Score*. We summarize the evaluation results on the Twitter and Facebook datasets in Tables 9.3 and 9.4, respectively. We observe that CoviDKG consistently outperforms all the baselines on both the Twitter and Facebook datasets in terms of all evaluation metrics. For example, we observe that CoviDKG outperforms the best-performing baseline (i.e., GUpdater) by 4.56% in terms of the F1 Score on the Facebook dataset. The performance gains can be mainly attributed to the distributed design of CoviDKG that explores the diversified COVID-19 knowledge facts in the community-contributed CCF across different social media platforms to effectively identify the incorrect COVID-19 social media posts.

Moreover, the performance improvements of CoviDKG over the knowledge graph based truth discovery baselines (i.e., GUpdater and DETERRENT) suggest the effectiveness of domain-aware knowledge integrator in CoviDKG that can efficiently integrate CD-KG with privacy-aware COVID-19 knowledge facts from

Table 9.3 Detection performance (Twitter dataset)

	Accuracy	Precision	Recall	F1 score
CoviDKG	**0.9089**	**0.9195**	**0.8065**	**0.8115**
GUpdater	0.7151	0.8991	0.6947	0.7838
DETERRENT	0.6948	0.8317	0.7389	0.7826
COVID-BKM	0.8802	0.8089	0.7183	0.7362
FedE	0.9020	0.8552	0.7455	0.7956

The bold values indicate the best performing results in each evaluation metric

Table 9.4 Detection performance (Facebook dataset)

	Accuracy	Precision	Recall	F1 score
CoviDKG	**0.9461**	**0.9074**	**0.8007**	**0.8498**
GUpdater	0.6983	0.8288	0.7811	0.8042
DETERRENT	0.7586	0.8429	0.7419	0.7892
COVID-BKM	0.9104	0.6961	0.7198	0.7066
FedE	0.9202	0.9027	0.6930	0.7816

The bold values indicate the best performing results in each evaluation metric

other social media platforms to enrich the COVID-19 knowledge facts in CD-KG. In addition, CoviDKG investigates the COVID-19 knowledge facts from CCF which includes both medical and non-medical COVID-19 knowledge facts that can greatly enhance the performance of identifying incorrect COVID-19 posts.

9.3.1.4 Robustness Study

In the second set of experiments, we investigate the robustness of CoviDKG by tuning two hyperparameters in CoviDKG, including: (1) the *number of exchanged knowledge triples* (Ω), and (2) the *number of rounds for knowledge exchange* (t). These two hyperparameters are key factors in CoviDKG to optimize the truth discovery performance. In particular, we vary Ω from 1 to 5, and t from 0 to 4. We evaluate the detection performance in terms of Accuracy and F1 Score. We present the results with respect to Ω and t in Figs. 9.8 and 9.9, respectively. We observe that the detection performance of CoviDKG gradually plateaus as Ω increases, especially after Ω reaches 4. This is because that increasing the number of exchanged knowledge triples may introduce additional knowledge triples that are less relevant to identifying incorrect COVID-19 posts. In addition, we also note that

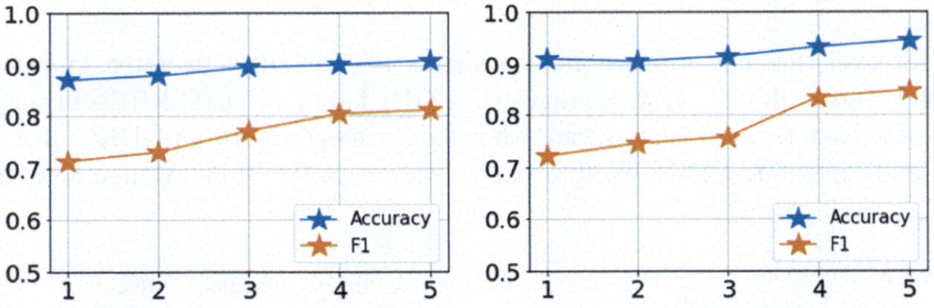

(a) (b)

Fig. 9.8 Robustness study: Knowledge triples (Ω). (**a**) Twitter dataset. (**b**) Facebook dataset

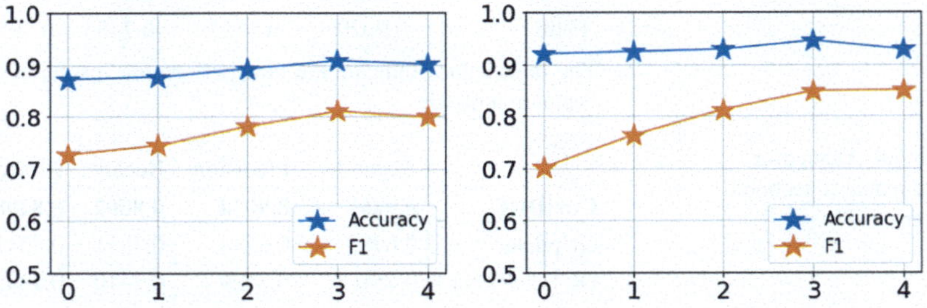

(a) (b)

Fig. 9.9 Robustness study: Knowledge exchange rounds (t). (**a**) Twitter dataset. (**b**) Facebook dataset

CoviDKG's performance increases as t increases from 1 to 3 and starts to plateaus afterwards. A possible reason is that there are not enough COVID-19 posts on each social media platform to optimize the knowledge graph as the size of the graph increases with more exchanged knowledge triples.

9.3.1.5 Ablation Study

In the third set of experiments, we conduct an ablation study to analyze the contribution of the main components in the CoviDKG framework. In particular, we consider three ablations of CoviDKG in the study:

- **CoviDKG\Z**: the variant of CoviDKG that excludes the Bhattacharyya distance measurement on domain discrepancy between the knowledge from different social media platforms in the DAKI module.
- **CoviDKG\A**: the variant of CoviDKG that excludes the binary adjacent matrix $\mathcal{A}_s^r$ as the additional mask in Eq. (9.3).
- **CoviDKG\U**: the variant of CoviDKG that does not update the relations between the exchanged knowledge triples and CD-KG by removing the knowledge graph updating process from the DAKI module.

We summarize the evaluation results of the ablation study on the Twitter and Facebook datasets in Tables 9.5 and 9.6, respectively. We observe that CoviDKG reaches the best performance when CoviDKG integrates all the components. The results demonstrate the effectiveness and necessity of key components in CoviDKG.

Table 9.5 Ablation study (Twitter dataset)

	Accuracy	Precision	Recall	F1 score
CoviDKG	**0.9089**	**0.9195**	**0.8065**	**0.8115**
CoviDKG\Z	0.9020	0.8552	0.7455	0.7956
CoviDKG\A	0.8837	0.7878	0.7647	0.7711
CoviDKG\U	0.8839	0.7762	0.7622	0.7635

The bold values indicate the best performing results in each evaluation metric

Table 9.6 Ablation study (Facebook dataset)

	Accuracy	Precision	Recall	F1 score
CoviDKG	**0.9461**	**0.9074**	**0.8007**	**0.8498**
CoviDKG\Z	0.9354	0.8846	0.7737	0.8153
CoviDKG\A	0.8339	0.8822	0.7956	0.8284
CoviDKG\U	0.9245	0.8977	0.7072	0.7850

The bold values indicate the best performing results in each evaluation metric

9.3.2 *Privacy-Aware Face Recognition*

We conduct extensive experiments on two real-world human-face datasets to evaluate the effectiveness of FaceCrowd in optimizing different face recognition models and protecting the identities of shared partial face images.

9.3.2.1 Data

We use CelebA [25] and LFW [19] as two large-scale public human face datasets in the experiments. CelebA [25] is a large-scale celebrity face dataset with 202,599 celebrity face images that belong to 10,177 unique identities. LFW [19] is a large-scale human face dataset that contains 38,581 public face images collected from the Internet with 5749 identities. Since there is no public human face dataset that contains personal human face images with identity labels from social media users, we randomly select 81,473 face images with 6000 identities from CelebA as public face dataset and 10,337 face images with 1720 identities from LFW as private face dataset. The reason for creating the public face dataset from CelebA is that celebrity images in CelebA are usually public and used for training the face recognition models [45]. In contrast, the LFW contains non-celebrity face images that are similar to the face images from common social media users in terms of face appearance and photo style. The identity labels of LFW are only used for evaluation purposes in the experiments. To simulate the action of social media users who select partial faces of their personal face images for sharing, we generate partial face images from LFW by randomly generating landmark-based partial faces (Definition 9.5) from the full face images.

9.3.2.2 Crowdsource Platform

Based on the collected partial face images, we generate 1500 crowdsourcing tasks with each task containing 16 different partial face images as shown in Fig. 9.6 from the CPGC module. For each crowdsourcing task, we assign five independent Amazon Mechanical Turk (AMT) crowd workers to perform the crowdsource face matching estimation. We define a set of screening pipelines to ensure the quality of the answers from crowd workers. In particular, the crowd workers are selected only if they have a 95% or higher Human Intelligence Task (HIT) rate. The crowd worker can choose to skip the task if they do not want to work on the assigned task for any reason. We set the payment to all crowd workers well above the minimum requirement from AMT [2]. After collecting the answers from crowd workers, we further filter out invalid answers from malicious crowd workers who complete each crowdsourcing task in an extremely short time (e.g., less than 3 seconds). We finally collected 5412 partial face image pairs with positive PFS and 5991 image pairs with negative PFS.

9.3.2.3 Baseline Methods and Experimental Setting

We choose a set of state-of-the-art face recognition models to evaluate the performance of FaceCrowd.

- **LightCNN** [44]: a face recognition framework that contains a lightweight convolutional module to learn compact human face features.
- **MobiFace** [16]: a face recognition framework designed for face recognition on edge devices that require efficient computing resources of the devices.
- **VGGFace** [29]: a face recognition framework that designs a VGG convolutional neural network [35] based model and trains the model by collecting a large-scale human face dataset.
- **SphereFace** [24]: a face recognition framework that builds a deep neural network architecture to learn discriminative face features by mapping the face features into an angular space.
- **VGGFace2** [5]: a face recognition framework trained on a large-scale face dataset that contains millions of face images with variations in pose, age and illumination.
- **CenterLoss** [43]: a face recognition framework that designs a new loss function to learn an identity-specific center representation for face images that belong to the same identity.
- **ArcFace** [12]: a face recognition framework that proposes a margin-based loss function that maximizes the inter-variance of embedded face image features that belong to different face identities.

In the experiments, we split the face images with 4000 identities from the public face dataset as a training set and randomly select 30% face images from the training set as the validation set. We further equally split the validation set into two subsets where the first subset is used to tune the parameters of each face recognition model and the second subset is used to test each model's face recognition performance. We create two types of testing sets that contain face images with exclusive identities from the training/validation set to extensively evaluate the performance of various face recognition models. The first type is N-shot face recognition testing set. In particular, we select 500 unique identities that contain at least $N + 1$ face images from the public and private face datasets respectively. For each identity, we define 1 face image as *probe* and the rest N face image with the same identity as *gallery*. The second type is the face verification testing set. We randomly select 500 face image pairs from both the public face dataset and the private face dataset, respectively.

9.3.2.4 Face Recognition Performance

In the first experiment, we evaluate the overall face recognition performance of all schemes on both validation and testing sets. We adopt $Prec@K$ as the evaluation metric for the face recognition performance on the validation set to represent the number of face images whose ground-truth identity labels are among the top

Table 9.7 Face recognition performance on validation set

Data	Public dataset		FaceCrowd	
Metric	Prec@1	Prec@5	Prec@1	Prec@5
LightCNN	74.40	85.80	**77.97**	**87.22**
MobiFace	72.70	83.95	**80.88**	**88.90**
VGGFace	79.80	88.22	**84.38**	**91.90**
SphereFace	79.45	90.95	**88.93**	**94.25**
VGGFace2	78.88	89.50	**85.83**	**93.38**
CenterLoss	80.85	87.22	**90.55**	**93.48**
ArcFace	83.58	91.90	**88.00**	**95.78**

The bold values indicate the best performing results in each evaluation metric

K predicted identity labels by a face recognition scheme. The evaluation results are shown in Table 9.7. We observe that FaceCrowd significantly improves the recognition performance of all compared schemes. The performance gains are mainly due to the fact that the FaceCrowd scheme creates a partial face graph to regulate the face image representations generated in the face recognition models by aggregating the representation of input full public face images with assembled partial face embeddings in the graph based on their estimated face similarities.

We further investigate the effectiveness of FaceCrowd on improving the face recognition performance of compared schemes on the testing sets with unseen face identities (i.e., N-shot recognition testing sets and the face verification testing set). We adopt two widely used evaluation metrics, *rank-r* [18] and *TMR@FMR=1.0%* [27], to evaluate the performance of compared schemes on. Given a *probe* image, the *rank-r* evaluates if a face recognition scheme can retrieve at least one of N face images with the same identity from the *gallery* and rank their similarity scores in Top-r. The *TMR@FMR=1.0%* calculates the True Match Rate (TMR) of the predicted results on the face verification set by a face recognition model at False Match Rate (FMR) of 1.0%. The evaluation results are shown in Table 9.8. We observe that the compared schemes achieve face recognition accuracy improvements on most of the evaluation metrics if they are optimized by FaceCrowd compared to the optimization on the public face dataset. The reason is that FaceCrowd optimizes the robustness of face recognition schemes on unseen face identities by developing a crowdsourcing-based partial face generator to explicitly consider the unique facial characteristics embedded in the personal face images from the private face dataset.

We visualize the face representations of a set of testing face images in Fig. 9.10 to demonstrate the effectiveness of FaceCrowd on generating more discriminative face representations (Fig. 9.10b) compared to the representations optimized on public face dataset (Fig. 9.10a). In particular, we randomly select 400 face images with 20 unseen face identities and embed them to 2D features by ArcFace model and t-SNE [40] since ArcFace is one of the representative models in the face recognition research. We observe that, compared to Fig. 9.10a, the face representations in Fig. 9.10b contains lower intra-identity variance and higher inter-identity variance.

Table 9.8 Evaluation of face recognition on testing sets

Data	Public dataset					FaceCrowd				
Gallery(N)	N=1		N=3		TMR@FMR=1.0%	N=1		N=3		TMR@FMR=1.0%
Rank(r)	r=1	r=3	r=1	r=3	–	r=1	r=3	r=1	r=3	–
LightCNN	51.7	64.9	65.1	79.8	78.8	**54.9**	**67.5**	**70.4**	**82.2**	**84.2**
MobiFace	49.3	61.7	66.3	79.8	71.8	**55.0**	**68.4**	**70.6**	**82.5**	**82.8**
VGGFace	53.6	67.0	70.5	80.9	**85.6**	**55.9**	**69.1**	**71.8**	**82.3**	82.6
SphereFace	54.3	66.1	70.0	81.9	77.2	**59.9**	**71.9**	**73.5**	**84.6**	**84.4**
VGGFace2	55.2	67.9	70.2	82.5	82.6	**60.1**	**71.7**	**73.2**	**84.5**	**85.2**
CenterLoss	55.4	69.5	72.0	82.5	79.8	**65.1**	**76.7**	**80.3**	**88.6**	**86.0**
ArcFace	57.2	69.4	72.8	85.6	78.6	**68.6**	**80.9**	**83.9**	**91.2**	**90.6**

The bold values indicate the best performing results in each evaluation metric

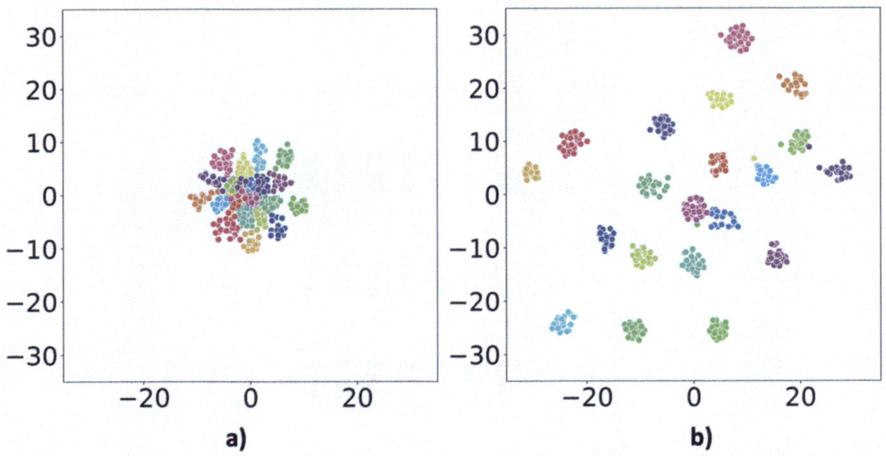

Fig. 9.10 Distribution of face representations. (**a**) Public dataset optimization. (**b**) FaceCrowd optimization

9.3.2.5 Identity Protection Performance

To answer question RQ2, we study the identity protection performance of FaceCrowd through a comprehensive real-world user study. In particular, we compare the partial face generation strategy of FaceCrowd with two different identity protection baselines: (1) AdversialNoise [23] adds random pixel-noise to manipulate the appearance of face images; (2) The GAN method [22] edits the specific components (e.g., mouth, nose) of original face images. We also added RawImage which makes no manipulation on the face images for a fair comparison. We first select 200 testing face images and process each image by the four compared schemes. For each testing face image, we randomly select N face images as candidate images from both public and private face datasets. We recruit three crowd workers for each testing face image to decide if there exists a candidate face image with the same identity as the testing face image. We define *face identification accuracy* as the fraction of the responses from the crowd workers that makes correct justifications. We then conduct an independent crowdsourcing user study by creating 32, 64, and 128 candidate face images for each testing face image. The results are summarized in Fig. 9.11.

We observe that the face recognition accuracy of FaceCrowd is significantly lower than all compared schemes with different number of candidate face images. The observation demonstrates that FaceCrowd can effectively protect the identity of human faces by generating partial face images with limited face regions. Moreover, as the number of candidate images increases, the face identification accuracy of FaceCrowd decreases more significantly than other schemes. The observation further verifies the effectiveness of the identity protection of FaceCrowd in more realistic scenarios where many social media users may view more than 128 face images on social media platforms [3].

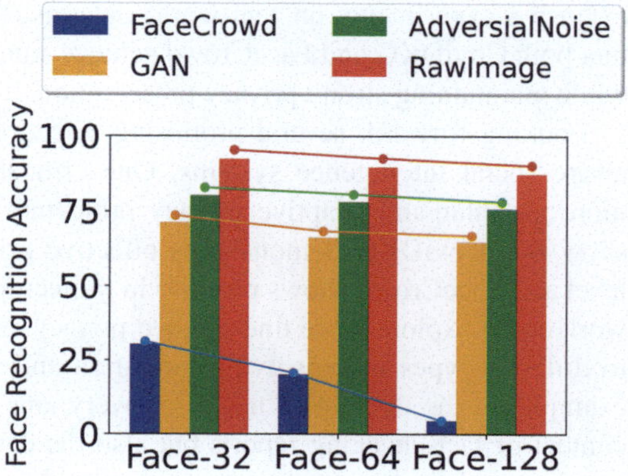

Fig. 9.11 Privacy protection evaluation on FaceCrowd

Table 9.9 Ablation study results with ArcFace

Gallery(N)	N=1		N=3		TMR@FMR=1.0%
Rank(r)	r=1	r=3	r=1	r=3	–
Partial-G	60.1	71.7	73.2	84.5	84.6
Partial-D	64.2	75.3	78.8	88.0	85.0
Partial-N	65.1	76.9	79.5	88.8	87.2
FaceCrowd	**68.6**	**80.9**	**83.9**	**91.2**	**90.6**

The bold values indicate the best performing results in each evaluation metric

9.3.2.6 Ablation Study

Finally, we perform a comprehensive *ablation study* to understand the contributions of important components in FaceCrowd. We create different variants of FaceCrowd by changing its key components: (1) *Partial-G*: we remove the PGDG module; (2) *FaceCrowd-D*: we remove the feature aggregation in MPID; and (3) *FaceCrowd-N*: we remove the negative relations in bPFG. The results are shown in Table 9.9. We observe FaceCrowd outperform other variants in terms of all evaluation metrics. The results demonstrate the importance and necessity of key components of FaceCrowd.

9.4 Discussion

This chapter presents novel approaches to addressing critical privacy challenges in social intelligence systems through two comprehensive case studies: CoviDKG for privacy-aware truth discovery and FaceCrowd for privacy-preserving face recognition. In particular, CoviDKG introduces a novel distributed knowledge graph approach that enables cross-platform collaboration for truth discovery while protecting both individual user privacy and platform-specific content. FaceCrowd presents a novel crowdsourcing-based partial face approach that leverages the collective intelligence of crowd workers to optimize face recognition models while preserving user privacy through the selective sharing of partial facial features. Through extensive experiments on real-world datasets, the evaluation results demonstrate that both CoviDKG and FaceCrowd achieve significant performance improvements while maintaining strong privacy preservation.

Looking forward, several promising directions emerge for advancing privacy-aware social intelligence systems. One critical direction is the development of more granular and adaptive privacy protection mechanisms. In this chapter, we show that CoviDKG demonstrates effective privacy preservation at the platform level and FaceCrowd shows promise in protecting individual facial features. Future work could explore more fine-grained privacy controls that can dynamically adjust to different types of sensitive information and varying privacy requirements. For example, in the domain of truth discovery, one may want to protect not only the content of fact-checking reports but also the contextual metadata, user interaction patterns, and temporal information that might also contain sensitive details about users or platforms. Similarly, in facial recognition applications, future research could investigate methods for selective feature sharing that adapt to different privacy preferences and cultural sensitivities regarding facial features, such as religious coverings, cultural markings, or age-related features that users may wish to keep private for personal or cultural reasons.

We envision that the advancement of social intelligence, combined with the growing awareness of privacy concerns, creates a rich landscape for novel solutions that can balance the competing demands of social intelligence data and privacy protection. Future work might explore the application of these approaches to other domains of social intelligence, such as mental health monitoring, online harassment detection, and recommendation systems, while preserving the privacy of individual users and platforms. For example, in mental health monitoring applications, distributed knowledge graphs could be developed to securely share patterns of concerning behavior across platforms while protecting individual user identities and specific post content. Such a system could help mental health professionals identify individuals at risk while maintaining the protection of sensitive personal information that may be unintentionally disclosed by individuals. Similarly, for recommendation systems, a privacy-aware approach could exchange user preference patterns through privacy-preserved feature representations which ensure the privacy of individual users while enhancing the recommendation quality with the collective knowledge/experience from multiple platforms and user communities. These applications would require careful consideration of privacy requirements and the development of sophisticated mechanisms to protect sensitive information while maintaining the effectiveness of social intelligence systems.

References

1. A. J. Adetayo. Fake news and social media censorship: Examining the librarian role. In *Deep Fakes, Fake News, and Misinformation in Online Teaching and Learning Technologies*, pages 69–92. IGI Global, 2021.
2. AMT, https://www.mturk.com/.

3. F. Benevenuto, T. Rodrigues, M. Cha, and V. Almeida. Characterizing user behavior in online social networks. In *Proceedings of the 9th ACM SIGCOMM Conference on Internet Measurement*, pages 49–62, 2009.
4. X. P. Burgos-Artizzu, P. Perona, and P. Dollár. Robust face landmark estimation under occlusion. In *Proceedings of the IEEE international conference on computer vision*, pages 1513–1520, 2013.
5. Q. Cao, L. Shen, W. Xie, O. M. Parkhi, and A. Zisserman. Vggface2: A dataset for recognising faces across pose and age. In *2018 13th IEEE international conference on automatic face & gesture recognition (FG 2018)*, pages 67–74. IEEE, 2018.
6. M. Chen, W. Zhang, Z. Yuan, Y. Jia, and H. Chen. Fede: Embedding knowledge graphs in federated setting. In *The 10th International Joint Conference on Knowledge Graphs*, pages 80–88, 2021.
7. E. Choi and C. Lee. Feature extraction based on the bhattacharyya distance. *Pattern Recognition*, 36(8):1703–1709, 2003.
8. J. Y. Choi, W. De Neve, K. N. Plataniotis, and Y. M. Ro. Collaborative face recognition for improved face annotation in personal photo collections shared on online social networks. *IEEE Transactions on Multimedia*, 13(1):14–28, 2010.
9. N. Colic and F. Rinaldi. Improving spacy dependency annotation and pos tagging web service using independent ner services. *Genomics & informatics*, 17(2), 2019.
10. L. Cui and D. Lee. Coaid: Covid-19 healthcare misinformation dataset, 2020.
11. L. Cui, H. Seo, M. Tabar, F. Ma, S. Wang, and D. Lee. Deterrent: Knowledge guided graph attention network for detecting healthcare misinformation. In *Proceedings of the 26th ACM SIGKDD International Conference on Knowledge Discovery & Data Mining*, pages 492–502, 2020.
12. J. Deng, J. Guo, N. Xue, and S. Zafeiriou. Arcface: Additive angular margin loss for deep face recognition. In *Proceedings of the IEEE/CVF Conference on Computer Vision and Pattern Recognition*, pages 4690–4699, 2019.
13. J. Devlin, M.-W. Chang, K. Lee, and K. Toutanova. Bert: Pre-training of deep bidirectional transformers for language understanding. *arXiv preprint arXiv:1810.04805*, 2018.
14. D. Domingo-Fernández, S. Baksi, B. Schultz, Y. Gadiya, R. Karki, T. Raschka, C. Ebeling, M. Hofmann-Apitius, et al. Covid-19 knowledge graph: a computable, multi-modal, cause-and-effect knowledge model of covid-19 pathophysiology. *BioRxiv*, 2020.
15. J. Dong, A. Roth, and W. J. Su. Gaussian differential privacy. *Journal of the Royal Statistical Society: Series B (Statistical Methodology)*, 84(1):3–37, 2022.
16. C. N. Duong, K. G. Quach, I. Jalata, N. Le, and K. Luu. Mobiface: A lightweight deep learning face recognition on mobile devices. In *2019 IEEE 10th International Conference on Biometrics Theory, Applications and Systems (BTAS)*, pages 1–6. IEEE, 2019.
17. K. He, X. Zhang, S. Ren, and J. Sun. Identity mappings in deep residual networks. In *European conference on computer vision*, pages 630–645. Springer, 2016.
18. L. He, H. Li, Q. Zhang, and Z. Sun. Dynamic feature matching for partial face recognition. *IEEE Transactions on Image Processing*, 28(2):791–802, 2018.
19. G. B. Huang, M. Mattar, T. Berg, and E. Learned-Miller. Labeled faces in the wild: A database forstudying face recognition in unconstrained environments. In *Workshop on faces in'Real-Life'Images: detection, alignment, and recognition*, 2008.
20. B. Knott, S. Venkataraman, A. Hannun, S. Sengupta, M. Ibrahim, and L. van der Maaten. Crypten: Secure multi-party computation meets machine learning. *Advances in Neural Information Processing Systems*, 34:4961–4973, 2021.
21. Z. Kou, L. Shang, Y. Zhang, S. Duan, and D. Wang. Can i only share my eyes? a web crowdsourcing based face partition approach towards privacy-aware face recognition. In *Proceedings of the ACM Web Conference 2022*, pages 3611–3622, 2022. https://doi.org/10.1145/3485447.3512256.
22. B. Liu, M. Ding, H. Xue, T. Zhu, D. Ye, L. Song, and W. Zhou. Dp-image: Differential privacy for image data in feature space. *arXiv preprint arXiv:2103.07073*, 2021.

23. B. Liu, M. Ding, T. Zhu, Y. Xiang, and W. Zhou. Adversaries or allies? privacy and deep learning in big data era. *Concurrency and Computation: Practice and Experience*, 31(19):e5102, 2019.
24. W. Liu, Y. Wen, Z. Yu, M. Li, B. Raj, and L. Song. Sphereface: Deep hypersphere embedding for face recognition. In *Proceedings of the IEEE conference on computer vision and pattern recognition*, pages 212–220, 2017.
25. Z. Liu, P. Luo, X. Wang, and X. Tang. Large-scale celebfaces attributes (celeba) dataset. *Retrieved August*, 15(2018):11, 2018.
26. Z. Luo, J. Hu, W. Deng, and H. Shen. Deep unsupervised domain adaptation for face recognition. In *2018 13th IEEE International Conference on Automatic Face & Gesture Recognition (FG 2018)*, pages 453–457. IEEE, 2018.
27. V. Mirjalili, S. Raschka, and A. Ross. Flowsan: Privacy-enhancing semi-adversarial networks to confound arbitrary face-based gender classifiers. *IEEE Access*, 7:99735–99745, 2019.
28. X. Ouyang, C. Antony, F. Gunning, H. Zhang, and Y. L. Guan. Discrete fresnel transform and its circular convolution. *arXiv preprint arXiv:1510.00574*, 2015.
29. O. M. Parkhi, A. Vedaldi, and A. Zisserman. *Deep face recognition*. British Machine Vision Association, 2015.
30. R. Pellungrini, L. Pappalardo, F. Pratesi, and A. Monreale. A data mining approach to assess privacy risk in human mobility data. *ACM Transactions on Intelligent Systems and Technology (TIST)*, 9(3):1–27, 2017.
31. N. Pröllochs. Community-based fact-checking on twitter's birdwatch platform. *arXiv preprint arXiv:2104.07175*, 2021.
32. Y. Qian, W. Deng, and J. Hu. Unsupervised face normalization with extreme pose and expression in the wild. In *Proceedings of the IEEE/CVF Conference on Computer Vision and Pattern Recognition*, pages 9851–9858, 2019.
33. M. Schlichtkrull, T. N. Kipf, P. Bloem, R. van den Berg, I. Titov, and M. Welling. Modeling relational data with graph convolutional networks, 2017.
34. L. Shang, Z. Kou, Y. Zhang, J. Chen, and D. Wang. A privacy-aware distributed knowledge graph approach to qois-driven covid-19 misinformation detection. In *2022 IEEE/ACM 30th International Symposium on Quality of Service (IWQoS)*, pages 1–10. IEEE, 2022. DOI:10.1109/IWQoS54832.2022.9812879, Reprinted with permission from IEEE.
35. K. Simonyan and A. Zisserman. Very deep convolutional networks for large-scale image recognition. *arXiv preprint arXiv:1409.1556*, 2014.
36. X. Song, J. Petrak, Y. Jiang, I. Singh, D. Maynard, and K. Bontcheva. Classification aware neural topic model for covid-19 disinformation categorisation. *PloS one*, 16(2):e0247086, 2021.
37. J. Tang, Y. Feng, and D. Zhao. Learning to update knowledge graphs by reading news. In *Proceedings of the 2019 Conference on Empirical Methods in Natural Language Processing and the 9th International Joint Conference on Natural Language Processing (EMNLP-IJCNLP)*, 2019.
38. C. Team. CrowdTangle Team (2020). CrowdTangle. Facebook, Menlo Park, California, United States.
39. T. University. Tulane University (2020). Key social media privacy issues for 2020. https://sopa.tulane.edu/blog/key-social-media-privacy-issues-2020
40. L. Van der Maaten and G. Hinton. Visualizing data using t-sne. *Journal of machine learning research*, 9(11), 2008.
41. A. Wani, I. Joshi, S. Khandve, V. Wagh, and R. Joshi. Evaluating deep learning approaches for covid19 fake news detection. In *International Workshop on Combating Online Hostile Posts in Regional Languages during Emergency Situation*, pages 153–163. Springer, 2021.
42. J. Wen, Z. Zhang, Y. Lan, Z. Cui, J. Cai, and W. Zhang. A survey on federated learning: challenges and applications. *International Journal of Machine Learning and Cybernetics*, 14(2):513–535, 2023.
43. Y. Wen, K. Zhang, Z. Li, and Y. Qiao. A discriminative feature learning approach for deep face recognition. In *European conference on computer vision*, pages 499–515. Springer, 2016.

44. X. Wu, R. He, Z. Sun, and T. Tan. A light cnn for deep face representation with noisy labels. *IEEE Transactions on Information Forensics and Security*, 13(11):2884–2896, 2018.
45. Z. Xiao, X. Gao, C. Fu, Y. Dong, W. Gao, X. Zhang, J. Zhou, and J. Zhu. Improving transferability of adversarial patches on face recognition with generative models. In *Proceedings of the IEEE/CVF Conference on Computer Vision and Pattern Recognition*, pages 11845–11854, 2021.
46. A. Yang, J. Shin, A. Zhou, K. M. Huang-Isherwood, E. Lee, C. Dong, H. M. Kim, Y. Zhang, J. Sun, Y. Li, et al. The battleground of covid-19 vaccine misinformation on facebook: Fact checkers vs. misinformation spreaders. *Harvard Kennedy School Misinformation Review*, 2021.
47. D. Y. Zhang, Z. Kou, and D. Wang. Fairfl: A fair federated learning approach to reducing demographic bias in privacy-sensitive classification models. In *2020 IEEE International Conference on Big Data (Big Data)*, pages 1051–1060. IEEE, 2020.
48. Z. Zhang, P. Luo, C. C. Loy, and X. Tang. Facial landmark detection by deep multi-task learning. In *European conference on computer vision*, pages 94–108. Springer, 2014.

Chapter 10
Further Readings

Abstract This chapter provides further readings related to the work presented in this book. The readers are recommended to take the content of this chapter as a reference if they would like to explore future problems from a broader perspective in Social Intelligence. Examples of the reviewed areas in this chapter include: human-AI systems, AI for social good, fairness and bias in social intelligence, privacy in social intelligence, AI ethics in social intelligence, and generative AI and LLM in social intelligence.

Keywords Human-AI systems · AI for social good · Fairness and bias · Privacy · AI ethics · Generative AI · LLM

10.1 Human-AI Systems

Humans have traditionally been an integral part of artificial intelligence systems as a means of generating labeled training data [5, 26, 42, 48, 54, 64, 73]. Such a paradigm has been proven to be effective in supervised learning tasks such as image classification [13], speech recognition [20], autonomous driving [65], social media mining [83], and virtual reality [61]. However, it also suffers from two key limitations. First, some applications (e.g., disaster response and damage assessment, online truth discovery) may require a large amount of training data to achieve reasonable performance, which could be impractical due to the labor cost [22, 37]. Second, the AI models are often black-box systems and it is difficult to diagnose in the event of failure or unsatisfactory performance. To address these limitations, a few human-AI hybrid frameworks have been developed in recent years. For example, Holzinger et al. proposed the notion of interactive human machine learning ("iML"), where humans directly interact with AI by identifying useful features that could be incorporated into the AI algorithms [23]. Branson et al. invented a human-in-the-loop visual recognition system to accurately classify the objects in the picture based on the descriptions of the picture from humans [7]. More recently, researchers have been interested in diagnosing the black-box AI algorithms to provide accountability. For example, Nushi et al. developed an accountable human-AI system that leverages workers on Amazon Mechanical Turk (AMT) to

D. Wang et al., *Social Intelligence*, https://doi.org/10.1007/978-3-031-90080-8_10

identify the limitations of the AI algorithms [49] and provide suggestions to improve them. However, the above solutions largely ignored the innate limitations of the AI algorithms that cannot be simply improved by retraining the model with more data. Human-AI interaction is a trending research area that aims at harnessing the power of human intelligence and AI to optimize the human-AI systems and improve human experience with AI [11, 40, 52, 56, 71]. Such a paradigm has been applied in many domains, including image classification [50, 60], natural language translation [6, 86], medical diagnosis [14, 39], and autonomous driving [74, 84]. More recently, a few human-AI interaction systems have been developed to explore the human intelligence of crowd workers through interactive crowdsourcing tasks [41, 46]. For example, Nguyen et al. designed a human-AI interactive news article fact-checking algorithm that checks the truthfulness of textual news and claims by assigning crowd workers to correct identification errors by AI models [46]. Mandel et al. developed a game-based crowdsourcing interface to incorporate a crowd of non-AI experts to reason the dynamics of AI misbehavior and improve AI performance in online advertisement recommendations [41]. However, these solutions either assume the human workers have sufficient domain knowledge or require them to be well-trained on domain-specific crowdsourcing tasks. Such approaches often suffer from noisy crowdsourcing results since the ordinary crowd workers usually do not have the essential domain knowledge for the domain-specific tasks or are not interested in those training tasks [29, 76]. Future works in the direction of human-AI collaboration systems are expected to address some of these limitations.

10.2 AI for Social Good

AI for social good has become an emerging area of research that focuses on studying the impact of AI technologies on humans and society. A recent comprehensive overview of AI for social good can be found in [63]. This trend has also been evidenced by several new multi-year special tracks on AI for (social) good in top AI and Web conferences such as AAAI,[1] IJCAI,[2] and the Web Conference.[3] Several examples of commonly discussed AI for social good application domains include AI for disaster response, AI for healthcare, AI for truth discovery, and AI for education. These application domains provide excellent opportunities to develop, analyze, and evaluate the new SI-based solutions in a human-AI immersive environment. We will review recent examples in some of these domains below. First, previous efforts have been made to address the disaster response and damage assessment in AI and deep learning [35, 36, 45, 47]. For example, Nguyen et al. developed a convolutional neural network approach to quantify the damage severity of affected

[1] https://aaai.org/conference/aaai/.

[2] https://www.ijcai.org/.

[3] https://thewebconf.org/.

areas from social media imagery data for disaster response [47]. Li et al. proposed a deep transfer learning approach for disaster damage assessment of an unfolding disaster event using a domain adaptation approach [36]. Mouzannar et al. developed a deep neural network framework that utilizes both text and image data from social media posts for damage identification via multimodal convolutional neural networks [45]. Kumar et al. developed an end-to-end deep learning based image processing system to detect disaster-affected cultural heritage sites using online social media images [35]. However, the deep neural network architectures in current AI solutions are mainly designed by AI experts, which often introduce non-negligible costs and errors into the design process [16]. There also exist several crowd-AI integrated approaches that leverage human intelligence to troubleshoot and retrain a single neural network architecture in disaster response and damage assessment applications [24, 81]. However, those approaches mainly rely on the existing neural network architecture and may not achieve optimal performance due to the manual neural network selection process [69]. Second, a significant amount of efforts have been made to combat the spread of false health information online [12, 32, 33, 67]. For example, Ghenai et al. proposed a user-centric model that identifies users who are prone to spreading incorrect health-related information by extracting features based on users' attitudes, writing styles, and sentiments from their posts on social media [18]. Zhao et al. designed a machine learning based detection framework to detect incorrect posts in online health communities by integrating a set of linguistic, topic, sentiment, and behavioral features extracted from the post content (e.g., XGBoost) [85]. Safarnejad et al. analyzed the propagation patterns of false health information on social media by reconstructing the dissemination networks of social media posts to identify incorrect health-related posts [55]. However, existing health truth discovery solutions primarily rely on user behaviors/activities (e.g., post content, user comments, and attitudes) to detect incorrect health information on social media. These solutions cannot fully address the problem of detecting false health information related to outbreaking diseases (e.g., COVID-19) since common social media users often lack disease-specific knowledge and can easily be misled by such false health information. The above limitations of existing solutions provide exciting directions for future work in the area of AI for social good.

10.3 Fairness and Bias in Social Intelligence

Fairness and bias are human-centered issues in social intelligence, where AI models often generate results with disparate qualities for groups of different demographic or sensitive attributes. An overview of AI bias and fairness and its impact is provided by a recent survey [17]. The bias of AI has a direct impact on several real-world social intelligence application domains such as online education, face recognition, healthcare, employment, and criminal justice. We review examples of recent works in two of these domains below. First, several efforts have been made to improve learning experiences and outcomes in online education with the recent advances in AI [91]. For example, Abdi et al. designs an AI-based learning system to assess students' knowledge state by tracing their performance on crowdsourcing knowledge assessment tasks [1]. Wambsganss et al. develops a deep-learning-based student argumentation self-evaluation system that leverages nudging theory techniques to help students write convincing texts [68]. Qadir et al. analyzes how to use large language models to benefit students (e.g., customized explanations) while minimizing negative impacts (e.g., false information) [51]. However, current AI approaches often ignore the algorithmic demographic bias in online education to ensure fairness. Additionally, there lacks systematic studies of the interactions between AI bias and human cognitive bias in the AI for education context. Second, several efforts have been made to address fairness issues for problems with human face images [4, 34, 72, 80]. For example, Alvi et al. [4] developed a face attribute classification framework that aims to remove demographic bias (e.g., age, gender) from the feature representations of face images. Zhang et al. [80] proposed an adversarial learning framework to improve the fairness performance of classification neural networks by removing demographic information embedded in input data representations. Wang et al. [72] designed a reinforcement learning based fair AI algorithm that achieves racial equality in face recognition by creating large margin losses of data samples with different races to reduce the skewness of input data representations. However, the above methods mainly focus on developing fairness AI algorithms to mitigate performance bias caused by the imbalanced training datasets with respect to different demographic attributes. More future work could be done to develop alternative solutions that explore the collective intelligence of both humans and AI to transform the biased dataset into a fairer one, which can potentially improve the fairness of a large category of existing solutions without making changes to the model/algorithm of the solutions.

10.4 Privacy in Social Intelligence

Privacy is another human-centered issue in social intelligence where sensitive data and information from humans need to be carefully protected during their engagement and interaction with social intelligence systems. An overview of privacy and AI can be found in a recent survey paper [15]. Privacy has a non-trivial implication in many real-world social intelligence applications [53]. Examples of research questions related to privacy in social intelligence include (1) how to protect the private data of patients in AI for healthcare applications where patients' medical records together with their demographic attributes are used to build accurate AI prediction/diagnosis models for diseases [28]? (2) How to protect student's privacy in AI for education applications where customized AI models are developed to help students better assess their academic performance by leveraging data from their individual learning activities [91]? (3) How to ensure the privacy perseverance of users' data from different online platforms (e.g., social media sites) where cross-platform models are built to detect and explain false information by constructing a comprehensive knowledge graph using online posts from those platforms [58]? (4) How to protect human face privacy in AI-based facial applications (e.g., face detection [2, 31, 38], face recognition [57, 90], face attribute prediction [30, 34]) where users' personal images are used to train and optimize the AI models? Recent techniques have been developed to address the above questions. Examples of such techniques include differential privacy [89], federated learning [82], homomorphic encryption [75] and synthetic data generation [19]. However, new research questions emerge. For example, when federated learning is adopted to protect user privacy in social intelligence applications, two issues often arise: data sparsity and data heterogeneity [77]. Both issues can be attributed to the distributed model learning paradigm in federated learning where the user's data is kept at the local clients instead of being shared at the global server to protect the user's privacy. In such a setting, each client (user) will only have access to its own limited data for the AI model training (data sparsity) and the data distributions are often different across clients (data heterogeneity) [78]. An interesting question in this context would be: how to optimize the performance of AI models by addressing the data sparsity and heterogeneity issues in federated learning while protecting user privacy in the federated learning framework? More future works are expected in this direction to further advance the research of privacy-aware AI in social intelligence contexts.

10.5 Ethics of AI in Social Intelligence

Ethics of AI is a set of principles that guide the development of AI techniques to optimize their beneficial impacts while reducing the risks and adversarial outcomes [21]. An overview of AI ethics can be found in a recent review [62]. Examples of AI ethics in social intelligence applications include fairness and bias mitigation, transparency and explainability, data responsibility and privacy, accountability and governance, human-AI collaboration, environmental sustainability, and global and cultural considerations [27]. We already discussed some of these issues (e.g., fairness, bias, and privacy) in the previous sections. We further elaborate on some of the examples of AI ethics in the social intelligence contexts below. As an example of AI transparency and explainability, IBM's Watson for Oncology is designed to assist in cancer treatment decisions by leveraging patients' data and medical literature. However, the system faced critiques for its lack of clear explanations that impose challenges for clinicians to fully understand the rationale of the recommendations from the system [10]. Efforts (e.g., employing SHARP or LIME for feature attribution) have been made to improve the system's interpretability and are highlighted in studies on healthcare AI transparency. As another example of AI accountability and governance, AI-driven autonomous driving imposes some challenging ethical questions [43]. For example, who will be legally responsible for accidents that involve AI-driven autonomous vehicles when the control decisions are made by AI or AI-human collaboration? Discussions on questions like this emphasize the critical need for shared responsibility among developers, companies, end users, and regulators. This example also underlines the need for clearer governance structures and policies, including performance standards and liability protocols [66]. Finally, as an example of global and cultural considerations, Large Language Models (LLMs) like GPT have faced challenges in addressing diverse linguistic and cultural nuances that are particularly evident in social intelligence tasks that need to capture regional idioms, cultural references, or social norms. For example, conversational AI agents trained on global datasets may inadvertently generate culturally insensitive responses because the training data may underrepresent specific cultural norms. A recent study highlighted such issues, noting that GPT models, while capable of producing coherent and grammatically correct text, often lack the depth of cultural understanding required for nuanced applications, particularly in multilingual settings [3]. More future works are needed to address the ethical issues of AI when it is integrated together with human intelligence in social intelligence domains.

10.6 Generative AI and LLM in Social Intelligence

With the recent advancement of Large Language Models (LLMs), there has been a trend toward exploring the context and generational capabilities of such models for social intelligence applications [79]. Generative models such as GPT, Llama, and Claude demonstrate great potential in-context learning and humanoid text generation, which can be applied to critical social intelligence tasks such as truth discovery, hate speech recognition, social media meme analysis, and smart cities [9, 59]. For example, in social media based truth discovery, Zhou et al. proposed a multimodal truth discovery system, MUSE, which uses LLMs for retrieving evidence and providing contextualized explanations to debunk false claims on social media [88]. In addition, Wan et al. introduced the DELL framework that provides accurate identification and explanation of false information by leveraging LLMs to synthesize user feedback and integrate domain-specific knowledge [70]. Caselli et al. introduced HateBERT, a retrained BERT model fine-tuned on data from banned Reddit communities to enhance the detection of nuanced hate speech and abusive language [8]. LLMs have also been applied to social media meme analysis. For example, Joshi et al. proposed a framework for contextualizing Internet memes across platforms by utilizing a vision transformer-based similarity approach to map memes to the Internet Meme Knowledge Graph [25]. Zhou et al. introduced the SemanticMemes dataset that leveraged computational clustering to analyze linguistic and semantic variations in meme usage on social media platforms [87]. Last but not least, in smart city applications, Meiling et al. presented the MONICA project in Hamburg, which incorporated LLMs to analyze IoT-generated data streams in real time that enables intelligent decision-making for public event management and urban safety enhancements [44]. All these advances make LLMs a promising solution to address critical challenges in social intelligence applications. However, several limitations remain to be addressed in future work.

Examples of such limitations include the potential for bias in LLM-generated outputs, lack of domain-specific knowledge, challenges in interpretability, and high computational costs [78]. Addressing these issues will require innovations in model architecture, fine-tuning approaches, and collaborative frameworks that integrate human expertise with AI in the social context to maximize the societal benefits of LLMs while mitigating their risks.

References

1. S. Abdi, H. Khosravi, and S. Sadiq. Modelling learners in crowdsourcing educational systems. In *International Conference on Artificial Intelligence in Education*, pages 3–9. Springer, 2020.
2. U. Ahmad, A. Baqir, F. ul Mustafa, S. Malik, S. A. Sani, and S. Z. H. Shah. Enhancing the authentication mechanism of social media websites using face detection. In *2019 4th International Conference on Emerging Trends in Engineering, Sciences and Technology (ICEEST)*, pages 1–5. IEEE, 2019.
3. M. Alawida, S. Mejri, A. Mehmood, B. Chikhaoui, and O. Isaac Abiodun. A comprehensive study of chatgpt: advancements, limitations, and ethical considerations in natural language processing and cybersecurity. *Information*, 14(8):462, 2023.
4. M. S. Alvi, A. Zisserman, and C. Nellåker. Turning a blind eye: Explicit removal of biases and variation from deep neural network embeddings. *CoRR*, abs/1809.02169, 2018.
5. S. Amershi, D. Weld, M. Vorvoreanu, A. Fourney, B. Nushi, P. Collisson, J. Suh, S. Iqbal, P. N. Bennett, and K. Inkpen. Guidelines for human-ai interaction. In *Proceedings of the 2019 CHI Conference on Human Factors in Computing Systems*, page 3. ACM, 2019.
6. M. Behnke, A. V. Miceli-Barone, R. Sennrich, V. Sosoni, T. Naskos, E. Takoulidou, M. Stasimioti, M. Van Zaanen, S. Castilho, and F. Gaspari. Improving machine translation of educational content via crowdsourcing. In *Proceedings of the Eleventh International Conference on Language Resources and Evaluation (LREC 2018)*, 2018.
7. S. Branson, C. Wah, F. Schroff, B. Babenko, P. Welinder, P. Perona, and S. Belongie. Visual recognition with humans in the loop. In *European Conference on Computer Vision*, pages 438–451. Springer, 2010.
8. T. Caselli, V. Basile, J. Mitrović, and M. Granitzer. Hatebert: Retraining bert for abusive language detection in english. *arXiv preprint arXiv:2010.12472*, 2020.
9. Y. Chang, X. Wang, J. Wang, Y. Wu, L. Yang, K. Zhu, H. Chen, X. Yi, C. Wang, Y. Wang, et al. A survey on evaluation of large language models. *ACM Transactions on Intelligent Systems and Technology*, 15(3):1–45, 2024.
10. I. S. Chua, M. Gaziel-Yablowitz, Z. T. Korach, K. L. Kehl, N. A. Levitan, Y. E. Arriaga, G. P. Jackson, D. W. Bates, and M. Hassett. Artificial intelligence in oncology: Path to implementation. *Cancer Medicine*, 10(12):4138–4149, 2021.
11. A. Cichocki and A. P. Kuleshov. Future trends for human-ai collaboration: A comprehensive taxonomy of ai/agi using multiple intelligences and learning styles. *Computational Intelligence and Neuroscience*, 2021, 2021.
12. L. Cui, H. Seo, M. Tabar, F. Ma, S. Wang, and D. Lee. Deterrent: Knowledge guided graph attention network for detecting healthcare misinformation. In *Proceedings of the 26th ACM SIGKDD International Conference on Knowledge Discovery & Data Mining*, pages 492–502, 2020.

13. J. Deng, W. Dong, R. Socher, L.-J. Li, K. Li, and L. Fei-Fei. Imagenet: A large-scale hierarchical image database. In *2009 IEEE conference on computer vision and pattern recognition*, pages 248–255. Ieee, 2009.
14. K. Dzobo, S. Adotey, N. E. Thomford, and W. Dzobo. Integrating artificial and human intelligence: a partnership for responsible innovation in biomedical engineering and medicine. *Omics: a journal of integrative biology*, 24(5):247–263, 2020.
15. D. Elliott and E. Soifer. Ai technologies, privacy, and security. *Frontiers in Artificial Intelligence*, 5:826737, 2022.
16. T. Elsken, J. H. Metzen, F. Hutter, et al. Neural architecture search: A survey. *J. Mach. Learn. Res.*, 20(55):1–21, 2019.
17. E. Ferrara. Fairness and bias in artificial intelligence: A brief survey of sources, impacts, and mitigation strategies. *Sci*, 6(1):3, 2023.
18. A. Ghenai and Y. Mejova. Fake cures: user-centric modeling of health misinformation in social media. *Proceedings of the ACM on human-computer interaction*, 2(CSCW):1–20, 2018.
19. M. Goyal and Q. H. Mahmoud. A systematic review of synthetic data generation techniques using generative ai. *Electronics*, 13(17):3509, 2024.
20. A. Graves, A.-r. Mohamed, and G. Hinton. Speech recognition with deep recurrent neural networks. *2013 IEEE International Conference on Acoustics, Speech and Signal Processing*, pages 6645–6649, 2013.
21. T. Hagendorff. The ethics of ai ethics: An evaluation of guidelines. *Minds and machines*, 30(1):99–120, 2020.
22. A. Holzinger, M. Plass, K. Holzinger, G. C. Crişan, C.-M. Pintea, and V. Palade. Towards interactive machine learning (iml): applying ant colony algorithms to solve the traveling salesman problem with the human-in-the-loop approach. In *International Conference on Availability, Reliability, and Security*, pages 81–95. Springer, 2016.
23. A. Holzinger, M. Plass, K. Holzinger, G. C. Crisan, C.-M. Pintea, and V. Palade. A glass-box interactive machine learning approach for solving np-hard problems with the human-in-the-loop. *arXiv preprint arXiv:1708.01104*, 2017.
24. J. Jarrett, I. Saleh, M. B. Blake, R. Malcolm, S. Thorpe, and T. Grandison. Combining human and machine computing elements for analysis via crowdsourcing. In *10th IEEE International Conference on Collaborative Computing: Networking, Applications and Worksharing*, pages 312–321. IEEE, 2014.
25. S. Joshi, F. Ilievski, and L. Luceri. Contextualizing internet memes across social media platforms. In *Companion Proceedings of the ACM on Web Conference 2024*, pages 1831–1840, 2024.
26. S. Kambhampati. Challenges of human-aware ai systems. *arXiv preprint arXiv:1910.07089*, 2019.
27. E. Kazim and A. S. Koshiyama. A high-level overview of ai ethics. *Patterns*, 2(9), 2021.
28. N. Khalid, A. Qayyum, M. Bilal, A. Al-Fuqaha, and J. Qadir. Privacy-preserving artificial intelligence in healthcare: Techniques and applications. *Computers in Biology and Medicine*, 158:106848, 2023.
29. J. A. Khan, L. Liu, L. Wen, and R. Ali. Crowd intelligence in requirements engineering: Current status and future directions. In *International working conference on requirements engineering: Foundation for software quality*, pages 245–261. Springer, 2019.
30. Z. Kou, L. Shang, H. Zeng, Y. Zhang, and D. Wang. Exgfair: A crowdsourcing data exchange approach to fair human face datasets augmentation. In *2021 IEEE International Conference on Big Data (Big Data)*, pages 1285–1290. IEEE, 2021.
31. Z. Kou, L. Shang, Y. Zhang, S. Duan, and D. Wang. Can i only share my eyes? a web crowdsourcing based face partition approach towards privacy-aware face recognition. In *Proceedings of the ACM Web Conference 2022*, pages 3611–3622, 2022. https://doi.org/10.1145/3485447.3512256.
32. Z. Kou, L. Shang, Y. Zhang, and D. Wang. Hc-covid: A hierarchical crowdsource knowledge graph approach to explainable covid-19 misinformation detection. *Proceedings of the ACM on Human-Computer Interaction*, 6(GROUP):1–25, 2022. https://doi.org/10.1145/3492855.

33. Z. Kou, L. Shang, Y. Zhang, Z. Yue, H. Zeng, and D. Wang. Crowd, expert & ai: A human-ai interactive approach towards natural language explanation based covid-19 misinformation detection. In *IJCAI*, 2022.
34. Z. Kou, Y. Zhang, L. Shang, and D. Wang. Faircrowd: Fair human face dataset sampling via batch-level crowdsourcing bias inference. In *2021 IEEE/ACM 29th International Symposium on Quality of Service (IWQOS)*, pages 1–10. IEEE, 2021, DOI:10.0.4.85/IWQOS52092.2021.9521312, Reprinted with permission from IEEE.
35. P. Kumar, F. Ofli, M. Imran, and C. Castillo. Detection of disaster-affected cultural heritage sites from social media images using deep learning techniques. *Journal on Computing and Cultural Heritage (JOCCH)*, 13(3):1–31, 2020.
36. X. Li, D. Caragea, C. Caragea, M. Imran, and F. Ofli. Identifying disaster damage images using a domain adaptation approach. In *Proceedings of the 16th International conference on information systems for crisis response and management*, 2019.
37. X. Li, D. Caragea, H. Zhang, and M. Imran. Localizing and quantifying damage in social media images. In *2018 IEEE/ACM International Conference on Advances in Social Networks Analysis and Mining (ASONAM)*, pages 194–201. IEEE, 2018.
38. Z. Liu, X. Qi, and P. H. Torr. Global texture enhancement for fake face detection in the wild. In *Proceedings of the IEEE/CVF Conference on Computer Vision and Pattern Recognition*, pages 8060–8069, 2020.
39. T. Lysaght, H. Y. Lim, V. Xafis, and K. Y. Ngiam. Ai-assisted decision-making in healthcare. *Asian Bioethics Review*, 11(3):299–314, 2019.
40. M. Maadi, H. Akbarzadeh Khorshidi, and U. Aickelin. A review on human–ai interaction in machine learning and insights for medical applications. *International journal of environmental research and public health*, 18(4):2121, 2021.
41. T. Mandel, J. Best, R. H. Tanaka, H. Temple, C. Haili, S. J. Carter, K. Schlechtinger, and R. Szeto. Using the crowd to prevent harmful ai behavior. *Proceedings of the ACM on Human-Computer Interaction*, 4(CSCW2):1–25, 2020.
42. J. Marshall and D. Wang. Mood-sensitive truth discovery for reliable recommendation systems in social sensing. In *Proceedings of the 10th ACM Conference on Recommender Systems*, pages 167–174. ACM, 2016.
43. A. Martinho, N. Herber, M. Kroesen, and C. Chorus. Ethical issues in focus by the autonomous vehicles industry. *Transport reviews*, 41(5):556–577, 2021.
44. S. Meiling, D. Purnomo, J.-A. Shiraishi, M. Fischer, and T. C. Schmidt. Monica in hamburg: Towards large-scale iot deployments in a smart city, 2018.
45. H. Mouzannar, Y. Rizk, and M. Awad. Damage identification in social media posts using multimodal deep learning. In *ISCRAM*, 2018.
46. A. T. Nguyen, A. Kharosekar, S. Krishnan, S. Krishnan, E. Tate, B. C. Wallace, and M. Lease. Believe it or not: Designing a human-ai partnership for mixed-initiative fact-checking. In *Proceedings of the 31st Annual ACM Symposium on User Interface Software and Technology*, pages 189–199, 2018.
47. D. T. Nguyen, F. Ofli, M. Imran, and P. Mitra. Damage assessment from social media imagery data during disasters. In *Proceedings of the 2017 IEEE/ACM International Conference on Advances in Social Networks Analysis and Mining 2017*, pages 569–576, 2017.
48. B. Nushi, E. Kamar, and E. Horvitz. Towards accountable ai: Hybrid human-machine analyses for characterizing system failure. *arXiv preprint arXiv:1809.07424*, 2018.
49. B. Nushi, E. Kamar, E. Horvitz, and D. Kossmann. On human intellect and machine failures: Troubleshooting integrative machine learning systems. In *AAAI*, pages 1017–1025, 2017.
50. S. Ørting, A. Doyle, A. van Hilten, M. Hirth, O. Inel, C. R. Madan, P. Mavridis, H. Spiers, and V. Cheplygina. A survey of crowdsourcing in medical image analysis. *arXiv preprint arXiv:1902.09159*, 2019.
51. J. Qadir. Engineering education in the era of chatgpt: Promise and pitfalls of generative ai for education. In *2023 IEEE Global Engineering Education Conference (EDUCON)*, pages 1–9. IEEE, 2023.

52. S. Rasp, H. Schulz, S. Bony, and B. Stevens. Combining crowdsourcing and deep learning to explore the mesoscale organization of shallow convection. *Bulletin of the American Meteorological Society*, 101(11):E1980–E1995, 2020.
53. K. V. Rønn and S. O. Søe. Is social media intelligence private? privacy in public and the nature of social media intelligence. In *Intelligence on the frontier between state and civil society*, pages 52–68. Routledge, 2020.
54. S. J. Russell and P. Norvig. *Artificial intelligence: a modern approach*. Malaysia; Pearson Education Limited,, 2016.
55. L. Safarnejad, Q. Xu, Y. Ge, S. Krishnan, A. Bagarvathi, and S. Chen. Contrasting misinformation and real-information dissemination network structures on social media during a health emergency. *American journal of public health*, 110(S3):S340–S347, 2020.
56. H. Schneider, M. Eiband, D. Ullrich, and A. Butz. Empowerment in hci-a survey and framework. In *Proceedings of the 2018 CHI Conference on Human Factors in Computing Systems*, pages 1–14, 2018.
57. S. I. Serengil and A. Ozpinar. Lightface: A hybrid deep face recognition framework. In *2020 Innovations in Intelligent Systems and Applications Conference (ASYU)*, pages 1–5. IEEE, 2020.
58. L. Shang, Z. Kou, Y. Zhang, and D. Wang. A duo-generative approach to explainable multimodal covid-19 misinformation detection. In *Proceedings of the ACM Web Conference 2022*, pages 3623–3631, New York, NY, USA, 2022. ACM. https://doi.org/10.1145/3485447.3512257.
59. L. Shang, D. Y. Zhang, M. Wang, and D. Wang. Vulnercheck: a content-agnostic detector for online hatred-vulnerable videos. In *2019 IEEE International Conference on Big Data (Big Data)*, pages 573–582. IEEE, 2019.
60. H. Shen, K. Liao, Z. Liao, J. Doornberg, M. Qiao, A. Van Den Hengel, and J. W. Verjans. Human-ai interactive and continuous sensemaking: A case study of image classification using scribble attention maps. In *Extended Abstracts of the 2021 CHI Conference on Human Factors in Computing Systems*, pages 1–8, 2021.
61. J. Shu, S. Kosta, R. Zheng, and P. Hui. Talk2me: A framework for device-to-device augmented reality social network. In *2018 IEEE International Conference on Pervasive Computing and Communications (PerCom)*, pages 1–10. IEEE, 2018.
62. K. Siau and W. Wang. Artificial intelligence (ai) ethics: ethics of ai and ethical ai. *Journal of Database Management (JDM)*, 31(2):74–87, 2020.
63. N. Tomašev, J. Cornebise, F. Hutter, S. Mohamed, A. Picciariello, B. Connelly, D. C. Belgrave, D. Ezer, F. C. v. d. Haert, F. Mugisha, et al. Ai for social good: unlocking the opportunity for positive impact. *Nature Communications*, 11(1):2468, 2020.
64. E. J. Topol. High-performance medicine: the convergence of human and artificial intelligence. *Nature medicine*, 25(1):44–56, 2019.
65. C. Urmson, J. Anhalt, D. Bagnell, C. Baker, R. Bittner, M. Clark, J. Dolan, D. Duggins, T. Galatali, and C. Geyer. Autonomous driving in urban environments: Boss and the urban challenge. *Journal of Field Robotics*, 25(8):425–466, 2008.
66. N. S. Uzougbo, C. G. Ikegwu, and A. O. Adewusi. Legal accountability and ethical considerations of ai in financial services. *GSC Advanced Research and Reviews*, 19(2):130–142, 2024.
67. E. K. Vraga and L. Bode. Using expert sources to correct health misinformation in social media. *Science Communication*, 39(5):621–645, 2017.
68. T. Wambsganss, A. Janson, T. Käser, and J. M. Leimeister. Improving students argumentation learning with adaptive self-evaluation nudging. *Proceedings of the ACM on Human-Computer Interaction*, 6(CSCW2):1–31, 2022.
69. A. Wan, X. Dai, P. Zhang, Z. He, Y. Tian, S. Xie, B. Wu, M. Yu, T. Xu, K. Chen, et al. Fbnetv2: Differentiable neural architecture search for spatial and channel dimensions. In *Proceedings of the IEEE/CVF Conference on Computer Vision and Pattern Recognition*, pages 12965–12974, 2020.
70. H. Wan, S. Feng, Z. Tan, H. Wang, Y. Tsvetkov, and M. Luo. Dell: Generating reactions and explanations for llm-based misinformation detection. *arXiv preprint arXiv:2402.10426*, 2024.

71. D. Wang, E. Churchill, P. Maes, X. Fan, B. Shneiderman, Y. Shi, and Q. Wang. From human-human collaboration to human-ai collaboration: Designing ai systems that can work together with people. In *Extended abstracts of the 2020 CHI conference on human factors in computing systems*, pages 1–6, 2020.
72. M. Wang and W. Deng. Mitigating bias in face recognition using skewness-aware reinforcement learning. In *Proceedings of the IEEE/CVF Conference on Computer Vision and Pattern Recognition (CVPR)*, June 2020.
73. B. G. Weber, M. Mateas, and A. Jhala. Building human-level ai for real-time strategy games. In *AAAI Fall Symposium: Advances in Cognitive Systems*, volume 11, page 01, 2011.
74. J. Wu, Z. Huang, C. Huang, Z. Hu, P. Hang, Y. Xing, and C. Lv. Human-in-the-loop deep reinforcement learning with application to autonomous driving. *arXiv preprint arXiv:2104.07246*, 2021.
75. S. Yaji, K. Bangera, and B. Neelima. Privacy preserving in blockchain based on partial homomorphic encryption system for ai applications. In *2018 IEEE 25th International Conference on High Performance Computing Workshops (HiPCW)*, pages 81–85. IEEE, 2018.
76. S. Yuasa, T. Nakai, T. Maruichi, M. Landsmann, K. Kise, M. Matsubara, and A. Morishima. Towards quality assessment of crowdworker output based on behavioral data. In *2019 IEEE International Conference on Big Data (Big Data)*, pages 4659–4661. IEEE, 2019.
77. H. Zeng, Z. Yue, Q. Jiang, Y. Zhang, L. Shang, R. Zong, and D. Wang. Mitigating demographic bias of federated learning models via robust-fair domain smoothing: A domain-shifting approach. In *2024 IEEE 44th International Conference on Distributed Computing Systems (ICDCS)*, pages 785–796. IEEE, 2024.
78. H. Zeng, Z. Yue, Y. Zhang, L. Shang, and D. Wang. Fair federated learning with biased vision-language models. In *Findings of the Association for Computational Linguistics ACL 2024*, pages 10002–10017, 2024.
79. J. Zeng, R. Huang, W. Malik, L. Yin, B. Babic, D. Shacham, X. Yan, J. Yang, and Q. He. Large language models for social networks: Applications, challenges, and solutions, 2024.
80. B. H. Zhang, B. Lemoine, and M. Mitchell. Mitigating unwanted biases with adversarial learning. *CoRR*, abs/1801.07593, 2018.
81. D. Zhang, Y. Zhang, Q. Li, T. Plummer, and D. Wang. Crowdlearn: A crowd-ai hybrid system for deep learning-based damage assessment applications. In *2019 IEEE 39th International Conference on Distributed Computing Systems (ICDCS)*, pages 1221–1232. IEEE, 2019.
82. D. Y. Zhang, Z. Kou, and D. Wang. Fairfl: A fair federated learning approach to reducing demographic bias in privacy-sensitive classification models. In *2020 IEEE International Conference on Big Data (Big Data)*, pages 1051–1060. IEEE, 2020.
83. D. Y. Zhang, L. Song, Q. Li, Y. Zhang, and D. Wang. Streamguard: A bayesian network approach to copyright infringement detection problem in large-scale live video sharing systems. In *2018 IEEE International Conference on Big Data (Big Data)*, pages 901–910. IEEE, 2018.
84. J. Zhang, Y. Shu, and H. Yu. Human-machine interaction for autonomous vehicles: A review. In *International Conference on Human-Computer Interaction*, pages 190–201. Springer, 2021.
85. Y. Zhao, J. Da, and J. Yan. Detecting health misinformation in online health communities: Incorporating behavioral features into machine learning based approaches. *Information Processing & Management*, 58(1):102390, 2021.
86. W. Zhaohui. Application of human-machine interactive translation model and its implications. *Advances in Social Science, Education and Humanities Research*, 347, 2019.
87. N. Zhou, D. Jurgens, and D. Bamman. Social meme-ing: Measuring linguistic variation in memes, 2023.
88. X. Zhou, A. Sharma, A. X. Zhang, and T. Althoff. Correcting misinformation on social media with a large language model. *arXiv preprint arXiv:2403.11169*, 2024.
89. T. Zhu, D. Ye, W. Wang, W. Zhou, and S. Y. Philip. More than privacy: Applying differential privacy in key areas of artificial intelligence. *IEEE Transactions on Knowledge and Data Engineering*, 34(6):2824–2843, 2020.

90. Z. Zhu, G. Huang, J. Deng, Y. Ye, J. Huang, X. Chen, J. Zhu, T. Yang, J. Lu, D. Du, et al. Webface260m: A benchmark unveiling the power of million-scale deep face recognition. In *Proceedings of the IEEE/CVF Conference on Computer Vision and Pattern Recognition*, pages 10492–10502, 2021.
91. R. Zong, Y. Zhang, F. Stinar, L. Shang, H. Zeng, N. Bosch, and D. Wang. A crowd–ai collaborative approach to address demographic bias for student performance prediction in online education. In *Proceedings of the AAAI Conference on Human Computation and Crowdsourcing*, volume 11, pages 198–210, 2023. https://doi.org/10.1609/hcomp.v11i1.27560.

Chapter 11
Conclusions and Remaining Challenges

Abstract In this chapter, we summarize the techniques, theories, models, and solutions reviewed in previous chapters. We also discuss a few remaining challenges and exciting directions for future research in the field of social intelligence. We expect interest in social intelligence from different research communities (e.g., AI, machine learning, NLP, computer vision, social computing, human-computer interaction, estimation theory and statistical learning, fairness, and privacy) will keep on increasing and more fundamental and interesting research work will be carried out in the future.

Keywords Conclusion · Summary · Remaining challenges · Future directions

11.1 Conclusion and Summary

This book presented a new paradigm, namely social intelligence, that explores the complementary power of human intelligence (HI) and artificial intelligence (AI) to address complex real-world challenges in the social space. The contributions of the book can be summarized as: (1) the book first presented a set of novel frameworks, such as DualGen, ContrastFaux, CrowdAdapt, and CollabGeneral, to overcome fundamental challenges in social intelligence, including data heterogeneity, sparsity, and model generalizability; (2) the book then discussed a series of human-AI hybrid approaches to enhance explainability and collaboration, such as HC-COVID and DExFC for explainable AI, and CrowdNAS and CrowdOptim for integrating crowd wisdom with AI design and optimization; (3) the book also presented pressing ethical concerns in the context of social intelligence by introducing FairCrowd and DebiasEdu to address fairness and bias, and CoviDKG and FaceCrowd to ensure privacy in social intelligence applications; (4) the book reviewed a rich set of literature related to social intelligence and outlined a few open research directions in this field. Through extensive real-world case studies across various domains, the book demonstrated the practical applicability and effectiveness of these proposed solutions in achieving substantial performance gains in prediction accuracy, model generalizability, explainability, algorithmic fairness, and system robustness. We briefly summarize the content and key ideas of each chapter in the book.

D. Wang et al., *Social Intelligence*, https://doi.org/10.1007/978-3-031-90080-8_11

In Chap. 1, we started the book with an introduction to an emerging intelligence paradigm called *social intelligence (SI)*. In SI, human intelligence and AI are integrated to explore their complementary strengths in the social space. We identified a few unique characteristics that help define SI and discussed several fundamental research challenges that are centered around the idea of exploring the collective intelligence from humans and AI. We also outlined the organization of the book at the end of the chapter.

In Chap. 2, we discussed the root of SI and its interdisciplinary nature in the context of related research fields. To demonstrate the real-world implications of SI, we also presented a set of real-world SI applications such as social media misbehavior identification and mitigation, multimodal truth discovery, explainable AI and machine learning, disaster response and damage assessment, AI and crowdsourcing for education, social sensing in smart city applications.

In Chap. 3, we summarized the mathematic foundations that are used in this book. These foundations include concepts and basic principles in estimation theory and statistics (e.g., MLE, EM, HMM, Bayesian Estimation, Subjective Logic), deep learning methods (e.g., MLP, CNN, GNN, Transformers), AI optimization techniques (e.g., contrastive learning, domain adaptation, few-shot learning, adversarial training). We reviewed the above math foundations with some simple examples to help readers understand and digest the underlying principles. We also discussed the pros and cons as well as application scenarios of the reviewed techniques.

In Chap. 4, we considered an important challenge in SI: the data heterogeneity where the data is obtained from diverse sources, modalities, and contexts. Several unique challenges related to data heterogeneity (e.g., cross-modal information inconsistency, sparse multimodal annotations, heterogeneous feature fusion) are identified. In this chapter, we reviewed two SI solutions (i.e., DualGen and ContrastFaux) to address the data heterogeneity in the context of multimodal truth discovery applications. Real-world case studies of the above solutions were also presented with a discussion on their limitations.

In Chap. 5, we investigated two fundamental challenges in SI: data sparsity and model generality where SI systems need to adapt to new domains or situations with limited or no training data. We introduced two human-AI hybrid SI solutions (i.e., CrowdAdapt and CollabGeneral) to address these two challenges. In particular, these two solutions address the domain discrepancy between the source and target domains and the optimal trade-off between model generality and domain specificity in the context of real case studies on health truth discovery and disaster damage assessment. The chapter concludes with a discussion on the limitations of the presented SI solutions and directions for future work for further improvements.

In Chap. 6, we explored the explainable AI (XAI) aspect of SI where collective intelligence from both humans and AI is explored to generate understandable, evidence-based, and well justified explanations for the results of SI systems. In this chapter, we reviewed two graph-based human-AI collaborative explanation approaches (i.e., HC-COVID and DExFC) to address the XAI problem in SI. In particular, the two reviewed SI approaches addressed several non-trivial technical challenges such as varied knowledge fact quality, lack of modality-level annotations, diverse cross-modal explanations. Two real-world case studies with real-world XAI applications have also been presented to study the effectiveness of the reviewed XAI approaches.

In Chap. 7, we studied one of the core challenges in SI: how to fuse human intelligence from crowd with AI to address complex problems that cannot be fully addressed by a HI only or AI only solution? We presented two crowd-AI collaborative SI frameworks (i.e., CrowdNAS and CrowdOptim) to address two fundamental problems in AI design and optimization: neural network architecture search and hyperparameter optimization. The presented frameworks were studied in the context of two real-world case studies and the results showed that the SI based solutions achieve improved application performance while reducing computational demands by fully exploring the collective intelligence of both HI and AI.

In Chap. 8, we explored one of the challenges of SI systems in the social dimension: fairness and bias. We reviewed two fairness-aware SI systems (i.e., FairCrowd and DebiasEdu) that explore the collective strengths of crowd intelligence and AI to address fairness issues in social intelligence applications. FairCrowd and DebiasEdu were evaluated in two different SI applications: face attribute prediction and student performance prediction. We demonstrated the combination of HI and AI is able to significantly improve the fairness of the SI systems. The chapter concludes with a discussion on the limitations of the reviewed SI frameworks and the direction to further study the potential interactions between human and AI biases.

In Chap. 9, we studied a critical challenge in social intelligence—privacy—where the goal is to protect sensitive and private information from humans in the social intelligence applications. We presented two privacy-preserving SI solutions (i.e., CoviDKG and FaceCrowd) to explicitly address the privacy challenge in social intelligence. CoviDKG designed a distributed knowledge graph framework to protect people privacy on multi-platform social networks while FaceCrowd developed a crowdsourcing based face participation approach to protect individual's privacy in face recognition and attribute prediction applications. Two case studies were presented to demonstrate the effectiveness of the presented solutions to protect people's privacy in social intelligence context.

In Chap. 10, we recommended a few directions of related work for further readings and future work in social intelligence. These directions include human-AI systems, AI for social good, fairness and bias, privacy, ethics of AI, generative AI and LLM in social intelligence.

11.2 Remaining Challenges

We highlight a few promising remaining challenges for future work directions in Social Intelligence.

11.2.1 Scalability in Social Intelligence

Scalability is a crucial factor in social intelligence given the tremendous amount of social intelligence data (e.g., social media feeds, crowdsourcing inputs) and the new emerging events (e.g., public health crisis, social unrest) in SI domains. First, the efficiency of analyzing social intelligence data is critical for providing timely outputs to ensure informative decision-making in mission-critical social intelligence applications such as early detection of false information and rapid response to disasters and emergencies. To achieve this goal, future work should focus on computationally efficient AI models and distributed computing systems capable of processing massive amounts of diverse SI data in real time. Examples of these efforts could include applying incremental learning [19], parallel computing [6], and edge computing techniques [11] to maximize the use of resources and reduce the latency in social intelligence applications. In addition to computational efficiency, the scaling of social intelligence solutions also depends on the efficient scaling of human intelligence. While this book has explored crowdsourcing techniques as a scalable solution to harness human intelligence for tasks such as knowledge fact verification, face attribution prediction, and online education, future work should investigate more scalable human-AI collaboration frameworks that can seamlessly integrate human insights into the AI pipeline in social intelligence. Such efforts can involve developing interactive interfaces and feedback mechanisms that allow both domain experts and general users to provide real-time guidance, feedback, and corrections to AI models [22]. Moreover, to ensure the fairness of human-AI collaboration, it is important to design incentive mechanisms and task allocation strategies that can motivate and reward human participants based on their contributions and expertise [20]. The integration of complementary competencies from both humans and AI will enable us to build more scalable and efficient social intelligence systems in the future.

With the rapid progress of large foundation models in recent years [25], the scalability issue of these models needs to be addressed for them to be effectively integrated with HI in social intelligence applications. It is noted that these foundation models often require a non-trivial amount of computational resources, limiting their applicability in resource-constrained social intelligence applications (e.g., disaster response scenarios with low accessibility to computing resources). To address such limitations, we could further optimize the trade-off between computational costs and the performance of these large foundation models in future research. For example, various methods (e.g., model compression, knowledge distillation, and pruning) can be explored to create more lightweight versions of foundation models that can run in low-resource settings. Similarly, new adaptive inference techniques can also be developed to dynamically adjust the complexity of large foundation models based on the inputs from HI in SI systems and available resources in the system. Last but not least, more modular architectures in SI architectures can also improve customization and fine-tuning of large foundation models for specific SI tasks, which reduces the need for training entire models from scratch.

11.2.2 Adaptation in Low-Resource Domains

The book has discussed the model generality and domain adaptation challenges in social intelligence applications (e.g., truth discovery, disaster damage assessment). The work in this direction can be further expanded into other social intelligence application domains with low resources. For instance, a significant portion of the world's population speaks languages of scarcity that lack labeled data and linguistic resources. False information in these languages can be particularly harmful as it impacts more vulnerable populations with lower media literacy. One future direction could be to create cross-linguistic social intelligence systems that can effectively adapt an SI system learned from the high-resource language domain to the low-resource language domain. Such a domain adaptation process may involve developing new cross-lingual representation learning [10] and leveraging multilingual knowledge bases [5] to reduce the domain discrepancy between high-resource and low-resource languages. Moreover, human intelligence from native speakers could also be effectively harnessed to obtain high-quality annotations and capture the cultural characteristics in low-resource languages. A potential direction is to create a cross-lingual crowdsourcing platform that can effectively recruit and train native speakers in low-resource languages to provide informative annotations and contexts for understanding the cultural appropriateness [1]. These annotations could then be used to tailor the cross-lingual AI models and adjust them to the linguistic and cultural contexts of specific low-resource language domains.

The robustness of the SI solutions in low-resource language domains can be further improved by exploring unsupervised or semi-supervised learning approaches. For instance, one can leverage cross-lingual data augmentation [9], adversarial learning [14], and contrastive learning [13] to take advantage of the large amount of unlabeled data in the low-resource languages and transfer the knowledge learned from the labeled data in the high-resource language domains. Additionally, the transparency of SI solutions in low-resource languages is also an important issue. It would be helpful to develop SI solutions that can provide contextually and culturally relevant explanations for the target language domains. These XAI solutions often involve integrating linguistic and cultural knowledge into the explanation generation process and working with communities in the low-resource language domains to co-design and validate the explanations [7]. By developing adaptive and explainable SI solutions for low-resource languages, we can empower underrepresented groups with low-resource languages to better assess information integrity and build trust and credibility of information in their native languages.

Rare diseases are another low-resource domain where adaptive social intelligence systems can be helpful. Rare conditions (e.g., Huntington's disease, progeria) do not normally have extensive research and clinical data, which could make them particularly vulnerable to false information and delayed diagnoses. The future of social intelligence research could focus on developing an adaptable SI model that can leverage the rich set of information from common diseases (e.g., cardiovascular disease and hypertension) to help researchers, healthcare providers, and patients better understand and manage rare diseases. In particular, these SI systems could use transfer learning and domain adaptation methods to transfer and adapt knowledge from well-known diseases to rare or new diseases and potentially uncover novel biological pathways or therapies for those diseases. For example, AI models that have been calibrated on massive sets of cardiovascular disease data can be adapted to identify the relevant patterns from the limited data on progeria, which often involves premature cardiovascular aging.

These SI systems can be further extended to be multimodal to accommodate various types of data sources (e.g., clinical evidence, doctors' diagnoses, and patient-reported symptoms). These systems could help identify subtle connections between rare and common diseases that might not be apparent through traditional research methods. For example, an adaptive multimodal SI system could analyze genetic data from patients with a rare neurodegenerative disorder alongside clinical observations and patient-reported symptoms. By analyzing such information in light of data on more general neurodegenerative disorders (e.g., Alzheimer's disease or Parkinson's disease), the AI could detect shared genetic pathways or symptomatic patterns. This line of research might provide new insights into the mechanisms of rare diseases, novel treatment options, or the discovery of new diseases.

11.2.3 Knowledge-Grounded Reasoning and Explanation

Health crisis response is a cornerstone of public health management in social intelligence applications, which involves the strategies and actions to deal with large-scale health emergencies, such as disease outbreaks, pandemics, and natural or man-made disasters. A future direction along this line of work is to empower AI-driven health crisis response solutions with the capability of providing interpretable and trustworthy explanations to ensure that healthcare stakeholders and common citizens can understand the rationale behind the predictions and recommendations of AI algorithms. This will require integrating causal inference methods (e.g., causal discovery and causal effect estimation) into the knowledge graph reasoning process to infer the causal structure and quantify the causal effects among different entities and their relationships. The integration of causal mechanisms into AI models can generate more robust and unbiased explanations that can identify the root causes of the observed outcomes and suggest effective interventions to mitigate the negative impacts of health crises.

Future work could also leverage recent language techniques (e.g., natural language inference [17] and large language models [12]) to generate human-understandable explanations. These techniques can translate the knowledge-grounded reasoning process into natural language explanations that are coherent, logical, and persuasive. For example, given a predicted intervention policy for controlling a disease outbreak, an explainable knowledge-grounded social intelligence model can use natural language inference and relevant knowledge triples retrieved from knowledge graphs to generate an explanation that highlights the key factors considered in the decision-making process, such as the disease transmission dynamics, population mobility patterns, resource constraints, and how these factors logically lead to the recommended policy. Moreover, it is possible to leverage large language models pre-trained on vast amounts of text data to generate explanations that are fluent, diverse, and tailored to the linguistic preferences of users with different backgrounds.

Another desirable feature of future SI systems is to develop adaptive and context-aware explanation models that can adjust the level of detail, complexity, and format of explanations based on the background, role, and information needs of its end users. Such explanations are particularly helpful in social intelligence applications, where different stakeholders and end users may require different types of explanations. For instance, a clinician might need detailed, technical explanations of treatment recommendations, while a policymaker might require high-level summaries of population-level trends and intervention impacts. To develop such customizable XAI capabilities, we can integrate AI models with human intelligence from both domain experts and stakeholders who can help infer the user's knowledge level, preferences, and context from their interactions and queries without the need for massive training data. Additionally, the XAI capabilities of future SI systems should also explore multimodal data from different sources to provide multimodal, engaging, and informative explanations. For example, complex epidemiological concepts could be illustrated through interactive simulations, while statistical trends could be visualized through dynamic charts and graphs. By providing tailored, multimodal explanations, we can enhance the accessibility and effectiveness of AI-driven health crisis response solutions that promote a more informed decision-making process across diverse stakeholder groups in human society.

11.2.4 Adoption of Large Foundation Models

One of the next frontiers for social intelligence is the large foundation models (LFMs)—trained on large and varied data sets [3]. LFMs are capable of generalizing across a wide variety of downstream applications and offering promising application performance in the realm of social intelligence. Their use in social intelligence applications, ranging from truth discovery, online education, disaster damage assessment, to public health monitoring, opens up unprecedented opportunities as well as a new set of non-trivial challenges that future research will need to carefully tackle. For example, one challenge is that the use of LFMs in social intelligence necessitates the invention of methodologies with special ethical and responsibility considerations. This is because LFMs trained on large amounts of data can sometimes generate outputs that either reflect inherent biases or contain inappropriate contents [26]. Fairness-aware training algorithms and post-hoc corrective techniques such as debiasing, adversarial training, and fairness constraints can be leveraged to address this issue. Efforts to enhance transparency and accountability by developing explainability tools and providing audit trails for LFMs should also be undertaken. Second, LFMs may also require strategies to enable their efficient deployment in different social intelligence scenarios. Given their computational requirements, LFMs could generate computational bottlenecks that prohibit their implementation in resource-constrained environments (e.g., embedded systems, IoT devices). To address this, future research should explore efficient LLM and neural network optimizing techniques such as quantization and distillation [23, 24], enabling efficient on-device processing and making LFM implementation feasible even in settings with limited Internet connectivity or computational resources [27].

Additionally, developing new techniques for adapting LFMs to social intelligence applications for different domains is an emerging research area. While LFMs can generalize well across multiple downstream tasks, their performance can be constrained by domain-specific discrepancies, such as distribution shifts or the absence of domain-relevant priors [15]. Recent advances in domain adaptation and transfer learning techniques can be used to address the above challenge, where LFMs can be fine-tuned on domain-specific social intelligence tasks [2]. Few-shot or zero-shot learning techniques can also be used for finetuning LFMs to achieve performance gains. Lastly, it is also important to explore human-AI collaboration in facilitating the adaptation of LFMs in social intelligence applications. LFMs can analyze vast amounts of data from large datasets, but their analysis can be better augmented by human knowledge, to provide context and corrective feedback and input [8]. However, integrating LFMs and HI in social intelligence applications faces challenges rooted in their complex interdependence [21]. For instance, in social media recommender systems, AI models optimize their recommendation contents based on user engagements, often reinforcing user biases and creating echo chambers [18]. These AI-driven recommendations influence user interactions, which in turn feed back into model training. This feedback loop could amplify biases in both AI and human behavior, leading to polarized content ecosystems [4]. One possible solution to address this problem is to design collaborative debiasing systems, where AI models are trained with diversity constraints such as fairness-based ranking (e.g., demographic parity or exposure fairness) and content diversification (e.g., minimizing topical redundancy). Meanwhile, human input is systematically diversified across a wide spectrum of viewpoints (e.g., using stratified sampling to ensure demographic representation and active learning to engage underrepresented groups) to enable mutual correction of biases in AI recommendations and human interactions [16].

References

1. B. Abraham, D. Goel, D. Siddarth, K. Bali, M. Chopra, M. Choudhury, P. Joshi, P. Jyoti, S. Sitaram, and V. Seshadri. Crowdsourcing speech data for low-resource languages from low-income workers. In *Proceedings of the Twelfth Language Resources and Evaluation Conference*, pages 2819–2826, 2020.
2. S. Aycock and R. Bawden. Topic-guided example selection for domain adaptation in llm-based machine translation. In *Proceedings of the 18th Conference of the European Chapter of the Association for Computational Linguistics: Student Research Workshop*, pages 175–195, 2024.
3. R. Bommasani, D. A. Hudson, E. Adeli, R. Altman, S. Arora, S. von Arx, et al. On the opportunities and risks of foundation models. *arXiv preprint arXiv:2108.07258*, 2021.
4. Y. Cheng and H. Jiang. How do ai-driven chatbots impact user experience? examining gratifications, perceived privacy risk, satisfaction, loyalty, and continued use. *Journal of Broadcasting & Electronic Media*, 64(4):592–614, 2020.
5. X. Jiang, Y. Liang, W. Chen, and N. Duan. Xlm-k: Improving cross-lingual language model pre-training with multilingual knowledge. In *Proceedings of the AAAI Conference on Artificial Intelligence*, volume 36, pages 10840–10848, 2022.
6. W. Kwon, G.-I. Yu, E. Jeong, and B.-G. Chun. Nimble: Lightweight and parallel gpu task scheduling for deep learning. *Advances in Neural Information Processing Systems*, 33:8343–8354, 2020.
7. H. Lakkaraju, D. Slack, Y. Chen, C. Tan, and S. Singh. Rethinking explainability as a dialogue: A practitioner's perspective. In *NeurIPS Workshop on Human Centered AI*, 2022.
8. H. Lee, S. Phatale, H. Mansoor, K. Lu, T. Mesnard, C. Bishop, V. Carbune, and A. Rastogi. Rlaif: Scaling reinforcement learning from human feedback with ai feedback. *arXiv e-prints*, pages arXiv–2309, 2023.
9. L. Liu, B. Ding, L. Bing, S. Joty, L. Si, and C. Miao. Mulda: A multilingual data augmentation framework for low-resource cross-lingual ner. In *Proceedings of the 59th Annual Meeting of the Association for Computational Linguistics and the 11th International Joint Conference on Natural Language Processing (Volume 1: Long Papers)*, pages 5834–5846, 2021.
10. Y. Lu, M. Huang, X. Qu, P. Wei, and Z. Ma. Language adaptive cross-lingual speech representation learning with sparse sharing sub-networks. In *ICASSP 2022–2022 IEEE International Conference on Acoustics, Speech and Signal Processing (ICASSP)*, pages 6882–6886. IEEE, 2022.
11. Q. Luo, S. Hu, C. Li, G. Li, and W. Shi. Resource scheduling in edge computing: A survey. *IEEE Communications Surveys & Tutorials*, 23(4):2131–2165, 2021.
12. S. Ma, Q. Chen, X. Wang, C. Zheng, Z. Peng, M. Yin, and X. Ma. Towards human-ai deliberation: Design and evaluation of llm-empowered deliberative ai for ai-assisted decision-making. *arXiv preprint arXiv:2403.16812*, 2024.
13. Y. Mo, J. Yang, J. Liu, Q. Wang, R. Chen, J. Wang, and Z. Li. mcl-ner: Cross-lingual named entity recognition via multi-view contrastive learning. In *Proceedings of the AAAI Conference on Artificial Intelligence*, volume 38, pages 18789–18797, 2024.
14. L. G. Nateras, M. Van Nguyen, and T. Nguyen. Cross-lingual event detection via optimized adversarial training. In *Proceedings of the 2022 conference of the north american chapter of the association for computational linguistics: Human language technologies*, pages 5588–5599, 2022.
15. J. Saad-Falcon, O. Khattab, K. Santhanam, R. Florian, M. Franz, S. Roukos, A. Sil, M. A. Sultan, and C. Potts. Udapdr: unsupervised domain adaptation via llm prompting and distillation of rerankers. *arXiv preprint arXiv:2303.00807*, 2023.
16. P. Schmidt and F. Biessmann. Calibrating human-ai collaboration: Impact of risk, ambiguity and transparency on algorithmic bias. In *Machine Learning and Knowledge Extraction: 4th IFIP TC 5, TC 12, WG 8.4, WG 8.9, WG 12.9 International Cross-Domain Conference, CD-MAKE 2020, Dublin, Ireland, August 25–28, 2020, Proceedings 4*, pages 431–449. Springer, 2020.

17. J. Stacey, Y. Belinkov, and M. Rei. Supervising model attention with human explanations for robust natural language inference. In *Proceedings of the AAAI conference on artificial intelligence*, volume 36, pages 11349–11357, 2022.
18. L. T. L. Terren and R. B.-B. R. Borge-Bravo. Echo chambers on social media: A systematic review of the literature. *Review of Communication Research*, 9, 2021.
19. G. M. Van de Ven, T. Tuytelaars, and A. S. Tolias. Three types of incremental learning. *Nature Machine Intelligence*, 4(12):1185–1197, 2022.
20. J. Wang, W. Ma, J. Li, H. Lu, M. Zhang, B. Li, Y. Liu, P. Jiang, and S. Ma. Make fairness more fair: Fair item utility estimation and exposure re-distribution. In *Proceedings of the 28th ACM SIGKDD Conference on Knowledge Discovery and Data Mining*, pages 1868–1877, 2022.
21. X. Wang, H. Kim, S. Rahman, K. Mitra, and Z. Miao. Human-llm collaborative annotation through effective verification of llm labels. In *Proceedings of the CHI Conference on Human Factors in Computing Systems*, pages 1–21, 2024.
22. Z. J. Wang, D. Choi, S. Xu, and D. Yang. Putting humans in the natural language processing loop: A survey. In *Proceedings of the First Workshop on Bridging Human–Computer Interaction and Natural Language Processing*, pages 47–52, 2021.
23. G. Xiao, J. Lin, M. Seznec, H. Wu, J. Demouth, and S. Han. Smoothquant: Accurate and efficient post-training quantization for large language models. In *International Conference on Machine Learning*, pages 38087–38099. PMLR, 2023.
24. M. Xu, W. Yin, D. Cai, R. Yi, D. Xu, Q. Wang, B. Wu, Y. Zhao, C. Yang, S. Wang, et al. A survey of resource-efficient llm and multimodal foundation models. *arXiv preprint arXiv:2401.08092*, 2024.
25. S. Yang, O. Nachum, Y. Du, J. Wei, P. Abbeel, and D. Schuurmans. Foundation models for decision making: Problems, methods, and opportunities. *arXiv preprint arXiv:2303.04129*, 2023.
26. Y. Yu, Y. Zhuang, J. Zhang, Y. Meng, A. J. Ratner, R. Krishna, J. Shen, and C. Zhang. Large language model as attributed training data generator: A tale of diversity and bias. *Advances in Neural Information Processing Systems*, 36, 2024.
27. J. Yuan, C. Yang, D. Cai, S. Wang, X. Yuan, Z. Zhang, X. Li, D. Zhang, H. Mei, X. Jia, et al. Mobile foundation model as firmware. *arXiv preprint arXiv:2308.14363*, 2023.

Index

D. Wang et al., *Social Intelligence*, https://doi.org/10.1007/978-3-031-90080-8

The manufacturer's authorised representative in the EU is Springer Nature Customer Service Centre GmbH, Europaplatz 3, 69115 Heidelberg, Germany. If you have any concerns regarding our products, please contact ProductSafety@springernature.com

Printed and bound by CPI Group (UK) Ltd, Croydon, CR0 4YY
01/10/2026
02225971-0009